Digital Transformation
Strategies

Thank you for choosing a SAGE product!
If you have any comment, observation or feedback,
I would like to personally hear from you.

Please write to me at contactceo@sagepub.in

Vivek Mehra, Managing Director and CEO, SAGE India.

Bulk Sales

SAGE India offers special discounts
for bulk institutional purchases.

For queries/orders/inspection copy requests,
write to **textbooksales@sagepub.in**

Publishing

Would you like to publish a textbook with SAGE?
Please send your proposal to **publishtextbook@sagepub.in**

Subscribe to our mailing list

Write to marketing@sagepub.in

This book is also available as an e-book.

Digital Transformation Strategies

Theory and Practice

Srinivas R. Pingali
Professor of Practice, Indian Institute of Management Udaipur

Shankar Prakash
Professor of Practice, Indian Institute of Management Udaipur

Jyothi R. Korem
*Former Managing Director, Technology Strategy and
Advisory Practice, Accenture*

Los Angeles | London | New Delhi
Singapore | Washington DC | Melbourne

First published in 2021 by

SAGE Publications India Pvt Ltd
B1/I-1 Mohan Cooperative Industrial Area
Mathura Road, New Delhi 110 044, India
www.sagepub.in

SAGE Publications Inc
2455 Teller Road
Thousand Oaks, California 91320, USA

SAGE Publications Ltd
1 Oliver's Yard, 55 City Road
London EC1Y 1SP, United Kingdom

SAGE Publications Asia-Pacific Pte Ltd
18 Cross Street #10-10/11/12
China Square Central
Singapore 048423

Published by Vivek Mehra for SAGE Publications India Pvt. Ltd. Typeset in 10/12 pt ITC Century by Zaza Eunice, Hosur, Tamil Nadu, India.

Library of Congress Control Number: 2021943209

ISBN: 978-93-91370-33-6 (PB)

SAGE Team: Amit Kumar, Ariba Zainab, Vandana Gupta, Sonam Rana and Rajinder Kaur

Contents

Detailed Contents

List of Exhibits

List of Abbreviations

3Is:	Instrumented, interconnected and intelligent
4Ps	Product, place, price and promotion
AC	Air conditioner
ADSL	Asymmetric digital subscriber line
AGI	Artificial general intelligence
AI	Artificial intelligence
ANI	Artificial narrow intelligence
API	Application programming interface
AR	Augmented reality
ASI	Artificial superintelligence
AVs	Autonomous vehicles
B2B	Business-to-business
B2C	Business-to-consumer
BIC	Brighton Insurance Company
BLE	Bluetooth low energy
BMI	Business model innovation
BPA	Business process automation
BPO	Business process outsourcing
CAGR	Compounded annual growth rate
CDO	Chief digital officer
CEO	Chief executive officer
CFO	Chief financial officer
CHRO	Chief human resources officer
CIO	Chief information officer
CMO	Chief marketing officer
CNC	Computer numeric control
CPA	Certified public accountant
CPC	Cost per click
CRM	Customer relationship management
CTO	Chief technology officer
CTR	Click-through rates
DAI	Dhanashree Agro Industries

DAI   Digital Acceleration Index
DAP   Diammonium phosphate
DSN   Digital supply networks
EDS   Electronic data systems
ERP   Enterprise resource planning
Fintech   Financial technology
FMCG   Fast-moving consumer goods
FSSAI   Food Safety and Standards Authority of India
GDP   Gross domestic product
GDPR   General Data Protection Regulation
GPS   Global positioning system
GRE   Global Real Estate
HMD   Head-mounted display
HR   Human resources
HVAC   Heating, ventilation and air conditioning
IaaS   Infrastructure as a service
IGBC   Indian Green Building Council
IoT   Internet of Things
IP   Intellectual property
IPv4   Internet Protocol Version 4
IPv6   Internet Protocol Version 6
ISO   International Organization for Standardization
IT   Information technology
ITU   International Telecommunication Union
IVR   Interactive voice response
JVs   Joint ventures
KYC   Know your customer
LAN   Local area network
LCAP   Low-code application platform
LEED   Leadership in Energy and Environmental Design
LEO   Low earth orbit
LiDAR   Light detection and ranging
LP-WAN   Low-power wide area network
LR-WPAN   Low-rate wireless personal area network
M&A   Mergers and acquisitions
MANET   Mobile ad hoc network
ML   Machine learning
MSPs   Multisided platforms
MVPs   Minimum viable products
NAS   Network attached storage
NB-IoT   Naroowband Internet of Things
NFC   Near-field communication
NLP   Natural language processing
NPD   New product development
OBCM   Osterwalder Business Canvas Model
OTC   Over-the-counter

OTT	Over-the-top
P2P	Peer-to-peer
PaaS	Platform as a service
PAN	Personal area networks
PPE	Personal protective equipment
RAD	Rapid application development
RBC	Royal Bank of Canada
RBV	Resource-based view
Regtech	Regulatory technology
RFID	Radio-frequency identification
RPA	Robotics process automation
RTVN	Resources, transactions, value and narrative
SaaS	Software as a service
SAN	Storage area network
SBI	State Bank of India
SCM	Supply chain management
SDLC	Software development life cycle
SEC	Socio-economic classification
SEM	Search engine marketing
SEO	Search engine optimization
SER	Search engine ranking
SFAS	Strategic Factors Analysis Matrix
SHS	Sharp Hardware Supplies
SKU	Stock keeping unit
SMEs	Small and medium enterprises
SWOT	Strengths, weaknesses, opportunities and threats
TPM	Total productive maintenance
TQM	Total quality management
TSG	The Sinusoid Group
VR	Virtual reality
VRIO	Value, rarity, imitability and organization
WAN	Wide area network
WAP	Wireless Application Protocol
WSN	Wireless sensor network
XP	Extreme Programming

Preface

Digital strategies and transformation are the topmost items on the agendas of most global CEOs. Open any business publication and you will see a plethora of articles on digital strategies across industries. Traditional industries such as manufacturing, FMCG, high tech, hospitality, healthcare, agriculture, government, and small and medium-sized enterprises (SMEs) are just some examples of industries being disrupted by digital. Technologies such as artificial intelligence, blockchain, the Internet of Things (IoT), cloud and augmented reality are all no longer science fiction and are becoming an integral part of mainstream business. From digital natives to traditional companies, all are in a race to win the digital war.

Digital strategy development is a new area, and we find a lack of understanding on what it entails and how a traditional company can go about transforming itself into a digital company. While digital transformation is led by CEOs, it is equally important for all layers of an organization to understand its mechanics. Several books have been written on digital strategies and transformation. However, most of these books are written with senior corporate executives and CEOs in mind. As academics and practitioners of strategy and digital transformation, we found a gap in a comprehensive book on digital strategies and transformation for junior and mid-level executives, and students.

Digital-related education is also entering academia. Most MOOC platforms have included courses on digital. Some graduate business programmes have launched specialized digital degrees focusing on digital strategies.

This book covers both theory and practice of digital strategies. It is based on academic research, over 70 years of combined personal experiences of the authors in leading global consulting companies and a multitude of cases across industries. It is structured in an easy-to-read fashion for academic instructors, students and junior and mid-level executives. It helps define digital strategies, transformation and digitalization and contrasts these with digitation and automation. It then goes on to provide a comprehensive digital strategy framework. Later chapters then describe each element of the digital strategy framework. The book provides industry-specific use cases and detailed templates for digital implementation. Finally, the book describes the risks of digitalization and potential mitigation strategy.

The book assumes no prior knowledge of strategy, product development or process innovation among its readers and starts with the basics of each of these topics. Many of the cases used in the book are from India; however, the theory and methodologies described in the book are universal. They are equally relevant for large companies, social enterprises and SMEs. The theories and examples in the book can be used by both start-ups and traditional businesses that need to transform.

Our hope is that this book will aid academicians and young practitioners to understand, teach and implement digital strategies.

Acknowledgements

I would like to thank my family, who bore the brunt of my mood swings as I was pursuing a late-life doctoral programme and writing books—my wife, Padma Priya Pingali, who was my chief editor and critique, and my children, Samyukta and Raghava Pingali, who were my cheerleaders through the process. I would like to thank my in-laws, Mrs Vedavani and Mr Krishna Mohan, and my parents, Dr Sunanda Rao and Mr P. S. Rao, for their constant encouragement.

Srinivas R. Pingali

I remember my late mother, Smt J. Nagasundari, for her perpetual enthusiasm and encouragement for every small and big step I took to fulfil my aspirations. I would like to thank my father, Shri G. Janakiraman, for his thoughtful guidance whenever I needed it. I would like to thank my wife, Jayshri, and son, Vedanth, for being the substratum of all my endeavours. Finally, I would like to thank Mr Rajesh Nambiar, a former colleague and a mentor, who untiringly shaped my thinking as a professional for many years.

Shankar Prakash

I would like to acknowledge my later father, Adi Reddy, who helped me to forge an untrodden path and inspired many other young girls in my family and village to follow.

Jyothi R. Korem

About the Authors

Srinivas R. Pingali is a Professor of Practice at the Indian Institute of Management Udaipur, India. He has close to 30 years of varied experience in product development and innovation, sales and marketing, market research and business operations in multinationals and entrepreneurial companies. He has never held a role that existed before he created it.

His areas of expertise include strategy, digital transformation and innovation. His research focus is on the intersection of digital transformation, traditional businesses including SMEs and emerging markets.

Professor Pingali is a regular speaker on platform-based services, innovation and SME strategies.

He is a Chemical Engineer from University College of Technology, Osmania University, India, and holds an MBA degree in marketing from the University of Illinois at Urbana-Champaign and is an Executive Fellow in Management (doctoral equivalent) from the Indian School of Business.

Shankar Prakash is a business transformation professional with 20 years of experience, spanning IT service operations, digital operations and supply chain, digital transformation and, service automation. He has worked with IBM for over 11 years and prior to that, has a diverse work experience including with Ernst & Young, Wipro and Brakes India.

He is a Professor of Practice at the Indian Institute of Management Udaipur. He teaches courses in digital technologies, artificial intelligence and IoT to MBA students. He is currently pursuing doctoral-level research in digital transformation and future of work at the Indian School of Business, Hyderabad. He is an avid artificial intelligence practitioner with research interests to apply machine learning and natural language processing for knowledge synthesis.

He is a mechanical engineer from Vellore Engineering College, University of Madras, and has completed the postgraduate programme in management from Indian School of Business, Hyderabad.

 **Jyothi R. Korem** was previously Managing Director of Technology Strategy and Advisory Practice with Accenture. She has more than 25 years of experience in leading technology-led business transformation engagements across various industries in different parts of the world. She has led more than 40 business transformation engagements including a billion-dollar transformation programme for a public service organization. She worked closely with CXOs in various industries across geographies during her years of experience covering the IT services value chain from transformation to outsourcing.

She brings unique perspective to digital transformation having worked across the value chain—product, consulting and IT service organizations. She is also currently engaged in developing a technology platform and ecosystem to bring best-in-class digital transformation services to SMEs through her start-up.

She has a master's in industrial engineering from National Institute of Industrial Engineering, Mumbai, and is currently doing the executive fellow programme in management (doctoral equivalent) from Indian School of Business, Hyderabad.

Introduction to Digital Strategies

Learning Objectives

This chapter introduces digital strategy and its individual components. The chapter is designed to help readers:

- Understand the concepts of business transformation and digital strategy
- Define digital strategy and its key elements
- Develop a digital strategy model
- Get insights into the drivers for digital strategy and transformation
- Assess the stages of the digital strategy of a company

Each element outlined in this chapter is explored in greater detail in further chapters.

Mini Case 1.1

Unilever is a global multinational consumer products company headquartered in London, UK.

The company has presence in over 190 countries with 400+ brands across food and refreshments, home care, and personal and beauty care. The company has been in existence for a hundred years and has grown organically as well as through acquisitions. For decades, the company followed a traditional marketing approach. Its products were available through large and small retailers around the world. The company promoted its products through a combination of above-the-line advertising on television and other traditional media. To complement these activities, the company participated in several below-the-line activities such as coupons and in-store sampling. Along with other consumer giants such as P&G and Nestlé, Unilever was a dominant consumer products company in most countries it operated in. It had a significant influence on traditional media, distributors and retailers in these countries. However, the advent of the internet and e-commerce began to change the market dynamics. As e-commerce and digital marketing grew, the role of traditional distribution and marketing began to diminish. These technologies also enabled newer companies and brands to launch their products and establish themselves quickly. For the first time in decades, Unilever was witnessing competition from a new breed of digital competitors. What did Unilever do to transform itself from a traditional company to a digital company? What elements of its overall strategy did it need to tweak? How was this transformation managed?

Source: The case has been compiled from multiple public sources.

1.1. DIGITAL STRATEGIES

All companies need to have a digital strategy. Many companies that came into existence in the last decade started as digital companies. These companies are often referred to as 'born digital' or 'digital natives' and include companies such as Uber and Airbnb. At the other end of the digital spectrum are traditional companies like GE that are transforming themselves to become digital companies. As digital strategies and digital technologies are evolving rapidly, even born-digital companies need to evolve or transform themselves to keep pace with the change. The concepts in this chapter are equally applicable to born digitals building a digital strategy for the first time and traditional companies transforming themselves into digital entities.

1.2. DEFINING DIGITAL STRATEGY

Digital strategy is often confused with technology strategy. Several academic papers (Exhibit 1.1) have attempted to define the term 'digital strategy'. The essence of these definitions is that it is a **strategy enabled by digital technologies**. For a traditional company, its digital strategy is referred to as a digital transformation strategy.

EXHIBIT 1.1 | *Definitions of Digital Transformation*

Definition	Authors
Organizational strategy formulated and executed by leveraging digital resources to create differential value.	Bharadwaj et al. (2013)
A pattern of deliberate competitive actions undertaken by a firm as it competes by offering digitally enabled products or services.	Woodard et al. (2013)
Digital transformation is concerned with the changes digital technologies can bring about in a company's business model, which result in changed products or organizational structures or in the automation of processes.	Hess et al. (2016)

Based on the key elements from each of the above definitions, a digital strategy has the following components:

Strategy led: A digital strategy is led by strategy and not technology. For example, the launch of ride-sharing companies was driven by a customer need for convenient and cost-effective local transport. Mobile, global positioning system (GPS) and other technologies just enabled the strategy of these companies. Similarly, e-commerce was driven by a customer need for convenience and technologies such as mobile, web and analytics enabled this need.

Innovation driven: Most digital strategies involve innovation at multiple levels. This could include product innovation, process innovation or people innovation. This is discussed in detail further in this chapter.

Business model changing: A significant impact of digital strategies is that they have enabled new business models. The lines between products and services are getting blurred as a result. For example, in the past, to listen to music, a customer had to go to a shop and buy a CD or a record. Today this same music is available on a subscription basis online.

Value chain altering: A digital strategy impacts all parts of a value chain. It not only changes the nature of the product or service but the entire chain that supports this delivery. For example, for a retail company that is moving from traditional brick and mortar to online, it is not enough to create a customer-facing platform. The company needs to rework the way it partners with suppliers, the ordering and payment process, the logistics process from the supplier to its warehouses and then from its warehouses to its end customers, and the way it markets its products while leveraging analytics. One of the primary reasons for companies faltering in their efforts to transform digitally is that they focus only on customer-facing changes and do not pay enough attention to the entire value chain.

Technology enabled: Technology forms a critically important component of a digital strategy. Going back to the ride-sharing example, the customer need for convenience and low-cost rides always existed. However, the current transformation was possible only due to the availability of newer technologies. As another example, companies were always seeking international markets. The high cost of entry, regulatory requirements and lack of knowledge and understanding of these markets prevented companies from expanding internationally. E-commerce platforms have enabled rapid internationalization. Companies now list their products on international e-commerce websites and ensure product availability. Technology has reduced the need for setting up expensive offices and hiring local resources.

1.3. INTRODUCTION TO BUSINESS TRANSFORMATION

Implementing digital strategies is far more complex in older and established organizations as it involves a significant amount of change and transformation. In this section, we describe business transformation and how industries have transformed over the last three hundred years.

Business transformation is about changing the way a company does business. Transformation is driven by external factors such as customer preferences, competition and regulatory environment. It can also be caused by internal drivers like change in leadership or availability of new processes or technology. It can be evolutionary or revolutionary:

Evolutionary transformation is gradual and takes place in incremental steps. It is sustained over a period and allows for a business to adapt to the changes. Evolutionary transformation can be caused by technology projects or process improvements through six-sigma or kaizen projects. It is usually not organization wide and limited to changes within a function.

Revolutionary transformation, on the other hand, is implementing large change in a short duration of time. This transformation could be driven by implementing new technologies or business model and impacts all aspect of a business.

1.3.1. Types of Business Transformation

Some of the common types of business transformation are described in this section.

1.3.1.1. Operational Transformation

Operational transformation is about making fundamental changes to processes and changing the way a company operates. For example, it could include developing new processes for procuring input material or a change in the core production process.

Key factors to consider for operational transformation are outlined in Exhibit 1.2.

EXHIBIT 1.2 | *Operational Transformation*

Factors	Illustration
What results does the work deliver?	Focus on lifetime customer value rather than the value from a single transaction.
Who performs the work?	One worker handles all issues relating to a customer service escalation rather than having multiple handoffs.
Where is the work performed?	Outsourcing of work that was traditionally handled in-house.
When is the work performed?	Specific tasks are moved to night-times for better utilization of infrastructure.
Whether the work is performed?	In a B2B sale, goods are shipped directly to a customer without transhipment at a distributors warehouse.
What information does the work employ?	A sales representative uses prior purchase data to offer solutions proactively.
How thoroughly the work is performed?	Based on data, preventive maintenance is used to avert issues proactively.

Source: Kotter (2007).

Operational transformation has an immediate and lasting impact. As an illustration, most manufacturing companies have gone through waves of operational transformation as newer production methods were developed.

1.3.1.2. Business Model Transformation

A business model defines how a company creates and captures value. To transform its value creation and value capture mechanism, a company needs to organize its internal and external processes differently. Outcomes of business model transformations are generally riskier and less predictable when compared to operational transformation. There are several examples of such transformations in the recent past. One of the most written-about business model transformations is how Amazon, with its e-commerce model, permanently changed the way books are produced and sold.

1.3.1.3. Strategic Transformation

Strategic transformation is about changing the essence of an organization. It is a combination of operational and business model transitions. It is the riskiest of transformations and can have a catastrophic impact on an organization if it fails. If such a transformation succeeds, then it will put the company way ahead of its competitors. Amazon and Apple are examples of two companies that embarked and succeeded in strategic transformations.

1.3.2. History of Business Transformation

Business transformation is not new. Industries have transformed themselves multiple times over the last few centuries. Individual industries were transformed due to the availability of new technology or equipment, discoveries and inventions or new processes. At a macro level, businesses and industries have gone through at least four stages of transformations over the last few centuries. These stages are more popularly referred to as the four industrial revolutions. It is essential to understand the previous industrial revolutions as they provide context to the current transformation, called the Fourth Industrial Revolution (Exhibit 1.3).

1.3.2.1. First Industrial Revolution (from ~1760 to ~1840)

The First Industrial Revolution started in the middle of the 18th century. The revolution that was centred in the UK and Europe was driven by three drivers: (a) mechanization of industrial processes, (b) harnessing of steam and (c) advances in iron and steel.

Till the start of the First Industrial Revolution, industries were mostly manual and unorganized. This revolution resulted in a significant shift in the way industries were organized. A good illustration is the textile industry. Until then, cotton was imported by Britain from its colonies, including India. It was then woven into fabric in the homes of spinners and weavers. Using a traditional spinning wheel, it took four to eight spinners to supply to one weaver. The invention of new weaving tools caused a further imbalance to this relationship.

EXHIBIT 1.3 | *The Four Industrial Revolutions*

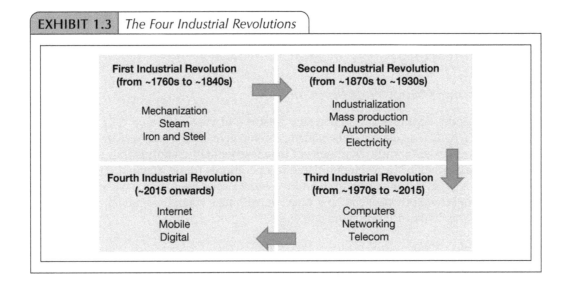

This imbalance was eventually corrected by the invention of the mechanized spinning wheel. As both these technologies evolved, some entrepreneurs saw this as an opportunity to consolidate the two processes under one roof, thus creating the first textile mill. These mills very rapidly evolved from using manually operated tools to steam-powered tools, thus increasing the output of textiles being produced. The quality of output was not the same as the handwoven textiles that were being produced in colonies like India. However, the sheer scale and lower cost led to the rapid collapse of the handwoven textile industry in India. Britain soon became the largest producer of cotton textiles. By the end of the 18th century, Britain controlled the entire textile supply from cotton growing (by then Britain was formally ruling over India), production and consumption. This is one of the earliest examples of platform dominance and predatory pricing enabled by a technology revolution.

Another key driver for the First Industrial Revolution was the harnessing of steam power through stationary steam engines. These engines could generate enough power, thus reducing the need for less-efficient sources of energy and manual labour. Steam power also led to drastic improvements in machining technologies such as lathes, plaining machines, milling machines and shaping machines which led to further improvement in industrial equipment.

The third driver for the First Industrial Revolution was technological advances in iron and steel manufacturing. High-powered steam engines led to the development of blast furnaces that made iron and steel making processes more efficient and scalable. Availability of steel and steam power drove much of the First Industrial Revolution.

The revolution also had a significant impact on society. Hitherto, society had been primarily rural and agrarian. Setting up of large factories led to urbanization as people moved to cities to work in these factories. This, in turn, led to a growing need for additional infrastructure such as housing, transport, water and food in the cities.

The First Industrial Revolution also changed the global economic power centres from China and India to Britain, Europe and America. It also set the base for another revolution to meet the growing needs of an affluent population.

1.3.2.2. The Second Industrial Revolution (from ~1870 to ~1930)

The Second Industrial Revolution, also known as the Technology Revolution, began in the late 19th century, about 30 years after the decline of the previous Industrial Revolution. Advancement in manufacturing technologies, large-scale infrastructure projects such as roads, railroads, water and sewerage, and newer technologies such as electric power and telephones enabled the second revolution. One of the most important developments of this period was the mass production of automobiles. Henry Ford, the founder of Ford Motor Company, and his team redesigned their production process into an assembly line. This assembly line structured machine tools in an organized sequence, based on the part of the car being produced. Workers along the line had access to all the tools they needed to work on the specific tasks allocated to them. This reorganization dramatically increased process efficiencies, eliminated wasteful tasks and eventually reduced costs. This was the first time that a complex product, with thousands of parts, was produced on a large scale. Ford Motor Company had operationally transformed the production process within the company and the manufacturing industry globally.

Another significant development of this age was electrification. The invention of the AC electric motor in the 1890s allowed for the electrification of industries and factories. Electric lighting in factories eliminated the heat and pollution caused by gas lights, reduced the cost of operations and significantly improved working conditions.

The Second Industrial Revolution witnessed the birth of what is the foundation of today's digital revolution—telecommunication. Alexander Graham Bell invented the modern telephone in the 1890s, and it was used to speed up business transactions replacing the slower and less efficient telegraph. The invention of the radio and the vacuum tube laid the basis for modern communications.

The Second Industrial Revolution was ended abruptly with the start of the First World War in 1914. However, much like the preceding revolution, it set the wheels in motion for the next set of transformations.

1.3.2.3. The Third Industrial Revolution (from ~1970s to ~2015)

The Third Industrial Revolution began in the 1960s with the advent of semiconductors, computers, the internet and mass communication. The second revolution had streamlined operations and brought in new technologies. The Third Industrial Revolution leveraged electronics and information technology (IT) to automate production to the next level.

The move from analogue electronic and mechanical devices towards digital technology dramatically disrupted industries. Electronics and IT began to automate production and helped companies globalize their production and supply chains. Companies very rapidly moved from outsourcing to offshoring. At a societal level, personal computing and mobile computing changed the way people operated their lives. Increased communication and exposure to information were some the positive impacts, while data security and privacy were some of the downsides of this transformation.

While the entire period from the 1970s to around 2015 has been clubbed as a single phase in popular literature, in reality, there have been sub-phases within this period. The late 1990s saw another round of acceleration in technologies with the availability of mobile connectivity and pervasiveness of the internet-based technologies.

1.3.2.4. Fourth Industrial Revolution (~2015 onwards)

The Third Industrial Revolution set the base for the Fourth Industrial Revolution, also known as the Digital Revolution, that is currently in the early stages. This revolution is based on increasing computing speeds, cheaper storage and faster transmission. These phenomena are best described by three 'laws':

1. **Moore's law (Schaller, 1997):** Gordon Moore, the co-founder of Intel Corporation, stated in 1965 that the number of transistors on a microchip would double about every two years, though the cost of computers will halve. This observation is often referred to as Moore's law and describes the exponential growth of processing power. The law held true for over 40 years, and it is only around 2019 that this exponential growth started to slow down due to thermal limitations, that is, the ability to effectively dissipate the heat that is generated by such a densely packed set of microchips.

2. **Butters law (Roser & Ritchie, 2013):** In 1997, Gerald Butters, the former head of Lucent's Optical Networking Group at Bell Labs, stated that the amount of data coming out of optical fibre will double every nine months. Thus, the cost of transmitting a bit over an optical network will decrease by half every nine months. As the world moved from copper lines to fibre optics and then to mobile data to 5G, this law has made a tremendous impact on industries such as telecom, communication, media and others. As 5G rolls in, the next wave of industries and technologies are likely to get disrupted.

3. **Kryder's law (Walter, 2005):** Propounded in 2005 by Mark Kryder of Seagate Technology, Kryder's law is the assumption that disk drive density will double every 13 months. Since the introduction of the disk drive in 1956, the density of information it can record has increased from 2,000 bits to 100 billion bits (gigabits), fitted into one square inch, which represents a 50-million-fold increase.

There are other laws such as Kecks law (that states that the number of bits per second that can be sent down an optical fibre increases exponentially) and Edholm's law (that states that the bandwidth of telecommunication networks (including the internet) is doubling every 18 months).

This combination of increasing computing speeds, cheaper storage and faster transmission has led to several new technological developments. These developments have facilitated new business models that form the basis for the Digital Revolution.

Although in its early stages, the Fourth Industrial Revolution has already disrupted most traditional industries. The media industry is a good example of the way customers consume media has changed. New over-the-top (OTT) platforms like Netflix have disrupted traditional television and movie industries. Discrete manufacturing is another sector that is undergoing rapid changes due to the availability of newer technologies. Artificial intelligence (AI), the Internet of Things (IoT) and analytics are changing the manufacturing processes. Proactive equipment management, remote management and automation through robots are some of the changes in this sector. Industries as varied as education, distribution, retail, healthcare and manufacturing are all getting disrupted by these technologies.

The rest of this book focuses on each building block of the Fourth Industrial Revolution, the impact it has on various industries and the capabilities that are required to be successful in this new business environment.

1.4. DIGITAL STRATEGY FRAMEWORK

A digital strategy is not all about implementing technology or solving discrete business issues. As previously discussed, it encompasses product changes, business model changes, process changes and organizational changes (Exhibit 1.4). It is often referred to as digitalization (as against digitization).

Our digital strategy framework has five key components:

1. **Process innovation:** This is a combination of moving processes to a digital form and making fundamental changes in operational processes. For example, an accounting company may transition from using traditional paper-based invoice processing into automating its accounts payable process by incorporating tools like workflow software. The company may also choose to handle a part of the accounting process in-house and outsource the low-end work to another provider who could provide low-cost services. Process innovations are not differentiators by themselves but are key to the success of other components of the digital strategy framework.
2. **Product innovation:** The next element of the framework is product or service innovation. This is where a company innovates its product and service offerings. Using the same above example of the accounting firm, the company could move its services to the cloud or provide self-service analytical tools. These innovations will start differentiating the product offerings of the accounting firm.

| EXHIBIT 1.4 | *The Digital Strategy Framework* |

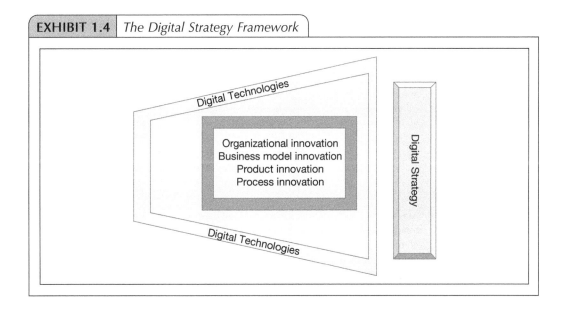

3. **Business model innovation (BMI):** The third element in the framework is BMI. BMI is about how a company earns revenues while providing value to its customers. In the accounting outsourcing company example, the company could innovate its business model by changing its charging mechanism from a 'per-hour fee' to a more flexible per-transaction price.

4. **Organizational innovation:** For any strategy to be successful, people are the most critical variables. Strategy and transformation start at the leadership level and flow down the entire organization. The top leaders need to be open to transformation, and they should have the ability to convey this across the organization. In older and legacy organizations, change management becomes one of the most critical parts of any digital transformation. In the accounting example, the changes in process, service and business model will require a combination of eliminating some roles, reskilling some roles and adding new ones. Unless its leadership plans people transition meticulously, the transformation of a traditional accounting company to a cloud-based service provider will fail.

5. **Technology innovation:** Encompassing the previous four elements is a digital technology layer that consists of automation, platforms and applications, networking and storage, and intelligence (data and analytics). It is these digital technologies that make this wave of transformation unique compared to earlier versions. Going back to the accounting company illustration, automation could include workflows, platforms could include enterprise resource planning (ERP) with multi-device access and mobile applications, networking and storage could include cloud-based hosting and intelligence could include analytical tools that provide customers more value.

Exhibit 1.5 summarizes the illustration of the digital transformation of the accounting company.

No two digital strategies are similar. Nor does a company need to tweak all five elements to digitally transform itself. A company needs to leverage elements of the framework that

EXHIBIT 1.5	*Illustrative Digital Transformation*

Stack	Pre-transformation	Transformed Company	Digital Technologies
Process innovation	• Manual processes • All processes handled in-house	• Workflow-driven processes • Implementation of ERP • Low value-added processes outsourced	• Workflows • Robotics process automation • Cloud ERPs • Collaboration tools • Application programming interface (API) integration
Product/ Service innovation	• Accounting handled by the company • Limited interaction and visibility for its clients	• Online and anytime access to reports and status reports • Self-help for reporting and analysis	• Mobile apps • Cloud-based self-service portal • Business intelligence and visualization tools

Stack	Pre-transformation	Transformed Company	Digital Technologies
Business model innovation	• Per accountant • Step-function linkage to the volume of business • Not easily scalable up or down	• Subscription-based services • Per transaction based pricing	• Billing engine • Automated transaction monitoring system
Organizational innovation	• Accountants handle all processes	• Skill-based accounting • Non-accountants and machines handle all routine functions • Accountants handle only value-added processes and spend more time consulting with clients	• Workflow tools • Single sign-on • Robotics process automation • AI-based knowledge base

best suit its needs based on its customer and industry contexts. The only constant across all digital strategies is the leveraging of digital technologies.

1.5. DIGITALIZATION VERSUS DIGITIZATION

There is often confusion between digitization and digitalization (or digital transformation). Digitization is simply automating a manual process. Digitalization, on the other hand, is *strategic change enabled by digital technologies*. Some simple illustrations of the difference between the two are given below.

1.5.1 Evolution of Watches

Till the 1980s, watches were analogue. Their primary function was to tell time. Analogue watches had mechanical moving parts that deteriorated over time. Also, they had limited functionality and were not very accurate. In the 1970s, the entire watch industry underwent digitization. These digital watches were far more accurate and had no moving parts. Soon they offered other functionalities such as stopwatch and dual time. The market for analogue watches eventually shrunk and digital watches gained a majority market share. By the early 2010s, the next wave of watches called 'smart watches' started to appear. Using the latest technologies such as GPS and sensors, they offered a lot more than a better way of telling time. In addition to all the features of digital watches, smartwatches could synchronize with various devices, measure physical activities and measure health parameters. They stored the data in the cloud and provided analytics on an individual's life. They became the hub of all other devices that an individual owned. The move from digital to smartwatches is a good representation of digitalization.

Another excellent example of digitization versus digitalization is the transformation of the music industry. Traditionally, music was sold on long-playing records or cassettes. These were cumbersome, prone to damage and could not reproduce good-quality sound. In the 1990s, digital music on CDs and DVDs started to replace the older forms of music. This digitization of music substantially improved the quality of music. However, consumers still had to buy full albums and had to go to retail stores to buy CDs. The launch of MP3 devices led the first round of digitalization of the music industry. Initially, these devices were essentially digital music being sold through a more convenient device. Soon Apple, with the iPod, changed the music business model. Consumers could now buy individual songs rather than entire albums, and these could be bought online. The next phase of digitalization happened in the mid-2010s, where the hardware device no longer mattered. Consumers could stream music on any device (laptop or phones); they could either purchase songs or subscribe to streaming music services. With in-depth analytics, the streaming providers made playlists and recommendations to the consumers.

By now, we have established the differences between digitization and digitalization or digital transformation. However, digitization of core processes is an antecedent to digital transformation and, therefore, equally critical. Without digitizing, digitalization is not possible. Some companies use the cost savings derived from digitization to fund their digital transformation programmes.

1.6. DIGITAL TECHNOLOGIES

Exhibit 1.6 illustrates commonly prevalent digital technologies across a digital organization.

EXHIBIT 1.6 *Illustrative Use of Digital Technologies*

Customers	Multi-channel communication (web/mobile) Customer Self-service platform Sales platforms Customer relationship management Field service management Social media Collaboration tools
Operations	Robotics AR/VR Big data Financial systems Supply chain platforms Payments Business intelligence E-commerce platforms
Employees	Hiring and onboarding Social media Collaboration tools Employee portal Learning Retention Payroll
Infrastructure	Cyber security Cloud Devices (mobile/tablets/wearables) IoT

Digital technologies can be broadly divided into four categories based on their use within a firm.

1. **Customer focused:** This encompasses both the customer acquisition processes and the customer management and retention processes. Social media, mobile and internet based marketing has rapidly grown in emerging markets. Social media platforms such as Google Reviews, Facebook, LinkedIn and WhatsApp are some examples.
2. **Operation focused:** This includes the processes and technology that form the backbone for delivery. Robotics and IoT based solutions for manufacturing, e-commerce platforms like Alibaba for supply chain management are some examples.
   Payment options have expanded beyond traditional cash-based transactions to the internet, credit card and mobile payments.
3. **Employee focused:** Employee life cycle management, from hiring to exit, forms the crux of this area. There are transactional elements like payroll and self-service portals and value-added processes such as training and skilling.
4. **Infrastructure focused:** This is the area where most progress has been made, with the growing adoption of cloud and virtualization.

Digital technologies are rapidly evolving. Lack of clear standards is making technology decisions very difficult for companies. It is, therefore, better to focus on the strategy and remain flexible on technology choices.

1.7. DRIVERS FOR DIGITAL STRATEGIES

There are several potential drivers for a firm embarking on a digital path (Exhibit 1.7). The internal drivers range from a dynamic chief executive officer (CEO) wanting to bring about change, need for growth and building process efficiencies. External drivers include customer needs, industry dynamics and competition.

1.7.1. External Drivers

1.7.1.1 Industry and Competition

As stated earlier, digital strategy is about strategic change above all else. Therefore, competition plays a critical role in developing this strategy. Competition and industry dynamics

EXHIBIT 1.7 *External and Internal Drivers for a Digital Strategy*

External Drivers	Internal Drivers
Industry and competition	Dynamic leadership
Customer expectations and needs	Growth
Governing agencies	Operational efficiencies
Availability of third-party platforms	Need to globalize
Government push	Attract the right talent

are vital influencers for digital strategy. A company requires a digital strategy to either get ahead of the competition or in many cases just to keep up with the competition. As far back as in early 1900, famed political economist, Joseph Schumpeter theorized that innovation and change come in waves. Innovation creates temporary monopolies, and this provokes other competitors to invest in catching up with the leader. Once they catch up, the entire cycle is repeated, possibly with a new innovator leading the way. Since the impact of digital is to innovate and get ahead of the competition, it has been argued that the Schumpeterian cycle is very applicable to digital transformation.

While competition focusses specifically on the dynamics that arise from what other players in the industry are doing, growth and turbulence are more related to the overall state of the industry. In other words, a company may reactively embark on a digital strategy based on what its competitors are doing (or not doing) or proactively initiate it based on the current state of its industry. In turbulent times, companies are forced to be agile and embark on strategic changes to survive. During industry growth periods, all companies are profitable and adding customers. The need for differentiation is less during these periods, and companies will invest in digital strategies only to the extent that it keeps them on par with the rest of the industry.

1.7.1.2 Customer Expectations

Customers who use digital in their personal lives are expecting the same technology and strategies in their business transactions. Companies are implementing digital strategies to provide customers with the right product at the right time and the right place to meet these expectations. In business-to-business (B2B) transactions, customers themselves are undergoing digital transformation, and they require their suppliers and partners to be in sync with them. Digital has enhanced customer expectations from their suppliers and merchants. This includes the availability of products online and across multiple channels, integration of supply chains or delivery, order-tracking mechanisms, multi-channel and real-time reports and customer support. The only way a company can achieve all these is by going digital.

1.7.1.3 Governing Agencies

As part of the boards of companies, governing agencies such as private equity, venture capital and bankers play a role in challenging management to find new ways to grow and transform, while also approving broad funding decisions. These agencies play a significant role across the digital transformation process of start-ups and when they are scaling up.

These agencies are involved in encouraging the company to start its digital journey, provide financial resources, monitor the impact, provide strategic directions, help build networks and make course corrections. Governing agencies have the luxury of being involved in the digital transformations of multiple investee companies, across industries. They provide company's leadership and management with strategic insights as well as best practices from these multiple industries. As described in the section on the role of leadership later in this chapter, leaders need to 'listen' to non-competitors as well in this age of disruption. Investors are a good source of such information. While prompting from investors is one of the antecedents for embarking of a digital journey, the reverse is also true—companies seeking funding start their digital journey to send a message to potential investors that they are on a growth trajectory.

1.7.1.4 Availability of Third-party Networks

Most companies have begun to leverage external platforms for sales, marketing and input sourcing. E-commerce platforms like Amazon and supply chain platforms such as Ariba and Alibaba are some examples.

1.7.1.5 Governmental Support

To boost the country's economy and generate employment, governments are encouraging companies to adopt digital strategies. Some examples are the technology hubs created by the Singapore government, Bharat Craft which is a B2B e-commerce platform launched by the Indian government, and the Epower forum launched in Kenya to encourage digital strategies and provide the necessary tools.

Interventions by the central government, governmental agencies and industry bodies are critical for digital adoption, especially among smaller companies. These include policy support, providing funding and subsidies and digital training. Governments themselves are adopting digital, and many countries are witnessing the co-evolution of digital in government agencies along with the industry.

1.7.2. Internal Drivers

1.7.2.1 Dynamic Leadership

Digital strategies are high on the agenda of the senior leadership of companies, and such leaders are critical for triggering these digital journeys. Multiple studies have shown that digital frontrunners have leadership with a strong vision of digital strategy. As digital strategies are multifunctional by nature, they need a fulcrum or focal point.

While the role of chief digital officer (CDO) is evolving in organizations, CEO is critical for providing the initial leadership towards the transformation. The role of CEO is to provide overall direction, be the moderator between the IT teams and functional leadership and lead a governance process for the transformation.

To provide overall direction, CEOs need to 'listen'. Traditionally, this 'listening' was restricted to within a firm's industry and adjacent industries. In this continually changing business environment, CEOs need to have an adaptive leadership style, where they are constantly receiving feedback from within the company itself and making course corrections as required. CEOs need to create a culture of open innovation where newer digital strategies are evaluated continuously (Chesbrough, 2004).

Another characteristic of leadership that influences digital innovation is their age cohort. Millennial-led companies move faster to embrace new technologies. Millennials and digital natives readily embrace technology in both their personal and business lives. In traditional family-run businesses, as the millennial generations take over or start playing a larger role, they start to bring in the concepts of digital transformation. Companies that are started by millennials are born digital and incorporate digital strategies from their inception. Another trigger for going digital is that traditional companies suddenly see themselves competing against born-digital companies or companies where the leadership had transitioned to millennials. The threat of being left behind increases their own need to transform digitally.

1.7.2.2 Growth and Customer Connect

One of the primary drivers for digital is increased customer connect and business growth.

A digital strategy increases customer connect by providing the right product and the right place and the right time. For example, using big data, data analytics and AI, a retail company can provide customized products to its customers at the right time. Omnichannel strategies make the buying process seamless and enable customers find the product at a place of their choice.

Digital also plays a significant role in enhancing customer satisfaction and retaining customers. It helps in developing customer orientation as well as customer response processes. Customer orientation relates to 'listening', while customer response is more focused on 'actions'. On the flip side, digital has dramatically increased the number of customer touchpoints, and it has become a complex task for companies to manage.

Growth and scaling in the digital era have taken a new dimension. Digital has allowed for lean growth at speeds that were not possible earlier. Another key difference from the past is that digital provides growth through flexibility. This flexibility, in turn, provides agility for innovation.

Digital allows for companies to globalize rapidly. E-commerce platforms have enabled access to global markets instantaneously. These platforms have allowed for smooth cross-border transfer of digital products such as books, music, other content and training. Digital technologies have enabled tracking of physical goods. For example, IoT devices and radio-frequency identification that allow for tracking of movement of goods have enabled the flow of physical goods, especially to and from emerging economies that lack infrastructure.

1.7.2.3 Increase Process Efficiencies

A 2016 MIT Sloan report found that 80 per cent of early-stage companies stated that improving efficiency and customer experiences is the reason for their digital strategy. Digital technologies help in increasing the efficiency of a company. They help in standardizing and integrating various parts of the value chain seamlessly. Digital technologies also help in eliminating inefficiencies in process workflow, automate manual interventions, provide reporting and monitoring mechanisms, predict process defects by proactive monitoring and so on. IoT, robotics and virtual reality (VR) are some important digital technologies that are implemented to enhance process efficiencies. The data that emerges from a digital implementation can be used to drive further process efficiencies.

Digital strategies have helped in implementing technologies that integrate business processes across a company and its network partners. As product life cycles shorten and R&D costs spiral, concepts such as open innovation enabled by digital technologies are becoming more prevalent.

Industry 4.0 has been used to describe the digital transformation of a production, and manufacturing environment technologies such as Cloud, Blockchain, IoT and Big Data are being integrated to build smart manufacturing.

Industry 4.0 brings value creation opportunities for all types of companies. For a supply chain process, Industry 4.0, sometimes referred to as Procurement 4.0, provides agility, dynamic co-operation and ability to operate beyond organizational and national boundaries. Digital has allowed for companies to rapidly set up new supply chain networks and gain a first-mover advantage for new products. Digital transformation of supply chains has helped increasing current efficiencies and enabled companies to build agile processes to develop, launch and market new products.

At production level, increased productivity and flexibility allow for smaller batch sizes and automate production decisions, and big data and analytics combined with IoT help in proactive detection of errors and defects. This helps in increasing customer experience and customer satisfaction.

Implementing a standard digital strategy across an organization, including ERP and supply chain management systems, can be complex and time-consuming. However, once implemented, it can lead to greater efficiencies and agility.

1.7.2.4 Need to Globalize

Going global and exploring new markets is one of the key triggers of a digital strategy. Digital enables instant cross-border trade. This cross-border trade encompasses a whole variety of transactions. E-commerce platforms have enabled sourcing of materials from a global supplier base. On the other end, these platforms have allowed for companies to expand their markets outside of their national boundaries. In the pre-digital era, companies, especially small companies, did not have the resources to go beyond their regional markets. Digital has enabled them to access these markets with very minimal set-up costs and efforts and has reduced the time to do so.

Another aspect of digital is accessing global talent. While this has been primarily in the services sector, digital platforms such as Flexjobs and WorkMarket have allowed companies to source talent globally.

1.7.2.5 Attract the Right Talent

Digital strategies have a significant impact on the 'people strategy' of companies. On the one hand, the platform layer of digital including AI, chatbots and robotic automation eliminates the need for manual interventions and, therefore, the need for large teams. Organizations will need to be relatively lean and, therefore, procure a larger number of outsourced and contract employees. Digital platforms will be used to source employees and teams as and when required. On the other hand, learning functions within organizations must leverage digital to provide training on innovation, change and agility in addition to skills required for digital transformation. A specialist will be the most sought-after employee.

Networking and collaboration will be vital for fostering innovation and agility. Creating a digital workplace that incorporates digital technologies such as big data, cloud and AI can help in enhancing individual and organizational productivity.

While implementing a digital strategy requires talent, companies also use their digital maturity to attract the right talent. The younger workforce, especially millennials, need to feel that they are a part of the next big opportunity. Therefore, a company needs to project that it is a digitally mature company or on its path to digital transformation. The word 'digital' has also been added into job titles to attract the right talent. A 2015 MIT Sloan study showed that employees between the wide age range of 22–60 years prefer to work for digital leaders (Kane et al., 2015).

1.8. DEGREE OF DIGITAL ADOPTION

Digital adoption is a continuum, and the line between digitization and digital transformation is very fine. Exhibit 1.8 provides the stages a company could potentially go through across its digital journey.

Most technology companies and start-ups are digital experts. At the other end of the spectrum, there are hardly any companies that fit into the digital unaware category. The COVID-19 pandemic has accelerated digital adoption. As a result, most companies are in the digital 'aware', 'starter' or 'proficient' phases. The degree of digital adoption also varies by industry. Specific industries such as financial services, healthcare and retail have seen greater adoption of digital. Manufacturing, small and medium enterprises, and agri industries are in the early stages of adoption.

EXHIBIT 1.8 | *Digital Adoption Phases*

Stage	Definition
Digital unaware	Unaware of digital transformation or digitalization Basic awareness of digitization and automation
Digital aware	Aware of digitalization Have considered implementing digital strategies
Digital starter	Implemented at least one digital technology
Digital proficient	Has a digital road map In the process of implementing multiple digital technologies Focus on business model changes
Digital expert	Fully digital (typically, only born-digital or digital-native companies)

MINI CASE 1.1. DISCUSSION

Digital transformation starts from the top and flows down in an organization. In 2016, Unilever appointed Rahul Welde as executive vice-president to lead the digital transformation initiatives of the company.[1] Rahul, who had joined the company in 1991, had worked across a range of roles in the global organization. The company initiated what it called the 5C framework for its transformation—consumers at the centre, with great content and connections, building communities and powering commerce.

To compete against the newer entrants, Unilever launched a 'Sustainable Living Plan' programme. The premise of the programme was for Unilever to get closer to its customer through holistic value proposition including sustainable sourcing, fair treatment of employees and partners and impact on climate change.

The company used digital marketing in addition to traditional channels to market its products to its customers. Platforms such as Instagram were used to communicate its digital and sustainability initiatives to its employees and partners. The company focused on digital upskilling of its employees through in-house training programmes.

The company also used technology to automate several processes such as payments, company communications and supply chain procedures. This turned bottlenecks into seamless processes and improved productivity and efficiency of its workforce. By 2019, the company had automated over 700 processes.

The company invested heavily in an omnichannel presence that provided its customers with a seamless experience across e-commerce and conventional retail stores. Unilever also began to extensively leverage data, using technology and tools, and engaged with its consumers more directly through a data-driven approach. The company began to use AI, machine learning (ML) and voice-related technologies to deliver personalized and immersive experiences to consumer platforms like Recipedia.

To accelerate innovation, Unilever launched the Unilever Foundry, a platform to partner with start-ups and develop a long-lasting ecosystem. The foundry helped the company to collaborate with start-ups in procurement, brand partnerships and product development, among others.

By 2019, the digital transformation of Unilever started to show tangible results. In February 2019, the company announced that the company had sold €3.12 billion (representing 6% of the total sales) through e-commerce channels like Amazon.[2] The company also reduced its reliance on big-box retailers with e-commerce growing 13 per cent globally.

[1] https://infotechlead.com/cio/unilever-reveals-how-digital-transformation-improves-consumer-relationship-58299
[2] https://infotechlead.com/cio/unilever-digital-transformation-lifts-e-commerce-sales-in-2019-60681

SUMMARY

A digital strategy is a strategy enabled by digital technologies. A comprehensive digital strategy consists of operational innovation, product or service innovation, business model innovation and organizational innovation, all of which are enabled by a set of new digital technologies that include networking and storage, platforms and applications, intelligence including data and analytics, and automation. These new technologies have become prevalent due to radical improvements in processing speeds, storage capacity and networking.

Traditional companies undergo a digital transformation for several reasons including enhancing operational efficiencies, growth and revenues, increased customer reach and customer satisfaction. The digital strategies of these companies are referred to as digital transformation strategies. For a successful transformation, a company needs the right leadership, robust change management processes, technology (in-house or outsourced) and most importantly, a need to change. This need to change could be driven by internal factors such as efficiencies and cost reduction, and external factors such as customer need, competition and regulatory changes.

Only born-digital or digital-native companies are wholly digital. Most traditional companies go through a long and phased process of restructuring to become digital companies.

Discussion Questions

1. Define digital strategy in your own words.
2. What is the relationship between digital strategy and technology strategy?
3. What are the four historical phases of industrial transformations? How is digital transformation different?
4. Give three key reasons for companies to begin their digital transformation journey.
5. What are some key antecedents to a successful digital strategy?
6. What are the stages of digital transformation? For each of the stages, describe one industry that you believe is that stage.

GLOSSARY

Digital strategy: Strategy enabled by digital technologies. It consists of innovation of processes, products and services, business models and organizations.

Digital technologies: The set of newer technologies that make digital transformation different from earlier transformations.

Industrial revolutions: Generally referred to the four phases of industry from the mid-18th century to current times. While the exact dates of each of the four phases can be debated, there is consensus on the broad timelines. Within each phase, there is a continuum of change.

Transformation: A company making fundamental changes to the way it works to deliver better stakeholder value.

REFERENCES

Bharadwaj, A., El Sawy, O. A., Pavlou, P. A., & Venkatraman, N. (2013). Digital business strategy: Toward a next generation of insights. *MIS Quarterly, 37*(2), 471–482.

Chesbrough, H. (2004). Managing open innovation. *Research-Technology Management, 47*(1), 23–26.

Hess, T., Matt, C., Benlian, A., & Wiesböck, F. (2016). Options for formulating a digital transformation strategy. *MIS Quarterly Executive, 15*(2), 123–139.

Kane, G. C., Palmer, D., Phillips, A. N., Kiron, D., & Buckley, N. (2015). Strategy, not technology, drives digital transformation: Becoming a digitally mature enterprise. *MIT Sloan Management Review* and Deloitte.

Kotter, J. P. (2012). *Leading change.* Harvard Business Press.

Roser, M., & Ritchie, H. (2013). Technological progress. *Our World in Data.*

Schaller, R. R. (1997). Moore's law: Past, present and future. *IEEE Spectrum, 34*(6), 52–59.

Walter, C. (2005). Kryder's law. *Scientific American,* 32–33.

Woodard, C. J., Ramasubbu, N., Tschang, F. T., & Sambamurthy, V. (2013). Design capital and design moves: The logic of digital business strategy. *MIS Quarterly, 37*(2), 537–564.

CHAPTER

2

Strategic Management

Learning Objectives

Chapter 1 helped define digital strategy and introduced the digital strategy framework. This chapter describes how to build an overall digital strategy using traditional frameworks. By the end of this chapter, readers will be able to:

- Define strategy.
- Understand the steps in a strategy development process.
- Understand how digital is impacting this process.
- Understand various frameworks in strategic management.
- Role of digital technologies in strategy development.

Mini Case 2.1

Priya Rao was a director of Sree Speciality Pharma (Sree), a paediatric pharmaceutical company that made a range of over-the-counter (OTC) baby products such as talcum powder and bath gels and skincare lotions. Sree was a family-owned pharmaceutical company headquartered in Coimbatore, India. It was founded by Priya's father Raj Rao three decades ago. Raj, who was a chemical engineer from Anna University, was formerly an employee of Indian Chemicals, a public sector company. In the late 1970s, Raj and a few colleagues from his former company decided to quit their jobs and found Sree. In three decades that followed, the company grew to a turnover of ₹100 crore with 150 employees. The company's products were sold primarily through paediatricians even though the products were OTC and could be sold without a prescription.

Raj's other co-founders had retired a few years ago, and it was now Raj's turn to step down from active management. The founders had decided that Priya would lead the company with the help of professional management. Priya, herself, was a chemical engineer from Anna University and had a management degree from the University of Wisconsin, Madison. As Priya was preparing to take over the company and bring in professional managers, she realized that the company did not have a formal strategy. The three founders managed the company based on weekly meetings, where they took both strategic and tactical decisions.

The co-founders were managing Sree like a traditional pharma company with limited technology on the production floor and in its back-office functions. On the customer front, Sree was facing severe competition from both international players and newer start-ups focusing on similar products. These start-ups were getting their products developed by outsourcing R&D and production while concentrating their efforts on marketing their products. They bypassed the traditional pharmaceutical channels and went directly to customers through digital channels. With their lean and agile structures, these newer companies were able to react to changing market needs much faster.

Sree was caught between the financial might of the large multinationals and the agility of these start-ups. However, the company had a good brand reputation as well as a competent distribution network in the southern and western states of India.

Priya realized that to take the company to its next phase of growth, she needed to develop a formal strategic plan. This plan would need to incorporate digital elements as it would provide direction to the company for the next five years.

She had learnt about strategy in her MBA programme and had attended multiple courses on digital strategy on Coursera but was struggling to develop a strategic plan for the company.

2.1. DEFINING STRATEGY

Simply put, strategy is a plan to achieve a business goal. A strategy sets the common goals and the boundaries within which a company operates. Strategic planning is the process of formulating a strategy, and strategic management is used in the context of formulating and executing a strategy.

At a firm or corporate level, it is referred to as corporate strategy; at the divisional or business level, it is a business strategy, and at a functional level, it could be a marketing or technology strategy (Exhibit 2.1). The corporate strategy provides the overall direction to business and functional strategy, and there is a continuous feedback process to keep all three synchronized. In companies that have a single division, there is a significant overlap between corporate and business strategy.

2.2. HOW IS STRATEGY CHANGING?

There is a considerable business and academic literature on formulating and implementing strategy. Concepts and frameworks such as Porter's five forces and strengths, weaknesses, opportunities and threats (SWOT) analysis have been used extensively by organizations of all sizes.

Traditionally, corporate strategies were developed for a 5–10-year horizon. However, the rapid evolution of technology and shorter life cycles of products and services is requiring strategies to be updated far more frequently. Professors Bill Fischer and Michael Wade of IMD have gone to the extent of stating that 'strategy is dead' as the world is

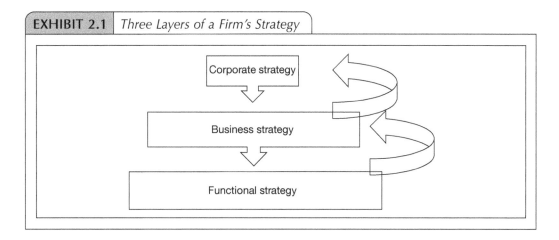

EXHIBIT 2.1 *Three Layers of a Firm's Strategy*

changing rapidly.[1] While this may be a radical thought, there is no doubt that the strategic planning process itself is transforming. Some of the critical changes are described below.

Driven by digital: The most significant change in the development of strategy is the incorporation of digital elements within the strategic plan.

For most companies, their digital strategy has become the primary strategic plan. As defined in the earlier chapter, a digital strategy is a strategy enabled by digital technologies. The need for strategic change is being caused by the availability of newer digital technologies and the strategic choices they enable.

The relationship between strategy and digital technologies is bidirectional. Strategy determines the choice of digital technologies, while the availability of digital technologies allows for new strategies. Companies need to balance the two while developing their strategy.

Changing horizons: Traditionally, companies developed a strategy with a 5–10-year horizon in mind. During this period, the overall direction of the company remained relatively stable, while there were minor changes at the implementation level. Rapid shifts in industry structures have shortened the life cycles of innovation, products and even executives. CEO tenure in the *Fortune* 500 has fallen from an average of 11 years in 2002 to 6 years by 2016. The average lifespan of a company in the *Fortune* 500© has shrunk from 25 years in 1980 to just 15 by 2016.[2] A long-term plan is now relevant for a maximum of 2–3 years.

A new set of competitors: The first task in any strategic planning is to scan the industry and map competitors. Digital has obscured the boundary between industries, and it is no longer enough to scan the traditional boundaries. The music industry was disrupted by a (then) PC company called Apple; the retail industry was disrupted by an internet bookseller called Amazon, and the taxi service industry was disrupted by a company that did not own a single cab. It is no longer easy to define which industry a company operates in. For example, is Apple a cell phone company or a music company or an OTT media channel? Which industries should Apple be benchmarking itself with? Alternately, which industries and companies should consider Apple as part of their competition set? The blurring of lines between industries requires careful thinking as to who a company's current and future competitors may be.

Changing customer needs: Millennial customers have an underlying need for change. Product life cycles have reduced to less than two years, and companies are being forced to innovate far more often than in the past. Companies can no longer make long-term product strategies and need to be able to react to rapidly changing consumer needs and industry disruptions

2.3. STRATEGIC MANAGEMENT FRAMEWORK

The steps involved in developing a digital strategy are similar to those used to develop a more traditional strategy. However, digital elements need to be brought in at every stage of strategy development. While there is no single 'right method', there are broadly four steps in building a ground-up digital strategy.

The first step is 'environment scanning' that consists of scanning the environment in which a company operates. The second step, 'strategy formulation', consists of several substeps, including 'business assessment', 'strategic objectives' and 'strategy development'. The final two steps in a strategy are 'implementation' and 'evaluation and control' (Exhibit 2.2).

EXHIBIT 2.2   *Overall Strategy Process*

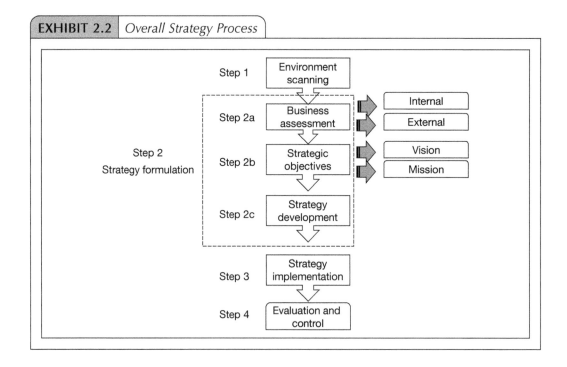

2.3.1. Environment Scanning (Step 1)

This step includes a systematic scanning, filtering and dissemination of relevant information on internal and external environments to stakeholders.

2.3.1.1. External Data

The starting point for any good strategy is gathering external industry data. The data can be primary or secondary.

Primary data is information that is gathered for the specific purpose it is required from the relevant stakeholders. It is usually gathered through interviews, panels or surveys. Most companies engage in some primary data collection activities throughout the year. An industry benchmarking survey initiated by a company is an example of primary data.

Secondary data is created for other purposes but can help in aiding the strategic planning process. Statistics relating to the health of the economy, billing and sales data, financial data and market share data are some examples of secondary data. In the digital world, data gathered from mining customer reviews on social media sites like Google Reviews or Yelp are examples of secondary data.

At a broad level, the external information required to build an effective strategy can be classified into five buckets—economic, policy and regulation, technological, sociocultural and industry (Exhibit 2.3).

Economic: This data relates to macro and microeconomic factors that impact a company. The data can be at a regional, national or global level depending on the scope of operations of a company. Typical economic data includes the gross domestic product (GDP), growth, employment rates and inflation.

Economic data can be collected from a variety of sources, including industry bodies, international financial bodies, such as the World Bank and Industrial Finance Corporation of India (IFCI), and central banks and economic surveys at a national level. For example, in India, economic data can be harnessed from the annual economic survey, annual budget reports and various reports published by the Reserve Bank of India.

Policy and regulation: Policy and regulations play an essential role in developing a company's strategy. Changes in tax laws, implementation of new taxation systems (like the introduction of GST in India), export incentives and opening or closing of sectors for foreign companies are some examples of policy changes. In the world of digital commerce, there is still a significant ambiguity on matters such as jurisdiction for taxation and the definition of services and products. For example, in India, there are restrictions on multi-brand retail companies entering the country. E-commerce companies need to ensure that there is no deviation from this policy when they market their house brands from their portals. Digital has also blurred the lines between product and services. These two categories are still governed by different policies and taxed at different rates in many countries. As a company develops its product strategy, it is critical to understand the policy and tax implications of such a strategy. Another significant implication for digital companies is their jurisdiction of operation as this governs the regulations they need to adhere to. Companies need to clearly understand the implications of intercountry and interstate commerce as

EXHIBIT 2.3 *Information for Environment Scanning*

Classification	Type of Data	Sources
Economic	GDP Inflation Unemployment Income growth Disposable income Currency rates Population growth Urbanization Population by socio-economic classification (SEC) Energy	World Bank IFCI reports Country economic surveys Annual budgets Central Bank reports
Policy and regulation	Tax laws Industry-specific regulations Intellectual property Patent laws Data privacy and security laws Incentives Labour laws Immigration laws Foreign trade regulations Environmental laws Corporate social responsibility laws	Government bodies Industry regulatory agencies (e.g., US Food and Drug Administration) Accounting firms Law firms
Technology	Digital technologies Improvements to current technologies Trends in mobility and internet penetration Automation	Technology reports Vendors and consultants Exhibitions and conferences Academic research Competition Industry associations
Sociocultural	Demographic data Age distribution Literacy Migration and urbanization Employee trends Unionization Customer preferences Customer lifestyles Media consumption	Government sources Census Customer surveys and reports Panel data Industry reports Sales team
Industry	Competitor set Adjacent industries Market share Trends in customers' industries Vendor set Trends in vendors' industries Start-ups and potential disruptors M&A activity	Industry reports News and media Company reports Panel data Sales team

part of their strategic plans. Intelligence on intellectual property, patent laws and data security laws are other critical pieces of information that are required in the digital age.

Sources for policy and regulations include government bodies, industry regulatory agencies and external consultants like accounting firms.

Technological: In the digital age, companies must scan for new technologies and platforms continuously. Technology information can be at two levels. At a macro level, it can relate to government policy on technology, availability of incentives and telecom laws, among others. At a micro-level, this can range from new technologies being developed, improvements to existing technologies or automation.

There are several sources for gathering technology information. Industry reports such as the 'Gartner Magic Quadrant', tracking of start-ups, vendors, exhibitions and conferences and competitor activities are some sources for technology information.

Sociocultural: Sociocultural information can be broadly classified into two types of data. Structured data is easier to collect and includes statistics relating to population, demographics, ageing and skill availability, among others. The more challenging part is sourcing data relating to employee and consumer preferences that are primarily unstructured and subjective. Sociocultural data forms an essential part of a product strategy. This data could range from changing customer lifestyles, the impact of digital on buying behaviour, attitudes to brands, willingness to pay premiums for organic or handcrafted goods or preferences between domestic and international brands. In addition to customers and products, sociocultural data also impacts the ability of a company to attract the right talent. For example, a digital culture plays a vital role in the decision of millennials to work for a company.

Sources for sociocultural data include demographic data from census and other government bodies, employee surveys and consumer reports.

Industry: This includes data on the industry a company operates in, the industries its customers are from (in the case of B2B customers) and its vendors' industries. Information on a company's own industry includes the competition, both current and potential. In the digital world, it is also important to track players in adjacent industries and other industries that could disrupt the company's industry. Start-ups are another set of companies that may not be current competitors. However, they could become one in the future or get acquired by an existing competitor. It is also important to track changes in a customer's industry, as changes here may have a direct impact on their purchase behaviours. This is especially true in B2B scenarios. Vendor industries also need to be tracked for consolidation, M&A, new materials and technologies as these may have an impact on the supply chain.

Industry and company reports and news and media activities are some sources for industry data.

Digital technologies have significantly impacted the process of external environmental scanning. On the one hand, data is readily available through online resources. On the other hand, there is an overload of data from multiple sources. The data is also available in both structured and unstructured formats. According to a *Harvard Business Review* article, less than half of an organization's structured data is actively used in making decisions, and less than 1 per cent of its unstructured data is analysed or used at all (DalleMule & Davenport, 2017). Companies, therefore, need to identify reliable sources of data and develop a mechanism to continuously collect, store, organize and analyse data. Data sources have been extended from traditional industry reports and customer surveys to social media platforms. Technologies such as AI and ML are being deployed to analyse data. Several data visualization tools are available to interpret the data and to make the insights easier.

2.3.1.2. Internal Data

The second source of data for building an effective strategy is internal data. This includes data on past performance across the organization. One of the challenges with internal data is that in large companies, the data lies across multiple systems and platforms in multiple geographies. Companies that have not implemented effective information management and business analytics tools struggle to collate effective and accurate internal data. Some types of internal data and potential sources are highlighted in Exhibit 2.4.

EXHIBIT 2.4	Internal Data for Environment Scanning

Classification	Type of Data	Sources
Financial	P&L and balance sheets Division, region and product-wise financial performance Budget versus actual performance	Financial systems (ERP) Budgets
Sales	Products and services sold Profitability and market share by product Cost of sale by product Sales team structure and size Salesforce effectiveness Sales stages and cycles Challenges in selling	Sales team Financial systems Point of sale systems Business intelligence tools Sales management CRMs
Technology	Technologies in use Projects and programmes underway and being planned Insourcing versus outsourcing Offshore strategy	Technology asset registers Technology team
Vendors/Suppliers	Vendors by product and service Preferred vendor list Cost of input products and services Geographic distribution Risk and challenges	Procurement or supply chain ERP Contracts Supply chain team
Employees	Employees break-up Wages and inflation Sourcing of employees Skills requirement Hiring and training challenges Attrition and retention strategies	HR systems HR team

Like external data, the challenge with internal data includes the volume and multiple sources of data. Digitization and digitalization have helped in organizing the data for better analysis. For example, implementing a salesforce customer relationship management (CRM) has helped in consolidating and organizing data relating to customers and the pipeline. Similarly, the implementation of supply chain platforms has helped in streamlining data relating to vendors, raw materials and logistics.

2.3.2. Business Assessment (Step 2a)

Several frameworks are available for analysing the data gathered in Step 1.

SWOT analysis (Helms & Nixon, 2010): SWOT was first developed in the 1960s and is still a commonly used method to analyse a firm's position (Exhibit 2.5).

Strengths refer to what the company does well and the unique resources it can draw on. Strengths can be operational efficiencies, profitability, revenue growth or market share. They can be tangible and intangible factors that contribute to a company's strengths. Tangible attributes may include the location of factories or technologies. Intangible attributes include the skill set of the workforce, company culture and so on.

Weaknesses are areas a company can improve and includes gaps in people, resources or product quality. These weaknesses are relative to competition and prevent the company from gaining from its customers. From a digital perspective, this could include poor automation, outdated technology and even poor data management.

Opportunities are areas where a company can build its strengths and gain against competitors. Opportunities can also be an outcome of industry and market trends. Some examples of opportunities in the digital context are analysing customer data and leveraging them against competition or building an asset-light model that allows a company to remain agile.

EXHIBIT 2.5 | *SWOT Analysis*

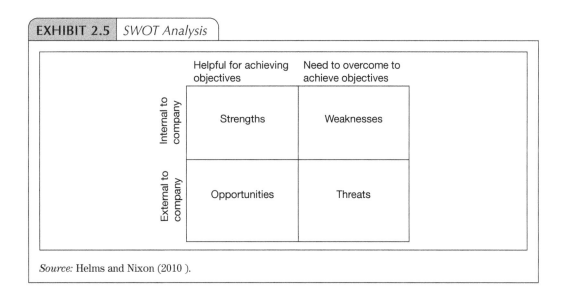

Source: Helms and Nixon (2010).

Threats are external factors that can harm a company exploiting its weaknesses. Threats could also be from regulatory changes (e.g., tax or foreign investment policy), institutional changes (e.g., change in government or government policy) and environmental changes (e.g., war or financial crisis).

SWOT is a simplistic analysis of a company and its environment, and there are more well-developed models for information analysis. Ideally, a separate analysis of a firm's internal and external environment provides a more comprehensive view of a company's strengths and weaknesses.

2.3.2.1. Assessment of Internal Environment

Internal scanning, also referred to as organizational analysis, focuses on identifying and strengthening an organization's internal resources.

A resource-based view (RBV) is a framework often used to evaluate a company's strengths and resources that it can use for competitive advantage. While RBV has existed in various forms since the 1930s, Jay Barney's 1991 article, 'Firm Resources and Sustained Competitive Advantage' (Barney, 1991), is the milestone that made RBV mainstream.

According to RBV, a company has two kinds of resources, which are as follows:

Tangible: These are physical assets such as infrastructure, machinery, equipment and capital. Most of these assets can be acquired and, therefore, do not offer too much of a competitive advantage unless there is something unique. For example, a company may have a factory that is uniquely located close to a critical input raw material, or it has an exclusive contract with a raw material supplier or key digital channel partner.

Intangible: These are assets that have no physical presence. Brand, trademarks, intellectual property, process know-how, work methods, customer relationships are all intangible assets.

Where resources are an organization's assets and its basic building blocks, capabilities are the ability of a company to harness these resources. Capabilities can be in the form of processes or routines that manage the interactions between the resources and turn inputs into outputs. Typical capabilities include marketing capabilities and technology capabilities.

At the next level, competency is an integration of multifunctional capabilities. For example, integrating a company's marketing and technology capabilities can lead to its digital e-commerce competency (see Exhibit 2.6).

A core competency is a competency that is unique to a company and differentiates it from other companies in its industry. For competencies to be able to provide a company competitive advantage, they need to meet the following criteria:

1. **Heterogenous:** The competencies are different from what competition possesses.
2. **Immobile:** The competencies are not mobile, at least in the short run—a stellar employee who can be poached by a competitor is not a unique advantage.

For example, as per Mukesh Ambani, chairman of Reliance Industries, the core competency of the company is to execute large-scale capital-intensive projects.[3] The competency

EXHIBIT 2.6 | *Resources–Capabilities–Competencies*

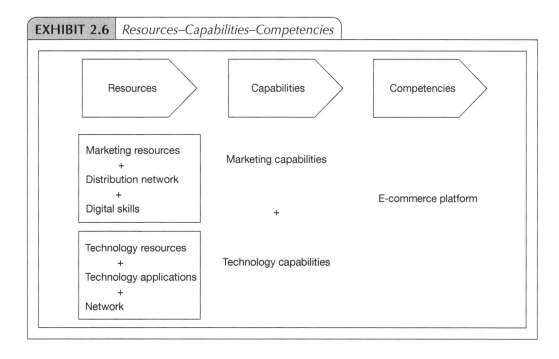

is based on multiple capabilities in the company, including project management, capital financing, technology and people. Reliance has fine-tuned its competencies from the learnings of multiple large-scale projects. The company now has the financial, people and process skills very few other companies in India can match. Thus, the competencies are both heterogeneous and immobile, making them core competencies.

Barney proposed the value, rarity, imitability and organization (VRIO) framework to test the sustainable advantage its resources offer (Exhibit 2.7). For a resource to provide a sustainable competitive advantage, it needs to pass through all the following four questions posed in the framework:

EXHIBIT 2.7 | *VRIO Framework*

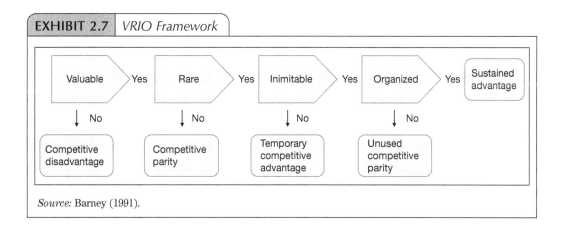

Source: Barney (1991).

1. **Valuable:** The first question of the framework asks if a resource adds value by enabling a firm to exploit opportunities or defend against threats. A resource can be valuable if it provides value to a company's customers. The value can be in the form of additional product features or reduced costs. The resources that cannot meet this condition lead to a competitive disadvantage. As market dynamics and competitor actions increase or decrease the value of a resource, a company needs to evaluate the value of its competencies continually.

2. **Rare:** It denotes resources that are unique to one or a few companies. Some of the questions that determine rarity is whether there is a persistent demand for the resource over time and relatively fewer companies control the resource. Rare and valuable resources lead to a company being on par with its competitors.

3. **Inimitable**: The next filter in the VRIO model is if a resource is difficult and costly to imitate by other organizations. Imitation can be in two forms. A competitor may be able to build the same resource (duplication) or build an alternate resource (substitution) that provides the same product or services. A firm that has valuable, rare and inimitable resource can achieve a temporary competitive advantage. Barney identified the following three reasons why resources can be hard to imitate:

    i. **Historical conditions:** Resources that were developed due to historical events or over a long period are costly to imitate.

    ii. **Causal ambiguity:** Companies cannot identify the resources that are the cause of their competitive advantage.

    iii. **Social complexity:** The resources and capabilities that are based on a company's culture or interpersonal relationships.

4. **Capturing the value:** The resources themselves do not confer any advantage for a company if it is not organized to capture the value from them. A firm must organize its management systems, processes, policies, organizational structure and culture to be able to fully realize the potential of its valuable, rare and costly to imitate resources, capabilities and competencies. Only then, the companies can achieve sustained competitive advantage.

Exhibit 2.8 provides a VRIO analysis of Reliance Jio, one of India's largest telecom company against its competitors Vodafone and Airtel. For this analysis, the attributes relevant to the telecom industry have been considered. These attributes vary by industry and type of service or products being offered.

EXHIBIT 2.8	*Reliance Jio VRIO*				
VRIO	**Extensive Network**	**Large Customer Base**	**Value Brand**	**Financial Strength**	**Value-added Products**
Valuable	Yes	Yes	Yes	Yes	Yes
Rare	No	No	Yes	Yes	Yes
Inimitable	No	No	Yes	Yes	Yes
Organized	Yes	Yes	Yes	Yes	Yes

According to the above analysis, Reliance Jio's network and customer base put in on par with other telecom players such as Vodafone and Airtel. Its sustained competitive advantage is derived from its financial strength, brand positioning of being a value player and the value-added products and services that it provides (including the Jiomart omnichannel grocery service).

2.3.2.2. Assessment of External Environment

Several factors make up for an external environment. Michael Porter's five forces (Porter, 2008) model is a well-known framework for industry analysis (Exhibit 2.9).

Industry: Industry analysis begins with the definition of the industry that a firm operates in.

As discussed earlier in the chapter, industry lines are blurring, and it is no longer an easy task. Many new-age companies compete in multiple industries. One way for a company to ensure that no relevant industry is left out of the analysis is to start with the revenue break-up of its products and services. Each line item on the revenue line will identify the industry the company operates. Exhibit 2.10 illustrates these new industries and competition for Reliance Jio.

One of the unique dynamics of digital companies is that two companies may partner for one service offering and compete on another service offering. For example, Jio may partner with Facebook for retail but compete on messaging services.

Once the industry(ies) has been defined, the next step is to analyse each of the industries. Some of the questions that are part of a typical analysis include the following:

- What are some of the trends in the industry?
- What is the growth rate of the industry?
- How is the industry growing in other emerging and advanced markets?
- Is the industry cyclical?

EXHIBIT 2.9 | *Assessment of External Environment*

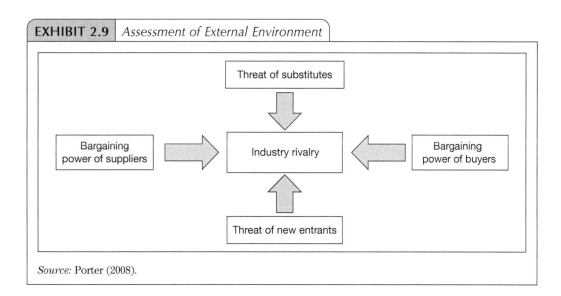

Source: Porter (2008).

EXHIBIT 2.10	*Industry Competition across Services for Reliance Jio*

Service	Industry	Industry Players
Voice	Telecom	Airtel, Vodafone
Data	Data services	Airtel, Vodafone, Sify, ACT
Streaming music	Music	Apple, Spotify, Amazon
Retail/e-commerce	Retail	Amazon, Flipkart
Messaging	Social media	Facebook, WhatsApp

Another aspect of industry analysis is policies and regulations. As discussed earlier in the chapter, policies and regulations are becoming more complex in the digital world. Some of the questions that need to be considered while developing a strategy include the following:

- Is the industry regulated?
- Who is the regulator (or regulators)?
- What are the trends in regulations?
- How is the regulation expected to change in the short term and medium term?
- Will the change in regulations be helpful or detrimental?
- What is the taxation regime for products/services? Is this expected to change?
- What are the laws under privacy, security and data protection for the relevant industry?

Industry analysis also includes an evaluation of the entry and exit barriers from the industry.

Competitors/new entrants: Along with industry dynamics, competitor strategy forms an important variable in a company's strategy. Some of the key questions that need to be analysed include the following:

- Who are the competitors?
- Are these start-ups or established companies?
- What differentiates the company from its competitors?
- What are the company's weaknesses when compared to its competitors?
- Which countries are the competitors from? Is this expected to change?

Digital has had an impact on competition on two fronts. First, it has enabled easy globalization, and a company needs to look beyond its national boundaries while defining competition. Second, ease of communication and cloud-based technologies have led to the formation of asset-light start-ups. Entry barriers that were once based on the time required to set up R&D teams and production facilities have been eliminated by contract R&D and manufacturing. Start-ups can take a product from concept to launch in much shorter time-lines and pose a real threat to incumbent players.

Suppliers: Suppliers form an important part of a company's strategy. The advent of digital has redefined supply chains. Many digital companies are platforms; they do not own their resources and are highly dependent on their suppliers. For example, Ola and Uber, the larg-est ride-share companies in India, have many individual and cab service operators as their suppliers. While this reduces their fixed costs, it also increases their dependencies on these suppliers. There have been several instances in the last few years of their suppliers striking or discontinuing their services, thereby impacting their market share and brand reputation. Another trend in the supply chain is the hyper-globalization of suppliers. Most companies now use a best-shoring strategy and have vendors and suppliers all over the world con-nected by technology. Any analysis of suppliers needs to consider these factors.

Some of the key questions that are critical for supplier analysis include the following:

- Who are the suppliers to the industry?
- Can suppliers put any constraints on the company's growth?
- What has been the pricing trends from suppliers? Is this expected to change?
- Are there any disruptions possible in the supply chain due to trade wars?
- What supply chain technologies will be required for managing an effective process?

Customers/buyers: Customers are the most critical part of any strategy development. This is also the element of the strategy that is most dynamic. Customers determine a com-pany's product strategy, business model and marketing strategies. Each of these elements is covered in subsequent chapters in the book.

Some of the key questions that a company needs to analyse about its customers are:

- Who are the company's customers?
- What are the various segments? Which are growing and which are not?
- What have been the recent customer trend? Are customers expected to consume more or less of the company's product? What factors will determine this?
- What products/services can potentially substitute a company's product portfolio?
- How sensitive are customers to price?
- What factors do customers value in the company's product/service? What is their benchmark product/service?
- What is the optimum product-pricing-promotion-distribution strategy?
- How can the company leverage omnichannel, e-commerce and platforms to enhance sales?

Exhibit 2.11 provides some examples of how digital is changing the way a company looks at its customer strategy.

EXHIBIT 2.11	*Impact of Digital on the Marketing Mix*

4P	Impact of Digital
Product	Integrated products and services, disruption from alternate business models
Place	Multichannel, omnichannel, e-commerce, instant globalization
Price	Subscription based, shared models
Promotion	Social media, information clutter

In addition to the constructs outlined by the above framework, companies also need to keep specific track of disruptions in their external environment. In the digital age, there is a need for companies to focus on three types of disruptions:

1. **Technology disruption:** Any strategy needs to explicitly include analyses of traditional technologies, recent technologies and future technologies and the role each will play in the future of the company. Examples of current technologies include enterprise resource planning (ERP) and automation; recent technologies include the IoT (AI) and robotics, and future technologies include VR and blockchain.
2. **Business model disruption:** Newer models such as shared services and 'product as a service' are disrupting industries. Companies need to evaluate all types of models and determine the ones most suitable for their product and industry.
3. **Start-up disruption:** Many industries and companies are getting disrupted by start-ups. As part of its strategy, a company needs to evaluate the start-ups in its industry and determine the right strategy to prevent being disrupted. The strategies could include partnering with these start-ups or acquiring them.

Environment scanning and business assessments force senior management to analyse their industry, competitors, regulations and internal strengths. Even for established companies, it is useful to go through this exercise every year.

2.3.3. Strategic Objectives (Step 2b)

The next step in the process is to develop the overall strategic objectives of the company. These will form the guiding principles for the rest of the process. The strategic objectives process has two parts.

2.3.3.1. Vision Statement

A vision statement describes the future direction of the business and its goals for the next three–five years. A vision statement needs to be crisp and something that very easily communicates the company's focus to all its stakeholders.

As described in Chapter 1, providing the digital vision for a company that is transforming itself from a traditional business to a digital business is critical. A change in the vision and mission statements signals the commencement of this transformation to a company's internal and external stakeholders.

2.3.3.2. Mission Statement

The mission statement goes hand in hand with the vision statement and outlines its primary objectives. This focuses on what needs to be done in the short term to realize the long-term vision. Exhibit 2.12 provides the vision and mission of some digital companies. As can be seen from the Exhibit, some companies combine their vision and mission statements.

2.3.4. Strategy Development (Step 2c)

The next step of the process is to develop a strategy that helps a company achieve its strategic objectives. This includes determining and developing the overall positioning of the company and its business model.

However, there is no perfect strategy! Frameworks and financial analysis provide inputs and structure to the decision-making process. The final strategy that a company chooses has to be a well-informed choice based on the analysis, tribal knowledge and intuition of key decision-makers.

There are several frameworks available for developing a strategy and positioning of a company.

Porter's generic strategies framework is one such framework (Porter, 2011) used to determine the basis for differentiation for a company (Exhibit 2.13).

EXHIBIT 2.12 | *Vision–Mission of Digital Companies*

Company	Vision	Mission
Disney	To be one of the world's leading producers and providers of entertainment and information.	To use our portfolio of brands to differentiate our content, services and consumer products. We seek to develop the most creative, innovative and profitable entertainment experiences and related products in the world for a delightful customer experience.
Asian Paints	We want to be an innovative, agile and responsive world-class research and technology organization that is aligned to future customer needs and catalyses the growth of the company across existing and future businesses.	To provide paints as per market demand, ensuring the desired level and quality of customer (dealer) service, continued availability of the right product mix of right quality at the right time.
Uber	Uber's mission is to bring transportation, for everyone, everywhere.	Smarter transportation with fewer cars and greater access. Transportation that is safer, cheaper and more reliable; transportation that creates more job opportunities and higher incomes for drivers.
TRRINGO (India)	TRRINGO is a foremost tractor and farm equipment rental business that aims to raise the level of mechanization in Indian farming through the power of technology and to build a strong franchise network to make farm mechanization easily accessible, affordable and reachable to farmers across India.	

EXHIBIT 2.13	Porter's Generic Strategies Framework (with Examples from the Retail Industry)

		Source of Competitive Advantage	
		Cost	**Differentiation**
Strategic Target	**Narrow**	Cost Focus (Aldi Supermarkets)	Focus in Differentiation (Apple Store)
	Broad	Cost Leadership (Walmart)	Differentiation (Nordstrom)

Source: Adapted from Porter (2011).

A company can choose to differentiate itself based on cost or differentiation, and its target segment can be broad or narrow. Based on the quadrant, a company's choice of the overall strategy that it needs to adopt will vary. For example, Aldi, a German supermarket, is a discount grocery store that largely stocks its own brands. This contrasts with another low-cost chain Walmart that carries a wide range of products. At the other end of the spectrum, Apple stores are high-end stores that focus exclusively on Apple products, while a brand like Nordstrom focuses on a wide range of fashion wear.

The *Strategic Factors Analysis Matrix* (SFAS) developed by Wheelan (Hunger & Wheelen, 2003) is another useful tool. In this tool, all factors, both internal and external, are weighted based on their importance to a company's strategic positioning and then rated based on the company's strength on that factor. The weighted score is used to determine the significance of the attribute and whether its impact would be short, medium or long term.

Another popular framework that has been used in the recent past to look at new target segments is the *Blue Ocean Framework*. Blue ocean refers to the creation by a company of a new uncontested market space that makes competitors irrelevant and that creates new consumer value often while decreasing costs. W. Chan Kim and Renée Mauborgne introduced it in their bestselling book titled *Blue Ocean Strategy* (Mauborgne & Kim, 2007). Blue oceans are preferred over 'bloody red oceans'. Red oceans are all the industries/markets in existence already or the known market spaces, where industry boundaries are defined, and companies try to outperform their rivals to grab a greater share of the existing market.

Another important aspect of strategy development is identifying the right business model. A business model is essentially the way a company earns revenue. Digital technologies have allowed for the creation of several newer business models. Many frameworks are available for innovating business models. The most common framework that is used is the *Business Model Canvas* by Osterwalder (Osterwalder & Pigneur, 2010). The canvas is an easy-to-use tool to outline a company's existing and new business models. Business models are covered in greater detail in Chapter 4.

A business case analysis is used to evaluate the feasibility and effectiveness of individual programmes within a strategy.

Some pitfalls of formulating a strategy include the following:

- **Blindly follow a competitor's strategy:** A company may not have a full understanding of the resource-capability-competency matrix of a competitor that is the backbone of its strategy.
- **Not do something because it is the strategy followed by a competitor:** Most markets are large enough to accommodate multiple players. A company can succeed by following a similar strategy as its competitor, and with better implementation, it can get ahead.

2.3.5. Implementation (Step 3)

The next step in the strategy development process is implementing the chosen strategy. The implementation has four elements: leadership, programmes, resource allocation and budgets.

The first step of any strategy implementation is to identify leaders and teams that will be responsible for its implementation. At an overall level, this could be the CEO and the board. At a programme level, this could be functional or divisional heads.

The overall strategy of a company can be broken down into individual programmes that can be implemented separately but coordinated by a central team. This makes the strategy implementation more manageable. Newer tools allow for better management of the programmes and project management activities.

The next element of a successful implementation is to identify the tangible and intangible assets and processes required for the implementation. This involves insourcing versus outsourcing decisions. As part of this process, companies may also decide to acquire or merge with other companies to enter the market with a shorter lead time.

Once the individual programmes and the resources required are identified, the final step is to create programme-level and company-level financial budgets.

2.3.6. Monitoring and Control (Step 4)

Once the implementation of a strategy has been rolled out, it is critical to monitor it with a governance process. The governance process consists of the following three elements:

- Who is governing?
  - o Company level and business/programme level leadership
  - o Reporting matrix
  - o Escalation matrix
- What is being governed?
  - o Metrics and reporting

    o Timelines
    o Project management
- How is it being governed?
    o Creation and monitoring of a project plan
    o Periodic and scheduled reviews
    o Troubleshooting and quality control
    o Course correction

As discussed earlier, product life cycles and strategies are getting disrupted must faster than in the past. The monitoring and control process has gained more significance, and a company may have to modify its strategy mid-implementation.

2.4. USE OF DIGITAL TECHNOLOGIES IN STRATEGY PLANNING

As discussed in Section 2.3.1.1, AI is being used to analyse the vast volumes of internal and external data. In the recent past, there have been discussions and experiments to use AI to develop entire strategic plans for companies.[4] While there is still a long way to go for AI and ML to develop entire strategic plans, there is value in using these technologies in elements of the planning process. Exhibit 2.14 maps the strategic planning process against the use of digital technologies.

EXHIBIT 2.14 | *Use of Digital Technologies in Strategy Development*

Stage	Illustrative Use of Digital Technologies
Environment scanning	Newer data sources including social media mobile data and digital publications Crowdsourcing platforms as a data source Use of geospatial data (GIS/GPS) to map distribution of retailers or potential consumers Data warehousing
Business assessment	AI to sort and analyse data Big data Natural language processing, and text and speech recognition to process unstructured data ERP, CRM and other internal platforms
Strategic objectives	NLP to analyse vision/mission statements of other digital companies and competitors Social media to communicate key messages
Strategy development	Advanced forecasting tools Simulation software to test alternate models
Strategy implementation	Collaboration tools to manage the implementation process and teams Project management platforms
Evaluation and controls	Mobile-based tracking tools Visualization tools to monitor progress

2.5. DOES EVERY COMPANY NEED A DIGITAL STRATEGY?

Every CEO is drowned in information about digital. At various forums and conferences and through mass media, CEOs and companies are bombarded with advice on digital being the panacea for all their challenges. 'Disrupt or be disrupted' is the common refrain. While there is some truth in this, CEOs and companies need to be careful not to get carried away.

The fundamentals of business strategy have not changed. A company needs to understand the current and future needs of its customers and map it against its internal and external strengths. As defined in Chapter 1, a digital strategy is a strategy enabled by digital technologies. Once a company develops its strategy, it needs to determine the best technologies that will allow it to implement its strategies. Some of these may be digital technologies, and some may be more traditional technologies. A few of the key questions that a company needs to take into consideration while deciding on a digital strategy are as follows:

- Is there some gap in the customer need that the company can fulfil using digital technologies?
- Does implementing digital technologies help the company expand its market or market share?
- Does digital allow the company to get and stay ahead of its competitors?
- Does the digital strategy help create any unique resource-capabilities-competencies?
- Is there a business case for digital transformation?

The responses to these questions should determine the extent of digital in a company's strategy. Implementing discrete digital technologies that do not contribute to a company's overall strategy can be a waste of resources and effort.

MINI CASE 2.1. DISCUSSION

The challenges being faced by Priya are typical of most mid-sized companies. As she takes over the company, she needs to build a strategic plan with a five-year horizon in mind.

The first task for building a plan is putting together a small team of business analysts. These could be a mix of current and new employees and could even include resources from a consulting company that can help us gather data and build a plan.

The next task for Priya is to use the four-step process to build a strategy.

External data: The sources for external data include census and reports from the pharma and fast-moving consumer goods (FMCG) industry bodies and retail panels in these industries.

Internal data: Internal data for Sree could be from the financial systems and the sales team.

External analysis: This includes the following:

Industry: Sree has been operating as a pharmaceutical company, but most of its newer competition is from FMCG companies. It needs to look beyond its traditional industry.

Policy and regulations: The FMCG industry is less regulated than the pharma industry. This may provide Sree with newer avenues to promote its products.

Customer segments: Primarily, new mothers in urban areas and with SEC of A&B.

Disruptions: The industry has already been disrupted by lean start-ups who have reworked the value chain and marketing activities.

Competitors: Start-ups and traditional companies.

Suppliers: This is Sree's strength, and it has had relationships with its suppliers for many years.

Internal analysis:

Clearly, the key valuable resources for Sree are its brand, customer base and trust enjoyed with doctors. Its weaknesses are its marketing, distribution, lack of national presence and high-cost structure. Exhibits 2.15 and 2.16 outline the internal analysis conducted by Sree.

Vision of Sree: To provide safe and secure baby care products.

Mission: To be India's largest baby care products company with a national presence and a full range of products.

Business model: Sree has been a traditional company and was selling its products through recommendations by paediatricians from pharmaceutical stores. These products were being sold like a typical product at a retail price. Some business model changes that Sree can consider are subscription-based services. For example, they could offer a discounted price for an annual subscription of baby products. Also, instead of selling individual products, they could create product bundles as part of the subscription.

Digital 4Ps:

If this strategy is implemented, Sree will be able to leverage the goodwill and brand reputation to build a modern baby care company with a national presence. This is summarized in Exhibit 2.17.

EXHIBIT 2.15 | *SWOT Analysis*

Strengths	**Weaknesses**
Strong brand	One single sales channel
Relationships with paediatrician	No systems
	Lack of sales analytics
Opportunities	**Threats**
Expand channels	Large pharma and FMCG companies
National coverage	Newer entrants

EXHIBIT 2.16 | *VRIO Analysis*

VRIO	Brand	Large Customer Base	Cost Structure	Doctor Trust	Distribution	Marketing
Valuable	Yes	Yes	No	Yes	Yes	No
Rare	Yes	Yes	No	Yes	No	No
Inimitable	Yes	Yes	No	Yes	No	No
Organized	Yes	Yes	No	Yes	No	No

EXHIBIT 2.17 | *Digital 4Ps*

4Ps	
Product	Products targeted at new mothers across India, SEC A&B
Place	In addition to pharma outlets, the products could be available through Sree's own e-commerce portals, baby care portals like babychakra.com and generic e-commerce portals like Amazon and Flipkart
Price	Subscription models, bundled models
Promotions	Digital boards at paediatricians Social media such as Facebook and Instagram Use of social influencers WhatsApp-based messaging Promotions on e-commerce portals

SUMMARY

A strategy is a plan to achieve a business goal. It sets the common goals and the boundaries within which a firm operates. A strategy that embraces digital across its elements is a digital strategy. A company's business strategy used to have a 5–10-year horizon. However, rapidly changing market dynamics have reduced strategy cycles to shorter timeframes.

There are several frameworks for strategy formulation and deployment. However, most of them revolve around four key steps: environment scanning, business assessment, strategy formulation, implementation and controls. This structure is applicable irrespective of the degree of digital transformation sought in a company's strategy. Frameworks such as Porter's five forces, SWOT, RBV and Barney's VRIO frameworks are commonly used to formulate and deploy business strategies.

There is no one correct strategy. While the data and tools help a company make an informed decision, a company's strategy still requires considerable human judgement, including past experiences and intuition.

The role of digital is increasing in strategy development, and strategy and digital strategy are almost being used as synonyms. However, it is essential for a company not to get carried away by the 'latest and greatest' in digital technologies. Digital must be incorporated into a company's strategy based on specific customer or market needs.

Discussion Questions

1. Define strategy and digital strategy. How are the two similar and different?
2. What are the four steps involved in developing a strategy?
3. What are the types of internal and external information? Provide some examples for each of these sources.
4. What are the elements of external environmental analysis?
5. What is the VRIO model?
6. Provide some examples of how the vision and mission of companies have evolved after they embraced digital strategies.
7. What are some key steps in monitoring and controlling strategy implementation?

GLOSSARY

Capability: These are the abilities of a company to harness resources. Capabilities can be in the form of processes and routines that manage the interactions between the resources and turns inputs into outputs. Typical capabilities include marketing capabilities and technology capabilities.

Competency: A competency is an integration of multifunctional capabilities. Competencies can be in the form of processes or routines that manage the interactions between the resources and turn inputs into outputs.

Digital strategy: It is a strategy that is enabled by digital capabilities.

Resource: Resources are an organization's assets and form their basic building blocks.

Strategy: A strategy sets the common goals and the boundaries within which a company operates. Strategic planning is the process of formulating a strategy, and strategic management is used in the context of formulating and executing a strategy.

NOTES

1. https://www.imd.org/research-knowledge/articles/strategy-is-dead/
2. https://www.strategy-business.com/article/Management-Is-All-in-the-Timing?gko=497a9
3. https://www.businesstoday.in/magazine/cover-story/reliance-industries—the-virtues-of-integration/story/1673.html
4. https://www.forbes.com/sites/danielshapiro1/2019/08/19/can-artificial-intelligence-generate-corporate-strategy/?sh=5def6cd6559f

REFERENCES

Barney, J. (1991). Firm resources and sustained competitive advantage. *Journal of Management, 17*(1), 99–120.

DalleMule, L., & Davenport, T. H. (2017). What's your data strategy. *Harvard Business Review, 95*(3), 112–121.

Helms, M. M., & Nixon, J. (2010). Exploring SWOT analysis: Where are we now? *Journal of Strategy and Management, 3*(3), 215–251.

Hunger, J. D., & Wheelen, T. L. (2003). *Essentials of strategic management* (vol. 4). Prentice Hall.

Mauborgne, R., & Kim, W. C. (2007). *Blue ocean strategy*. Gildan Media.

Osterwalder, A., & Pigneur, Y. (2010). *Business model canvas*. Self-published.

Porter, M. E. (2008). The five competitive forces that shape strategy. *Harvard Business Review, 86*(1), 25–40.

Porter, M. E. (2011). *Competitive advantage of nations: creating and sustaining superior performance*. Simon and Schuster.

3

Process and Product Innovation

Learning Objectives

Chapter 1 helped define digital transformation, and Chapter 2 described how digital could be incorporated into a company's strategic planning process. Chapter 3 delves further into the digital strategy framework outlined in Chapter 1 (Exhibit 1.2) and focuses on operational innovation and product innovation. By the end of this chapter, readers will be able to:

- Define process innovation.
- Understand the elements of process innovation and the impact of digital.
- Understand how process efficiencies can be enhanced through digital.
- Understand how processes can be fundamentally altered and the impact of digital on process reconstruction.
- Define product/service innovation.
- Understand the product development process.
- Appreciate the impact of digital strategies on product development.

Mini Case 3.1

Antonio Silva was recently appointed CEO of Europak Packaging, Brazil. Europak had taken over two packaging companies in Brazil and had hired Antonio to consolidate the operations of the two companies and integrate them into Europak. Europak was one of Europe's largest packaging companies, headquartered in Hamburg, Germany. It had operations in 30 countries and catered to clients in the pharmaceutical and food industries. Europak was known around the globe for its quality and supply chain processes. This 50-year-old company had many global clients who had operations around the world, and it supplied packaging to their factories by distributing its manufacturing across Europak's own plants. Using technology and sophisticated supply chain processes, Europak ensured that its clients' factories had sufficient stock of high-quality packaging material.

One of the major countries Europak was not present in was Brazil. Brazil was rapidly growing to become one of the largest markets for packaging. In 2015, Europak decided to acquire a company in Brazil to accelerate its entry into the country. However, given that most of the existing companies in Brazil were relatively small, Europak had to acquire two companies simultaneously and merge them to have scaled operations. The two companies were family-owned and, in combination, had factories in 10 locations across the country.

Europak hired industry veteran Antonio as the CEO of its Brazil operations. Antonio had close to three decades of experience in the packaging industry and had worked for both Brazilian and multinational packaging companies. With a degree in mechanical engineering and an MBA, Antonio effortlessly straddled both production and marketing roles. The first task given to him was to merge the two companies and integrate their operations into the Europak ecosystem. The charter for Antonio was to make the 10 factories in Brazil additional nodes in Europak's global factory network, both in terms of quality and supply chain efficiencies.

As soon as Antonio joined the company, he visited the offices and factories of the two acquired companies. He realized that the companies had very rudimentary processes, were labour intensive and lacked any automation or technology. Integrating the companies into Europak's network would require a lot of effort.

Antonio had to grapple with several questions. What processes would be needed to be implemented? What quality programmes would the company need to run for its operations? What quality standards would be required? How could he reduce the number of manual processes? What automation would be necessary?

3.1. PROCESS INNOVATION

3.1.1. Introduction to Process Innovation

Process innovation focuses on improving a company's business processes such as procurement, logistics and customer support, among others. Process innovation can be achieved through a combination of enhancing efficiencies through quality management and process automation and reconstructing processes fundamentally through outsourcing and offshoring and unbundling of value chains.

3.1.2. Quality Management

Most companies have basic quality management programmes to continuously evaluate, manage and control process quality. A quality programme helps in increasing efficiency, reducing product defects, enhancing customer satisfaction and helps to manage risk. A comprehensive quality management programme can be divided into the following two sets of activities:

1. **Quality standards:** This includes generic regulation-based standards such as ISI mark, industry-specific standards such as Food Safety and Standards Authority of India (FSSAI) and universal industry standards like International Organization for Standardization (ISO) 7001

2. **Quality methodologies:** These are tools and methods for managing, measuring, reporting and improving quality (e.g., Six Sigma, Lean, etc.)

Some of the commonly used quality methods include the following:

Six Sigma: It is a rigorous and disciplined methodology that uses data and statistical analysis to measure and improve operational performance by identifying and eliminating 'defects' in manufacturing and service-related processes and limiting it to 3.4 defects per million samples.

Total productive maintenance (TPM): TPM involves operators, maintenance staff and management working together to improve the overall operation of any equipment. Operators are the first to identify issues. They are trained to make many simple repairs to prevent major and costly breakdowns. Keeping an overall equipment effectiveness record can help to monitor performance reduction. These reports monitor three key areas: availability, performance and quality of output.

Total quality management (TQM): TQM is an enhancement to the traditional way of doing business. It is, for the most part, common sense. Analysing the three words, total (made up of the whole), quality (degree of excellence a product or service provides) and management (act or manner of handling or controlling). Therefore, TQM is the art of managing the whole to achieve excellence. TQM integrates fundamental management techniques, existing improvement efforts and technical tools.

Kaizen: Kaizen is an approach towards creating continuous improvements based on the idea that small ongoing positive changes can reap significant improvements. Typically, it is based on cooperation and commitment and stands in contrast to approaches that use radical changes or top-down edicts to achieve transformation.

Lean: Lean is a systematic method for the minimization of waste (muda) within a manufacturing system without sacrificing productivity, which can cause problems. Lean also considers waste created through overburden (muri) and unevenness in workloads (mura).

Software quality assurance and testing: In addition to the frameworks discussed above, there are specialized quality and testing measures used in a software development life cycle (SDLC). These include design review, code review and test plan review. All software developed also undergoes rigorous internal and user testing. The states of testing include unit testing, where individual components of the software are tested and integration testing, where the integrated components are tested. At a level above is system testing, where the software is tested to check if it is delivering the output it was expected to and, finally, acceptance testing, where the end-user tests the software before acceptance. Other types of testing include stress testing and security testing.

While obvious, the benefits of a quality programme are multifold.

- **Customer focus:** Maintain and exceed customer expectations for product/service quality
- **Leadership and people:** Keeping leadership and all employees motivated and focused on achieving organizational goals

- **Improving network relationships:** Help improving relationship with all network partners, including suppliers and platforms
- **Gain efficiencies:** Enhance process productivity, reduce wastage and lower costs
- **Transparency:** Help making effective decisions which are based on the analysis of data and information
- **Culture of continuous improvement:** Helps continuous improvement to be ingrained into the culture of the organization allowing for innovations from evolutionary changes and revolutionary disruptions

For a company to successfully transform its operations, it needs to have a culture of quality. This forms the basic building block to process innovation.

Digital strategies require rapid innovation to a company's products and services. This change, in turn, requires equally rapid changes in underlying production, software development and business processes. In such a dynamic environment, the role of quality programmes becomes even more significant.

On the customer-facing side, any defect in product or service quality immediately gets amplified on social media, impacting the overall brand reputation of the company.

Internally, rapid product development cycles require an effective quality management programme to eliminate the need for rework and keep costs under control.

Apple hires former NASA employees to test its autonomous cars. This has been interpreted as a move from Apple to enhance the quality of testing and increase customer confidence in its driverless cars.

Digital technologies also play a role in quality management and testing. Technologies such as digital twins and digital simulators help in the testing of products and services. Other technologies such as IoT and AI help in proactively managing product and process quality by predicting potential failures. Robots are also being used to automate processes, and technologies like drones are being used in quality management in large production facilities.

3.1.3. Process Automation

Process automation is the use of technology to automate business or production processes. In a manufacturing company, an example of automation could be the commissioning of a forklift to load material into a machine, replacing manual labour. In a back-office setting, an example of automation is scanning paper documents and transferring them via an electronic workflow thus eliminating the need for physical transfer of paper. Process automation is another essential step for operational innovation. Unless a process is automated, the opportunity to innovate is minimal.

There are multiple benefits of process automation, which are as follows:

- Standardized operations help in producing consistent outcomes independent of human behaviour, thus increasing product and process quality.

- Streamlined processes enable clear accountability, faster turnaround times and waste reduction.
  Operational efficiencies increase productivity, including speed of operations, lower manual interventions and reduction in costs.
- Monitoring and compliance provide automation tools for robust reporting at a transactional level. This betters proactive monitoring and reactive audits.
- Increased customer satisfaction resulting from better quality and lower costs.
- Process automation is the first step towards implementing digital technologies in production and business processes.

3.1.3.1. Production Automation

Production automation is a type of process automation but is mainly used in the context of manufacturing. It is typically classified into three categories:

1. **Fixed automation** is hard automation that has a specific purpose and can handle large volumes and eliminates manual handling. A conveyor belt connecting two parts of a manufacturing plant is an example of fixed automation. Fixed automation is the lowest cost of automation and can be used only for the purpose it was implemented.
2. **Programmable automation** is soft automation used for batch processes. For example, in the pharma industry, each batch can be controlled through automation equipment that controls the mix of chemicals and then monitors parameters such as temperature and pressure. Programmable automation is costlier than fixed automation and is typically used for lower speed processes that need periodic changes.
3. **Flexible automation** is a variation of programmable automation. This type of automation is controlled through a central command system. It is used in situations where the batch sizes are smaller, and the number of products is higher. In such cases, programmable automation results in higher downtimes and wastage. An example is a robotic arm that has the flexibility to conduct a variety of movement and tasks and that has changeable heads. Depending on the specific part required, the robot can be reprogrammed quickly. Digital technologies such as IoT and robotics form essential components in flexible automation.

Automaker Tesla's manufacturing facility in Fremont, California, is a good example of flexible automation. The company developed, in-house, what it calls the Tesla Manufacturing Operating System. The system allows the company to reconfigure its automation processes and equipment, including robots, rapidly. According to experts, this system enables Tesla to come up with improvements or new products at a significantly faster speed than any traditional auto manufacturer.

3.1.3.2. Business Process Automation (BPA)

BPA is similar to production automation. However, it is used in the context of automating businesses, including sales, supply chain or finance and accounting. It is the automation of repetitive tasks in business operations. BPA forms the basis for efficient business process management.

Some examples of BPA include automation of accounts payable processes and automation of sales reporting processes.

The next phase of BPA is robotics process automation (RPA). In RPA, digital tools such as software robots (bots) or AI-based digital workers are used for automation.

In traditional BPA, technologies such as workflows and application programming interface (APIs or software connectors) are used to automate processes. In RPA, the system uses tools like AI to watch a user perform a task and then repeats the tasks. AI-based chatbots are an excellent example of RPA and now being used extensively in customer service.

3.1.4. Process Reconstruction

Traditionally, companies were vertically integrated, and they owned all parts of the value chain. Some of the reasons for vertical integration included:

- **High transaction costs:** Lack of technology and telecom made the process of managing multiple suppliers across geographies very costly.
- **Supply uncertainty:** Integration removed the dependencies on suppliers. Companies had complete control over their cost structure, and there was less risk of disruption in the supply of raw materials.
- **Raise entry barriers:** By controlling all critical elements in a supply chain, companies ensured that no other competitor could enter the market.

However, vertical integration is no longer a popular strategy. There are several factors for this shift. By vertically integrating, companies had become large and unwieldy. They lost their edge in innovation, and costs grew due to layers of overheads required to manage a complex conglomerate. There were also clashes of culture across the various teams within an organization.

Companies are now using outsourcing, offshoring and unbundling of value chains to reduce their complexity and become nimbler to meet customer needs.

3.1.4.1. Outsourcing and Offshoring

Outsourcing is the practice of moving part of a production or business process to external suppliers. Outsourcing as a strategy has been in existence for over 100 years. Ford Motor Company, one of the pioneers in manufacturing and the company that led the second industrial revolution, was vertically integrated across its value chain. In the early 1920s, Ford controlled more than 50% of the automobile industry. However, within a decade, competition from another large automobile company, General Motors, reduced its share to less than 20%.

Alfred Sloan, the founder of General Motors, adopted a very different strategy. He felt that his company should focus only on the areas that were core to the company. All other processes should be outsourced to specialist companies which had the expertise and scale to produce better quality components at a lower cost. Eventually, Ford Motors was forced to move to an outsourcing model to compete with General Motors. Almost seven decades, before outsourcing became a mainstream strategy, it was already in use.

In IT and business process management, outsourcing became mainstream in the late 1960s due to the initiatives of companies like electronic data systems (EDS). By the 1980s, most large companies were outsourcing their IT. Some examples included the extensive engagement that Kodak had with IBM and General Motors with EDS.

The next phase of outsourcing, offshoring, began on a large scale in the 1990s. The availability of telecom infrastructure allowed companies to move a part of their operations to overseas locations that offered lower costs and had a large population of skilled resources. China for manufacturing and India for IT and business process outsourcing (BPO) became large offshoring destinations. Companies either set up their 'captive centres' or outsourced to suppliers who had operations in these countries.

Outsourcing and offshoring help companies innovate their business processes. Some of the specific benefits of these strategies include the following:

- **Cost reduction:** Reduce costs in comparison to in-house operations and enhance operational efficiencies.
- **Access to skilled resources:** By relocating operations to global locations, companies get access to hard-to-find skills.
- **Quality management:** Most suppliers have extensive quality management and continuous innovation processes. By outsourcing to multiple vendors, companies get access to innovation ideas from numerous sources.
- **Internal focus:** By outsourcing all non-core functions, companies can focus their internal efforts on value-added activities such as innovation and R&D.

Outsourcing and offshoring have a two-way relationship with digital technologies and digital strategies. Digital communications and collaboration tools have enabled extensive outsourcing and offshoring. In turn, offshoring and outsourcing have allowed companies access to digital technologies, innovations and skilled resources that they lacked internally.

3.1.4.2. Unbundling of Value Chains

A value chain is a set of activities that a firm operating in a specific industry performs in order to deliver a valuable product.

Reduction in telecom costs, improvement in the quality of communication and the advent of digital technologies have all led to the emergence of a new model of hyper-outsourcing.

Many start-up companies retain marketing and ownership of intellectual property (IP) of technology and processes internally. All other elements of their value chain are outsourced. This helps them remain lean and scale very rapidly.

Ola in the ride-sharing space, Flipkart in the retail industry and many of the newer cosmetic companies are examples of such organizations. Each of these companies owns the IP, technology and processes and leverages partners for all other parts of the value chain. Exhibit 3.1 illustrates the value chain of a new-age cosmetics company.

EXHIBIT 3.1 | *Unbundling of a Process Company: Illustration*

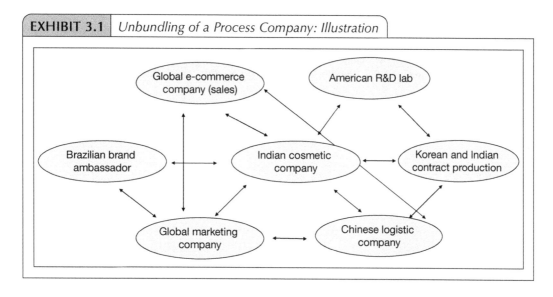

In this illustration, the Indian cosmetic company owns IP for the cosmetic formulations and the brands. All other processes are outsourced to global suppliers. For example, the company outsources its R&D to a lab in the USA and crowdsources a part of its innovation through platforms like InnoCentive. The company gets its products manufactured in India and Korea through outsourced partners. The products are sold through global e-commerce platforms such as Amazon and Sephora, and an international marketing company handles all brand activities. The company has become an orchestrator of the value chain without owning every element. By adopting this structure, the company can remain lean, be an innovator and build a global brand presence rapidly.

While the above example is of a new-age company, even traditional companies are unbundling their value chains. In the automobile industry, it is no longer uncommon for competitors to share engines or platforms. While this trend began with sharing platforms across different lines of the same company (Audi and Skoda sharing platforms and engines), it has now extended across competitors (Toyota and Suzuki in India). In this rapidly changing world, companies are preferring to invest in assets that are controllable in the longer term such as design, brand and distribution and allow for collaboration on all other elements of the value chain.

MINI CASE 3.1. DISCUSSION

Antonio had a very challenging task of simultaneous integrating two companies while enhancing their operational efficiencies.

The first task for Antonio was to create a process innovation team. The team consisted of quality and production personnel from both the acquired companies and was led by a veteran quality executive from Europak. This ensured that there was representation from both the companies as well as the parent company.

The team created an inventory of all the processes in both companies. As both the companies were in the same business, there was significant overlap in types of processes, even though the way a particular process was being handled was different. The processes were across the value chain and included accounting, supplier interaction, production, client interaction, warehousing and logistics.

The inventory of processes was then evaluated for best practices and opportunities for automation. Exhibit 3.2 provides an outline of the process comparison conducted by the team.

EXHIBIT 3.2 *Evaluation of Processes*

Inventory	Company 1	Company 2	Europak	Best Practices	Automation
Process 1	As-is	As-is	As-is	To-be	To-be
Process 2	As-is	As-is	As-is	To-be	To-be
Process n	As-is	As-is	As-is	To-be	To-be

For each process, the 'as-is' process being followed by each of the company and at Europak's global operations were compared. Based on brainstorming sessions, a 'to-be' process was designed for each of these processes. The 'to-be' process took into consideration the best practices from all three organizations and their ability to integrate into the global organization. Opportunities to automate were also identified during these sessions.

The recommendations from the brainstorming sessions were then presented to Antonio and Europak's global management for approval.

The next step was to implement the 'to-be' processes and build a quality culture within the combined Brazilian companies. This included introducing quality standards and quality programmes.

As outlined in the Exhibit 3.3, Europak Brazil chose Lean and Six Sigma as the basis of their quality programme. The company selected ISO 9001 and IS 27001 and People Capability Maturity Model (for people management) as their quality standards. The company split its quality programme across three pillars—people, process and technology. To implement and manage the programme, the company identified Master Black Belts and Black Belts to be the leads. All employees were trained on Kaizen and Lean to develop a culture of innovation.

For each of the areas where automation was identified, the technology team at Europak Global recommended specific tools and equipment that would help in integrating the Brazilian operations into its global network. Production automation included simple equipment, such as forklifts and conveyor belts (fixed automation), to high-end equipment that had inbuilt IoT devices for better monitoring and reporting. Labour cost in Brazil was lower than in other parts of the world. The team had to balance the need for automation with its financial viability given the low labour costs.

As the team evaluated the companies, they also realized that many processes could be outsourced. For example, both the companies had large in-house teams handling accounting, payroll and taxation. The process innovation team recommended that these processes

EXHIBIT 3.3 | *Quality Programme*

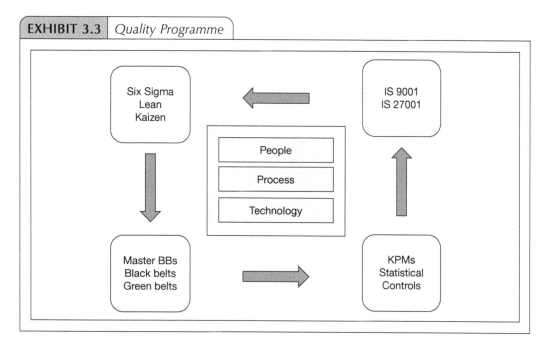

be outsourced to an accounting firm retaining minimal staff in-house. Similarly, since both companies had many contract workers, the team recommended that all the contract labour be consolidated through a single outsourced company to simplify processes and reduce paperwork.

In two years, Antonio was able to successfully integrate the two acquired entities into Europak and bring in operational efficiencies. Soon, some of the operational innovations emerging from the Brazilian entity were being incorporated into Europak's global operations.

3.2. PRODUCT INNOVATION

Mini Case 3.2

Vinay Singh was CEO of Trend BPO, a BPO company headquartered in Surat, India. Trend was a 10-year-old BPO that provided accounting services to certified public accountant (CPA) firms in North America. Vinay, a BPO veteran, was hired as CEO by the founders of Trend three years ago. When Vinay joined Trend, it was a $15 million business and had three major CPA firms as clients who accounted for 90% of its revenues. The clients had been sourced through the founder's brother in the USA who also was a CPA, and Trend ran almost like a captive unit with its clients controlling most decisions. There were some issues relating to quality and standardization, but overall, the relationships were stable. When Vinay was hired, his principal task was to leverage the capabilities that existed within Trend to grow the business to $50 million.

In two years, Vinay hired two business development executives in the USA, and he spent 15 days every other month on sales calls. However, acquiring new clients was a challenge. Most of the prospective CPA firms felt that Trend was a captive, and they did not want to outsource to a competitor.

On a long flight back to India, Vinay had plenty of time to think. Maybe the solution for Trend's growth issues was to target end customers (customers of CPA firms). This was possibly the only way to overcome the 'captive' issues. How would he be able to achieve this? What product offerings would Trend need to build and offer? What new capabilities would Trend need to build? How could he leverage the learnings that existed within Trend? Could he create products out of these capabilities and offer self-service capabilities to his customers?

3.2.1. Introduction

Product innovation is the creation or improvement of a product or service. It can be incremental with continuous but evolutionary improvements. An excellent example of this is the annual release of cellphones, where each new phone release has a newer chip, more random-access memory or a better display.

Product innovation can also be radical or revolutionary with the launch of a completely new product or service. The launch of shared cabs is an example of revolutionary innovation. Revolutionary products are rare and riskier, while evolutionary products are less risky and have become a norm. Going back to the cell phone example, there are times when the differences between the two versions are minimal. However, companies are forced to launch them as a signal to their consumers that they are continually innovating.

Another method to classify innovation developed by Henderson and Clark (1990) is based on the type of markets and technology (Exhibit 3.4).

According to this model, innovations can be classified based on the type of markets and technologies. Incremental innovations are those that require limited changes to technology and targeted towards existing markets. On the other hand, innovations that rely on new technologies to target new markets have been classified as radical innovations. Between these two extremes lie architectural innovation that requires minimum technology changes

EXHIBIT 3.4 *Henderson and Clark Model for Innovation*

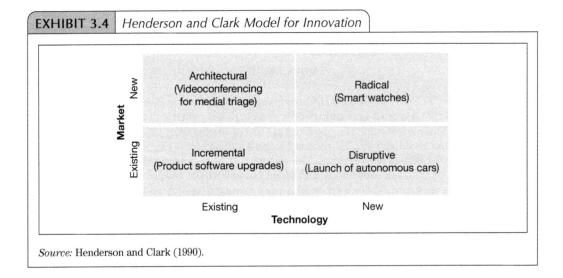

Source: Henderson and Clark (1990).

to address a new market and disruptive innovation where new technologies are developed to target existing segments.

3.2.2. Product Development

A new product development (NPD) process is a systemic methodology, from ideation to market launch of new products. All companies, irrespective of size and industry sector or whether in the services or product industries, need an NPD process.

NPD is complex and fraught with risks. According to a Harvard Business School study, there are over 30,000 new products introduced every year, and 80 per cent fail.[1] Therefore, it is essential to have a formal framework and team that works exclusively on product development.

NPD frameworks can be used to improve existing products or develop new ones.

Consulting company Booz Allen Hamilton developed a framework (Exhibit 3.5) that helps in classifying new products. A company may choose one or multiple quadrants to introduce products as part of its new product portfolio. The framework can also be used to determine the resources a company may allocate across the various type of new products.

New products can be plotted on two axes in the framework. One axis represents the newness of the product to the market, and the other axis represents the newness of the product to the company. For example, a telecom company that launches a data plan that is cheaper than what it and its competitors offered in the past (possibly through process innovation) falls into the lower left quadrant of cost reduction. At the other end of the spectrum, the launch of ridesharing by Uber was a new product/service from a new company. Similarly, a new version of a cell phone is a product improvement, and a low-cost airline targeting corporate flyers is an example of repositioning.

EXHIBIT 3.5 | *Classification of New Products*

Newness to the Company			
High	New to the company		Revolutionary products (new to the world)
	Product improvement	Addition to existing product lines	
	Cost reductions (to existing products)	Re-positioning: Existing products can be targeted to new markets or market segments	
	Low	**Newness to Market**	**High**

Source: Hamilton (1982).

Some of the questions that help a company in determining the allocation of resources across the various types of new products include the following:

- Customer focus
  - o How are customers evolving?
  - o Is there a gap in the expectations of customers and product performance?
  - o Do customers expect new products regularly?
- Competitive advantage
  - o How competitive is the industry?
  - o How frequently are products launched?
  - o Who is gaining market share in the industry? What are they doing differently?

3.2.3. NPD Process

Digital strategies and technologies are increasingly disrupting industries and products. It is, therefore, critical for companies to have a prescribed NPD process that will keep them agile and relevant in the market.

There are several NPD frameworks used by companies. However, at a broad level, they all prescribe similar steps.

This section provides a basic product development framework (Exhibit 3.6). Every company needs to further tailor this based on its unique needs and past experiences.

STEP 1. MARKET/ENVIRONMENT SCANNING

This topic has been covered extensively in Chapter 2 and includes scanning the company's industry, competitors and customers. Market scanning needs to be a continuous process, and many companies outsource the process. Some sources for market information are as follows:

- Industry reports
- Industry organizations
- Market reports
- Feedback from the sales team
- Internal win–loss analysis
- Customer feedback (informal and formal surveys)

Sales personnel are an important but often ignored source of market information, and many companies have set up a formal process to collect and process information from their sales team.

A win–loss analysis is the analysis of sales wins and losses against the competition. It gives a company a clear indicator of customer requirements and why a company is either winning or losing in the marketplace.

STEP 2. IDEA GENERATION

Information received from market screening forms an important input to idea generation. Companies map customer needs against the products and product features available to

EXHIBIT 3.6 | *NPD Framework*

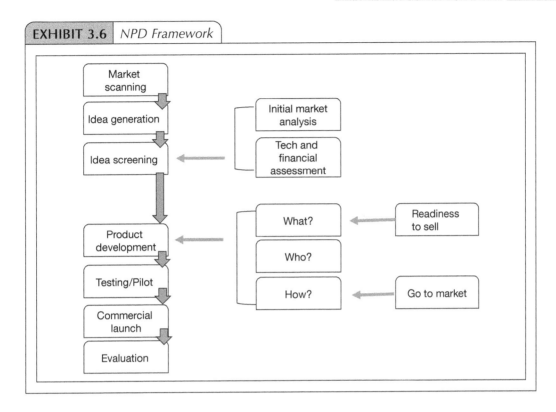

their customers to help generate product ideas. Several frameworks are available in helping in this 'out-of-the-box' thinking.

Christensen's (2013) theory of disruption innovation: This theory was developed by Professor of Strategy at Harvard University, Clayton Christensen. According to this theory, incumbent companies are on a path of continuous innovation. At some point in time, their products and services overshoot the expectation of their customers, especially the lower end of the market. This creates a gap for newer players to launch products or services. Initially, these new players are not direct competitors for the incumbents. However, as they continue to innovate, their products become mainstream, and they become threats to incumbents. According to the theory, for a company to be a disruptive innovator, the following four industry conditions need to be fulfilled.

- Incumbents in a market are improving along a trajectory of sustaining innovation.
- They overshoot or exceed customer needs.
- They possess the capability to respond to disruptive threats by newer competitors (but may not respond).
- Incumbents end up floundering because of the disruptions caused by the newer competitors that eventually dislodge them.

The theory is useful for both incumbent and start-up companies to ideate the products and services they could launch. For start-ups, studying the market using this theory helps in identifying gaps in product or service offerings. For incumbents, the theory helps in understanding what gaps they have created by over innovating.

Using the cell phone example, as phones got more sophisticated and expensive, there was a gap created for lower-end phones that were cheaper and had basic features that most customers use. Several manufacturers such as OnePlus and Oppo launched phones to fill this gap and eventually became market leaders, taking away share from industry leaders Samsung and Apple.

Blue Ocean Strategy (Mauborgne & Kim, 2007): As outlined in Chapter 2, this is another framework that is used to identify new markets and develop new products. According to this theory, companies can simultaneously pursue a strategy of lowering costs and increasing buyer value. They can achieve this by looking beyond their current markets and customer segments. These companies identify adjacent markets that are 'blue ocean' or less crowded. The companies launch new products and services in the 'blue oceans' that can be both differentiated and profitable.

There are several techniques for idea generation. The following are some commonly used methods:

Brainstorming: A simple process where a group of people are brought together into a room, and ideas are thrown up. Some rules for brainstorming include the following:
- There are no right or wrong ideas.
- No judgements—all ideas are welcome.
- The more the ideas, the better.

It is essential to have a facilitator whose role is to set the context, warm up the group, manage time, keep the discussion on track and keep the process visual with the use of whiteboards, stickies and so on. Once the ideas are generated, they are grouped and consolidated into a few good ideas.

Mind mapping: It is an idea popularized by Tony Buzan, a UK author. It is a graphical technique for imagining connections between various pieces of information or ideas. Each fact or idea is written down and then connected by curves or lines to its minor or major (previous or following) fact or idea, thus building a web of relationships.

Role-playing: Each participant takes on a personality or role different from their own. As the technique is fun, it can help people reduce their inhibitions and come out with unexpected ideas.

STEP 3. IDEA SCREENING
The next step of the innovation process is to screen and shortlist the ideas generated through the previous step. The shortlisted ideas are put through two levels of screening.

- **Initial market analysis:** A preliminary test is conducted with a sample of potential customers. Some of the steps taken to test a concept include the following:
    - o Creation of a storyboard of the product
        - → What is the product about?
        - → What customer issue is the product solving?

→ How is it different from other solutions currently available?
→ What benefits can the customer expect (cost/features/ease of use/etc.)?
o Identification of a set of customers/potential customers with whom the storyboard can be tested
→ Current customers
→ 'Friendly customers'
→ Potential customers
→ Non-customers (customers currently using alternate product categories)
o Conduct qualitative interviews
→ Get customer views of existing products
→ What is the gap between their expectations and these products?
→ Expose customers to the new concept(s)
→ What is their view of the concept(s)? Positives/negatives?
→ How can the concept(s) be improved?
→ Would they buy the product, if available?
- **Technology and financial assessment:** While conducting market tests, companies need to perform a high-level assessment of the new product and innovation. Technology assessment at this stage is a quick exercise on what it would take to build the product. Would existing infrastructure suffice or would new investments be required? What is the cost of the additional investment? Technology assessment is a crucial input to financial assessment where a full business case is prepared for the product ideas. This requires building a revenue model with sales projections, sales growth and potential pricing along with a cost model.

The business case, along with customer feedback, helps in shortlisting the product ideas that can move to the product development stage.

STEP 4. PRODUCT DEVELOPMENT
The product development phase can be defined by the what-who-how model. 'What' defines the product, 'who' is the target segment and 'how' is how the product is going to be distributed and sold. The 'what', also referred to as 'readiness to serve', defines what it takes for a product to be ready to be offered to customers. The 'how' is referred to as the 'go-to market' as it outlines how a product will be marketed.

- **What—defining the product:** Exhibit 3.7 provides a high-level checklist of some of the issues that need to be taken into consideration to get a product 'ready to serve'.
- **Who—defining the target segment:** Identify the target:
  o By processes within the industry
  o By buyers or buyer groups within the industry
  o By size and operations range
  o By geography/region
  o Key decision-makers
  o Key influencers
  o Alternate segments (e.g., small and medium enterprises)

EXHIBIT 3.7 | *Product Readiness Checklist*

Product	People	Infrastructure	Quality	Regulatory and Legal
Product specs Product design Production plan Workflows Material sourcing In-house versus outsourcing versus global sourcing	Team design Org structure Skills required/ training Talent pool creation Certifications Compensation and incentives Retention plan	Infrastructure required Location decisions BCP Plan Redundancy needs Security	Design for six sigma Key metrics Project planning Reporting and governance	Regulatory clearances Intellectual property Trademarks, copyrights and so on Data protection

- **How—defining the sales and distribution process:** Some of the key decisions that need to be taken for defining the 'how' are:
  - o Distribution channels—online versus offline sales
  - o Channel partners
  - o Aggregator strategy (e.g., Amazon and Alibaba)
  - o Digital marketing strategies (search engine optimization [SEO] and search engine marketing [SEM])
  - o Offline sales strategy
  - o Product and sales material
  - o Sales plan
  - o Product pricing and pricing models
  - o Sales incentive structures
  - o Launch plan

STEP 5. THE TEST PRODUCTION AND LAUNCH

On completion of 'readiness to serve' and 'go-to market', a product is ready for a test launch. Test launches are usually in a well-defined market or among 'friendly customers'. Testing provides feedback from a contained market and allows for ironing out any issues before a full-scale launch. It is vital to have a well-defined feedback process during this phase.

Several new digital solutions, like simulators and digital twins, are being used to accelerate the testing process.

STEP 6. COMMERCIAL LAUNCH

Once the feedback from the Test phase is received and any course corrections are made, a product is ready for full-scale commercial launch.

STEP 7. EVALUATION

Product satisfaction and customer satisfaction surveys are essential for continuous feedback on new products, especially in the initial post-launch period.

There is a stage-gate between every step in the NPD process where a go/no go decision needs to be taken. Developing new products is expensive and taking a 'no go' decision at every stage is as critical as following the process.

3.2.4. Accelerating Product Innovation

Partnerships, outsourcing and launching minimum viable products (MVPs) are some standard methods used to accelerate product innovation.

Partner with start-ups: Start-up entrepreneurs are always seeking test cases and pilots. Many companies scan the start-up world and interact with those companies that are relevant to their industry. Many of these start-ups offer point solutions but can help accelerate parts of the product development process.

Use of outsourcing: Outsourcing helps in accelerating product development. Companies outsource part of their R&D to outsourced partners who have the resources and skills to handle aspects of the innovation process.

MVP: MVP is defined as a new product with sufficient features to satisfy early adopters. This approach helps in accelerating a company's product launch and gain a first-mover advantage. Feedback from these initial customers also helps in providing valuable inputs for further product development.

3.2.5. Impact of Digital on NPD Process

Digital has had a significant impact on the product development process. It has allowed for the development of new products and reduced the time required to develop and launch a new product.

Digital products: Digital transformation has led to the development of new products that have incorporated digital technologies into them. Almost every product across industries is going through this change. For example, payments have moved to mobile-based applications with QR code and proximity-based features, and most media and entertainment companies have launched stream services leveraging technologies such as cloud and AI. Industrial equipment companies are launching machines that incorporate the latest in digital technologies, including IoT, embedded software and virtual reality.

Digital tools: Several tools and platforms are available to aid and accelerate NPD. These tools are being used across the NPD process, including ideation, prototyping, production and testing.

Sophisticated knowledge management tools with AI-based functionalities are helping companies generate new product ideas.

The 3D printing allows for rapid prototyping without the need for an entire manufacturing process. This technology is moving beyond prototypes towards finished products.

Virtual reality (VR) and augmented reality (AR) are being used to test pilot versions of products. They can be used to simulate the user's environment so that test customers can try the product in its intended setting.

Simulations through digital twins are being used to test products and process changes before they are implemented in a real environment. For example, most automobile companies now simulate production line changes in a digital twin environment to check for impact on the overall line.

Crowdsourcing of innovation through dedicated innovation platforms and collaboration platforms are being used to expand the team working on innovation beyond the four walls of an R&D centre. Social media is being used to test products and receive consumer feedback extensively.

Agile development: In traditional software development frameworks, like the waterfall model, requirements for a project must be agreed upon upfront. The entire scope of the project is planned, and timelines agreed upon between the stakeholders. Although these methodologies provide a structure to the development and save the customer time, they are rigid and do not have the flexibility to adapt to customer and market changes that may happen along the development process. The methodologies have lag market needs and have no mechanism for interim feedback. They also disconnect the customer from the development process and are effective only when where all requirements are unknown. Agile development overcomes many of the weaknesses of these traditional methodologies.

Agile has existed since the late 1950s but became mainstream only in the 2000s. Reducing product lifespans and the need for customer connect with the development processes have increased the usage of agile development. Agile methods make the following tradeoffs:

- Individuals and interactions over processes and tools
- Working software over comprehensive documentation
- Customer collaboration over contract negotiation
- Responding to change over following a plan

Some of the popular methods used in agile development include scrum, extreme programming, rapid application development and kanban.

Development of digital platforms: In traditional automobile manufacturing, engine and chassis platforms are shared across product lines and companies. In the digital world, similar platforms are changing the way new products are being developed and launched. The most common example is the android platform developed by Google that allows for companies to launch new services leveraging the platform. There are many other such platforms that provide underlying infrastructure and tools for developing and operating tailored and customized services and processes. These platforms are now extending to combining physical products with technology, sometimes referred to as Phygital.

For example, Tetra Pak, a leading food packaging company, has launched a packaging platform.

Tetra Pak has today announced the launch of its connected packaging platform, which will transform milk and juice cartons into interactive information channels, full-scale data carriers and digital tools.

Driven by the trends behind Industry 4.0 and with code generation, digital printing and data management at its core, the connected packaging platform will bring new benefits to food producers, retailers and shoppers.

For 'producers', the new packaging platform will offer end-to-end traceability to improve the production of the product, quality control and supply chain transparency. It will have the ability to track and trace the history or location of any product, making it possible to monitor for market performance and any potential issues.

For 'retailers', it will offer greater supply chain visibility and real-time insights, enabling distributors to track stock movements, be alerted when issues occur and monitor for delivery performance.

For 'shoppers', it will mean the ability to access vast amounts of information such as where the product was made, the farm that the ingredients came from and where the package can be recycled.

Source: https://www.tetrapak.com/en-in/about-tetra-pak/news-and-events/newsarchive/connected-packaging-platform

3.2.6. Ambidextrous Organization

As discussed earlier in this chapter, digital has led to a disruption of products and services. Many traditional companies have core products and services that account for a large part of their revenue base that are profitable. These traditional companies sometimes ignore disruptions and disruptors in their early stages, as these disruptions conflict with the core revenue-earning products of the company. A well-documented example of this is how photography giant Kodak could never migrate to digital despite being the first to develop a digital camera. Their traditional business at that point of time (selling camera rolls) did not allow this idea to germinate.

A significant amount of academic research has been conducted on this issue of strategic tension between core businesses and digital disruptions. This concept has been discussed in greater detail in Chapter 5.

MINI CASE 3.2. DISCUSSION

As soon as Vinay got back to his office in India, he put together a product innovation team that consisted of leaders from his sales, finance and operations teams and a few research analysts. The team scanned internal and external data to look at the universe of potential clients. Based on the analysis, the team realized that there were two types of clients they could target. The first target was CPA firms themselves. This was a relatively easier segment to service as Trend had direct experience in providing services to CPA firms. Analysis of the clients of the three current CPA firms showed that 90% of these companies were small- and medium enterprises (SMEs), quick service restaurants and small groceries. While Trend had not directly interacted with these clients, the company was proficient in handling accounting for these segments. Vinay felt that he needed to target both CPA firms and end customers to put the company on the path of exponential growth. However, he would need to manage the conflict of interest as many CPA firms may object to Trend directly servicing their clients.

To handle this need for ambidexterity and avoid conflict, Vinay split Trend into two operating divisions. The first division included the company's current operations and continued to target CPA firms. The second division was started with a focus on SMEs in the retail and restaurant industries.

To directly target SMEs, the new division needed to invest in a cloud-based accounting platform. This platform was multi-tenanted so that licence costs could be apportioned across multiple SMEs. Some of the other innovations in this entity included using shared resources across clients, the introduction of sophisticated workflow tools, client-self-service portals, reporting and analytics and hiring domain experts in restaurant and grocery accounting to build processes and best practices. Effectively, what the new entity had done was assemble a 'CFO-in-a-box' solution. The customer paid based on 'per transaction' or 'outcome' instead of per full-time equivalent pricing that had been the norm in the BPO industry.

All of this would not have been possible if not for the leadership provided by Vinay.

SUMMARY

The chapter covers two important concepts in the digital strategy framework: process innovation and product innovation. Process innovation is a combination of enhancing efficiencies through process changes, process automation and making fundamental changes in production and supply chain processes. Each of these types of innovations is an essential building block for digital transformation. Product innovation is the creation or improvement of a product or service. Product innovation can be incremental or evolutionary, on the one hand, and discrete and revolutionary, on the other hand. A successful organization needs to be able to balance both types of innovation.

Organizations must have a structured process for innovation. While there are several innovation frameworks available, most of them have similar essential components: market scanning, ideation, product development, testing, launch and feedback. Digital transformation has an impact on the product development process. Digital technologies, platforms and methods like agile development are increasing the speed of innovation. Finally, to be successful innovators, companies need to balance the growth of core products with new innovations. Ambidextrous structures and adaptive leadership enable this balance.

Discussion Questions

1. What is process innovation? What are the types of this form of transformation?
2. Provide examples of each type of process innovation for any one industry.
3. Why is process innovation an essential building block for digital transformation?
4. What is product innovation?
5. What are the steps in production innovation?
6. How has digital transformation impacted the product development process?

GLOSSARY

Adaptive leadership: Adaptive leadership is a practical leadership framework that helps individuals and organizations to adapt to changing environments and effectively respond to recurring problems.

Ambidextrous organization: It is an organization's ability to be aligned and efficient in its management of current business demands and being adaptive to changes in the environment at the same time.

Disruptive innovation: Disruptive innovation refers to a technology, application of which significantly affects the way a market or industry functions.

Process innovation: This is a combination of enhancing efficiencies through process changes, process automation and making fundamental changes in production and supply chain processes.

Product innovation: It is the creation and subsequent introduction of a product or service that is either a new or an improved version of the company's previous product or service.

NOTE

1. https://www.forbes.com/sites/shamahyder/2019/10/17/how-to-launch-a-new-product-or-service-what-the-latest-research-teaches-us-about-successful-launches/?sh<hig>=</hig>41355190412a

REFERENCES

Christensen, C. M. (2013). *The innovator's dilemma: when new technologies cause great firms to fail.* Harvard Business Review Press.

Henderson, R. M., & Clark, K. B. (1990). Architectural innovation: The reconfiguration of existing product technologies and the failure of established firms. *Administrative Science Quarterly, 35*(1), 9–30.

Mauborgne, R., & Kim, W. C. (2007). *Blue ocean strategy.* Gildan Media.

Business Model Innovation

Learning Objectives

Chapter 3 focused on process and product innovation. This chapter takes another step into the digital strategy framework and introduces the concept of business model innovation (BMI). By the end of the chapter, readers will be able to:

- Define business models.
- Appreciate why business models are transforming.
- Understand the types of business models.
- Use multiple tools to define business models.

Mini Case 4.1

Google is one of the largest technology companies globally and focuses on providing various internet and technology-related products and services. The company was founded in the late 1990s by two Stanford University graduates, Larry Page and Sergey Brin. One of Google's most important services is its search engine that is free for all users. Larry Page, during the public listing of the company, stated:

Sergey and I founded Google because we believed we could provide an important service to the world - instantly delivering relevant information on virtually any topic. Serving our end users is at the heart of what we do and remains our number one priority.

Our goal is to develop services that significantly improve the lives of as many people as possible. In pursuing this goal, we may do things that we believe have a positive impact on the world, even if the near-term financial returns are not obvious. For example, we make our services as widely available as we can by supporting over 90 languages and by providing most services for free. Advertising is our principal source of revenue, and the ads we provide are relevant and useful rather than intrusive and annoying. We strive to provide users with great commercial information. (Securities and Exchange Commission, 2004)

Since its initial launch, the main business of Google has been searching and advertising. Google Search continues to be free for consumers. The Google home page remains advertisement free though a significant amount of search has moved away from the home page to Google widgets and mobile search. Google continues to have a dominant market share among search engines, and its revenue from advertising was $135 billion in 2019.

What is the business model for Google's search business? Who are the players in the ecosystem? Who are Google's current and future competitors in the advertising business? What investments does Google need to make to become a dominant player in the advertising industry? How does Google maximize its revenues?

4.1. DEFINING BUSINESS MODELS

The business model is one of the most-used buzzwords in the corporate world in recent times. The usage spans across both investors, start-ups and large conglomerates.

However, the term is also not clearly understood. What is a business model? Why has it become so important? Is there a precise/perfect/business model for every company? How often do companies need to have a relook at their business model? Can a company have multiple business models?

In academic literature (Osterwalder et al. 2005), business model has been described as:

A conceptual tool containing a set of objects, concepts and their relationships with the objective to express the business logic of a specific firm. Therefore, we must consider which concepts and relationships allow a simplified description and representation of what value is provided to customers, how this is done and with which financial consequences.

In popular literature, it has been described as:

A term of art. And like art itself, it's one of those things many people feel they can recognise when they see it (especially a particularly clever or terrible one) but can't quite define. All it really meant was how you planned to make money. (Lewis, 2014)

To put it simply, a business model is a way a company creates and captures value and the processes and technology that enable this endeavour (Chesbrough, 2007).

In Chapter 2, we covered strategic planning. A business model is often confused with strategy but is not the same. While strategy focuses on the overall direction of a company, a business model is restricted to the way a company generates and retains value. BMI is also different from product and process innovations covered in Chapter 3. A business model does not create a new service or product. Instead, it focuses on new ways to generate revenues from these products and services (Björkdahl & Holmén, 2013). However, BMI is often implemented in conjunction with product and service innovation.

4.2. TYPES OF BMI

Digital strategies and digital technologies have primarily driven the proliferation of BMI in the last decade. Digital technologies are enabling completely new services and the delivery

EXHIBIT 4.1	Industry versus Company Matrix for BMI

Industry Company	Traditional Industry	New Industry
Traditional company	Hilti Asian Paints	Apple (launch of iTunes) Amazon (launch of web services)
New company	Uber Netflix	Most social media companies including Facebook

of existing products and services through new models. These new models can be broadly classified into four buckets (Exhibit 4.1).

1. **Traditional industry, newer company:** Some industries have been ripe for BMI. This category has several examples, including Uber (taxi services), Airbnb (hotel) and Netflix (movie rentals). In Uber's case, the taxi services industry was controlled by a few players in each geography, difficult to access, expensive and low on customer service. Uber, leveraging digital technologies, launched a new 'pay-as-you-go' ride-share business model that disrupted a traditional industry.

2. **Traditional industry, traditional company:** In some industries, current players have themselves transformed their business models. Hilti (power tools)[1] and Asian Paints (paint industry) are some well-documented examples. Hilti, a Liechtenstein-based power tool company, was in existence since the 1940s. The company sold its power tools to various construction companies and other industrial end-users. In the early 2000s, Hilti disrupted the market by shifting its business from outright sale of equipment to a rental business model. Power tools are complex, and there is a wide range of tools required depending on the material being worked on or the specific use. Customers, especially construction companies, found it expensive to own every kind of tool in multiple construction sites. It was also cumbersome to maintain a variety of tools in multiple locations. Hilti tackled this issue by introducing a tool rental business where the tools are managed and maintained by Hilti and made available to their customers on demand. The service was managed through a new Hilti Tool Fleet Management solution backed by an online tool management portal.

3. **New industry, new company:** Several industries that did not exist earlier were created by newer entrants which introduced innovative business models. For example, when they first emerged, social media platforms such as Facebook, YouTube and Instagram created an industry that did not exist before. These platforms' primary purpose was to allow consumers to exchange messages, pictures and videos among friends and followers. As the number of users on these platforms grew, the need to invest in technology and infrastructure also grew. To sustain their businesses on such scales, all these social media companies developed advertising-based revenue models. For example, Instagram allowed brands to advertise on its platform through product pages, hashtags and links, thereby generating advertising revenues.

4. **New industry, traditional company:** There are fewer examples of traditional players diversifying into a completely new industry with a new business model. Amazon Web Services is one such example of a company in the retail and e-commerce business setting up a rental-based cloud infrastructure business. Apple diversifying into

music with a subscription-based business model is another example of such diversification.

4.3. WHY IS BMI IMPORTANT?

According to a study by IBM (Rometty, 2006; Exhibit 4.2), companies that have innovative business models are more likely to be outperformers.

BMI provides companies with several benefits.

Increased growth: As discussed in the previous section, BMI allows for business growth even in traditional industries. As an example, Hilti grew in an otherwise stable power tools industry because of its BMI in conjunction with its product/service innovation.

Targeting new segments: Related to the previous benefit, newer business models that require lower one-time fee payments allow for newer segments to access the services. For example, as many ERPs moved to cloud-based subscription models, they could expand their customer base into SMEs. This segment could not earlier afford the large one-time licence and implementation costs.

Smoothened cash flows: By moving to annuity subscription models from one-time licence fees, companies have been able to smoothen out their revenues across a financial year. This increased the predictability of cash flow.

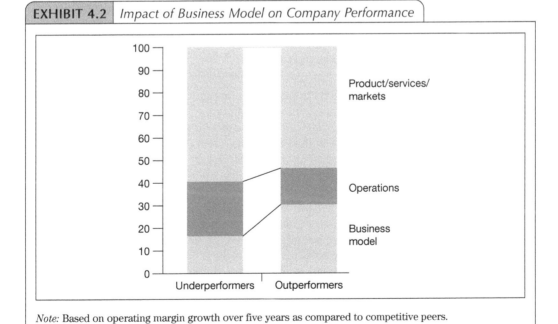

EXHIBIT 4.2 | *Impact of Business Model on Company Performance*

Note: Based on operating margin growth over five years as compared to competitive peers.

Source: Rometty (2006).

Competitive advantage: Business models are innovative and provide a competitive advantage at least in the short run. By launching a shared-taxi model, Uber not only expanded the taxi market but also created a relatively lower cost offering that traditional taxi companies could not easily compete with. Similarly, Intuit has been a dominant player in the small business accounting market through its subscription-based software model that has been difficult for others to copy. The likes of HP could not replicate Dell's direct selling model as Dells' entire value chain was rebuilt to support the business model.

Realigning operations: To sustain a new business model, an organization needs to evaluate its entire business operations. It needs to realign its operating model to deliver the cost structure and value that the new business model requires. This itself drives an organization to enhance its operational efficiencies. For example, studies have shown that when a low-cost airline launches in a new market, the existing full-service carriers are forced to relook at their operations and reduce costs. In many cases, these established airlines launched their low-cost services, leveraging the operational efficiencies gained due to the competition. An example of this is the launch of Jetstar by Qantas in response to the entry of Virgin Air into the Australian market.

Increased customer connect: Annuity business models also enhance customer connect, resulting in higher customer satisfaction. ERP companies that sold one-time licences to companies found a decline in the use of their products over a period. When they switched to subscription models, it was found that both vendors and customers evaluated the usage of the ERP more often. In some cases, customers have been the co-creators of the new business models. An example of this is how Volvo trucks created a 'maintenance-on-demand' service in conjunction with DHL, a large corporate customer.

4.4. THE RECENT FOCUS ON BMI

After understanding what BMI is and its impact on a company, it is also important to understand why it has gained such prominence in recent times.

BMI is not a new concept. It has existed for as long as companies have existed. It can be argued that by launching the Model T in the early 1900s, Henry Ford created a new business model for the automobile industry. The initial Model T costs around $800 against $2,000–3,000 that most cars cost at that time. This was achieved through superior manufacturing and quality processes.

However, there has been heightened activity around BMI in the last decade. This activity has been enabled by digital technologies that allow for greater innovation. As discussed in earlier chapters, digital technologies, including IoT, GPS, cloud and AI, have enabled new ways of developing and delivering services and products with newer revenue models. Uber's BMI was enabled by a combination of digital technologies, including mobile apps, GPS and data analytics. Mahindra, a leading automobile and farm equipment company in India, launched Trringo, the country's foremost farm equipment rental company. Trringo has enabled farmers of all sizes to rent the latest farm equipment on a 'pay-by-use' model using digital technologies.

Globalization is another factor that has led to a greater focus on BMI. The globalization of markets and production has allowed product innovations to flow rapidly across geographies. These trends have reduced a company's ability to compete on manufacturing costs as most competitors use the same global suppliers and contract manufactures. This has resulted in companies looking at BMI as an alternative to product and process-based competitiveness. Companies are trying to address the same segments with the same products but different business models to differentiate.

4.5. TYPES OF PRICING MODELS

We referred to pricing models such as subscription, rentals and 'pay-by-use' in the previous sections. This section provides an overview of some of the more prevalent pricing models that are part of newer business models:

Subscription-based: This is the most common business model and is based purely on the timeline the consumer is willing to contract for a product or services. Subscriptions usually range from a month to a year and multiple years. The pricing in a subscription plan declines as the commitment increases. For example, if a user subscribes to a service for a month, they may have to pay $10 per month. As the period increases, they receive a discount on this base price. A three-year subscription for the same product or service is, maybe, as low as $4 a month (or $144 for the entire period). Companies allow for subscriptions to be paid in advance or monthly. If paid in advance, a further discount may be available. Once customers decide on the duration of the plan when purchasing the service, they are not permitted to reduce the timelines for the commitment. Exhibit 4.3 provides an illustration of a company transitioning from licence-based to subscription-based business model and the impact this had on its channel partners.

EXHIBIT 4.3 | *The Office 365 Business Model*

In the mid-2010s, Microsoft© transitioned its Office products from a pure licence model to a subscription-based model known as Office 365 for end consumers and SME customers. The move provided the company with several benefits. It allowed for the conversion of a one-time licence fee to annuity revenues. The new business model also decreased the one-time cash outflow for home customers and SMEs, thus making the product more affordable. This itself led to lower piracy of the product. By offering Office 365 from the cloud, Microsoft provided its customers with regular updates and ensured that there was a single version of the product in the market. In the previous licence model, the company released a new version annually resulting in several versions of the product being in use simultaneously. This caused many challenges, including maintaining teams to manage and support multiple versions of the product. The multiple versions also led to integration issues with hardware original equipment manufacturers who were also launching new products at regular intervals.

The launch of Office 365 also required changes in the way the product was being billed and sold. Microsoft sold its Office product to home customers and SMEs through distributors, value-added resellers and retailers. These channel partners were equipped to handle one-time invoicing

(Continued)

(Continued)

when selling the product. However, the move to the Office 365 subscription model required channel partners to create billing systems that could handle monthly subscription billing. Improved billing platforms were needed to raise monthly invoices, charge the monthly fee to their customers' preferred payment methods, turn the subscriptions 'on' and 'off' based on receipt of payments, reconcile cash receipts with the number of subscriptions sold and provide reports back to Microsoft. The channel partners had to also provide billing-related customer services to help their customers with billing and subscription-related issues. All these investments by channel partners increased their cost of sale. However, it also allowed for an ongoing relationship with their customers based on which they could upsell other services. For the channel partners, who themselves were mainly SMEs, this was a significant change in their business model.

Usage-based: Usage-based or consumption-based business models have existed for a long time in the utility industry. Most electricity and water bills have always been usage-based. This model is now being extended to several other products and services. 'Pay-as-you-go' cellular plans to 'per-email' charging mechanism of direct marketing companies are some examples of such a model. One of the critical requirements for a company to implement usage-based plans is that there should be a precise and easily measurable mechanism to determine the usage. For example, in direct marketing, the unit of usage is an email sent, or for electricity consumption, the usage is measured as the number of units consumed.

This model's primary benefit is that it provides both the provider and consumer the flexibility to increase or decrease consumption based on requirements. For producers, the plan ensures that they are being paid for heavy usage. For consumers, they can manage their budgets and costs based on actual usage. On the other hand, this model removes the predictability in billing for both parties.

Usage-based models are more suited to high volume and varying volume businesses. From a producer's perspective, the model is ideal where the cost for the producer is mostly variable. Most cloud storage platforms charge based on the size of data stored and equipment-leasing companies like Trrigno charge per hour of usage.

Usage models can be entirely linear, like taxi companies, who charge per distance travelled. They can also be step-functions, like cloud storage model or data services providers, who change the prices at step intervals (e.g., the price for cloud storage could be one price up to 10 GB and then higher pricing for intervals of 10–100 GB and 100–500 GB).

A variation of a usage-based model is a hybrid 'fixed charge plus usage-based model'. Most utility billing models are hybrid, where they levy a minimum monthly payment in addition to usage-based charges. This combination allows for predictability for a portion of the provider's revenues in the form of the fixed charge. Simultaneously, the variable element enables users to increase or decrease their usage based on requirements.

Freemium: Freemium has become the dominant business model for most internet-based start-ups in the last decade. The model consists of a free base offering with charges for premium or advanced services. Business networking platform LinkedIn is a typical example of freemium where the base service is free, but most additional services such as search beyond the monthly limit, advanced search, direct mails to non-contacts and direct marketing activities are available only on subscribing to LinkedIn premium. Freemium is an attractive option for most platforms as the 'free' attracts initial users with minimal marketing spends. Once the users have signed up and used the free service, it is easier for the company to upsell premium services. Companies have traditionally offered 'free trials' for limited periods. Freemium is more effective than 'free trials' as customers are wary of providing payment details upfront and cumbersome cancellation and refund processes in the latter. However, freemium has also its downsides. Many customers never upgrade to the premium services as they are content with what is being offered as part of the free services. Therefore, providers need to be very judicious in determining the product features that are part of the free and premium services. If the free component is very limited, customers may not sign up or drop off from the service rapidly. If the free service features are very extensive, a customer may not be incentivized to upgrade. Finding the right balance between the two is critical for the success of a freemium model.

Marketplace: This business model is common among most e-commerce platforms. These platforms attract both buyers and sellers and earn a commission on every transaction. Uber and Amazon are two popular examples of this model. In both these cases, the platform companies have a large number of sellers and buyers. In the case of Uber, the sellers are the drivers, and the passengers are the buyers. In Amazon, a variety of large and small companies are sellers, and individuals are typically the buyers. Platform providers earn a share of the revenue from every transaction that gets consummated through the platform. In some cases, the providers also collect other fees such as listing fees and paid promotion fees (where the platform supports the seller in targeted sales campaigns).

Auction: A variation of the marketplace business model is an auction. eBay is the best-known example of this model. Unlike a traditional marketplace in the auctions model, the transaction price is set through an auction. Platforms like eBay earn revenue through a listing fee that is a percentage of the final value at which a product is sold. All stock markets and art dealers like Christie's and Sotheby's essentially use the auction models.

Crowdsourcing: In this business model, companies co-create their products or services with their customers and the general public. Crowdsourcing is being extensively used for activities such as information, analytics, innovation and funding. Platforms such as Wikipedia and Kaggle facilitate information and analytics crowdsourcing. Innocentive is an example of an open innovation platform, while Kickstarter is an example of a crowdsourcing funding platform.

Advertising: Several new-age companies generate revenues primarily from advertising. They achieve this by attracting a large number of users to use their free services. Facebook and Google are both examples of this business model. Google uses its search feature to attract users, while Facebook and Instagram offer free information-sharing platforms for personal news and views, pictures and videos.

The platforms are data-rich and have exhaustive customer and segmentation data. This segmented data is used to sell targeted promotion campaigns aimed at product companies.

In this section, we have discussed several business models. However, these models are not exclusive, and companies may use a combination of these to generate revenues. For example, YouTube crowdsources its content, but its revenue model is primarily from advertising.

4.6. MANAGING MULTIPLE BUSINESS MODELS

One of the challenges for traditional companies is how to manage multiple and often conflicting business models. One of the most written examples is Kodak (Exhibit 4.4).

How do companies manage two different and often conflicting business models? This topic has received significant attention in the last decade. Companies can take either of two paths to a new business model. The first path is to transition from one business model to another, while the second path is to manage both simultaneously. In the former, which is sequential, the challenge for a company is to drive change. In the latter, which is parallel or simultaneous, the challenge is on managing conflict. In the fast-changing business world of today, parallel change is more likely than sequential change.

According to a study published in the *MIT Sloan Management Review* (Sund et al., 2016), three key tensions exist in any company launching a new business model. One is to carefully think through the organizational structure before deciding on one that works. The second is to balance top management support and experimentation. If the new business model is overloaded with existing management and policies, it will lose its ability to experiment. Finally, top management has to plan for tensions between the current business and the new business for the allocation of resources. For example, IT budgets may be critical for both traditional and new businesses. However, due to strong pre-existing relationships between the traditional business and the IT department, the newer business may lose out in the allocation of budgets.

Finally, ambidextrous organizations are better equipped to handle business model conflicts.

The concept of ambidextrous organizations was introduced in Chapter 3 and will be discussed in greater detail in Chapter 5.

EXHIBIT 4.4 | *Kodak: Conflicting Business Models*

Kodak, a company based out of Rochester, New York, was founded in the late 1880s. For over a hundred years, the company dominated the photography industry with very few rivals. The company followed a 'razor and blade' business model by selling inexpensive cameras and earning its revenues through film. It had over an 80 per cent share in both these products in the USA. In the mid-1970s, the company invented the digital camera that required no film reel. The company felt that introducing the digital camera would harm its business model and did not actively pursue digital cameras. Within a decade, digital cameras became the norm, and Kodak rapidly lost share to Japanese competitors Canon and Sony. In the next few decades, cameras became integrated into cell phones, and the entire camera industry got disrupted. In 2012, one of the most valuable brands in the world filed for Chapter 11 bankruptcy protection.

4.7. DETERMINING THE RIGHT BUSINESS MODEL

While there is no perfect business model, some of the key characteristics of a good business model are described below:

Meets customer needs: All business models are designed to meet an existing customer's needs or allow a company to expand its target segment. For example, a full-service airline launches a low-cost airline to meet the needs of a new segment of travellers that it may not attract with its current model.

Provides competitive advantage: As discussed earlier in the chapter, more and more companies are looking at business models to provide them with a competitive advantage. Mere cost or price-based differentiators, as in the traditional models, are no longer sustainable.

Creates value for the entire value chain: In addition to providing value to a company and its customers, the new business model should also provide value to the whole value chain. In the Office 365 illustration, described in Exhibit 4.2, the shift from the licence fee model to the subscription-based business model provided value to its channel partners as well. Without adding value to all the stakeholders in the value chain, the new business model will not succeed.

Stays sustainable in the near term: Transitioning to a new business model requires significant changes in the company organization structure and operational processes. Unless a new model is sustainable, for a considerable period, it does not justify all the cost of change management.

Leaves room for further innovation: A business model cannot be thoroughly tested in a pilot environment. A broader acceptance of the model is known only with a scaled roll-out. Therefore, companies must plan for changes and tweaks to their business plan after their initial launch.

Captures network effects: A network effect is a phenomenon by which the value a user derives from a good or service or platform depends on the number of similar users. Business models aid in rapidly gaining customers and market share. This, in turn, enhances the network effects. The value of some companies, especially platform companies, grows only with an increased number of participants. Studies have shown that unless there is a tangible reason for signing up to multiple platforms, a customer prefers to be a member of one platform (Zhu & Iansiti, 2019). As a result, network effects have resulted in one or a few companies dominating an industry with a new business model. For example, in India, WhatsApp has become the dominant platform for messaging due to network effects. At the same time, subscribers are not motivated to be available on multiple messaging platforms. It is now challenging for a new messaging platform to break through into the markets.

Paves a path to revenues and profitability: Earlier in the chapter, we introduced the business model of freemium. One of the challenges of such a model is that customers are content using the free service and do not migrate to the premium and paid services. Therefore, companies need to have a clearly defined path to paid services and revenue. Companies spend a disproportionate amount of capital on customer acquisition to reap the benefits of network effects. As a result, several scaled companies are not profitable after many years of launching services.

4.8. BUILDING A BUSINESS MODEL

Several frameworks have been developed for building business models. In this section, three of the more popular models are discussed.

1. **The 4i framework (Frankenberger et al., 2013; Exhibit 4.5):** The 4i Framework outlines four steps (Exhibit 4.5), which are as follows:

   Initiation phase: The first phase includes understanding the ecosystem a company operates in. The ecosystem consists of customers, suppliers, competitors, government and investors. Understanding the ecosystem helps a company understand the needs of the players and any changes that might have to be made to the business model.

   Ideation phase: Once a company understands its ecosystem, the next activity is to generate ideas for potential new business models that address the evolving market.

   Integration: This is the third phase and involves detailing the ideas generated in the ideation phase. The four dimensions of this phase are best described by the questions: who, what, why and how. This phase also necessitates understanding how the business model options impact various ecosystem members and the change management process that will have to be executed for a successful implementation.

   Implementation: The final phase is the development of a detailed implementation plan based on all the aspects evolving from the previous phases. It involves prioritization of implementation, investments, project management and programme management. As business models cannot be easily tested before launch, this phase involves managing and mitigating business risk.

2. **Framework by Pynnönen et al. (2012):** This framework involves customers in the business model generation process (Exhibit 4.6).

   As illustrated in Exhibit 4.6, this framework has four phases. Phase 1 is similar to the initiation phase of the 4i framework and involves understanding the customer value and the ecosystem that generates this value. Phase 2 focuses on developing business model ideas based on the needs discovered in Phase 1. The next phase is to test the model using customer surveys and other techniques. The final phase is to adjust the model based on feedback received and then roll out its implementation. The significant difference between this framework and other BMI frameworks is that it recommends an iterative process with changes in the business model as and when customer feedback is received, and the model is tested in the marketplace.

3. **Osterwalder and Pigneur (Osterwalder et al., 2011) framework:** This framework consists of five phases: mobilize, understand, design, implement and manage.

   In the first phase, a company mobilizes all the required information to design a new business model. During this phase, awareness is created across the organization about the upcoming project and project teams are formed.

EXHIBIT 4.5   *4I Framework for Business Models*

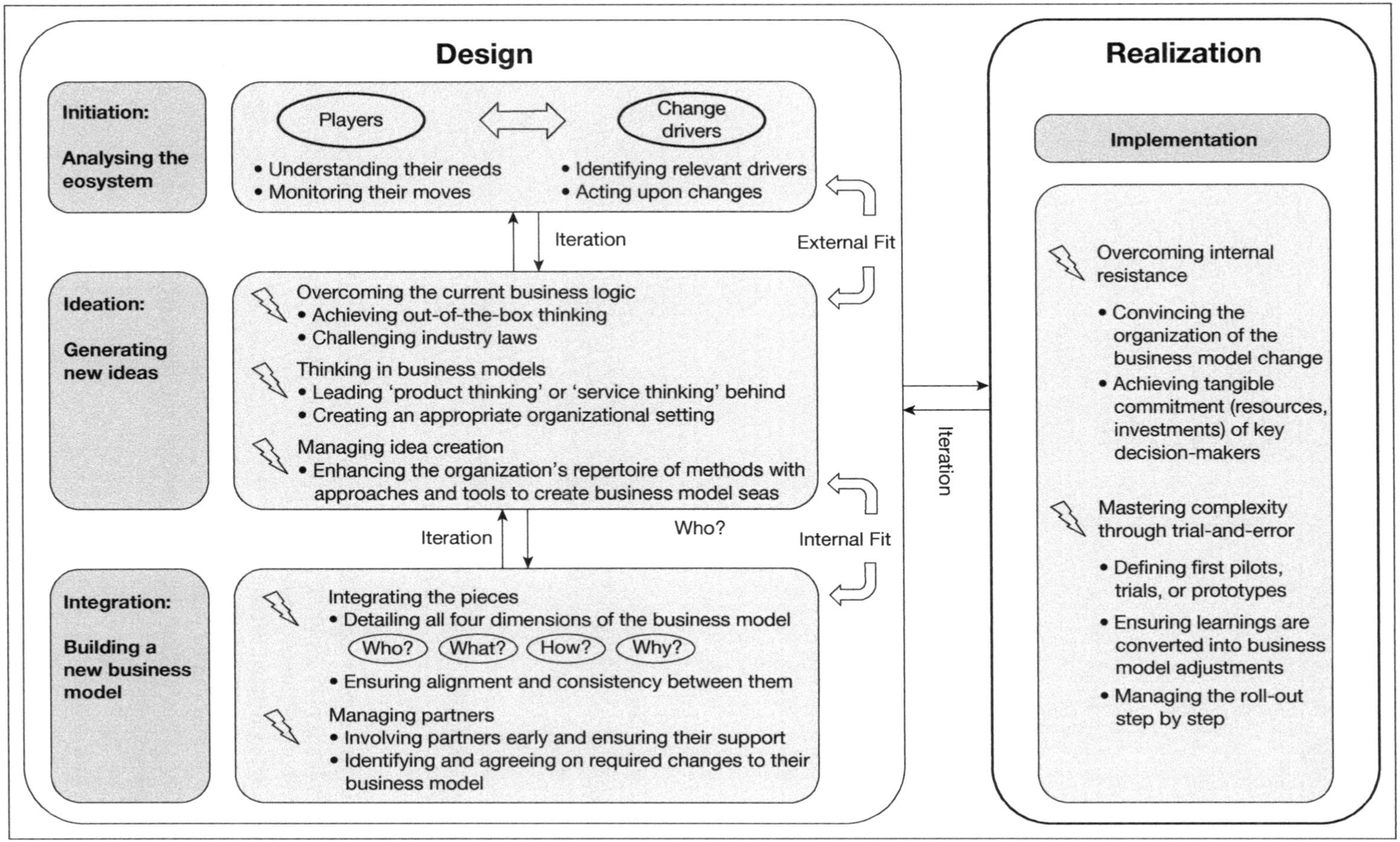

Design

Initiation:
Analysing the ecosystem

(Players) ⇕ (Change drivers)

- Understanding their needs
- Monitoring their moves
- Identifying relevant drivers
- Acting upon changes

Iteration

Ideation:
Generating new ideas

Overcoming the current business logic
- Achieving out-of-the-box thinking
- Challenging industry laws

Thinking in business models
- Leading 'product thinking' or 'service thinking' behind
- Creating an appropriate organizational setting

Managing idea creation
- Enhancing the organization's repertoire of methods with approaches and tools to create business model seas

External Fit

Who?

Internal Fit

Integration:
Building a new business model

Integrating the pieces
- Detailing all four dimensions of the business model

(Who?) (What?) (How?) (Why?)

- Ensuring alignment and consistency between them

Managing partners
- Involving partners early and ensuring their support
- Identifying and agreeing on required changes to their business model

Iteration

Realization

Implementation

Overcoming internal resistance
- Convincing the organization of the business model change
- Achieving tangible commitment (resources, investments) of key decision-makers

Mastering complexity through trial-and-error
- Defining first pilots, trials, or prototypes
- Ensuring learnings are converted into business model adjustments
- Managing the roll-out step by step

Iteration

Source: Frankenberger et al. (2013).

EXHIBIT 4.6 | *Business Model Framework*

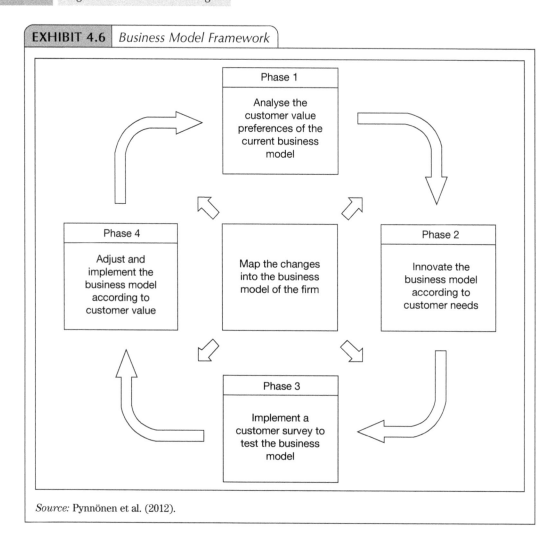

Source: Pynnönen et al. (2012).

In the understand phase, the company analyses the information gathered in the mobilize phase. The understanding is developed by interviewing experts and key members of the ecosystem.

Once the need is established, the design phase is all about creating the right business models. This phase also involves creating prototypes of the more promising models that can be tested in the marketplace.

The fourth stage involves testing the prototypes and rolling out large-scale implementation.

The final stage is monitoring the newly launched business model and making changes if required.

As can be seen, the three models follow similar paths that included data gathering, analysis, developing options, testing, implementation and course correction.

| EXHIBIT 4.7 | *Building Blocks of a Business Model* |

Building Block	Key Questions
Customers	Who are the key customers? What are the key segments? How are the relationships managed?
Product/Service offering	What is the portfolio of current offerings? What is the value proposition? What are the gaps in the proposition?
Competitors	Who are the current competitors? What are the competitor industry segments? What are the newer industry segments that could become potential competitors in the future? What are the gaps in the services being offered by competitors?
Partners	Who are the partners required to deliver the service?
Resources	What are the key resources/assets required to deliver the service?
Processes	What are the key processes/activities? What is the information flow?
Cost and revenue	What are the factors that contribute to the cost structure of the product and services? What are the current and potential revenue streams?

4.9. THE BUILDING BLOCKS OF BUSINESS MODELS

The previous section covered the process of building a business model. This section focuses on the essential building blocks of a successful business model. Exhibit 4.7 provides a comprehensive list of these building blocks. As can be seen later in this chapter, these building blocks have been converted into useful frameworks to build business models.

4.10. BUSINESS MODEL FRAMEWORKS

Several models are available to structure the information gathered around each of the building blocks. This section discusses three such models: Business Model Canvas used by growth companies, the Lean Canvas used by start-ups and resources, transactions, value and the narrative (RTVN) framework for pre-start-ups.

4.10.1. Osterwalder Business Canvas Model (OBCM)

This is the most popular framework introduced by Alexander Osterwalder in his book *Business Model Generation* (Osterwalder & Pigneur, 2010; Exhibit 4.8). (Several YouTube videos by the author and part of the book are available for free download.)

EXHIBIT 4.8 | *The Business Canvas Model*

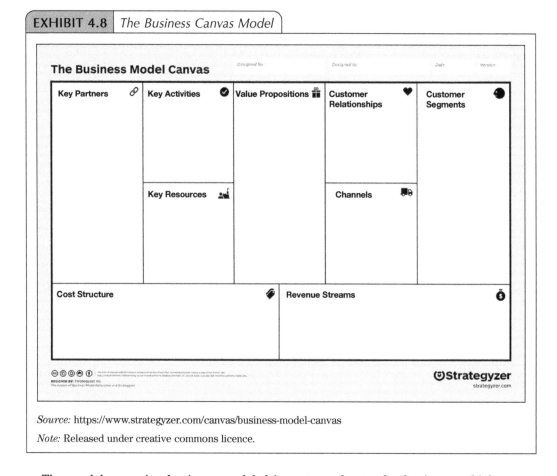

Source: https://www.strategyzer.com/canvas/business-model-canvas

Note: Released under creative commons licence.

The model uses nine business model drivers to understand a business, which are as follows:

Customer segments: The canvas first outlines all the types of 'customers' that a company is targeting. This could be individual customers, small business customers or large corporations.

Value propositions: The next step is to define the products or services that create 'value' for each of these customer segments based on their specific needs. What specific customer issues are these propositions solving?

Channels: The various methods of connecting the value propositions with the customer segments are called channels. These could be owned channels (owned by the company) or partner channels (owned by partners).

Customer relationships: What kind of relationships do customers expect from the company? How will these relationships be managed? Will it be virtual (digital) through a website or an app, or would it be in-person?

Revenue streams: How and through which business model is the value being captured? For what value are customers willing to pay? How are they currently paying and are there more preferred models for the value?

Key resources: What is the infrastructure required to create, deliver and capture the value? These could be human, physical, intellectual or financial resources. This will help to identify the assets that are indispensable for the business model.

Key activities: These are processes that are key to leveraging the resources and providing the value proposition. The activities can include manufacturing, platform development or analytics.

Key partners: The key partners are those who can help a company leverage its business model. The partners can include government, regulatory bodies, investors, marketing partners, outsourced vendors or suppliers.

Cost structure: Once the rest of the business model canvas is laid out, the final step is to determine the costs involved for all the activities required to deliver the value proposition.

The OBCM helps a company summarize its entire business in one simple framework. It allows leaders to understand how all the individual elements fit together, brainstorm on the gaps and exhibit out how to develop a new business model.

The OBCM framework has been applied to discuss the solution for the mini case at the end of the chapter.

4.10.2. Lean Canvas Model

Exhibit 4.9 provides the Lean Canvas Model structure that was developed as part of the lean start-up framework (Maurya, 2012). The model has been adapted from the OBCM to suit start-ups. Start-ups are different from growth companies. Many of the building blocks suggested in OBCM have not yet evolved in the case of start-ups or are not relevant.

The framework has the following building blocks:

- **Problem:** What is the problem users have that the business is trying to address? Is the business meeting this need?
- **Solution:** How will the start-up help solve this problem? Is there a minimum viable product?
- **Key metrics:** What are the key metrics that the company will focus on? This could be the number of users in the first year, revenue generated and so on.
- **Unique value proposition:** What is the USP for the company?
- **Unfair advantage:** What is the competitive advantage the start-up has over its competition and industry?
- **Channels:** What are all the channels available?
- **Customer segments:** What are the target segments?
- **Cost structure:** What are the cost elements of the product/services (e.g., salaries, cost of the materials, cost of maintenance, marketing, etc.).
- **Revenue streams:** How will the product/service generate revenue (e.g., sales, subscription)?

As an illustration, Exhibit 4.10 provides the Lean Canvas Model for Uber's ride-sharing service.

EXHIBIT 4.9 | *Lean Canvas Model*

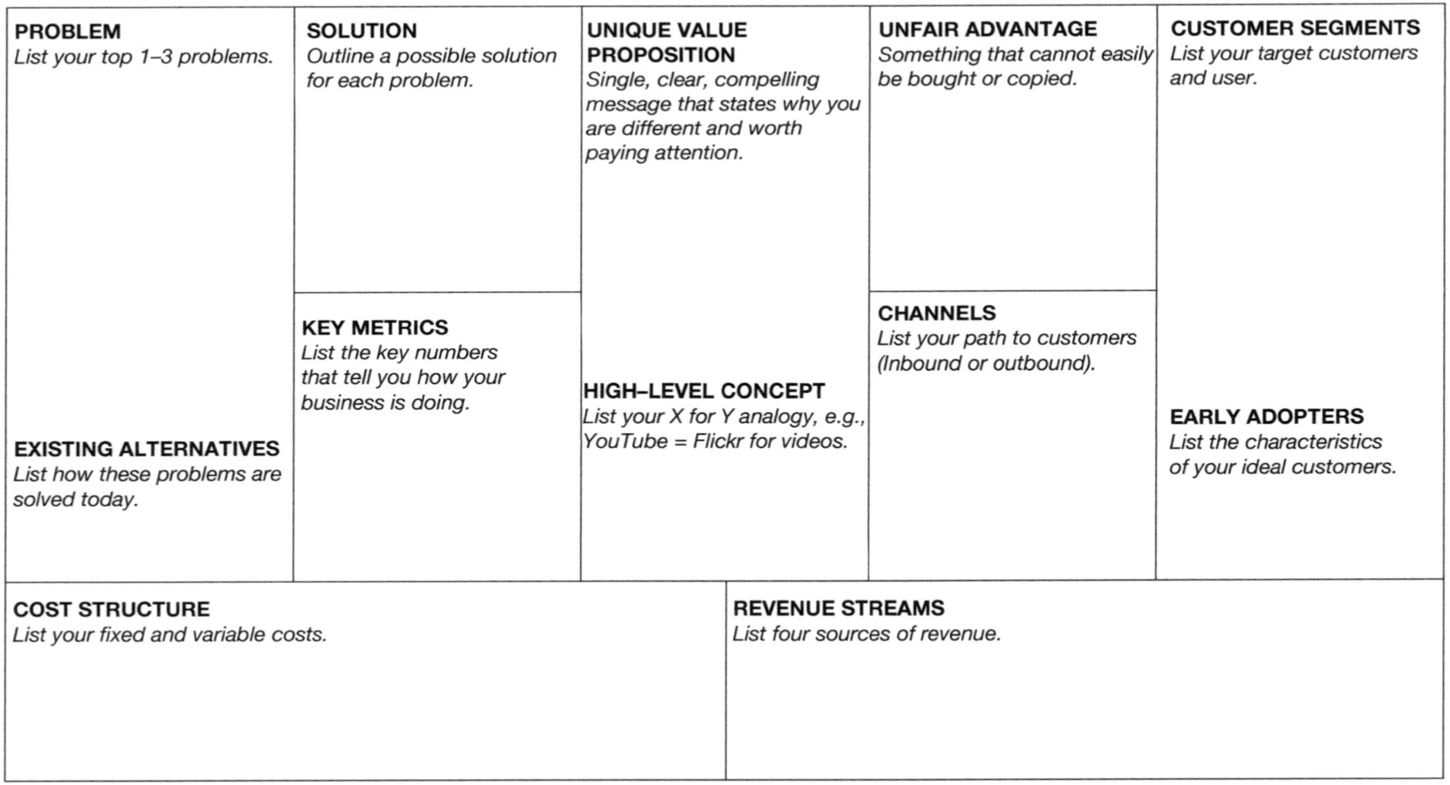

PROBLEM List your top 1–3 problems.	SOLUTION Outline a possible solution for each problem.	UNIQUE VALUE PROPOSITION Single, clear, compelling message that states why you are different and worth paying attention.	UNFAIR ADVANTAGE Something that cannot easily be bought or copied.	CUSTOMER SEGMENTS List your target customers and user.
	KEY METRICS List the key numbers that tell you how your business is doing.	HIGH-LEVEL CONCEPT List your X for Y analogy, e.g., YouTube = Flickr for videos.	CHANNELS List your path to customers (Inbound or outbound).	
EXISTING ALTERNATIVES List how these problems are solved today.				EARLY ADOPTERS List the characteristics of your ideal customers.
COST STRUCTURE List your fixed and variable costs.		REVENUE STREAMS List four sources of revenue.		

Source: https://blog.leanstack.com/why-lean-canvas-vs-business-model-canvas/

Note: Lean canvas is adapted from the busines model canvas (https://www.strategyzer.com/canvas/business-model-canvas released under creative commons licence).

EXHIBIT 4.10 | *Lean Canvas Model for Uber*

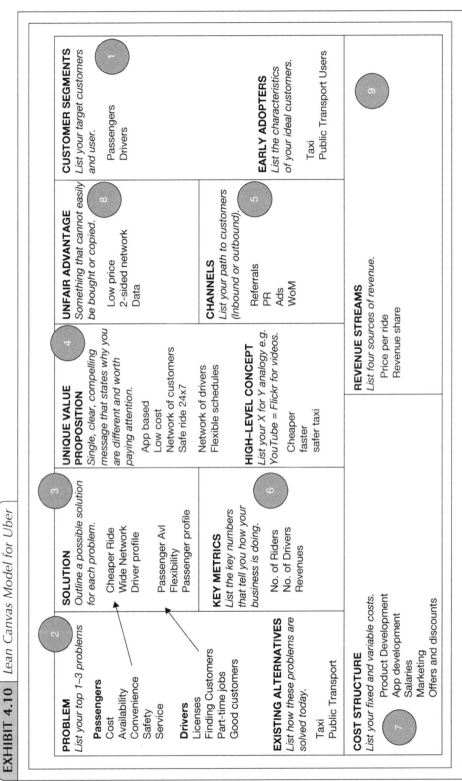

PROBLEM (2)
List your top 1–3 problems

Passengers
Cost
Availability
Convenience
Safety
Service

Drivers
Licenses
Finding Customers
Part-time jobs
Good customers

EXISTING ALTERNATIVES
List how these problems are solved today.

Taxi
Public Transport

SOLUTION (3)
Outline a possible solution for each problem.

Cheaper Ride
Wide Network
Driver profile

Passenger Avl
Flexibility
Passenger profile

KEY METRICS (6)
List the key numbers that tell you how your business is doing.

No. of Riders
No. of Drivers
Revenues

UNIQUE VALUE PROPOSITION (4)
Single, clear, compelling message that states why you are different and worth paying attention.

App based
Low cost
Network of customers
Safe ride 24x7

Network of drivers
Flexible schedules

HIGH–LEVEL CONCEPT
List your X for Y analogy e.g. YouTube = Flickr for videos.

Cheaper
faster
safer taxi

UNFAIR ADVANTAGE (8)
Something that cannot easily be bought or copied.

Low price
2-sided network
Data

CHANNELS (5)
List your path to customers (Inbound or outbound).

Referrals
PR
Ads
WoM

CUSTOMER SEGMENTS (1)
List your target customers and user.

Passengers
Drivers

EARLY ADOPTERS
List the characteristics of your ideal customers.

Taxi
Public Transport Users (9)

COST STRUCTURE (7)
List your fixed and variable costs.

Product Development
App development
Salaries
Marketing
Offers and discounts

REVENUE STREAMS
List four sources of revenue.

Price per ride
Revenue share

Source: https://blog.leanstack.com/why-lean-canvas-vs-business-model-canvas/

Note: Lean canvas is adapted from the busines model canvas (https://www.strategyzer.com/canvas/business-model-canvas released under creative commons licence).

As the Uber platform was being developed, there were two potential customer segments. These were passengers who were looking for rides and car owners who were willing to provide rides. This was different from the existing taxi model, where the taxis were part of licenced organizations, and individuals could not become taxi operators without going through cumbersome and expensive processes. This resulted in mini-regional monopolies with a limited number of taxi services that were charging high rates. As in any industry with limited competition, the services did not score high on service quality, convenience and availability.

Uber's solution was to provide a digital technology-based platform where individual car owners can offer rides to passengers. In the new model, the entire process of ride-hailing, interaction with drivers and payment were managed through a mobile app using technologies such as GPS. This overcame many of the challenges of traditional taxi services. The services were cheaper than regular taxi companies as Uber did not have any overheads like car maintenance, and there was a larger supply of drivers. Uber earned a share of the revenue, and its primary cost was product development, logistics and marketing.

4.10.3. RTVN Framework for Pre-start-ups (Bock & George, 2017)

The RTVN is a simple framework that helps entrepreneurs tie together their business idea into a model and narrative. The framework has four key components, which are as follows:

Resources: This defines the key resources available to an entrepreneur or the key resources that an entrepreneur will need to start a company. This could be financial resources, intellectual property, industry advisors or market access.

Transactions: Transactions are connectors for the various resources outlined. These could be internal, external or boundary-spanning transactions or processes. The transactions that add value to a company are those a company can be good at, important in delivering the value and differentiating from its competitors.

Value: Simply put, this is how resources and transactions can be combined to create and provide intangible or tangible value to customers.

The RTVN framework focuses on the intersection of these three attributes.

The 'resource-value' intersection helps define the resources that help in generating value to customers.

The 'resource-transaction' intersection helps determine how a company will link its key resources to its primary transactions and if it has suitable transactions to deliver its resources to its clients.

The 'transaction-value' intersection links transactions to the value of the delivery. For example, do customers have complex transaction requirements, or do customers avoid adopting new products from start-ups?

Narrative: The final element of the RTVN framework is to build a 'narrative' around the R-T-V that a company is developing. This is an inexpensive method to test out the initial analysis of a new product or service offering.

MINI CASE 4.1. DISCUSSION

Google Search's revenues are primarily driven by advertising. Exhibit 4.11 illustrates the application of the OBCM to Google Search.

Google Search targets two customer segments. The first is search users who could be any individual or business seeking information. The second set of users are owners of content (like media companies), businesses and advertisers. The key partners for Google Search are, therefore, content creators, advertising and marketing companies and corporations. Governments and local advertising regulators can also be considered to be partners. The primary resources that Google Search provides are the search platform algorithms that drive the search and search data. This is used to drive an effective search. The main costs for google are platform maintenance, R&D and marketing. The Google Search platform is available on the web, through a mobile app and in-built into third-party websites. The search platform is free for search users. Businesses can advertise (SEM) or appear high on the ranking when specific search terms are searched (SEO).

Google Search is the largest search engine and dominates the advertising industry. However, it is facing increased competition from Amazon and Facebook for search-based revenues in the recent past.

EXHIBIT 4.11 | *BCM for Google Search*

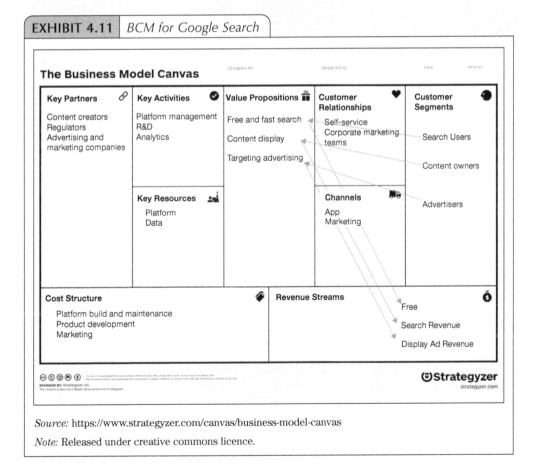

Source: https://www.strategyzer.com/canvas/business-model-canvas

Note: Released under creative commons licence.

SUMMARY

A business model is how a company creates and captures value and the processes and technology that enable this endeavour (Chesbrough, 2007). Digital technologies have enabled newer business models. Both traditional and newer companies focus on BMI as a differentiator as conventional differentiators such as manufacturing costs and efficiencies are no longer sustainable. Many companies are forced to manage multiple business models during this transitionary period.

BMI is high-risk as it is not possible to fully understand its impact until the launch. To mitigate this risk, several models are available to evaluate the drivers for BMI. The Osterwalder Business Model Canvas and its variation, the Lean Model Canvas, are two frameworks popularly used to structure a company's business model.

Discussion Questions

1. Define business model. How is it different from strategy?
2. Discuss the factors that are making BMI more and more relevant.
3. What are some of the building blocks of BMI?
4. What are some of the key frameworks for BMI? Compare and contrast them.

GLOSSARY

Business model canvas: A framework to evaluate the drivers for a business model.
Business model: The way a company generates and captures value.

NOTE

1. https://www.wurzer-kollegen.de/wp-content/uploads/2019/12/Hilti_MIPLM-Industry-Case-Study-Series.pdf

REFERENCES

Björkdahl, J., & Holmén, M. (2013). Business model innovation: The challenges ahead. *International Journal of Product Development, 18*(3/4), 213–225.

Bock, A. J., & George, G. (2017). *The business model book: Design, build and adapt business ideas that drive business growth.* Pearson.

Chesbrough, H. (2007). Business model innovation: It's not just about technology anymore. *Strategy & leadership, 35*(6), 12–17.

Frankenberger, K., Weiblen, T., Csik, M., & Gassmann, O. (2013). The 4I-framework of business model innovation: A structured view on process phases and challenges. *International Journal of Product Development, 18*(3–4), 249–273.

Lewis, M. (1999). *The new thing: A Silicon Valley story.* WW Norton & Company.

Osterwalder, A., & Pigneur, Y. (2010). *Business model generation: A handbook for visionaries, game changers, and challengers.* John Wiley & Sons.

Maurya, A. (2012). Why lean canvas vs business model canvas? https://blog.leanstack.com/why-lean-canvas-vs-business-model-canvas/

Osterwalder, A., Pigneur, Y., & Tucci, C. L. (2005). Clarifying business models: Origins, present, and future of the concept. *Communications of the Association for Information Systems, 16*(1), 1.

Osterwalder, A., Pigneur, Y., Oliveira, M. A. Y., & Ferreira, J. J. P. (2011). Business model generation: A handbook for visionaries, game changers and challengers. *African Journal of Business Management, 5*(7), 22–30.

Pynnönen, M., Hallikas, J., & Ritala, P. (2012). Managing customer-driven business model innovation. *International Journal of Innovation Management, 16*(04), 1250022.

Rometty, V. G. (2006). *Expanding the innovation horizon: The global CEO study 2006.* IBM Business Consulting Services.

Securities and Exchange Commission. (2004). Form S–1: Registration statement. Google Inc. https://www.sec.gov/Archives/edgar/data/1288776/000119312504073639/ds1.htm

Sund, K. J., Bogers, M., Villarroel, J. A., & Foss, N. (2016). Managing tensions between new and existing business models. *MIT Sloan Management Review, 57*(4), 8.

Zhu, F., & Iansiti, M. (2019). Why some platforms thrive and others don't. https://hbr.org/2019/01/why-some-platforms-thrive-and-others-dont

CHAPTER

Leadership and People

Learning Objectives

Digital strategies and transformation are all-pervasive and impact every part of an organization, whether customer facing, internal or support functions. Given the nature of the change, people form a critical part of digital strategies. Digital strategy implementation is led by the CEO, supported by the CXOs and managed at every level within an organization.

This chapter outlines the role of people in digital strategies and the characteristics and skills required at individual and organizational level and will help readers understand:

- Transformational versus transactional leadership.
- Role of the board and CEO.
- Role of a chief digital officer.
- Concepts of adaptive leadership and ambidexterity.
- Characteristics of a digital organization.
- Building a culture of innovation.
- Skills required for a successful digital organization.

Mini Case 5.1

Ron Hardy was the chairman of Brighton Insurance Company (BIC), a mid-sized general insurance company headquartered in Brighton, UK. The company offered a range of products, including motor, home, pet and travel insurance. The company focused primarily on individual customers and small businesses across the UK and had a niche market of loyal customers. The privately held company was founded almost a century ago by Hardy's great-grandfather and had survived several acquisition attempts. BIC had an independent board and a professional CEO to manage the company.

Over the last decade, BIC had made significant investments in technology and most of its sales, services and claims processing were on custom-built technology platforms. However, the board had been advising Hardy that the company was due for a digital makeover. Digital technologies such as mobile apps, AI-driven customer services and blockchain-based claims processing was already in use by newer and more digitally savvy insurers.

Hugh Jackson currently led BIC. Jackson had joined the company as a trainee four decades ago and had worked in various roles across the organization. He had become president seven years ago, and his contract was coming to an end next year. Hardy had a lot to think about. Was Jackson the right individual to lead BIC through its next round of transformation? Jackson had extensive experience and was well respected within the company and across the industry. However, did he have the necessary skills to rebuild BIC into a digital organization? What kind of leadership team would BIC need to build to traverse the next five years? What impact would digital transformation have on BIC employees, many of whom had worked there for almost their entire careers? What change management practices would BIC need to implement?

5.1. TRANSFORMATIONAL AND TRANSACTIONAL LEADERSHIP

Transformational leadership as a concept was first proposed in 1978 by Pulitzer Prize winner James MacGregor Burns in his seminal book *Leadership* (2004). The book describes how leaders interact with society and their efforts to shape society. Burns classified leadership as transactional and transformational. Transactional leaders lead through social exchange. For example, these leaders provide incentives or favours to achieve a goal. On the other hand, transformational leaders inspire others to follow and also mentor others to become transformational leaders themselves. Bernard M. Bass, an American scholar, developed Burn's ideas to what is known as the Bass transformational leadership theory or the 4I theory (Bass & Avolio, 1994). According to this theory, transformational leadership can be explained by using four attributes.

1. **Idealized influence:** A leader shares a vision and mission with the team. The team trusts the leader and the vision, and is motivated to accept radical and innovative solutions to achieve the leader's vision.
2. **Inspirational motivation:** A leader communicates effectively and with clarity. This communication generates optimism and enthusiasm.
3. **Intellectual stimulation:** A leader encourages the team to explore new ways of looking for solutions. The solutions are innovative and path breaking.
4. **Individualized consideration:** A leader provides personal attention to the team and makes each member feel valued and important. The leader is involved in the development of all the team members.

The authors also define the types of transactional leadership as follows.

Contingent reward: A leader gives the team a clear understanding of what needs to be done and sets expectations of/from each team member. To achieve these goals, a leader also outlines rewards and incentives, both monetary and non-monetary.

Management by exception: In active management, a leader proactively monitors the team's performance and takes corrective action, if required. In passive management, a leader intervenes only when there are deviations from the plan.

Laissez-faire: These leaders are not involved with their teams and are indecisive and not motivational.

The authors conclude that ideal leaders blend transformational and transactional styles, and transactional elements add to transformational leadership's effectiveness. They also conclude that contingent rewarding leaders are generally more effective in transactional leadership than those practising management by exception. Laissez-faire leaders are the least effective.

5.2. ROLE OF THE LEADER IN DIGITAL STRATEGIES

Digital strategies are on corporate boards' agenda and have risen to the top of CEOs' strategic priorities. According to a Gartner study conducted among CEOs in 2018,[1] growth continues to be the topmost priority of most CEOs. Through the years, though growth has been the key for CEOs, what has changed is the driver for this growth, which is, digital strategies.

According to the survey, every executive committee member needs to be engaged in developing, implementing and managing digital strategies. The survey also showed that CEOs are concerned that many of their executives do not possess sufficient digital skills to help the company's future. The survey determined that IT, sales, manufacturing, technology, supply chain and human resource (HR) executives are most in need of digital skills. Without these skills being imbibed by their entire executive team, CEOs stated that implementing a company-wide digital strategy would be challenging.

When asked which organizational competencies their company needs to develop the most, CEOs named talent management closely followed by technology enablement, digitalization and data centricity or data management. CEOs stated that data literacy and data centricity are critical for the overall growth of the company.

The roles expected from CEOs when leading the digital transformation of their companies are manifold and well summarized by Dan Shapero, vice-president, Global Solutions at LinkedIn (Ready et al., 2020).

> What makes a great leader in this new economy? In a way, it boils down to a few things: Do they build great teams? Do they understand the implications of technology on the business? Are they able to adapt to the speed at which business is happening? Can they operate at a high level and a low level simultaneously? And do they have the ability to build trust across the organization to get things done?

Some of the key characteristics that a successful digital CEO needs to exhibit include the following.

Vision: As discussed in Chapter 1, a digital strategy combines several elements of a business including operational innovation, product/service innovation, business model innovation and people innovation. Without a vision for both short-term and long-term goals, digital transformation will not be possible. There has been a considerable debate in academic and business literature on whether a leader from outside the industry will bring in a fresh mindset and accelerate the transformation. However, there is no evidence to prove this conclusively. This is related to the idealized influence and inspirational motivation attributes of transformational leaders.

Collaboration and networking: According to recent studies, Fortune 500 companies lose around $31.5 billion per year by failing to share knowledge (Myers, 2015). Successful digital transformation requires collaboration among various internal and external parties. The internal groups include sales and marketing, technology, operations and manufacturing, supply chain, finance and HR functions. External parties can consist of customers, suppliers, technology partners, system integrators, consultants, government and other policymaking bodies. A digital leader will need to implement internal communication processes that encourage the inter-functional sharing of information and ideas. They also need to create similar structures to exchange knowledge and interact with various external bodies.

Experimentation: Digital strategies require CEOs to encourage experimentation as, in most cases, there is no established path to success. The level of ambiguity in the marketplace makes it impossible for leaders to know precisely what will work and what technological and analytical capabilities they may need to acquire.

At the same time, this experimentation must be backed by data and analytics, scenario planning, contingency measures and the ability to modify plans rapidly. CEOs need to build a culture of measured risk-taking and inspire people to take decisions. Leaders also need to introduce agile ways of working in their organization.

This can be linked to the intellectual stimulation attribute of transformational leaders.

Learning from the outside: In developing traditional strategies, companies conduct market scans of the industry within which they operate. However, in the digital world, boundaries between sectors are getting blurred. For example, is Amazon a cloud infrastructure company, a media streaming company or an e-commerce company. Companies are getting disrupted by players who were not their traditional competition—a decade ago, a Swiss watch manufacturer never considered Apple to be a competitor. Another aspect of learning from outside is that business models transcend industry boundaries. Companies can learn from and adapt business models from both digital natives within their industries and companies in other industries which have digitally transformed.

Building a digital team: A digital strategy is only as good as the team executing it. A CEO needs to build good teams to handle digital transformation, starting from the change programme leader like a CDO. The CEO needs to ensure that there is a culture across the organization that can embrace change.

This can be linked to the individualized consideration of transformational leadership.

Execution focus: Another characteristic of a successful digital transformation is the CEO's focus on executing the vision. CEOs need to ensure proper governance structure, milestones, and feedback mechanisms. Incentives of/for the teams need to be aligned to the new vision of the company. For example, in a traditional company that has both legacy IT and digital technologies, the incentives for the IT team must be managed in such a way that both strategies receive appropriate focus from the team.

This is the transactional element of the role of a CEO.

5.3. ROLE OF INVESTORS AND BOARDS

Boards play a role across the digital transformation process. They are involved in encouraging the company to start its digital journey, approve financial resources, monitor the impact, provide strategic directions, help build networks and make course corrections.

Boards are responsible for balancing the company's short-term goals with its need to create a sustainable advantage for the long term. As per the BDO's 2018 Cyber Governance Survey,[2] public company board directors are increasingly recognizing the necessity and competitive advantages of embracing a digital transformation strategy. Boards need to understand the benefits and risks of digital transformation and, equally important, the downsides of not going digital.

Many digital companies, especially start-ups, focus on growing their user base in the short and medium terms. This focus on growth is at the cost of profitability and requires significant financial resources to sustain the 'burn rate'. Companies need to have a good relationship with their boards during this high-risk phase of their growth.

Board members are typically involved in the digital transformation of multiple companies, across industries. They provide a company's leadership strategic insights and best practices from multiple industries. As described in the section on the CEO's role, leaders need to 'listen' to non-competitors in this age of disruption. Investors and boards are a good source for such information.

5.4. THE CHIEF DIGITAL OFFICER

Companies worldwide are creating a new role of CDO or a chief digital officer to drive digital strategies and transformation across their businesses. Born-digital companies have digital embedded in their organization and culture. However, traditional companies need to create this culture with the direction of the CEO and the board. As discussed earlier, digital strategies involve all parts of an organization and not just technology. In traditional companies, these roles are spread across chief marketing officer (CMO), chief sales officer, chief information officer (CIO), chief technology officer (CTO), chief financial officer (CFO), chief human resources officer (CHRO) and chief operating officer, among others. The only point of convergence of all these functions is the CEO. As the CEO has multiple priorities, there was a need for a new fulcrum for this activity. This led to the rise of the position of CDO in companies across the globe. A 2017 study by Strategy& found that approximately 19% of top global companies have created a CDO role, mostly in the last five years.[3]

5.4.1. CIO versus CTO versus CDO

There is considerable confusion between the CIO and CTO's roles as both are focused on technology. CIOs, in general, are focused within the company and responsible for IT applications and infrastructure. The CIO deals internally with business groups, the IT team, and externally with vendors of IT services and products. The CTO, on the other hand, is focused externally on customers and works on developing products and services that are sold to customers. For example, an IT products company may have a CIO responsible for all internal infrastructure, while the CTO focuses on designing and developing products being sold to customers. The CDO is responsible for developing and implementing digital strategies and may not have a technology background. Stated in another way, a CIO focuses on continuity, a CTO focuses on growth and a CDO focuses on change.

Each of these roles requires different skills and companies have been found to struggle when CIOs or CTOs are given a CDO's responsibilities. According to a global survey of IT leaders (conducted by Harvey Nash and KPMG),[4] companies started to be effective in digital transformation only after creating the role of a dedicated CDO. The study found that half of the organizations with a dedicated CDO had a clear digital strategy, compared with only 21 per cent without a CDO.

5.4.2. Profile and Reporting Structure

Another issue that many companies have struggled with is the ideal profile of a CDO and who the CDO should report to. It has been argued that as CDOs need to bring together several functions in a company, they should be an insider or tenured employee. On the other hand, tenured employees may not be the most suited to drive change. An outsider who can bring in fresh ideas and best practices from other industries and companies may be a better change agent. Many companies have brought back senior professionals, who have had the tenure and then went to work for other companies, to become CDOs. Such individuals satisfy both the conditions of tenure and breadth of experiences. Diversified conglomerates have also picked individuals who have worked across multiple group companies as this provides them with a wide range of experiences.

In the early days of this role, CDOs reported to the CIO. Companies soon realized that this was less than ideal, and today most CDOs report directly to the CEO.

5.4.3. Key Responsibilities

The CDO holds several responsibilities relating to the design and implementation of digital strategies.

- **Designing the digital strategy:** The primary role of the CDO is to formulate the digital strategy of an organization. In most companies, CDOs invite several external consultants to provide their perspectives on potential digital strategies. Based on these inputs, CDOs work closely with the CEO to formulate a company's digital strategy.
- **Prioritize elements of a digital strategy:** A company transforming itself will undergo massive change across various functions. This takes time and resources and, therefore, it is essential to prioritize elements of transformation.
- **Building an innovation ecosystem:** Implementing digital requires an extensive range of skills including consulting, design, implementation and testing. For large

transformations, these skills are not available internally or wholly with an external partner. The CDO needs to build an ecosystem of partners, internal and external. In many cases, this also includes start-ups, research labs and academic institutions.

- **Driving change:** As discussed earlier in the chapter, digital transformation involves changes across an organization including changes in people, culture, work methods and technologies. A CDO is responsible for working with various stakeholders to build a culture of change.
- **Driving implementation:** A CDO works with cross-functional teams to ensure implementation of the transformation. This includes programme and project management, governance and reporting.
- **Measuring return on investment and goals:** The primary reason for digital innovation is to create value and remain competitive. The CDO sets up a mechanism to measure and report the progress of the transformation, including the achievement of return on investment.
- **Developing digital talent:** The CDO works closely with HR to attract and retain top talent and build digital capabilities.
- **Communication:** A CDO is also responsible for communication of the objectives and the status of transformation, to both internal and external stakeholders.

The role of a CDO is gaining recognition across companies. This is getting reflected in the number of CDOs who have taken over as CEOs of companies.

These include Ganesh Bell, CDO of GE, who became the president of Uptake; Adam Brotman, CDO of Starbucks Coffee, who later became president of retailer J.Crew; and James Hackett who was the head of Ford's Smart Mobility, a unit responsible for experimenting with car-sharing programmes, who took over as the president of Ford.

5.5. ROLE AND IMPACT ON TEAMS: THE FUTURE OF WORK

The role and impact of digital transformation on employees has been often referred to as the 'future of work'.

To successfully implement digital strategies, companies need to bring in many diverse capabilities together. At the front end, these include strategy experts, design thinkers, business modellers and business analysts. At the back end, digital implementations require solution architects who can design the appropriate technology architecture. These architects need to be supported by a range of digital technology experts including specialists in blockchain, IoT or AI. Companies also need expertise in change management, and programme and project management.

Digital transformation impacts all aspects of people management including talent acquisition, talent management or talent engagement.

5.5.1. Talent Acquisition

Talent acquisition starts with identifying the type of HR required in a company, then developing sources for hiring and moving on to the actual hiring and onboarding process.

To build a successful digital organization, companies need to attract and hire a new set of skills. A report published by the World Economic Forum[5] highlights a few technological trends that will be essential for organizations to go digital (Exhibit 5.1).

As many of these skills are new, in short supply and may not be required for extended periods, companies will need to innovate their talent-sourcing strategies. This could include moving to hybrid models where some employees are full-time, while others, especially those with specialist skills, can be leveraged from a talent ecosystem.

In addition to having in-house and outsourced employees, companies can leverage contract workers, gig workers and crowdsourced talent. Contract workers are provided by third-party staffing agencies and are typically used for short-term, high-volume work. Gig workers are independent contractors who have specialist skills and do not want to be tied down to any organization. While gig work is getting popular among millennials, it has challenges for hiring organizations and workers as the labour laws in many countries are not clear on the laws applicable to this class of workers. Platforms such as Flexjobs[6] connect gig workers with employers.

Platforms have also led to the rise of crowdsourcing of workers. As an example, companies post issues that require complex analytics on platforms like Kaggle.[7] Teams and individuals from around the world compete to solve these issues for prize money.

The entire talent acquisition process from sourcing talent, shortlisting, interviewing, offer acceptance and onboarding can also be completed on digital platforms.

EXHIBIT 5.1 | *Future of Jobs*

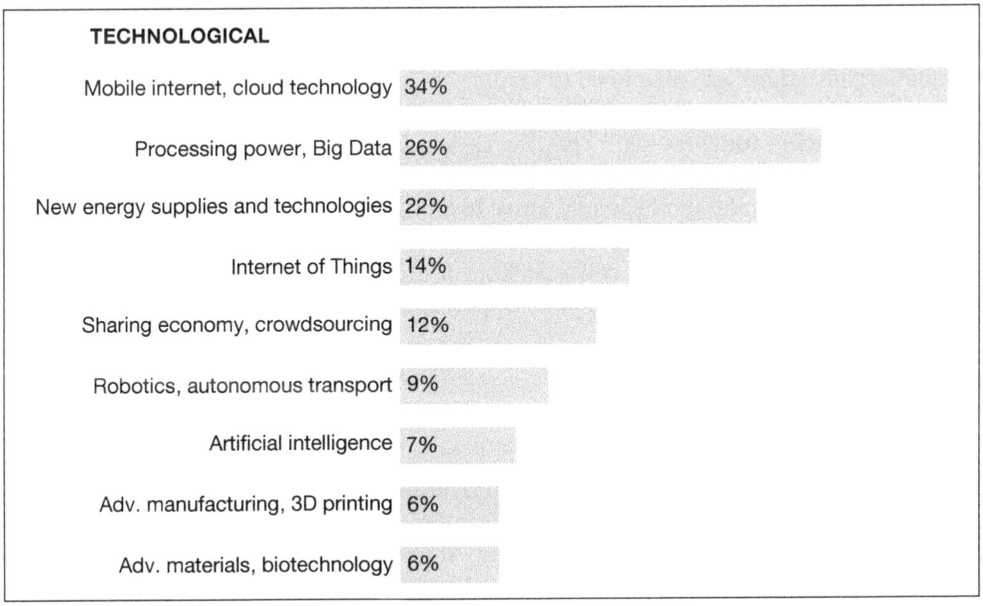

TECHNOLOGICAL

Mobile internet, cloud technology	34%
Processing power, Big Data	26%
New energy supplies and technologies	22%
Internet of Things	14%
Sharing economy, crowdsourcing	12%
Robotics, autonomous transport	9%
Artificial intelligence	7%
Adv. manufacturing, 3D printing	6%
Adv. materials, biotechnology	6%

Source: https://www.weforum.org/projects/future-of-work
Note: Names of drivers have been abbreviated to ensure legibility.

EXHIBIT 5.2 | *Redefining Goals*

	Traditional	Digital Organization
Basis for goals	Individual performance	Greater weightage on the team and business performance
Definition of success	Individual or team success	Business outcomes
Emphasis	Performance in the past period	Learning and new skill development—focus on the future
Process	Year-end appraisal	Continuous feedback with coaching
Evaluators	Managers	360-degree rating including internal and external customers
The outcome of the performance process	Upward mobility	Upward and sideway mobility

5.5.2. Talent Management

Talent management refers to the process of managing employees. This includes goal setting, evaluation, compensation and benefits.

Digital requires people to work as part of extended teams. The individuals and teams also need to adapt to rapidly changing scenarios and work in agile work environments. Traditional performance management processes are based mostly on individual performances and well-defined goals and are not suited for such scenarios. Companies will therefore have to create new ways of defining goals (Exhibit 5.2).

Digital organizations will also need to change their compensation structures. According to a study by Mercer on the future of compensation,[8] base pay will be pegged to 'skill clusters'. As the demand for these skill clusters varies, so will the compensation. Employees seeking higher wages will be encouraged to move to higher-paying clusters by reskilling themselves. This will take the base pay away from the tenure or experience-based benchmarks. The study also predicts that variable or performance-linked pay will become flexible. Employees will choose their rewards from a bouquet of benefits rather than a fixed percentage of base pay. This could include opportunities for reskilling, time off to travel or greater work-life balance.

5.5.3. Talent Motivation

Talent motivation focuses on retaining and motivating employees.

One of the critical impacts of digital and 'future of work' is that several IT and manufacturing roles will be automated. Workflow tools, AI and robotics are some of the drivers for this automation. This loss of jobs will require companies to find ways to reskill their employees or find better opportunities for them.

Organizations will have to provide continuous learning opportunities to their employees to keep pace with the rapid evolution of technologies. In the past, this learning was based on classroom training using internal or external instructors to conduct training programmes. However, the advent of specialized learning and education platforms has simplified this process. Many organizations are tying up with these platforms to support their continuing education initiatives. Reskilling of employees from legacy technology to digital technologies is another initiative undertaken by most companies as they embark on their digital journeys.

The physical location of where IT work is performed is also changing. The proliferation of collaboration and conferencing tools has enabled remote working and reduced the need for employees to be co-located. The COVID-19 crisis accelerated the concept of virtual working and 'work from home'. The new workplace strategies will reduce the need for centralized office space and increase employees' opportunities to work from the most suitable location, with periodic visits to an office. Concepts such as hot-desking and shared office space are replacing dedicated office spaces.

Workplace diversity is an important focus area in the 'future of work'. In addition to skills, diversity could be across multiple dimensions, including gender, age, education, religion and sexual orientation. A study by McKinsey has shown that diversity in the workforce is more than a fad.[9] As per the study, diversity has a direct impact on the quality of innovation and business results.

5.6. DESIGNING AN ADAPTIVE ORGANIZATION

An organization that is striving to be a digital leader needs to anticipate and adapt to change. As CEOs and CDOs develop their digital strategies, they need to evaluate if they have the right teams for the change. This includes people in key leadership roles who need to be able to plan and deploy the change. The leadership also needs to gauge their teams and assess if they can shift exiting people to new roles or if they would need to onboard new people with the required skills.

In most transformations, companies are deploying their newer digital strategies, while the existing legacy business continues to operate. Organizations need to decide on what proportion of existing resources they will engage in the change process without disturbing the current business. The people strategy must include evaluating processes and systems that need to be adapted to be in sync with the new business strategy. Company culture is another critical element of people strategy. A company needs to determine what facets of its culture need to evolve and if information, functional or business silos are likely to be hurdles as the company evolves. As discussed earlier, people strategy also needs to evaluate the three pillars of HR—talent acquisition, management and retention.

The concept of adaptive organizations refers to what organizations must do to survive and thrive in a rapidly evolving social-economic environment. This idea was popularized by the book *The Adaptive Corporation* in 1985, by management futurists Alvin and Heidi Toffler (Toffler & Shapiro, 1985). In 2019, the American Management Association organized a small group of executives to discuss organizational adaptiveness.[10] Some of the key vital attributes of adaptive organizations that emerged are as follows:

- The ability of all internal employees and departments to work together effectively, collaborate and share information.

- The ability of all employees to network with external stakeholders including customers, suppliers, industry experts and consultants, even competitors.
- The ability of all employees across an organization to innovate and experiment without the fear of failure, supported by the right incentives and culture that encourages innovation.

Sometimes when you innovate, you make mistakes. It is best to admit them quickly and get on with improving your other innovations.

—Steve Jobs, CEO and Founder of Apple

To enable this culture of change and innovation, companies have to empower and support individuals and teams with several initiatives.

Creation of self-directed teams: All bottom-up transformation starts with the empowerment of self-motivated teams. Overburdening teams with structures and processes reduces collaboration and constrains innovation. Smaller groups are found to be better at developing innovative solutions.

Breakdown of traditional barriers: Most large organizations work in silos with a limited flow of information and ideas across these silos. Exchange of ideas across these silos will help get a comprehensive view of problems and develop effective solutions.

EXHIBIT 5.3 | *Nokia: Adapting for over 150 Years*

From its humble beginning in 1865 as a single paper mill operation, Nokia has found and nurtured success over the years in a range of industrial sectors including cable, paper products, rubber boots, tires, televisions and mobile phones.

Nokia's transition to a primary focus on telecommunications began in the 1990s. The first GSM call was made in 1991 using Nokia equipment. Rapid success in the mobile phone sector allowed Nokia to become, by 1998, the best-selling mobile phone brand in the world. In 2003, Nokia introduced the first camera phone. In 2011, to address increasing competition from iOS and Android operating systems, Nokia entered into a strategic partnership with Microsoft. In 2014, Nokia sold its mobile and devices division to Microsoft.

Following the buyout of joint venture partner Siemens in 2013, the creation of Nokia Networks laid the foundation for Nokia's transformation into primarily a network hardware and software provider. The 2015 acquisition of Franco-American telecommunications equipment provider Alcatel-Lucent significantly broadened the scope of Nokia's portfolio and customer base. Additional acquisitions have positioned Nokia to be an industry leader in the transition to 5G wireless technology by offering the only end-to-end 5G network portfolio available globally.

In 2016, the Nokia brand re-entered the mobile handset market through a licensing agreement with HMD Global, allowing them to offer phones under the Nokia brand.

Source: https://www.nokia.com/about-us/company/our-history/

Creating spaces: Organizations need to create space and time for innovation. These could be physical spaces like innovation labs or virtual spaces where 'innovation teams' are formed to brainstorm and arrive at ideas for the future. These spaces allow employees to think 'out of the box' and provide a non-judgemental environment for free generation and exchange of ideas.

5.7. AMBIDEXTROUS ORGANIZATIONS

The concept of ambidextrous organizations has been around for over two decades. However, digital has brought this back to the forefront of discussions on strategy and transformation. As the word suggests, ambidexterity is the need for a company to focus on the current and future simultaneously. As digital transformation is a long process, companies need to continue with the existing ways of doing things while simultaneously launching their digital businesses. There are several such examples around the world. The State Bank of India (SBI), the largest public sector bank in India, is the most prominent bank in the country and services its customers through its 200,000 employees spread across a network of 22,000 branches around the world. The bank simultaneously launched SBI YONO, its digital banking business, to target and acquire clients. SBI continues to maintain and expand both these business models.

Professors Chares O'Rilley of Stanford University and Michael Tushman of Harvard University studied ambidexterity in the context of innovation (O'Reilly & Tushman, 2004). According to their research, companies need to maintain a variety of innovation efforts. They need to have a culture and process of continuous and incremental innovation, often referred to as exploitation innovation. Organizations and teams are usually comfortable with such innovation as they deal with questions familiar to them: improving existing products for existing customers. They know the customers and their expectations and, thus, find it relatively easy to address the challenge of exploiting. Companies also need to pursue radical innovation, that is, architectural innovations of applying processes and technologies that fundamentally change how an organization works. Finally, companies need to make discontinuous changes where the entire product or service and business model is transformed. Digital transformation mostly falls into the last category.

The organizational characteristics required for the two types of business are different, as shown in Exhibit 5.4.

The author studied companies with four types of organizational structures attempting discontinuous innovations (Exhibit 5.5).

In a functional structure, the new and old businesses are integrated into one organizational structure.

In an unsupported structure, the new business is carved out into a new entity. This structure allows for the building of a new culture and organization that is not 'contaminated' by the existing structure.

In a cross-functional structure, the new or emerging business has its own operating management, but its support functions are integrated into the existing support functions.

Finally, in an ambidextrous structure, the emerging business has its own structure but is linked back to the legacy business at the leadership level.

EXHIBIT 5.4 | *Managing an Ambidextrous Organization*

Alignment	Exploitative Business (Traditional Business Model)	Explorative Business (New Business Model)
Strategic intent	Cost, profit	Innovation, growth
Critical tasks	Operational efficiency, incremental innovation	Adaptability, new products breakthrough innovation
Competencies	Operational	Entrepreneurial
Structure	Format, mechanistic	Adaptive, loose
Control, rewards	Margins, productivity	Milestones, growth
Culture	Efficiency, low risk	Risk-taking, speed, flexibility
Leadership role	Authoritative, top-down	Visionary, involved

Source: O'Reilly and Tushman (2004).

The study found that 90 per cent of ambidextrous organizations and 25 per cent of functional organizations succeeded in their goals. No company with cross-functional or unsupported teams succeeded.

Other researchers, including Sunil Gupta, a digital transformation expert and professor at Harvard University, have further explored organizational structure and design in the context of digital transformation. In his book, *Driving Digital Strategy*, Gupta (2018) examines large companies that are undergoing digital transformation and the structures they adapted. Some companies adopt what Gupta refers to as the 'speedboat strategy' where they create a separate entity with a new structure, culture and technology platforms for the digital enterprise. This is similar to the ambidextrous structure discussed earlier in this section. While these companies do succeed, the challenge faced by them is that they are unable to integrate the new culture back into the parent organization. As these emerging companies or 'speedboats' grow larger, at some point in time, they start to clash with the parent company in terms of both internal resources and external market share.

Gupta also examines companies which try to create a digital culture within the central organization by creating 'landing docks'. In this model, CEOs focus on transforming the central organization by developing an ecosystem of partners and making the company accessible to entrepreneurs and start-ups. Some of the methods adopted to create these linkages include the following:

Innovation labs: As discussed earlier in this chapter, labs help in creating physical spaces for innovation. Internal employees can use the labs to brainstorm and develop new business ideas. Mastercard, for example, has a network of innovation labs around the globe that focus on fintech innovations.[11]

We create and deliver the new products and services that are going to drive our growth in the future. Clearly, not everything is in my shop. We bring it down to risk because there's a risk, or at least commercial uncertainty, associated with every new product. That is, where there's a new idea or a new twist on one, the project begins in Mastercard Labs unless the effort is so close to something the company is already doing that it makes sense to keep it in one of the company's product groups.

EXHIBIT 5.5 *Types of Innovation Structures*

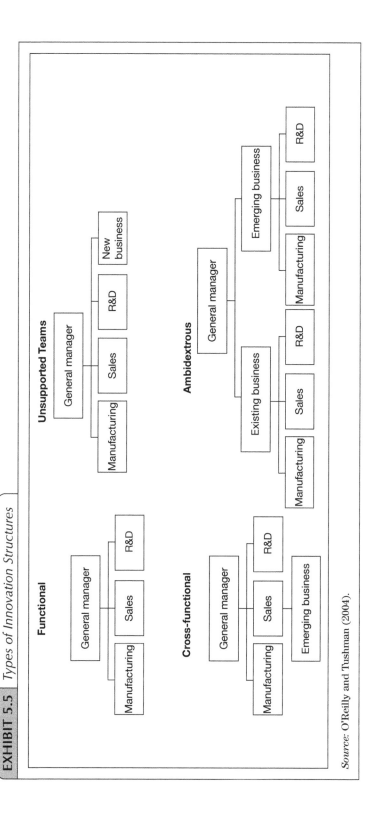

Source: O'Reilly and Tushman (2004).

Incubation labs: These are like innovation labs but focus on supporting external start-ups. These incubators can be created alone by companies or in conjunction with other incubators and government bodies. Incubation labs provide companies access to start-ups and innovations external to their organization. For example, in 2016, Intel started the Intel India Maker Lab programme to create a hardware-based innovation ecosystem in India.

Investments and joint ventures (JVs): Companies also make investments or create JVs to accelerate innovation. ZF, the German auto parts maker, made a series of investments and JVs to access innovation including the purchase of Ibeo, a LiDAR system manufacturer and TRW that became its Active Passive Safety Technology Division.

Internal start-ups: Internal start-ups are a form of corporate entrepreneurship. Large companies promote innovation by setting up new business divisions that operate at an arm's length from the rest of the company. Examples include Bell Labs, a research unit within Bell Corporation and Target Corporation (which began as an internal start-up of the Dayton's department store chain).

In recent times, more companies are taking the approach of 'landing docks' rather than 'speedboats'. While companies have been successful with speedboats, they have not successfully integrated these into the main company or transferred the culture. 'Landing docks', on the other hand, are by design a part of the main company and do not have many challenges of integration.

MINI CASE 5.1. DISCUSSION

Hardy convened a special board meeting that included Jackson to discuss the digital transformation of BIC. Jackson presented the board with the trends and disruptions in the insurance industry, the industry's future, the role digital would play and the potential disruptors. Jackson also gave an overview of where BIC was in relation to its competition where it showed that they were falling behind. The board decided that Jackson would continue to lead the organization and its transformation. Jackson was highly respected and a vision for the future conveyed by him would be well-accepted by all employees. The board also decided to bring back Ron Wixon, a tenured employee of BIC, who had left a few years ago to join a digital consulting company. Wixon would be offered the role of CDO and report directly to Jackson.

Wixon accepted the offer and joined BIC in a few months. He quickly formed a digital task force consisting of the CIO, CMO, CFO and CHRO of BIC. Wixon invited a select few digital consulting companies to present their credentials and their vision for the industry and the company. Based on the presentations, a leading consulting company was brought in as the lead digital consultant.

The consulting company worked along with the task force to develop a five-year digital transformation plan for BIC. The plan was to be implemented in phases to de-risk any implementation challenges. Customer-facing assets such as mobile apps, analytics and customer service were prioritized in the plan with an implementation timeline. This was done to prevent customers from moving to more digitally advanced insurers. The company also decided to hasten automation in its back office and move some work offshore. BIC used the savings from these initiatives to fund the first phase of digital roll-out. The company named its digital transformation programme BIC+ + and this logo was displayed at all BIC locations to inform customers and employees of the company's plans for its digital future.

Hardy and Wixon held press conferences and shared the company's digital plans with the press and investment managers. Internally, town halls were organized to inform employees about the digital plans, answer questions and address any concerns. The company also announced out-placement and retraining programmes for employees impacted by automation and digital trans-formation. Once the transformation scope was disseminated, the company allowed employees to form groups and volunteer for various programmes and projects. These groups were set up as part of an internal innovation centre. The company also created a venture fund to fund employees and other entrepreneurs who had innovative ideas relating to insurance. For example, some employees of BIC's IT organization had an idea of using blockchain in insurance processing and successfully received funding. In less than a year, BIC+ + announced the launch of its first fully digital insurance product.

SUMMARY

People form the most critical part of digital transformation. While digital starts with the board and CEO of companies, a culture of innovation needs to permeate throughout the organization to transform successfully. Companies need CEOs who can blend both trans-formational and transactional elements into their leadership style. To lead digital transfor-mation, leaders need to have the vision, be able to communicate this vision and build a culture of innovation. They also need to allow for the development of an innovation ecosys-tem outside the company. Leaders need to build and motivate their teams and provide incen-tives for the right behaviours and actions. Many organizations have supplemented their leadership with a CDO to help CEOs drive their digital agendas. Studies have shown that companies with CDOs have been more successful in transforming, and many CDOs have gone on to lead companies themselves. As digital transformation is top-down, the board of a company plays a large role in shaping a company's digital vision. Boards help in bringing the balance between short-term and medium-term goals of a company. They also help in providing valuable inputs from other industries. Beyond the leadership, digital impacts every level in the organizational structure of a company. To inculcate change and a culture of innovation, companies need to have the right organizational structure. Companies have used structures such as incubation centres, innovation centres, JVs, investments and partnerships to increase the pace of change.

Discussion Questions

1. What is the difference between transformational and transactional leadership? Explain with some examples.
2. What are the 4Is of transformational leadership?
3. What are some of the key responsibilities of the CDO?
4. What is adaptive leadership?
5. What are some of the organizational structures that companies have adopted to create new and innovative businesses? Which have succeeded more?

GLOSSARY

Adaptive leadership: It is a practical leadership framework that helps individuals and organizations adapt and thrive in challenging and rapidly evolving environments.

Ambidextrous organization: The ability to simultaneously pursue both incremental and discontinuous innovation, from hosting multiple contradictory structures, processes and cultures within the same firm.

Chief digital officer: A new role emerging in companies with the sole responsibility of driving digital strategies and transformation.

Transactional leadership: A transactional leader is someone who values order and structure. Transactional leadership depends on self-motivated people who work well in a structured, directed environment.

Transformational leadership: It is a leadership style in which leaders encourage, inspire and motivate employees to innovate and create change that will help grow and shape the company's future success.

NOTES

1. https://www.gartner.com/en/newsroom/press-releases/2018-05-01-gartner-survey-reveals-that-ceo-priorities-are-shifting-to-embrace-digital-business#:~:text=CEOs%20recognize%20the%20need%20for,change%20is%20needed%20by%202020
2. https://www.bdo.com/insights/assurance/corporate-governance/2018-bdo-cyber-governance-survey-board-perspecti
3. https://theleadershipnetwork.com/article/the-rise-and-role-of-the-chief-digital-officer
4. https://home.kpmg/xx/en/home/insights/2018/06/harvey-nash-kpmg-cio-survey-2018.html
5. https://www.weforum.org/projects/future-of-work
6. https://www.flexjobs.com/
7. https://www.kaggle.com/
8. https://www.mercer.us/content/dam/mercer/attachments/private/us-2019-performance-transformation-in-the-future-of-work.pdf
9. https://www.mckinsey.com/business-functions/organization/our-insights/the-organization-blog/employee-experience-essential-to-compete
10. https://www.amanet.org/articles/creating-adaptive-organizations/
11. https://thefinancialbrand.com/93733/digital-fintech-innovation-financial-lab-mastercard/

REFERENCES

Bass, B. M., & Avolio, B. J. (Eds.). (1994). *Improving organisational effectiveness through transformational leadership*. SAGE Publications.

Burns, J. M. (2004). *Transforming leadership: A new pursuit of happiness* (Vol. 213). Grove Press.

Gupta, S. (2018). *Driving digital strategy: A guide to reimagining your business*. Harvard Business Press.

Myers, C. (2015). Is your company encouraging employees to share what they know? *Harvard Business Review*.

Ready, D., Cohen, C., Kiron, D., & Pring, B. (2020). The new leadership playbook for the digital age. *MIT Sloan Management Review*.

O'Reilly III, C. A., & Tushman, M. L. (2004). The ambidextrous organisation. *Harvard Business Review, 82*(4), 74.

Toffler, A., & Shapiro, M. (1985). *Adaptive corporation*. McGraw-Hill.

Digital Technologies I

Learning Objectives

Chapters 6, 7 and 8 are focused on demystifying the various digital computing technologies in the context of digital transformation strategies for businesses. Chapters 6 and 7 focus on basic categories of digital technologies based on the nature of capabilities they enable for business. Chapter 8 focuses on composite technologies that build from a combination of the basic technologies covered in Chapters 6 and 7. At the end of Chapters 6 and 7, students will learn the following:

- A taxonomy of digital technologies
- Different levels of capabilities enabled by digital technologies and their relevance to business
- What makes digital era technologies distinct from earlier technology era
- Current state of each technology category and what to expect in the foreseeable future
- In Chapter 6, the following three Technology Categories are covered:
  o Computation
  o Instrumentation
  o Communication
- In Chapter 7, the following three Technology Categories are covered:
  o Data management
  o Interfaces (human–machine interfaces)
  o Digital security

6.1. INTRODUCTION

Digital technologies encompass a plethora of discrete and interrelated technologies. It is not uncommon in contemporary business and managerial vernacular to come across phrases like 'digital era' or 'digital enterprise'. When the word 'digital' is used in such phrases, there are a distinct set of characteristics that are implied. However, there is a lack of consistency in articulating or understanding those distinct characteristics. This lack of consistency in articulation and understanding exists among both students of management and practising managers. This section presents taxonomy that provides a simplified view of digital technologies. This taxonomy is discussed in detail in the later part of this chapter and the next chapter (Chapter 7). It is further leveraged in several chapters of this text to discuss the associated capabilities and their relevance to business.

Mini Case 6.1

The Sinusoid Group (TSG) is a family-owned business group. TSG has been in the business of manufacturing automotive components for the past 60 years. TSG's management is known to be conservative, with an exceptional track record of consistent growth and market leadership. Over the decades, they have successfully diversified into related business areas such as two-wheelers, computer peripherals, automotive maintenance services, multi-brand component distribution and automotive finance.

A fourth-generation family member, Aaryan (27), who has recently completed a master's degree in business administration, is pushing for the extensive implementation of digital technologies into TSG's existing businesses. Additionally, he is also building a case to manufacture and supply smart electronics components to the consumer durables industry in India. Aaryan intended to leverage the emerging momentum in the manufacturing opportunities in India, especially owing to the self-reliance push by the Government of India after the COVID-19 pandemic.

Aaryan assembled a small team of enthusiastic, young engineers and managers from TSG's businesses. The goal for the team was to build a comprehensive vision and business justifications for the two key ideas he is pursuing.

The initial objective of Aaryan's team is to survey the landscape of digital technologies and map them to the twin objectives set by Aaryan based on their relevance and viability. The team started to work on this exciting project with the immediate goal of making an investment proposal to TSG's board of directors.

Note: As the chapters progress, the characters in the mini case are assumed to follow and assimilate the contents in these chapters and evolve their understanding of digital technologies. A few select scenes from Aaryan's project will be used for putting in perspective the importance of understanding the fundamentals of digital technologies for managers.

Mini Case Revisited: Context 1
Technical Terminologies: A Minefield of Jargons

Aaryan wanted to have a simplified understanding of digital technologies before getting into the use cases for the digital transformation of TSG. Control systems engineer, Khushi, and technology expert, Ishaan, from the Information Technology and Practices Department started brainstorming about various digital technologies that need to be understood thoroughly. In the first week of exploration, the team was hit with a hailstorm of technical jargons. They needed a simplified framework to organize the inventory of technologies and eventually prioritize those that require a deep dive.

6.2. TAXONOMY OF DIGITAL TECHNOLOGIES: A MANAGERIAL ABSTRACTION

6.2.1. First-order Capabilities: The Basis for Defining the Taxonomy

ITs have evolved over several decades and have morphed into what is commonly referred to as digital technologies. The role of IT in business has been to provide capabilities for improving the gathering and dissemination of appropriate information to appropriate people and at the appropriate time. Herbert Simon once remarked that IT has had a great impact on the way information is gathered and disseminated (Simon, 1990). This elemental observation made by Simon nearly three decades ago has been reinforced further with the advent of digital technologies. As digital technologies evolved, three more dimensions of capabilities and information gathering, and dissemination have been added to the spectrum of IT. The five dimensions of capabilities are as follows:

1. Information gathering
2. Information dissemination
3. Information processing capabilities at unprecedented scale (as manifested in cloud computing)
4. Computational intelligence (as manifested in analytics, AI and ML)
5. User-centric/usage-centric interfaces for interaction between humans and digital systems (as manifested in systems of engagement[1] using mobile, augmented/virtual reality and so on)

These five capabilities (which we call first-order capabilities are depicted in Exhibit 6.1) enabled by digital technologies are available for businesses to improve decision-making and execution.

Any classification or taxonomy's objective is to encapsulate the differences and similarities among the items being classified. Any technology finds its place in business because it enables a set of fundamental or first-order capabilities that help in value-addition. For the purposes of this text, we use the first-order capability that a particular technology enables as the criteria for classification.

6.2.2. A Taxonomy for Managers

Digital technologies are highly heterogeneous and are evolving at different velocities across multiple dimensions. A good understanding of digital technologies and associated

> **EXHIBIT 6.1** *Taxonomy of Digital Technologies: Classification Based on First-order Capabilities*

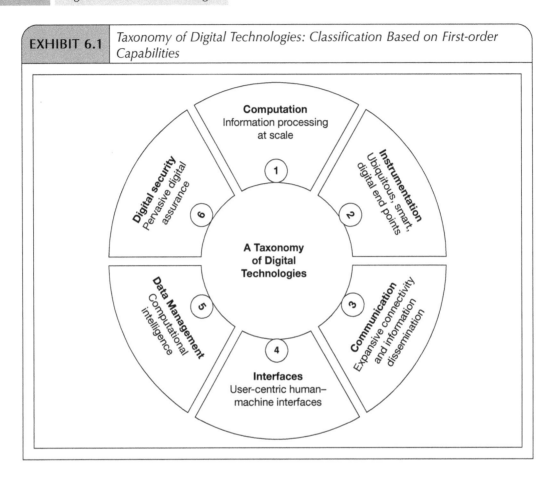

capabilities enables managers to make informed decisions about technology investments, implementation and business outcomes. This chapter provides such a taxonomy for managers.

Digital technologies can be classified into six broad categories based on the first-order/fundamental capabilities that they enable. This taxonomy will be used at several points in this text to understand the impact of digital technologies on business. Exhibits 6.1 and 6.2 provide an overview of the taxonomy and the associated first-order capabilities. The taxonomy is discussed in detail in a subsequent section titled 'Distinguishing Characteristics of Digital Technologies'.

When dealing with digital technologies, practitioners encounter a persistent question in different forms and forums. What makes 'digital' technologies different from the technologies prior to this digital era?

In the following sections, the salient characteristics of the digital-era technology capabilities have been juxtaposed with that of pre-digital (or) early internet era technologies (Exhibits 6.8, 6.11 and 6.13). This juxtaposition provides clarity on what has changed and provides a line of sight to how these changes are enabling newer capabilities for businesses.

EXHIBIT 6.2 | *Classification of Digital Technologies Based on First-order Capabilities*

	Taxonomy Category (First-order Capability)	Sub-category/Examples	Description of First-order Capabilities
1.	Computation (information processing at scale)	Cloud/Edge for • IaaS • PaaS • SaaS	Provide scalable, reliable and resilient computing capabilities with agility
2.	Instrumentation (ubiquitous, smart, digital end points)	Embedded systems • IoT devices, sensors, actuators	Provide special-purpose computing capability. Capability to connect to networks and optionally provide sensing and actuation/response. These systems are typically embedded into non-computing devices (things) with the purpose of enhancing and extending their functionality and manageability.
3.	Communication (expansive connectivity and information dissemination)	Device-to-device communication • Mobile/Wireless ad hoc networks (MANET/WANET) Network communication • LANs • WANs • Internet • Low-power personal area networks	Provide long-range/short-range communication capability between devices and networks with optimal levels of capacity (bandwidth), speed, latency and energy efficiency.
4.	Interface (user-centric human–machine interfaces)	Human to machine • Web • Mobile • AR/VR • Co-bots Machine to machine • Swarm drones • Drones: Aerial pass-the-parcel[2]	Provide an interface for interaction between humans and machines. The interface category also includes interfaces for machine-to-machine interaction in the physical world. *Note:* When machine-to-machine interaction happens through the virtual world, they could be categorized under the 'communication' technologies.
5.	Data management (computational intelligence)	Data storage • Big data • Real-time databases • NoSQL databases Data processing • Analytics and data visualization • Machine learning	Provide the capability to store massive amounts of data in distributed data stores typically beyond the scale of conventional database technologies. Provide capabilities to suitably store and handle persistent data as well as time-sensitive data in real time. Provide capabilities to process data

(Continued)

(Continued)

Taxonomy Category (First-order Capability)	Sub-category/Examples	Description of First-order Capabilities
		for analysis, reporting and visualization for descriptive and diagnostic analytics. Provide predictive capabilities through data processing for machine learning and predictive analytics.
6. Digital security (pervasive digital assurance)	Device-level security • Network security • Application security • Data privacy • Ethical AI	Provide assurance on availability, integrity and confidentiality of data across the entire digital technologies stack. Data privacy and data protection

6.3. SECOND-ORDER AND HIGHER-ORDER CAPABILITIES UNDERPINNED BY DIGITAL TECHNOLOGIES

The first-order capabilities enabled by digital technologies, when brought together in the context of business processes, enable second- and higher-order capabilities that have the potential to improve business performance. Second-order capabilities essentially manifest in two forms.

First, they enable improved decision-making through granular, relevant and timely (sometimes predictive) information. Second, they enable decision execution and actions through automation.

For example, an IoT sensor provides the capability of sensing the state of operation (a first-order capability in the form of capturing granular information) of an industrial asset like a wind turbine. This first-order capability of sensing the state of operation contributes to a second-order capability of making improved decisions. The second-order capability, in this case, could manifest as information regarding turbine performance in near real time. Such a second-order capability of improved visibility for decision-making when applied to the process of turbine maintenance results in more effective predictive maintenance.

The capabilities flowing from digital technologies (Exhibit 6.3), that is, the first-order, second-order and higher-order capabilities, progress from technologies at one end of the spectrum to business outcomes at the other end. The elemental capabilities are more identifiable closer to technology, while the more complex/sophisticated capabilities are identifiable closer to and have a line of sight to business outcomes. Exhibit 6.4 provides an expanded view of the second-order capabilities introduced in Exhibit 6.3.

Mini Case Revisited: Context 2
Perspective Gives Clarity: Aaryan Motivated for Deeper Understanding

With the perspectives gained from the taxonomy of digital technologies and the capability-centric basis for the classification, both Aaryan and the members of the team felt highly

EXHIBIT 6.3 *Continuum of Capabilities Spanning from Digital Technologies to Business Outcomes*

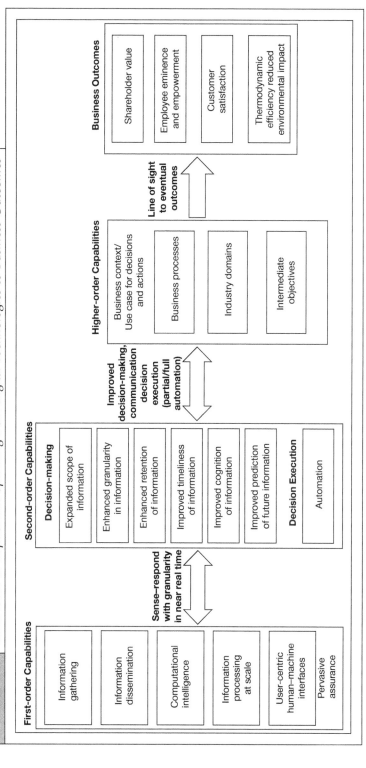

encouraged to get a deeper understanding of the categories of technologies. Maran, from the marketing team, was extremely optimistic that talking about these technologies to TSG's enterprise customers will position the group as a leading innovator in the automotive industry. Reacting to Maran's optimism, Manu, though soft-spoken, forcefully tried to impress upon the group that TSG's differentiation arises from its 'manufacturing' capabilities and experience. He also added that the flashy discussion on 'digital' would not help in solving real-life problems of the group. He concluded his opinion curtly, saying, 'all this is just the same old wine in a new bottle'. To substantiate his point, he argued that all these technology categories could be applied to the pre-digital era information technologies as well. For example, 'computation' as a category existed since computers were invented or for that matter 'communication' as a category existed so conspicuously as the internet for over a couple of decades prior to the notion of the 'digital era'. Aaryan was intrigued by these remarks and seemed to agree with the cynicism partially. He looked up to Ishaan to respond.

EXHIBIT 6.4 | *Expanded View of Second-order Capabilities*

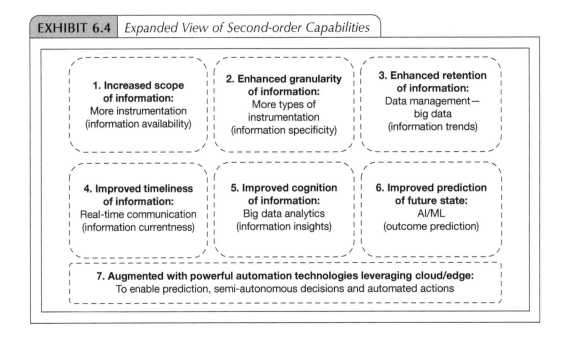

1. **Increased scope of information:**
More instrumentation (information availability)

2. **Enhanced granularity of information:**
More types of instrumentation (information specificity)

3. **Enhanced retention of information:**
Data management—big data (information trends)

4. **Improved timeliness of information:**
Real-time communication (information currency)

5. **Improved cognition of information:**
Big data analytics (information insights)

6. **Improved prediction of future state:**
AI/ML (outcome prediction)

7. **Augmented with powerful automation technologies leveraging cloud/edge:**
To enable prediction, semi-autonomous decisions and automated actions

6.4. DISTINGUISHING CHARACTERISTICS OF DIGITAL TECHNOLOGIES

All the categories of the taxonomy are applicable to various stages of the evolution of IT in the past, and most likely in the future. However, in the digital era, these capabilities have become even more powerful at relatively lower costs. This shift is because new capabilities are rapidly evolving across all the categories concurrently. Such a convergence is making them a force multiplier of each other, leading to unprecedented possibilities in the digital era. The following sections present the salient aspects of digital technology categories and highlight their distinction when compared to the pre-digital phases.

6.4.1. Computation: Information Processing at Scale with Agility

Digital era computation, underpinned by cloud computing, provides scalable, elastic, reliable and resilient computing capabilities with agility.

Cloud computing is at the foundation of the computational capabilities in the digital era. Exhibit 6.5 highlights Cloud Computing capabilities in the context of digital technology taxonomies. The cloud has transformed the fabric of computational capabilities available to enterprises and individuals. The use of the cloud metaphor for virtualized computing services dates at least to General Magic in 1994 and is credited to General Magic communications employee David Hoffman.[3] Computation capabilities of the digital era gained prominence at the beginning of the 21st century through cloud computing companies such as Amazon Web Services and Google. The trend was reinforced by offerings from incumbents such as Microsoft and IBM.

Cloud computing refers to the use of a network of remote computers hosted on the internet (public cloud) or within the logical boundary of a company (private cloud). With cloud, computational infrastructure shifted from a server-centric paradigm (a hardware

| EXHIBIT 6.5 | *Taxonomical Context for Computation Technologies* |

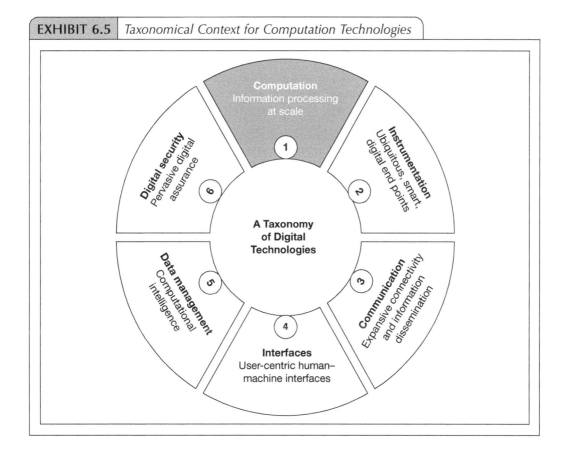

product) to a virtualized service-centric paradigm which made the computational capabilities more elastic accessible on demand with agility.

Cloud computing capabilities can be described across two dimensions. The first with the logical layers of computing capabilities available in the cloud and the other, along with the physical layers of cloud configuration. Exhibit 6.6 lays out an overview of the two dimensions.

Cloud computing provides logical layers of computational capabilities.

1. Infrastructure as a service (IaaS)
2. Platform as a service (PaaS)
3. Software as a service (SaaS)

These three logical layers of capabilities provide differing levels of pre-built computational architecture components. Description of capabilities available in the logical layers is depicted in Exhibit 6.7.

6.4.1.1. Cloud to Edge: The Evolving Continuum of the Spatial Distribution of Computation

The spatial distribution of cloud infrastructure can be used as the basis of the classification of physical layers of cloud computing. Cloud computing relies heavily on the internet, which is a public network. While the internet works exceedingly well in enabling global connectivity across systems, it comes with its limitations in terms of latency in information access at the end point/end user.

An end point/user device, when accessing a cloud resource over the internet, needs to go through a large, uncertain number of hops which induce latency/time to execute the

EXHIBIT 6.6 | *An Overview of the Logical and Physical Layers of Cloud Computing*

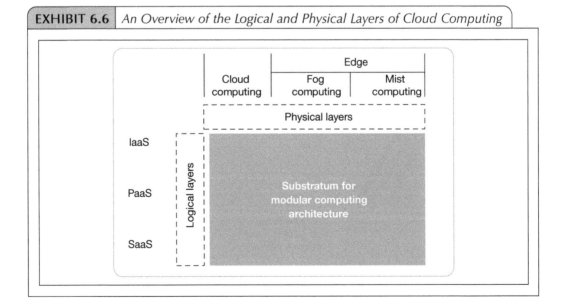

EXHIBIT 6.7 | *Description of Capabilities at Various Levels of Cloud Computing*

	Cloud Layer	Description of Capabilities
1.	IaaS	IaaS is equivalent to raw compute power or hardware power along with operating systems to run software applications.
2.	PaaS	PaaS is equivalent to middleware which provides common services (e.g., data management, messaging, APIs) to software applications beyond what is provided by operating systems.
3.	SaaS	SaaS is equivalent to pre-built software applications that can be customized for different enterprise/user needs (e.g., productivity tools such as Microsoft Office, cloud-based e-mail services, enterprise applications for finance, procurement, HR and so on).

---

communication. In some use cases which are highly time sensitive (e.g., multimedia content, autonomous cars and so on), the latency involved in leveraging cloud needs to be minimized or eliminated. To reduce latency, newer configurations have been developed with part of the essential computing capability replicated closer to the end user (edge computing). Edge computing configurations augment cloud computing by provisioning time/latency-sensitive computing capability closer to the end point while relying on the cloud for other computing needs which are tolerant to the latency of the internet. Suitable configurations for latency reduction can be implemented at different spatial distances from the end point (Exhibit 6.8).

6.4.1.2. Public Cloud versus Private Cloud versus Hybrid Cloud

In the digital era, any computational workloads that are not using cloud computing are referred to as legacy systems. In the year 2020, more than 80% of enterprise computing workloads[5, 6] have not moved to the cloud. This estimate is in sharp contrast to the high levels of mindshare that cloud commands among business and technology thought leaders. Cloud computing offers several benefits over conventional computing but the constraints such as time, cost and complexities involved in migrating to cloud have limited its usage.

These constraints can be overcome by leveraging cloud a few different mechanisms such as public cloud, private cloud and hybrid cloud.

Public cloud: Cloud computing offers maximum flexibility when availed in a public cloud configuration, that is, the computing capabilities (either some or all of IaaS, PaaS and SaaS) provided by cloud services are shared by multiple enterprises and individuals. This configuration may not suit the needs of large enterprises for two reasons. First, large businesses have significant investments in dedicated compute infrastructure, which escalates the cost of migration to the cloud. Second, the nature of business requires a high level of security/confidentiality, making publicly shared compute infrastructure unfit for the purpose. In such cases, an enterprise could avail the benefits of cloud within the constraints of security/confidentiality of their workloads using alternate mechanisms like public or hybrid cloud.

	Nomenclature	Description	Analogy[4]/Examples
1.	Cloud computing	Centralized compute power accessed through the internet or other private networks over requiring multiple hops between the cloud resource and the end point resulting in a high level of latency in network communications.	Metrologically, cloud in the real world is dense with heavy condensed water, literally far away from the surface of the earth/end point. Example(s): Cloud-based e-mail services Cloud-hosted news website
2.	Fog computing	The configuration of moving relevant part of the computing power/resource from a central cloud to an intermediate computing device (e.g., a network gateway) device that is connected to the end device either directly or with much fewer hops when compared to cloud.	Metrologically, fog is less dense than cloud, located below the cloud. Example(s): Multimedia content servers that are distributed away from the central cloud, closer to the end users to improve user experience.
3.	Mist computing	The configuration in which the computing power is at the very edge of the network, that is, within the end point/device.	Metrologically, mist is a thin layer of floating droplets on the ground/end point. Example(s): Smart objects or sensor devices that have embedded processing power, like in the case of autonomous cars.
4.	Edge computing	Edge is not a homogenous category by itself. It is used to refer to any configuration in which a relevant part of the computing power/resource from a central cloud is made available closer to the end point.	Edge is used loosely but directionally to mean getting the compute power closer to the end user/edge of the cloud.

EXHIBIT 6.8 *Cloud to Edge: The Evolving Continuum of the Spatial Distribution of Computation*

Private cloud: Private cloud is a mechanism where an enterprise's internal IT services could emulate a cloud service provider. In this case, an internal service provider could set up a private cloud infrastructure (privately owned by the company) which is shared on a subscription basis only among the internal business units/group companies. The individual business units within the company experience the advantages of cloud while the enterprise creates a private environment that is not exposed to public cloud vulnerabilities. Such private cloud configurations are only suitable for large enterprises.

Hybrid cloud: Hybrid cloud is the third configuration that emerges from harnessing the unique merits of legacy/private compute infrastructure and public cloud. To embrace a hybrid cloud configuration, enterprises first classify their workloads into two parts. The first part may be called core (which supports proprietary processes and data, requiring a higher level of security, like core banking applications in a bank). The second part could include peripheral workloads (which are important but support relatively standard processes like payroll processing). In a hybrid cloud configuration, the core workloads are run in an upgraded legacy computing infrastructure or a private cloud infrastructure, while the peripheral workloads leverage the public cloud. These two parts are made interoperable from a data and process perspective to provide a seamless end-user experience.

6.4.1.3. The Salience of Computation Technologies of the Digital Era

The nuances with respect to capabilities and deployment considerations of cloud computing were discussed in the preceding sections. This section deconstructs relevant attributes of cloud computing to highlight the salience of computation technologies in the digital era as an evolution from the pre-digital era (Exhibit 6.9).

EXHIBIT 6.9	*Salience of Computation Technologies of the Digital Era*	
	Attribute	**Pre-digital**	**Digital Era**
1.	Unit of capacity	Servers hosted in enterprise data centres	Virtualized servers hosted in distributed locations (cloud)
2.	Unit of access	Consumed as hardware/perpetual software licence	Consumed as a service subscriptions
3.	Scalability	Achieved by adding more servers	Achieved by subscribing to more computing power as and when needed
4.	Elasticity	Capacity is rigid and cannot be scaled down when there is surplus capacity	Capacity is elastic and can be scaled up or down based on computation loads
5.	Agility	Significant lead times to scale up capacity (potentially in months). Scaling down possibly very slowly with the age/depreciation/obsolescence of hardware	In most cases, scaling up and scaling down usage can be made within a matter of minutes or seconds
6.	Maintenance	Maintenance of the computational capability (like physical hardware failures or software version patches/version upgrades) is a distinct responsibility of the business/user	Maintenance is typically packaged (and often automated) as part of the subscription service
7.	Pricing/Cost	Priced for hardware units and typically deemed as capital expenditure for businesses	Usage-based subscription fees typically deemed as operating expenditure for businesses

6.4.1.4. Current State of Adoption and Future Expectations

Companies intending to leverage the digital era computation capabilities must essentially 'shift to the cloud'. The current state of cloud adoption in enterprises is at an early stage. Most of the use cases for the initial adoption of cloud have been for 'non-core' workloads such as e-mail and HR processes. A vast majority of workloads (about 80%) that are core to businesses are yet to achieve cloud potential. Hybrid cloud strategies are being pursued by larger companies to help them migrate both non-core and core applications.

Cloud computing will be the default choice for all new digital initiatives. However, despite the promise, cloud adoption will be tempered by extending the longevity of legacy systems, cost of change and security risks associated with public cloud. For companies, it is going to be a long journey to cloud that is likely to stretch, at least, for another decade, 2020–2030.

6.4.2. Instrumentation: Ubiquitous, Smart, Digital End Points

Digital era instrumentation, underpinned by capable, miniaturized and affordable digital end points, provides ubiquitous sense-and-respond capabilities at the boundary of the 'physical–analogue' and the 'virtual–digital' worlds.

Instrumentation, in general, refers to instruments used for measuring physical quantities that characterize the physical world, that is, temperature, pressure, volume, mass and so on. Exhibit 6.10 highlights Instrumentation capabilities in the context of digital technology taxonomies. Transducers are devices that convert one form of energy to another. They are among the most common devices used in instrumentation. Example of transducers include microphones that convert mechanical sound energy to electrical signals and speakers which convert electrical signals to sound energy.

Transducers operate as sensors when deployed to convert physical quantities in the environment to electrical signals (like in the case of microphones). Transducers operate as actuators when deployed to convert electrical signals from the computational upstream (mist/fog/cloud computing) to effect changes to the physical environment (like in the case of speakers).

Transducers, as the basic elements of instrumentation, provide sense-and-respond capabilities in three broad steps as follows (depicted in Exhibit 6.11).

1. Digitalize the physical world objects into the virtual world
2. Apply computational intelligence to the various attributes being sensed
3. Respond by affecting changes to the environment, either to interact with human users (like voice interfaces) or to automate physical world tasks (autonomous vehicles)

The digital era has seen explosive growth in the variety of sensors and actuators. The sensing and actuation capabilities are explored in greater detail in the IoT section of this book (Chapter 8). Amplifying the impact of growing volume and variety of instrumentation, they

EXHIBIT 6.10 | *Taxonomical Context for Instrumentation Technologies*

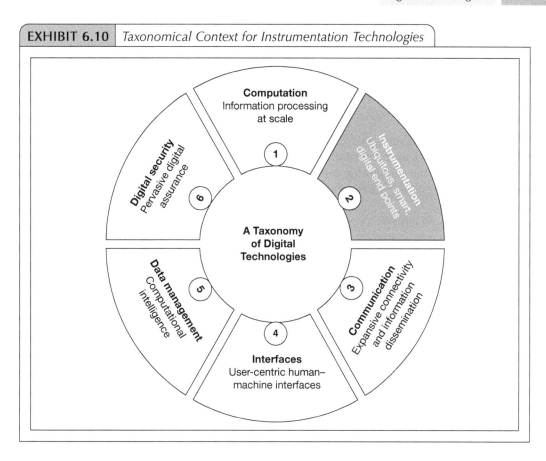

EXHIBIT 6.11 | *Basic Mechanism of Sense and Respond Capabilities*

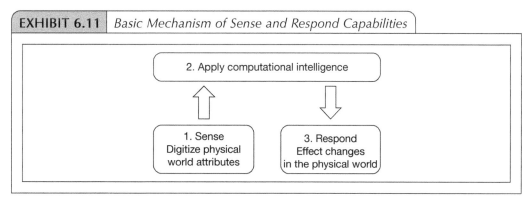

can be easily embedded with meaningful and miniaturized computing and wireless communication capabilities.

In the context of this text, instrumentation refers to these augmented instrumentation devices (sensors and actuators) that exhibit varying combinations of the following capabilities:

1. Measure physical quantities from the environment
2. Digitize the measured quantities for electronic processing (e.g., microphone)
3. Communicate with other devices and computers in a network, through either wired or wireless connections
4. Effect changes to physical quantities of the environment (e.g., speakers, light-emitting diodes etc.)

As the computing technologies rapidly evolved to be exponentially more powerful each year and far cheaper over the past few decades, there has been a spontaneous impact on the lower end of the computing power that provides meaningful, relatively small scale, miniaturized computational capability at extremely affordable prices (e.g., microcontrollers).

As the digital era unfolded, these microcontrollers attained computational power equivalence that existed in erstwhile full-scale computers. This has opened up possibilities for ubiquitous and smart instrumentation devices that could not be achieved in the past. This trend can be understood by comparing computer processors and their applications over the past three to four decades. Such a comparison, though not theoretically precise, helps in appreciating the increase in computational power and falling costs from an order-of-magnitude perspective. For instance, ATmega328 microcontroller (cost under $2,[7] in 2020 dollars) has the comparable computational capability with Intel's 8088 microprocessor (cost ~$125,[8] in 1979 dollars). From an end-use perspective, ATmega328 microcontroller is used in experimental digital projects and low-cost digital devices like Arduino Uno, while Intel 8088 was used in IBM PC in 1981.

6.4.2.1. Salience of Instrumentation Technologies of the Digital Era

This section deconstructs relevant attributes of instrumentation technologies to highlight their salience in the digital era as an evolution from the pre-digital era (Exhibit 6.12).

| EXHIBIT 6.12 | Salience of Instrumentation Technologies of the Digital Era |

	Attribute	Pre-digital	Digital Era
1.	Dominant use cases	Instrumentation typically entailed instruments to monitor devices, machines, processes and processing environments in industrial settings	Expanded instrumentation in industrial settings. Exponential use of instrumentation at the consumer end of the supply chain, in appliances (washing machines, refrigerators and so on), in personal health monitors (smart watches, step counters and so on) and so on
2.	Device identification/Addressing	IPv4 addressing scheme used to identify computers and devices connected to the internet	IPv6 addressing scheme used to identify devices and things that are connected to the internet
3.	Computational capability	Specialized computational capabilities severely constrained	General purpose computational capabilities with aggressive price to performance

	Attribute	Pre-digital	Digital Era
		by cost of computation as well as price to performance ratios	ratios creating the potential for sophisticated computational intelligence available in the edge devices/mist (e.g., ML algorithms are being run effectively on low-end edge devices/instrumentation devices)
4.	Communication/ Connectivity	Instrumentation predominantly was connected to industrial monitoring control systems like SCADA through wired communication	Wireless communication underpins the potential to achieve ubiquitous instrumentation in both industrial and consumer/citizen settings
5.	Scale and scope	Scale and scope were limited to industrial use cases. Adoption was relatively stable. Adoption is driven by new investments in modernization and automation in industrial entities (e.g., oil and gas, factory automation and so on)	Scale and scope growing exponentially with annual shipment of IoT devices (a reasonable proxy for digital-era instrumentation) projected to exceed 26 billion units in 2020 and expected to grow to 67 billion units by 2026[9]
6.	Energy efficiency	Energy efficiency, not a dominant criterion in system design as the instrumentation devices were typically stationary and connected to grid power	Energy efficiency is a primary criterion as the instrumentation devices are increasingly mobile and are not connected to grid power, relying on battery or energy from the environment
7.	Cost	Relatively more expensive driven by relatively lower volumes of Industry centric use-cases	Becoming very inexpensive due to the cost of technology and scale driven by explosive expansion in industrial use cases and new opportunities in consumer/domestic use cases
8.	Information security	Vulnerabilities limited to insider tampering or negligence as the industrial instrumentation devices were not connected to the internet or any other public network	Vulnerabilities are exponentially higher not only due to connectivity to the internet but also due to the non-standard and commodity instrumentation devices flooding the market

6.4.2.2. Current State of Adoption and Future Expectations

IoT is accelerating the proliferation of instrumentation. Industrial IoT is the primary driver of high-impact instrumentation. Consumer IoT has a huge scope in terms of volume of instrumentation but is yet to be deployed in use cases that generate substantial economic value.

Going forward, instrumentation is likely to expand in both scale and scope. Scale expansion will be driven by the existing range of sensors and actuators finding new uses in both industrial and consumer settings. Further miniaturization of computational end points with increased capability will be another driver for increasing the potential for instrumentation in the future. Scope expansion will be driven by the emergence of new types of sensors and actuators. A few examples of sensors that are in early stage development are listed as follows:

- Olfactory sensors—Internet of Smell using nanomechanical sensors (Ngo et al., 2019)
- Electronic tongue—used in pharmaceutical, food and beverage industries (Podrażka et al., 2018)
- Flexible electronics for implanted body sensor networks (Lee et al., 2019)

Digital instrumentation as a link between the real world and its digitization for the virtual world has nearly infinite potential. This potential is likely to progressively manifest in economic value creation over the following years and decades to come.

6.4.3 Communication: Expansive Connectivity and Information Dissemination

---

Digital era communication technologies, stratified by spatial range, network speed and bandwidth capacity, provide capabilities to interconnect a practically unlimited number of devices with optimal energy efficiency.

The IT era that preceded the digital era was primarily driven by a revolution in communication technologies that connected computers around the world seamlessly over a massive network of networks, the internet. The internet powered a new communication revolution that resulted in the democratization of data from the perspective of both content creation and content consumption. The focus of internet communication technologies was to connect data networks over very long distances effectively. The devices connected to the internet were mostly full-scale computers starting from high performance servers to the desktop computers of end users. In the digital era, the internet paradigm is being expanded to connect new 'things', potentially everything that is not connected to the internet yet.

6.4.3.1. Identifying Things of the Digital Era

When devices are connected over the internet, it becomes a necessity for assigning unique, global address/identifiers for each device. In the pre-digital internet era, the number of devices connected was in the order of a few billion. The digital era strives to connect everything on the planet and beyond. This requires a multi-fold increase in the range of unique addresses. The internet era was anchored on Internet Protocol Version 4 (IPv4) that had the ability to identify about 4.3 billion devices. The Internet Protocol Version 6 (IPv6), which is the most recent version of the internet protocol addressing, is driving the identification and addressing requirements for connected devices in the digital era. IPv6 provides the

EXHIBIT 6.13 | *Taxonomical Context for Communication Technologies*

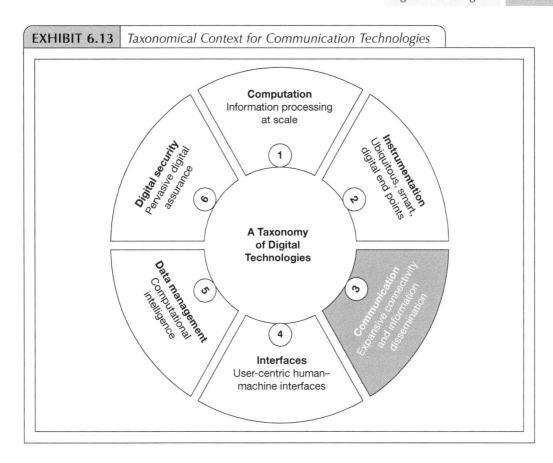

capability to identify and address a practically unlimited number of devices. Exhibit 6.14 illustrates the differences between IPv4 and IPv6 and highlights the potential of IPv6.

6.4.3.2. Salience of Communication Technologies of the Digital Era

The emerging requirements for communication in the digital era heavily leverage the capabilities enabled by the internet and seek to broaden further and deepen the level of connectivity between the physical (analogue) and virtual (digital) worlds. The salient features of this digital era communication technologies are depicted in Exhibit 6.15.

6.4.3.3. Current State of Adoption and Future Expectations

The internet will continue to be the backbone of global communication between devices and networks. The ongoing revolution in connecting billions of things to the internet is being driven by the evolution of low-bitrate, low-band, low-power, low-cost wireless communications. On the other hand, the need for low latency requirements for autonomous devices such as connected cars and drones is driving the evolution of high-speed,

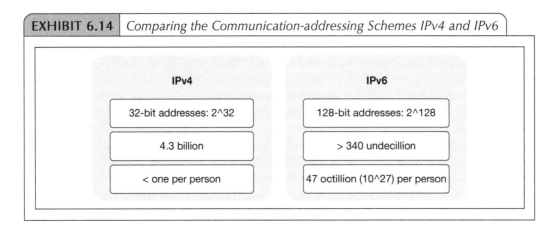

EXHIBIT 6.14 | *Comparing the Communication-addressing Schemes IPv4 and IPv6*

IPv4	IPv6
32-bit addresses: 2^32	128-bit addresses: 2^128
4.3 billion	> 340 undecillion
< one per person	47 octillion (10^27) per person

low-latency communication. The key innovations in the communication capabilities can be expected to evolve in two distinct directions: (a) low-speed, low-power/energy networks and (b) high-speed, low-latency networks.

> **Low-speed, low-power/energy networks:** One of the two aspects of these categories of networks is device communication technologies. Highly energy efficient, almost self-powered network end points that will connect billions of things to the internet.
>
> The second aspect of the low-power networks is emerging global coverage. The billions of things need to connect to an omnipresent low power wide area network that acts as a gateway to the internet for all the devices that are getting onboarded into the expansive realm of connected things.
>
> For example, the implementation of Sigfox (Lauridsen et al., 2017) networks for low-bitrate, low-power applications covering several countries with relatively limited physical infrastructure is a precursor to the future of communication capabilities.
>
> **High-speed, low-latency networks:** Most parts of the connected world would demand high-speed, low-latency, wireless applications such as autonomous cars and swarm drones. These applications will require the next evolution of the cellular network, which is likely to manifest as the 5G revolution.

6.4.3.4. The Heterogeneous Future

The future of device connectivity and global coverage can be expected to land with highly energy-efficient/self-powered end points that connect to the ubiquitous coverage provided by low-bitrate wireless networks. Connectivity for billions of such devices would be underpinned by the new type of networks, that is, WSN, PAN, MANET and so on. The communications capabilities for the foreseeable future will push the frontier to achieve performance within two distinct categories of applications. The first category is extreme energy efficiency balanced with optimal speed, and the second category is extremely low latency with high speeds and bandwidths. This expanding communication technology frontier will provide connectivity for a wide spectrum of applications when billions of heterogeneous devices connect with each other over the internet.

EXHIBIT 6.15	*Salience of Communication Technologies in the Digital Era*

	Attribute	Pre-digital	Digital Era
1.	Spatial range	Characterized by the internet with wired networks proliferating LAN and WAN leading to network of networks, that is, the internet.	Characterized by a continuum of spatial range with PAN, WSN, MANET, creating more heterogeneity to the internet.
2.	Network speed	Increasing speed had been the focus of technology development. This was required to support the ever-increasing size of transacted content, going from simple websites to high-definition video streaming. For example, Ethernet evolving to Gigabit Ethernet.	Lower bit rate applications are the new driving force due to exponential growth in IoT devices, sensors and so on. The key design consideration was to trade off transmission speed to other constraints such as power requirement and wireless range. For example, LR-WPAN.
3.	Bandwidth	Increasing bandwidth for communication has been the focus of technology development. For example, ADSL, fibre broadband, 3G, 4G and so on.	Alongside high bandwidth, narrow band communication becomes essential and useful to increase digitization with IoT. For example, NB-IoT standards, Sigfox protocol stack and so on.
4.	Energy efficiency	Internet revolution was powered by computers typically connected to the electricity grid power. They were not constrained in energy consumption. Hence, energy efficiency was not the main driver for technology development.	Internet of everything means that energy efficiency is a key design driver for instrumenting billions of things around the world. Hence, energy-efficient communication is at the frontier of innovation in digital era communications.
5.	Protocols standards	TCP/IP protocol suite emerged as the standard for the internet communication.	Multiple competing technologies using various combinations of spatial range, bit rate, energy efficiency leading to a lack of standard, both at device-level and network-level communications. For example, Zigbee, 6LoWPAN, BLE, LP-WAN and so on.
6.	Wireless networks	The wireless medium was considered a good-to-have alternative and gradually Wi-Fi and cellular connectivity became pervasive in the last mile of connectivity. Wired networks continue to dominate the bulk of data communication requirements.	Wireless communication becomes a necessity as connectivity requirements grow from a few billion devices overall to a few billion devices every few months. Wired communication is neither feasible nor affordable at the scale of digitalization envisaged in the digital era.
7.	Network addressing schemes	IPv4 addressing scheme used to identify computers and devices connected to the internet.	IPv6 addressing scheme used to identify devices and things that are connected to the internet.

SUMMARY

Digital technologies are a part of the continuing evolution of IT. Digital technologies encompass a wide variety of technologies which are changing at a pace faster than they have changed in the past. The wide variety of technologies, the unprecedented velocity of their evolution and the deep impact they have on businesses together form the foundation for the ongoing digital revolution.

This digital revolution is promising profound impact on how businesses serve customers and create value, making it important for managers to acquire a good grasp of digital. This chapter introduces a taxonomy of digital technologies categorizing them into six broad categories (or six elements) based on the capabilities they enable for businesses. Using this taxonomy, managers can organize their understanding of the plethora of digital technologies and gain a conceptual clarity on how they add value to business.

The capabilities enabled by the six technology elements provide the structure for a detailed discussion on how they add value to businesses. An overview of the three out of the six elements covered in this chapter is presented as follows:

1. **Computation:** Cloud Computing is at the foundation of the computational capabilities for the digital era. Cloud transforms the fabric of computational capabilities available to enterprises and individuals. Digital era computation, underpinned by cloud computing, provides scalable, elastic, reliable and resilient computing capabilities with agility.
2. **Instrumentation:** Instrumentation in general refers to instruments used for measuring physical quantities that characterize the physical world, that is, temperature, pressure, volume, mass and so on. The digital era instrumentation, underpinned by capable, miniaturized and affordable digital end points, provides ubiquitous sense-and-respond capabilities at the boundary of the 'physical–analogue' and the 'virtual–digital' worlds.
3. **Communication:** The pre-digital era which saw the growth of the internet was mainly driven by a revolution in communication technologies that connected computers around the world seamlessly over a massive network of networks, the internet. The digital era communication technologies, stratified by spatial range, network speed and bandwidth capacity, provide capabilities to interconnect practically unlimited number of devices with optimal energy efficiency.

Discussion Questions

1. What are the key elements of digital technologies?
2. What are the first-order capabilities enabled by digital technologies?
3. What are the second-order capabilities? How do they add value to business?
4. How do capabilities enabled by digital technologies contribute to shareholder value?

5. What are the physical and logical layers of cloud computing? What capabilities do they enable for business?
6. What are the business drivers for adoption of public cloud versus private cloud versus hybrid cloud?
7. Both computation and instrumentation elements have computational capabilities. What are the characteristics that differentiate these two elements?
8. What is the significance of low-power/high-energy efficiency in communication technologies for the digital era?
9. When identifying devices in a digital network, what is the significance of IPv6 when compared to IPv4? Why is this important for digital use cases for business?
10. What are the salient characteristics of the following digital technology elements in the digital era when compared to the pre-digital era?
    a. Computation
    b. Instrumentation
    c. Communication
11. What to expect in the foreseeable future with respect to the evolution of the following digital technology elements?
    a. Computation
    b. Instrumentation
    c. Communication

GLOSSARY

The technical terminologies defined below are not essential for managers. These are terms, and associated descriptions are neither comprehensive nor mandatory for the purposes of this book. A basic understanding of some of these terms will familiarize managers with key esoteric technical terminologies of the digital era. These will also provide managers with an opportunity to appreciate the trajectory of the evolution of digital technologies both from the past and into the future.

3G[10]: 3G is a mobile communication technology that is characterized by deep technical nuances. For the sake of managerial abstraction, 3G can be simply referred to as the third-generation wireless cellular communications technology. More details and nuances are discussed in an International Telecommunication Union (ITU) document provided in the references section.

4G[11]: 4G is a mobile communication technology that provides higher data rates and better spectral efficiency than 3G. More technical but relevant details are available in the ITU document provided in the references section.

6LoWPAN[12]: 6LoWPAN stands for IPv6 network over low-power wireless personal area network. This is a networking technology that has the potential for extensive use in IoT. For the sake of managerial abstraction, this could be considered as a technology that enables connecting billions of low-power IoT devices directly to the internet.

ADSL[13]**:** ADSL stands for asymmetric digital subscriber line. ADSL is a data communication technology that enables faster data transmission rates over a copper cable. This was an evolution in data transmission over copper lines used in conventional telephone lines.

BLE[14]**:** BLE stands for Bluetooth low energy. BLE is a wireless protocol that is suitable for low-energy devices in personal area network (PAN) targeted towards innovative applications in healthcare, fitness and so on.

Ethernet[15]**:** Ethernet is a wired communication technology used for connecting computers in a variety of computer networks such as local area network (LAN) and wide area network (WAN). Almost all the wired networks to which a typical user connects their computer at home or in an office are based on Ethernet technology.

Fibre broadband[16]**:** Fibre broadband is a high-speed communication technology that uses fibre optic cables. Fibre optic cables are better than copper cables (used in ADSL) for transferring data.

LAN[17]**:** LAN stands for local area network. LANs are used to connect computers within a home, building or campus. A LAN can be implemented with wired or wireless technologies or a combination of both.

LP-WAN[18]**:** LP-WAN stands for low-power wide area network. It is a type of wireless network that enables connecting low-power (consequently low-bitrate) devices over a long range. The range of LP-WAN could be several kilometres. Devices that use LP-WAN are optimized for power consumption and can operate for several years continuously using inexpensive batteries.

LR-WPAN: LR-WPAN stands for low-rate wireless personal area network. It is a category of network used to connect low data rate/bitrate devices within a very small area (personal area). Several network protocols belong to this category of networks such as Zigbee and 6LoWPAN, which have extensive potential in IoT applications.

MANET: MANET stands for mobile ad hoc network. It is also called WANET (wireless ad hoc network). It is a unique type of network that does not require a fixed physical network infrastructure[19] (unlike networks like home Wi-Fi networks that require a router). For example, MANET-enabled devices can form ad hoc networks when they come in adequate proximity to one another. This has extensive potential in IoT applications.

Microcontroller[20]**:** It is a small computer processor. It is used extensively in IoT devices and embedded systems. A microcontroller is functionally comparable to microprocessors. They have technical differences, which is beyond the scope of this discussion. For the sake of managerial abstraction, a microcontroller is typically used in embedded systems, while a microprocessor is typically used in computers.

Microprocessor[21]**:** A microprocessor is the core component of a computer that provides the computational capability for the computer. A microprocessor is functionally comparable to microcontrollers. They have technical differences, which is beyond the scope of this discussion. For the sake of managerial abstraction, a microprocessor is typically used in computers, while a microcontroller is used in embedded systems.

NB-IoT[22]**:** NB-IoT stands for narrowband Internet of Things. It is a communication technology that uses mobile cellular networks for low-power, narrow-band applications. NB-IoT provides long-range communication and can be categorized as part of LP-WAN technologies.[23]

Operating systems[24]: In the context of IT, operating system refers to a class of software that acts as an interface between computer hardware and users (and user applications). Some examples of operating systems are Linux, Windows, macOS, iOS and Android.

PAN[25]: PAN stands for personal area network. This simply refers to a network of devices around a person. Both wireless and wired connectivity are possible in a PAN. Computer peripherals with Bluetooth connectivity is a common example of PAN.

Sigfox[26]: Sigfox is a company that provides network services for IoT. Their technology enables low-cost, low-power and low-bitrate requirements across several industries. Sigfox uses an LP-WAN network to provide connectivity to IoT devices with low-power characteristics such as smart metres and IoT devices for assets tracking in supply chains.

TCP/IP[27]: TCP/IP stands for transfer control protocol/internet protocol. It refers to a suite of computer networking protocols used on the internet. This suite of protocols provides specifications for end-to-end data communication. These specifications include aspects such as how data needs to be broken down into packets (smaller units of data), how devices in the network get addressed/identified and how the packets get routed between devices.

WAN[28]: WAN stands for wide area network. This is a computer network that spans over a large geographic area. It is typically used to connect members of an organization, its suppliers and customers spread across multiple locations, cities and countries. A WAN is made up of other types of networks such as LANs, WSNs and PANs, suitably connected for data communication among them.

Wi-Fi[29]: Wi-Fi is a family of networking protocols used in LANs for wireless communication. Wi-Fi networks are designed to work seamlessly with wired LANs. This is a very commonly used technology for wireless connectivity at homes, offices and LAN settings.

WSN[30]: WSN stands for wireless sensor network. WSNs are extensively used in IoT. As the name implies, this type of network connects a large number of sensors and actuators that have wireless capability and connect with each other directly or through IoT gateways (discussed in detail in Chapter 8). WSNs enable the collection of sensor data from the environment and communicate the data to a central data management system for storing, processing and analysing data.

Zigbee[31]: Zigbee is a wireless communication technology used for IoT networks that need low-cost, low-power and low-bitrate data communication. Zigbee is used in short-range communication requirements such as wireless PANs, home automation and industrial IoT settings.

NOTES

1. https://www.forbes.com/sites/joshbersin/2012/08/16/the-move-from-systems-of-record-to-systems-of-engagement/?sh=21ecfec447f5

2. https://newsroom.ibm.com/2017-04-28-IBM-Inventors-Patent-Invention-for-Transferring-Packages-between-Aerial-Drones

3. https://en.wikipedia.org/wiki/Cloud_computing

4. https://developer.ibm.com/technologies/iot/articles/how-cloud-fog-and-mist-computing-can-work-together/
5. https://www.ibm.com/blogs/cloud-computing/2019/03/05/20-percent-cloud-transformation/
6. https://www.forbes.com/sites/louiscolumbus/2018/01/07/83-of-enterprise-workloads-will-be-in-the-cloud-by-2020/?sh=777f59246261
7. https://www.electronicscomp.com/atmega328p-microcontroller-india
8. https://en.wikipedia.org/wiki/Intel_8088
9. https://store.frost.com/2020-update-global-internet-of-things-iot-devices-forecast-2017-2026.html
10. https://www.itu.int/ITU-D/tech/FORMER_PAGE_IMT2000/DocumentsIMT2000/What_really_3G.pdf
11. https://www.itu.int/en/ITU-D/Regional-Presence/AsiaPacific/SiteAssets/Pages/Events/2019/ITU-ASP-CoE-Training-on-/3GPP_4G%20to%205G%20networks%20evolution%20and%20releases.pdf
12. https://en.wikipedia.org/wiki/6LoWPAN
13. https://en.wikipedia.org/wiki/Asymmetric_digital_subscriber_line
14. https://en.wikipedia.org/wiki/Bluetooth_Low_Energy
15. https://en.wikipedia.org/wiki/Ethernet
16. https://en.wikipedia.org/wiki/Fiber-optic_communication
17. https://en.wikipedia.org/wiki/Local_area_network
18. https://en.wikipedia.org/wiki/LPWAN
19. https://en.wikipedia.org/wiki/Wireless_ad_hoc_network
20. https://en.wikipedia.org/wiki/Microcontroller
21. https://en.wikipedia.org/wiki/Microprocessor
22. https://en.wikipedia.org/wiki/Narrowband_IoT
23. https://www.iotforall.com/iot-connectivity-comparison-lora-sigfox-rpma-lpwan-technologies
24. https://en.wikipedia.org/wiki/Operating_system
25. https://en.wikipedia.org/wiki/Personal_area_network
26. https://www.sigfox.com/en/sigfox-story
27. https://en.wikipedia.org/wiki/Internet_protocol_suite
28. https://en.wikipedia.org/wiki/Wide_area_network
29. https://en.wikipedia.org/wiki/Wi-Fi
30. https://en.wikipedia.org/wiki/Wireless_sensor_network
31. https://en.wikipedia.org/wiki/Zigbee

REFERENCES

Lauridsen, M., Nguyen, H., Vejlgaard, B., Kovács, I. Z., Mogensen, P., & Sorensen, M. (2017, June). *Coverage comparison of GPRS, NB-IoT, LoRa, and SigFox in a 7800 km² area*, 1–5. 2017 IEEE 85th Vehicular Technology Conference: VTC-2017 Spring, IEEE, Sydney.

Lee, S., Shi, Q., & Lee, C. (2019). From flexible electronics technology in the era of IoT and artificial intelligence toward future implanted body sensor networks. *APL Materials, 7*(3), 031302.

Ngo, H. T., Minami, K., Imamura, G., Shiba, K., & Yoshikawa, G. (2019). Membrane-type surface stress sensor (MSS) for an artificial olfactory system. In K. Mitsubayashi, O. Niwa, & Y. Ueno (Eds), *Chemical, gas, and biosensors for internet of things and related applications*, 27–38. Elsevier.

Podrażka, M., Bączyńska, E., Kundys, M., Jeleń, P. S., & Witkowska Nery, E. (2018). Electronic tongue—a tool for all tastes? *Biosensors, 8*(1), 3.

Simon, H. A. (1990). Information technologies and organisations. *Accounting Review, 65*(3), 658–667.

Digital Technologies II

Learning Objectives

This chapter is a continuation of Digital Technologies I (Chapter 6).

Chapters 6, 7 and 8 focus on demystifying the various digital computing technologies in the context of digital transformation. These three chapters provide a managerial abstraction of digital technologies that help map the technological underpinnings of digital transformation. Chapters 6 and 7 focus on elemental categories of digital technologies based on the nature of capabilities they enable for business. Chapter 8 focuses on composite technologies built from a combination of the elemental technologies covered in Chapters 6 and 7. At the end of Chapters 6 and 7, students will learn the following:

- A managerial abstraction of key digital technologies in the form of a taxonomy
- Different levels of capabilities enabled by digital technologies and their relevance to business
- What makes digital era technologies distinct from earlier technology era
- The current state of each technology category and what to expect in the foreseeable future
- The following technology categories are covered in Chapter 6:
  o Computation
  o Instrumentation
  o Communication

Chapter 7 builds on the content discussed in Chapter 6 and provides a deep dive into the following three technology categories:

- Data management
- Interfaces (human–machine interfaces)
- Digital security

7.1. DISTINGUISHING CHARACTERISTICS OF DIGITAL TECHNOLOGIES: SEGUE FROM CHAPTER 6

Chapter 6 presented a managerial abstraction of various categories of digital technologies in the form of a taxonomy. The distinguishing characteristics of the first three categories in the taxonomy (computation, instrumentation and communication) were discussed in Chapter 6. The digital technologies taxonomy is revisited in Exhibit 7.1. The exhibit also highlights the next three categories in the taxonomy that will be addressed in this chapter.

7.1.1. Interface: User-centric Human–machine Interfaces

Digital era interface technologies, underpinned by user-centric design, provide capabilities that enable intuitive machine-to-human interactions in the physical world that emulate natural human gestures and preferences.

| EXHIBIT 7.1 | *Taxonomy of Digital Technologies: Revisited from Chapter 6* |

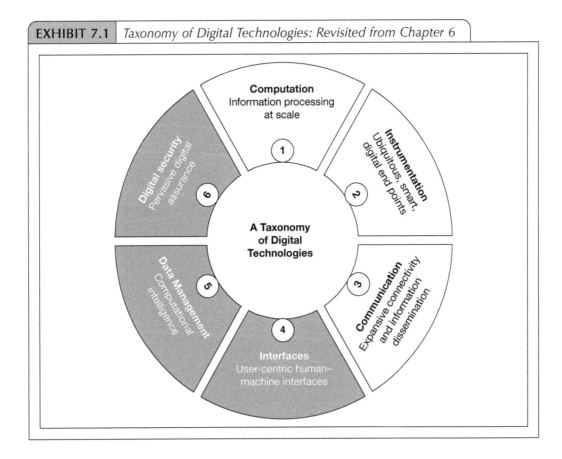

EXHIBIT 7.2 | *Taxonomical Context for Interface Technologies*

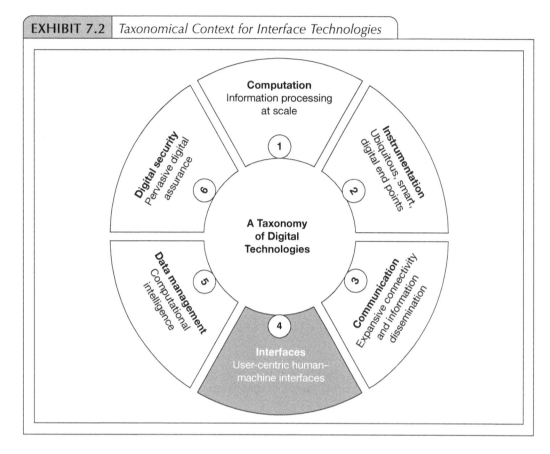

Computer interfaces with users have evolved from being mediated through specialist computer operators to directly using computers. Exhibit 7.2 highlights computer-user Interface capabilities in the context of digital technology taxonomies. These interfaces were still designed for computers (within the constraints of available technologies). For example, users had to learn newer skills like using a keyboard and mouse for using computers. Another aspect of design that impacted user interfaces was the purpose of software that ran on computers. The software that ran on computers were mostly designed for processes, that is, workflows, information flows and so on. The term systems of record[1] encapsulates the form and function of these systems. Systems of record are those that are used to run the core of business operations. Such systems were designed with a process-centric philosophy owing to their focus on the implementation of business processes. In the digital era, human–computer interfaces are being strongly influenced by developments in technologies such as touchscreen, voice controls and other gesture-based interfaces like those available in gaming consoles. These digital era interface technologies are closer to natural human communication preferences when compared to the keyboard and mouse interfaces that dominated the pre-digital era of IT. In the digital age, computer applications are being designed with the human user as a core design mainly enabled by the availability of intuitive human interface technologies. The term systems of engagement[2] encapsulates the form and function of these systems. Systems of engagement increase user engagement with their

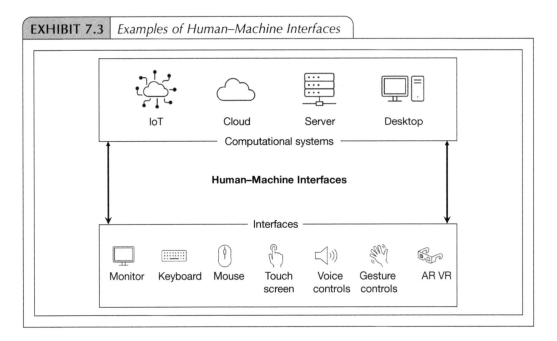

EXHIBIT 7.3 *Examples of Human–Machine Interfaces*

easy to use and intuitive user interfaces. Computer interfaces and applications, thus, designed require no specialized training for the user, as evident in devices like smartphones. Exhibit 7.3 presents some examples of human–machine interfaces.

7.1.1.1. Salience of Interface Technologies of the Digital Era

Nuances with respect to the nature of human–computer interfaces were discussed in the preceding section. This section deconstructs relevant attributes of interface technologies to highlight the salience of interface technologies in the digital era. This depiction also provides a perspective on the evolution of interfaces from the pre-digital age (Exhibit 7.4).

7.1.1.2. Current State of Adoption and Future Expectations

As the digital era unfolds, computing systems will get more sophisticated in terms of user engagement. More power will be available with users with far better ease of use. The initial days of the digital era saw unprecedented growth in mobile devices with intuitive touch screen interfaces. Such devices will become capable of recognizing a wide variety of human gestures, be cheaper and have more pervasive biometric security and other highly user-friendly alternatives to conventional interfaces.

The next frontier of interfaces would include AR and VR. AR and VR are gradually shifting from niche business and defence use cases like flight simulators to the realm of consumer devices. AR and VR will lead to more intuitive ways for humans to engage with computers. This is evident in their early adoption of gaming devices. We will witness a

	EXHIBIT 7.4	*Salience of Interface Technologies in the Digital Era*

	Attribute	Pre-digital	Digital Era
1.	Application context	Applications were mostly built for business uses. Most of the applications were used to automate business processes such as finance and HR.	Applications are increasingly being built for use by untrained users, like mobile apps. These applications are used by businesses for engaging consumers in social or peer-to-peer use cases.
2.	Dominant interfaces	Computer interfaces were mostly conventional, such as keyboard, mouse and joystick.	Digital devices were invented with a variety of intuitive interfaces, such as touch screens and gesture-based controls.
3.	Design philosophy	Computer systems were predominantly designed with a process-centric approach.	Computer systems were predominantly with a user-centric approach.
4.	End-user training	Users need to be trained for specialized uses due to a process-centric design.	End user training needs are minimal or sometimes not needed due to the user-centric design applied to computational devices in the digital era.
5.	Duration of user interactions	Duration of use limited to office hours and limited personal uses such as e-mail and office productivity applications.	Duration of use is almost perpetual, with digital-era computing devices being used as a part of day-to-day living.

plethora of applications for AR and VR in education, business for remote meetings, retail and so on. These applications will lead to a greater effectiveness in processes and improvements in user experience.

A new category of interfaces that is evolving is the interface between humans and robots/co-bots. Semi-autonomous or fully autonomous robots have started to operate alongside humans in industrial contexts (like industrial co-bots) and consumer context (like robots for customer service in the hospitality industry). For such use-case contexts, interface design should cater to ease of use (intuitive) and safety of humans amidst co-habiting machines. We are likely to witness these applications becoming mainstream in the foreseeable future.

7.1.2. Data Management: The Foundation of Computational Intelligence

Data management technologies in the digital era cater to effective and efficient life cycle management of rapidly growing large volumes of structured and unstructured data. These technologies enable applications for historical, real-time and predictive insights working, using real-time data streams and persistent data stores.

EXHIBIT 7.5 | *Taxonomical Context for Data Management Technologies*

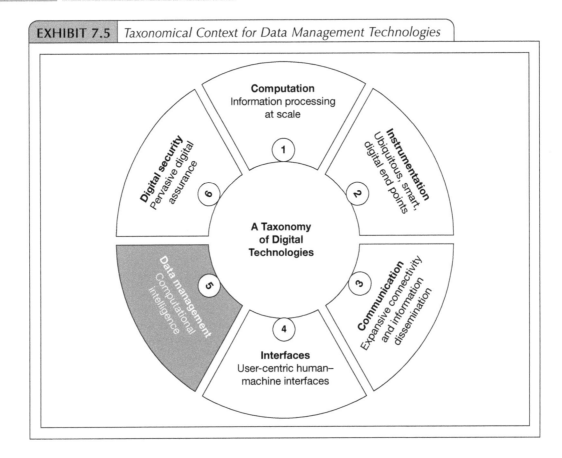

Data is considered the new oil and the most pervasive yet powerful value source for the 21st century. Data is the core driver of the digital revolution. Digital data is a collection of various attributes and states of the physical world (both natural and human-made), resulting in a digital representation or digitization. Exhibit 7.5 highlights Data Management capabilities in the context of digital technology taxonomies. The terms digital world, virtual world and information world have been used synonymously in this chapter. The following few examples reinforce this fundamental idea of how data creates a digital representation of the real world in a virtual environment.

Examples

Weather data collected by sensors essentially converts physical quantities manifesting as a natural phenomenon in the real world into digital quantities, which manifest at data (structured data) that describe the physical quantities in the virtual world.

A tweet by a customer about the quality of a product or experience converts the perception of quality into digital text data (unstructured data) that describes the customer's perception in the virtual world.

Digital data, thus created, forms the substance that shapes the digital universe. Such elemental significance of digital data and the fact that it is one of the most complex and expansive topics under the umbrella of digital technologies make this section relatively more elaborate than most other topics. As indicated earlier in Chapter 6, the conceptualizations provided in this section are intended to give a managerial abstraction of capabilities provided by data management technologies for building and transforming businesses in the digital era. It is important to note that the objective is not to provide the most comprehensive treatment of all the theory and practices of data management, which is beyond the scope of this text. Distinguishing characteristics of data in the digital era provide a reasonable basis for understanding the technologies and associated capabilities in the context of their potential for business impact.

7.1.2.1. Distinguishing Characteristics of Digital Era Data

The digital era has given rise to data characterized by three powerful and distinct characteristics: high volumes, high varieties and high velocity of data generation. Several other characteristics of data such as veracity, quality and durability characterize data in the digital era. But volume, variety and velocity elaborated in this chapter, to no small extent, capture the essential aspects of data management technologies. Distinguishing characteristics of digital data are depicted in Exhibit 7.6. Building on the three characteristics, this chapter presents data management technologies and associated capabilities as a managerial abstraction (Exhibit 7.7).

EXHIBIT 7.6 | *Salience of Digital Data*

	Attribute	Pre-digital	Digital era
1.	Origin of data	Most of the relevant data were generated within the company by business users.	A significant volume of relevant data getting generated outside the bounds of the company by customers, prospects and influencers on social media.
2.	Volume	The annual volume of data created, captured, copied and consumed was 2 zeta bytes in 2010.	The annual volume of data created, captured, copied and consumed estimated to be 74 zeta bytes in 2021.
3.	Variety	Mostly structured with some unstructured text and multimedia content.	Mostly unstructured with lots of variety, and a big bulk of it is multimedia content.
4.	Velocity	Typically, batch processing with limited real-time requirements.	Continuous processing of real-time data streams becomes the new normal.
5.	Temporal focus	Predominantly, historical data analysis for descriptive and diagnostic purposes.	Historical data analysis is still relevant; additionally, real-time streaming and predictive analytics gain prominence.

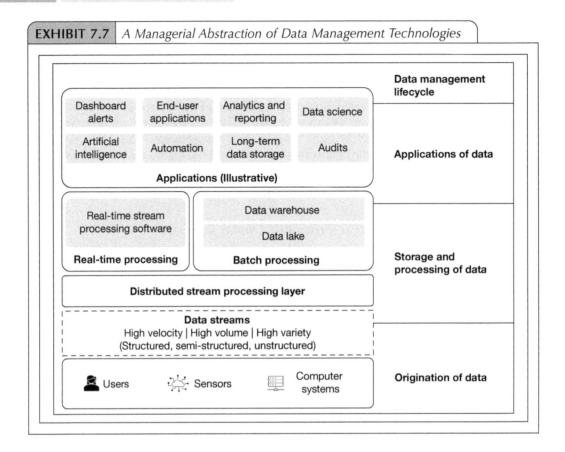

EXHIBIT 7.7 | *A Managerial Abstraction of Data Management Technologies*

7.1.2.2. Data Variety: Structured, Semi-structured and Unstructured Data

Digital data is broadly classified into structured and unstructured data. Structured data is tabular with a specified set of columns that correspond to each data variable (schema) and rows that have specific values for the data variable depicted by the corresponding column. Structured data has been the mainstay of computing in the pre-digital era of IT. Unstructured data is characterized by multimedia that includes text data, images, voice and video. With the proliferation of social media and multimedia content, most of the data in the digital era is unstructured. Nearly 80% of data in an organization data is unstructured.[3] Semi-structured data does not follow a strict tabular structure but has a hierarchy of attribute-value pairs like JSON files. Semi-structured data structures are sometimes applied to make unstructured data more processable for computer programs. Data management technologies to harness structured, semi-structured and unstructured data become essential for businesses to achieve potential with digital data.

7.1.2.3. Data Volume: Big Data

Data volume refers to the quantity of data that gets generated and needs to be stored and processed. Data volume in the context of digital data has two implications for data management technologies. The first implication is to cope with the challenges of storing and processing voluminous data. The second implication is to cope with the expectation that voluminous data needs to be processed both in real-time and in a batch mode. A common term used to describe the explosion in the volume of digital era data is big data. The idea of big data is not based on an absolute volume threshold. Instead, it is defined as the volume of data that conventional stand-alone computer systems cannot easily handle. The scale of data that requires parallel computing tools (typically involving multiple computers systems) can be classified as big data. Big data is also characterized by a more heterogeneous data variety that includes varying combinations of structured, semi-structured and unstructured data. Data management technologies to harness big data are essential for businesses to achieve potential with digital data.

Example
Google BigQuery is a data warehousing software in the cloud used to store and query large volumes of data. It can store data running into several exabytes.[4] It can support a petabyte scale[5] query data within a few seconds or minutes. This exemplifies contemporary data management technologies for handling large volumes of data with speed.

7.1.2.4. Data Velocity: Data Generation Velocity and Speed to Insights

Velocity refers to both the rate at which data gets generated and the time sensitivity of the data for decision-making, that is, their real-time or near-real-time relevance. For example, billions of sensors sensing data from their operating environment at periodic intervals, several times every hour, generate data with velocity, which has real-time relevance. During the pre-digital era, the bulk of enterprise data was generated through business users using computers as part of business processes. Data originating dominantly from end users/consumers on social media platforms and IoT sensors drives data velocity. These two developments have added high-velocity data streams that companies must deal with. Additional complexity in dealing with high-velocity data growth is that most data gets generated from outside the boundaries of a company. The following examples illustrate the massive rise in the velocity of potentially relevant data generated outside the bounds of the company.

1. Employees, customers, prospects and other stakeholders with their presence in public social media
2. Sensors sensing weather information
3. The geographic information from public cloud services that provide data on traffic conditions

Data management technologies to deal with high-velocity data streams of time-sensitive data are essential for businesses to extract value from real-time insights.

7.1.2.5. Origination of Data

Data sources: Data originates through multiple mechanisms. The three key mechanisms are as follows:

1. Produced by human users and captured through digital interfaces
2. Produced by sensors that are a part of digital instrumentation
3. Produced during data processing by computational systems

These data sources operate perpetually, driving the variety, volume and velocity of data generated, manifesting as data streams.

Data streams: Data, in general, and digital era data, in particular, can be conceived as data streams disparate in terms of the volume, variety and velocity attributes. Data streams originate from different computational endpoints supporting various users, machines, and processes. Data thus generated needs to be centrally managed (captured, stored, and processed) to unlock the potential inherent value.

7.1.2.6. Storage and Processing of Data

The capability to efficiently store and process heterogeneous types and formats of data is essential to realize digital data's potential. Data storage and processing capabilities include both hardware and software technologies. Hardware for storing and accessing high volume and variety of data has evolved significantly from general purpose hard drives to specialized storage appliances such as network attached storage (NAS) and storage area network (SAN). These hardware are made available as an on-premises infrastructure for enterprises or are made available as storage capabilities in the cloud. While the hardware elements are foundational to storing and processing data and provide capacity for scaling, the most impactful innovations in data management are mostly software driven.

From a software perspective, data storage and processing technologies are shaped based on the inputs (origins of data) and outputs (applications of data). Data storage and processing are at the core of the software architecture for data management and is a continuously and rapidly evolving area. The architectural elements that enable storing and processing of data, as represented in Exhibit 7.6, are based on software architecture practices promulgated by leading cloud service provides such as Google Cloud Platform, Amazon Web Services and Microsoft Azure. Various software architectural elements discussed in this section are functional representations. They may not necessarily manifest as distinct elements in commercial data management software. In real-life implementations, one software could perform the role of multiple functional elements. Capabilities provided by various architectural elements in data storage and processing are described in the following sub-sections.

7.1.2.7. Distributed Data Stream Processing

Data streams that occur need to be stored and processed for unlocking value from data. The first step in processing high-volume, high-velocity, high-variety data streams is fast and reliable processing of data streams. One of the architectural innovations that enables capabilities to handle high-velocity data is the distributed data stream processing software that acts as a mediator between high-velocity data streams and heterogeneous uses of data such as real-time streaming analytics and batch processing applications. Streaming analytics could include real-time dashboards, alerting engines and interfaces to automation software. Batch processing applications could consist of data mining, analysis, reporting, data audits and so on. The data stream processing layer is typically distributed. It needs to provide rapid scalability and needs to be highly resilient. It is the first level data store that is expected to feed the downstream data processing applications. This layer prioritizes the goal of reliably storing real-time data feeds and then making them available for downstream data processing applications in a flexible manner. An example of a stream processing layer is the Apache Kafka stream processing software platform that aims to provide a unified, high-throughput, low-latency platform for handling real-time data feeds. Once the high throughput data streams are stored reliably, they can be used for real-time processing or batch processing.

Real-time processing: Real-time stream processing involves querying and analysing continuous streams of data and respond to essential or preconfigured events within a concise timeframe. The response times could be as low as milliseconds. Thus, the capability provided by real-time stream processing software is to provide the ability to query and analyse high-volume and high-velocity data with very low latency so that the performance objectives ranging in milliseconds can be achieved. This capability that existed in the past in high-performance scientific and defence applications has become a mainstream capability available to businesses in the digital era. A few following use cases explained can exemplify the relevance of this capability for businesses.

The example of use cases for real-time stream processing:

1. To track connected things such as goods under shipment and transportation fleet to trigger real-time actions like alerts and provide location information to fleet monitoring dashboards
2. To track connected vehicles on the road and feed into traffic management dashboards and trigger alerts
3. Data from sensors in industrial assets such as wind generators and earth-moving (https://www.lexico.com/definition/earth_moving) equipment to monitor aberrant conditions and initiate alerts and automated actions

Batch processing: The second type of applications that are downstream of distributed data stream processing applications is used for batch processing of data. Data warehouses and data lakes are at the foundation of storing big data. Typically, data lakes are software applications that store a vast pool of raw data (a combination of structured, semi-structured and unstructured types) which are persistently stored. Data in data lakes are not yet processed and are not geared towards a specific purpose (reporting, data science, etc.). Some examples of cloud-based data lake software are Google Cloud Dataflow, Amazon S3 and so on. Data from a data lake are moved to a data warehouse after due processing and structuring for specific purposes. A data warehouse is a software application used as a central repository of data from disparate sources to serve multiple, predefined sets of applications/ end uses. Conventional data warehouses were designed to store structured data from business operations. These data warehouses supported data processing for analysis and reporting for business decision-making. In the digital era, the expectation of capabilities associated with data warehouses is becoming more demanding and complex. Data warehouses in the digital age provide capabilities on the volume dimension to horizontally scale for storing exabytes of data and offer querying capabilities that could process queries returning petabytes of data within a short time frame. Cloud-based data warehouses provide additional capabilities in terms of scalability, flexible scaling and managed services. Managed services in data warehousing mask the complexities of managing the underlying compute infrastructure (serverless data warehouses), the geographic distribution of capacity and the overall resilience of the services. Some examples of cloud-based data warehousing software are Google BigQuery, Amazon Redshift and so on.

7.1.2.8. Applications of Data

Applications that leverage the various types and streams of data may be classified based on their purpose. They are as follows:

1. **Historical data:** Stored, retrieved and analysed to understand the past
2. **Real-time data:** Stored, retrieved and analysed to perceive the present
3. **Predictive modelling:** Analysed, modelled and applied to automate human expertise or anticipate the future

There are several high-level use cases that focus on either or a combination of the above purposes. Some of the illustrative use cases for applications of data are as follows:

Analytics and reporting: Analytics and reporting are a category of application use case that is primarily fulfilling historical data analysis. These set of applications leverage historical data and provides two common types of analytics: descriptive analytics and diagnostic analysis. Descriptive analytics is focused on the question 'what' happened in the past based on historical data. A diagnostic analysis is focused on answering the question 'why' by providing various levels of drill down to descriptive reports. Some examples of business intelligence tools and reporting tools are Tableau, SAP Crystal Reports, IBM Cognos Analytics and so on. Advanced analytics is a high-impact application category and is discussed in more detail in Chapter 8.

Dashboard and alerts: Dashboard applications are typically used for depicting the current state of monitored objects, processes, events and so on. Dashboards are usually fed from real-time data streams enabled by the distributed stream processing layer. Dashboard applications are highly domain-specific, like IT operations dashboards that are used for monitoring IT objects and services or a traffic management dashboard monitoring traffic conditions in a city. Dashboards are typically accompanied by alerting engines to trigger alerts through email or phone calls to specific operational users based on predefined thresholds and rules. Sometimes, the threshold definitions may also be used to trigger automated actions, like restarting a service running in a web server or provisioning additional computational power in the cloud when the user traffic to a website is increasing, suddenly breaching a predefined threshold. Real-time data analysis is one of the feeds/triggers for automation applications.

Data science and applied AI: Data science applications use vast amounts of historical data to extract insights for human users or train models for ML applications. Data science applications are used for building and training AI models. Trained AI models are deployed in AI applications to achieve their intended purposes, such as cluster analysis and predictive analytics. Some examples of data science applications are exploratory data analysis to identifying patterns (unsupervised learning), build and train supervised training models and so on. Once the models are trained and tested, they may be deployed as part of applied artificial intelligence, getting embedded into other software applications like business applications, web sites or automation applications. Data science and AI applications use historical data for modelling and ML and apply them to automate or augment human expertise or predict the future.

Automation: Automation applications are used for performing predefined repetitive tasks without human intervention. RPA is a category of applications that take trigger from real-time data processing applications or AI applications or any other business or IT applications and execute repetitive tasks. Sometimes, RPA is paired with AI to embed a certain degree of learning into the RPA use cases. Some of the RPA software companies have templatized the RPA bots or agents to perform standardized functions. For example, 'Automation Anywhere' provides bots preconfigured for several tasks like the following.[6]

1. Automating Microsoft Excel-based operations
2. Administrative/user management functions in packaged applications such as SAP and salesforce

The preconfigured bots improve time to value with automation.

Long-term data storage and audits: In addition to historical, real-time and predictive applications of data, a vital capability of data management is to store transactions and other types of data for long-term retention (data archives) and audit purposes. There are several mature technologies that are used for highly durable and cost-effective archiving of data like tape storage. Cold cloud storage is a less expensive cloud storage service that can be used to store rarely used data. Some examples of cloud-based services for storing less frequently accessed data or archived data are Amazon S3 Glacier, Google Cloud storage classes—Nearline, Coldline or Archive—and Microsoft Azure Blob Storage. The objective of storing data should guide managers in making decisions with respect to longer-term data storage. Some of the typical objectives are as follows:

1. Mandatory data storage based on regulation
2. Mandated based on company policy
3. Decision-based on managerial discretion on the potential future use of retained data

There is a shelf life for data beyond which that data could become useless, for example, high-volume data from real-time applications like autonomous vehicles (AVs). In AVs, it will be necessary to collect all the data and store them for training the ML model. Once the AV system is out of the learning testing mode and moves into an operational mode, it may not be useful to retain the continuous feed from vehicle sensors during uneventful rides. In such cases, it is important to choose to discard data that are past their useful shelf life. A company could incur costs for storing data that is not useful anymore. These are important nuances for managers to understand and apply with respect to longer-term data storage applications.

7.1.2.9. Current State of Adoption and Future Expectations

Data management technologies are the most elemental force that is powering the digital revolution. The current state-of-the-art in data management is geared towards dealing with high-volume, high-variety and high-velocity data, reliably storing them and making them available for real-time and batch processing applications. One of the dimensions of the evolution of data management in the future is scale, and it is reasonable to expect the scaling of these platforms to store and retrieve zettabytes of data. The other dimension of evolution soon is improved querying speed and volume, that is, current petabyte-scale queries can be processed in a few minutes. This will improve to reach a query time of a few seconds. The third dimension of evolution is data variety—the evolution that is likely to happen in the mix of varieties. Structured and semi-structured data will continue to grow. Their contribution to the blend of varieties is expected to go down with the increasing volume of high-quality digital multimedia content generated from social media. The most profound changes in data management technologies will happen as part of AI, discussed in greater detail in Chapter 8.

7.1.3. Digital Security: Pervasive Assurance across the Complete Digital Stack

Digital security technologies and practices provide assurance on four critical attributes of information security—availability, integrity, confidentiality and data privacy. Ethics in AI is an emerging frontier of digital security.

Conceptualization of data as the new oil for the 21st century is appropriate since data drives a significant majority of decisions and actions that occur in society and businesses. The digital era has also introduced unprecedented levels of automation in decision-making and the execution of actions. Given the degree of dependency on data, it is extremely critical to ensure it is secure, accurate and available to support business decisions and actions continuously. Exhibit 7.8 highlights Digital Security capabilities in the context of digital technology taxonomies. Digital security deals with providing this assurance with the use of several tools and techniques that include, but not limited to, the following:

1. Software such as antivirus and anti-spyware
2. Appliances such as firewalls and network security appliances
3. Security tools that support practices such as penetration testing and vulnerability assessment
4. Security monitoring tools for various components such as application security, system security, communication network security and IoT device security

EXHIBIT 7.8   *Taxonomical Context for Digital Security Technologies*

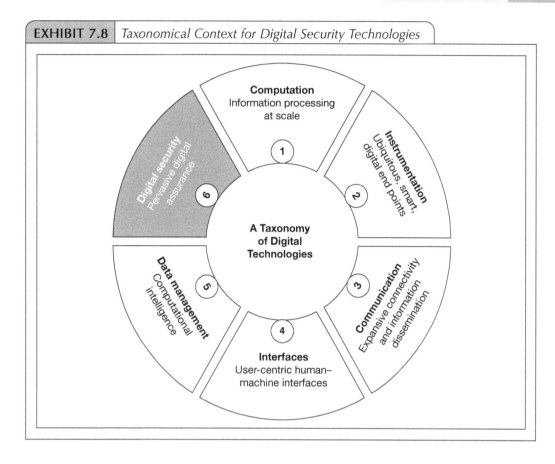

5. Security operations processes that implement and govern digital security standards and best practices like ISO 27000 family of standards for information security management[7]

Since data security can be compromised at any level in the digital stack, this topic is relevant across all the taxonomical categories of digital technology (computation, communication, etc.). Given the pervasiveness and significance of security, this text presents it as a distinct category of digital technology. In this section, the terms data and information are used synonymously.

7.1.3.1. Salience of Digital Security Technologies and Practices of the Digital Era

The primary goal of securing various elements of the digital stack is to secure the information contained in the virtual world and to assure transparency in the use of digital information. The ideas that underpinned information security in the pre-digital era are equally important in the digital age. But they are not adequate to address the new security risks. This text covers the three core aspects of information security (availability, integrity and confidentiality). It introduces two additional elements (ethics in AI and data privacy) that are becoming more prominent in the digital era. This text simplifies the vast digital security area under five core ideas to provide a managerial abstraction of digital security. The five core aspects are availability, integrity, confidentiality, privacy and ethical AI. The salience of the core aspects of the digital era is presented in Exhibit 7.9.

Distinct tools, technologies and practices are available for providing assurance around the five core aspects of digital security. Deep dive into tools, technologies and practices for each of these aspects is beyond this text's scope. The following subsections provide a basic overview of the five core aspects of digital security. This basic overview is intended to enable managers to appreciate the nuances of digital security and its implications for technology adoption in business.

Availability Availability is defined as a state when authorized personnel and systems can access relevant data when and where they need them. The following examples illustrate the significance of data availability.

Examples

When a bank teller needs to access data related to a customer from a core banking system, the information should be available to them through a computational endpoint like a

---

EXHIBIT 7.9 | *Salience of Digital Security Technologies and Practices of the Digital Era*

	Attribute	Pre-digital	Digital Era
1.	Availability	Data availability challenges were limited to the high availability/ redundancy of infrastructure, applications and databases within an enterprise data centre.	Data availability challenges have grown exponentially with exabytes of data distributed over highly virtualized, distributed infrastructure in the cloud.
2.	Integrity	Assurance of data integrity mostly focused on equipment failure concerned with storage and retrieval of data.	Assurance of data integrity increasingly focused on data capture from billions of IoT devices operating in uncontrolled natural environments.
3.	Confidentiality	Confidentiality of data mostly concerned with role-based access control within enterprises.	Confidentiality concerns of data expanded to cover the massive social media platforms.
4.	Privacy	It was essential but was limited to protecting privacy on information purposefully collected from users.	Has gained the most dominant attention due to digitization of highly granular, near real-time information that is personally identifiable.
5.	Ethics in AI	It was not a major area of focus as the proliferation and impact of AI were very limited.	Likely to be the most important focus area when trying to govern the application of direction of AI evolution.

desktop or a mobile device. For some reason, if the information is not available when needed, then it is an issue with data availability. Data availability can be disrupted due to several reasons like equipment malfunction (network, server, etc.) or human error or malicious behaviour of hackers.

Consider the case of autonomous cars. A self-driven car requires at least two sets of information to achieve its objectives of safe and quick transportation. The first set of information is about the immediate environment, roads, pedestrians and other vehicles on the road available to the car navigation control system from the instrumentation available in the car (cameras, LiDAR, etc.). The other set of information is about real-time traffic conditions in different routes to the destination will be available from a centralized compute service (potentially in the cloud or another edge device). Suppose the car's connectivity to the real-time service is disrupted. In that case, part of the data required to identify the best route in real-time suffers from a data availability problem.

Digital security technologies and practices accomplish the goal of assuring the necessary level of information available through the following various approaches.

- Proactive monitoring of equipment and events using specialized security software and appliances
- Periodic maintenance of systems
- Regular training of users and engineers involved in IT projects and operations
- Testing and governance for security vulnerabilities in system design, software development, deployment and operations

Integrity: Integrity is the aspect of information security defined as the accuracy of data at any point in time and, consequently, the consistency of data over its entire life cycle. In other words, assuring data integrity would entail protecting data from getting corrupted either inadvertently or maliciously throughout the entire data management life cycle stages of capture, storage, retrieval, processing, archival and so on. The following examples illustrate the significance of data integrity.

Examples

- Data integrity issue can be envisaged in storing and fetching data in some storage hardware. If a storage system malfunctions due to either a power failure or any other degradation of the physical hardware, then the stored data could get corrupted, compromising the integrity of data.
- In the case of a car connected to the internet, a hacker could hack the system and corrupt the data that controls the functioning of various systems, say the car air-conditioning system. If the hacker maliciously corrupts the data from the temperature sensors that control the air-conditioning system, it will prevent the system from performing as desired by the user. Data integrity issues in a connected car or AV could not only result in inconveniencing the passengers but also result in more severe malfunction and potentially put the passengers' life in danger.

Digital security technologies and practices accomplish the goal of assuring the necessary data integrity levels through various approaches. These include proactive monitoring of equipment and events, periodic maintenance of systems and hardening the system to make it impervious to hacking. Testing and governance around system design, software development, deployment and operations are other critical practices.

Confidentiality: Confidentiality is an aspect of information security that deals with unauthorized (unintentional or malicious) access to data. There are several consequences of compromised data confidentiality. Typically, a breach of data confidentiality could have cascading effects on data integrity and data availability. The following examples illustrate the significance of data confidentiality.

Examples

- Consider an authorized user's password being made available to another person, which means the first step towards breach of confidentiality. The password itself is confidential data, but more than that, a compromised password is likely to lead to further unauthorized access to the user's data leading to further breach of confidentiality.
- When a malicious user hacks an autonomous car, then the user can further compromise the integrity of data and impact the functioning of the system.

Digital security technology/approaches that assure confidentiality include identity and access control systems that could use passwords, voice phrases, biometric authentication and so on.

Privacy: Information privacy is the aspect of information security that deals with the use of data consistent with a user's privacy preferences and protecting personally identifiable information. Increasing scope and pace of digitization also lead to the digitization of several personal and personally identifiable information. For example, individual health records, medical conditions, food habits, purchase patterns may be generated to address specific convenience requirements known and acknowledged by the user. However, it is possible to put together various details about an individual from different contexts (retail, healthcare, internet habits, etc.) and generate a comprehensive profile of the individual, and it could potentially be put to exploitative purposes without explicit consent from the individual.

Digitization is expected to grow multi-fold in the coming years. This is expected to result in massive, growing volumes of personally-identifiable, granular information history. As a natural consequence, information privacy concerns will continue to persist and intensify. Sometimes, privacy is also seen as a compulsive trade-off that users end up making due to their preference for certain conveniences. The issue of information privacy is a substantive topic that needs to be kept in consideration when a manager makes decisions related to digitization in their businesses. Tools and technologies used for assuring confidentiality of data are also useful to ensure data privacy. While tools assist in managing data privacy, most data privacy management requirements are assured through practices based on policies, standards and procedures. These practices are defined either to meet statutory requirements like General Data Protection Regulation (GDPR) or to meet a company's internal policy requirements.

Ethical AI: AI is a kind of superpower available to those that have to understand its potential and promise. Within just a decade of progress with commercially viable supervised ML applications, a lot of things (autonomous cars, swarm drones, etc.) have been made possible. Supervised learning, in its current state, is a minuscule manifestation of the vast potential of AI technologies. AI techniques, today, have the capability to build on themselves through learning using the direction and objective set by humans. It is very much within the realm of possibility for humans to provide malicious or dubious direction and objective to develop powerful AI systems. Such sinister possibilities are giving rise to the question of ethics in AI. This topic, at some level, is philosophical and, at the same time, carries material implications to the business and society. Ethical considerations for AI are still at a nascent stage of development and are likely to evolve significantly over the next few years. It is essential for managers to be aware of the longer-term implications of the decisions they make with respect to AI. At a very high level, managers will need to keep in mind the moral dimension when providing directions or reviewing the goals and objectives that get defined when designing AI systems.

7.1.3.2. Current State of Adoption and Future Expectations

Information security in the digital era is evolving beyond the three primary objectives of availability, integrity and confidentiality. Data privacy and data protection are gaining significant attention in government and regulation, as evidenced by the importance of the GDPR of the European Union. The focus of regulations will initially be centred on data privacy. In the foreseeable future, as AI technologies proliferate more and more into the life of citizens, ethical considerations in AI will take a lot of mind share among policymakers. Just like the continuous duel between malware and antivirus, software engineers and researchers will devote substantial efforts to dealing with the impending battle between good and bad AI. For example, as much as AI is being applied to fake news detection, it can also be used for synthesizing fake news. It is not unreasonable to expect ethics in AI to evolve as a substantial segment within digital security in the foreseeable future.

Mini Case Revisited: Context 3

'With a strong foundation, the team geared for an informed discussion on frontier technologies to create a competitive advantage for TSG.'

Manu seemed satisfied with the detailed perspectives presented by his IT colleagues. Manu especially appreciated the contrast elucidated under each taxonomical category on what is different between the erstwhile internet era and the emerging digital era. He already started thinking about problem contexts in his manufacturing division and TSG's supply chain that could be addressed using the capabilities enabled by digital era IT. As he expressed his satisfaction with the clarity provided by the team and was about to bring up real-life problem contexts, Aaryan interrupted. Although Aaryan liked the clarity provided by the team to get a grasp on digital technologies, he was surprised that some of the most talked-about technology areas such as AI and blockchain had not featured adequately in the taxonomy discussions. He felt the approach so far has been bottom-up. While the debate was rigorous, it was missing the bigger picture. Shifting gears, he suggested that the team should consider three key emerging technologies that are expected to have a very high impact on economic value creation—a top-down approach. Aaryan reinforced his thinking by calling out AI and blockchain as having very high mindshare among entrepreneurs based on his experience. Ishaan and Khushi agreed that both of them are among the top three, and Khushi called out the IoT as another high impact area that deserves the team's understanding before they went on to identifying business use cases for building proof of concepts.

SUMMARY

As discussed in Chapter 6, the digital revolution is promising a profound impact on how businesses serve customers and create value, making it important for managers to acquire a good grasp of digital. Chapter 6 also introduced a taxonomy of digital technologies, categorizing them into six broad categories (or six elements) based on the capabilities they enable for businesses. It was also discussed that using this taxonomy managers can organize their understanding of the plethora of digital technologies and gain conceptual clarity on how they add value to the business.

Based on the structure provided by the six digital technology elements, this chapter presents a detailed discussion on how they add value to businesses. Chapter 6 presented a detailed discussion on the first three out of six technology elements. This chapter presents a detailed discussion on the next three of the six technology elements. An overview of the three technology elements covered in this chapter is presented as follows:

Interfaces: Computer interfaces for users have evolved from being mediated through specialist computer operators to having end users directly use computers. Digital era interface technologies, underpinned by user-centric design, provide capabilities that enable intuitive machine-to-human interactions in the physical world that emulate natural human gestures and preferences.

Data management: Data is considered as the new oil and the most pervasive yet powerful source of value for the 21st century. Data is the core driver of the digital revolution. Data management technologies in the digital era cater to effective and efficient life cycle management of rapidly growing large volumes of structured and unstructured data. These technologies enable applications for historical, real-time and predictive insights working, using real-time data streams and persistent data stores.

Digital security: Digital era has also introduced unprecedented levels of automation in decision-making and execution of actions. Given the degree of dependency on data, it is extremely critical to ensure it is secure, accurate and available to continuously support business decisions and actions. Digital security technologies and practices provide assurance on four critical attributes of information security—availability, integrity, confidentiality and data privacy. Ethics in AI is an emerging frontier of digital security.

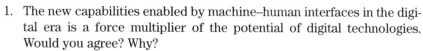

Discussion Questions

1. The new capabilities enabled by machine–human interfaces in the digital era is a force multiplier of the potential of digital technologies. Would you agree? Why?
2. What are the distinguishing characteristics of structured data, semi-structured data and unstructured data? Recall a few examples of each category of data from your personal experience.
3. The three forces of variety, volume and velocity are driving the digital data revolution. Try a thought experiment to envision an alternate universe where only one or any two of these forces were in action. Would the digital data revolution look different? What would be the hypothetical implications for businesses?
4. Although digital security is relevant and important in every technology element, why is it important for managers to understand and address it as a distinct element?
5. Why is data privacy important today? Do you expect the people's willingness to trade-off more of their privacy for greater convenience and economic benefit to change over a period of time? Why?
6. What are the salient characteristics of the following digital technology elements in the digital era when compared to the pre-digital era?
   a. Interfaces
   b. Data management
   c. Digital security
7. What to expect in the foreseeable future with respect to the evolution of the following digital technology elements?
   a. Interfaces
   b. Data management
   c. Digital security

GLOSSARY

Appliance: Appliances are special-purpose computers that are built with integrated hardware, software and firmware to provide a specific computing capability. Some examples of devices are storage appliances, network appliances (to provide firewall protection, network security, etc.), IoT gateway, appliances and so on.[8]

GDPR: GDPR stands for General Data Protection Regulation. It is a European privacy framework that is based on the idea of privacy as a fundamental human right.

JSON[9]: JSON stands for JavaScript Object Notation. It is a data format used to store semi-structured data. It is in human-readable form in which data is stored in attribute-value pairs.

LiDAR: LiDAR is used as an acronym for light detection and ranging. It is a method used for measuring distances by using light illumination of the targets. It is one of the promising technologies that have potential in autonomous vehicles serving as the eye of the vehicle. LiDAR has potential in diverse fields such as agriculture and terrain mapping.[10]

Petabyte, exabyte, zettabyte: These are the units of data size. Digital data sizes are defined in bits and bytes. A bit is a single binary digit, and 8 bits make up a byte. Multiple byte units are defined in powers of 10. For example, 10^3 is called a kilobyte in the decimal-metric system. In this system, a petabyte equals 10^{15} bytes, an exabyte equals 10^{18} bytes, and a zettabyte equals 10^{21} bytes.[11]

NOTES

1. https://www.forbes.com/sites/joshbersin/2012/08/16/the-move-from-systems-of-record-to-systems-of-engagement/?sh=21ecfec447f5
2. https://www.forbes.com/sites/joshbersin/2012/08/16/the-move-from-systems-of-record-to-systems-of-engagement/?sh=21ecfec447f5
3. https://blogs.oracle.com/bigdata/structured-vs-unstructured-data
4. https://cloud.google.com/bigquery
5. https://cloud.google.com/blog/products/data-analytics/new-blog-series-bigquery-explained-overview
6. https://www.automationanywhere.com/products/botstore
7. https://www.iso.org/isoiec-27001-information-security.html
8. https://en.wikipedia.org/wiki/Computer_appliance
9. https://en.wikipedia.org/wiki/Semi-structured_data
10. https://www.geospatialworld.net/blogs/why-lidar-is-important-for-autonomous-vehicle/
11. https://en.wikipedia.org/wiki/Byte

Composite Technologies

Learning Objectives

Chapters 6, 7 and 8 are focused on demystifying the various digital computing technologies in the context of digital transformation strategies for businesses. These three chapters provide a managerial abstraction of digital technologies that helps map the technological underpinnings of digital transformation. Chapters 6 and 7 focus on elemental categories of digital technologies based on the nature of capabilities they enable for business. Chapter 8 focuses on composite technologies built from a combination of the elemental technologies covered in Chapters 6 and 7. At the end of Chapters 8, the students will learn the following:

- Important definitions related to composite technologies covered in this chapter
- How the first-order capabilities discussed in Chapter 6 are brought to bear in composite technologies
- Second and higher-order capabilities enabled by composite technologies
- The elements of digital taxonomy as building blocks of composite technologies
- The following composite technologies are covered in Chapter 8:
  - o The IoT
  - o AI
  - o Blockchain

8.1. INTRODUCTION

Digital technology elements based on first-order capabilities were discussed in Chapters 6 and 7. These technology elements can be used singularly or in combination with other technology elements when architecting solutions for addressing business problems. This text uses the term composite technologies to denote distinct technology areas that are built using a combination of individual technology elements of the digital technology taxonomy. The following example scenarios are presented to illustrate how business objectives can be achieved using either individual technology elements or a combination of elements.

Example Scenarios

Consider the case of a business planning to move its enterprise applications from a legacy on-premises infrastructure to a modern cloud infrastructure to reduce costs and increase flexibility. In this case, the solution would involve primarily the *computational* elements discussed in Chapter 6. This scenario is an example of a technology element being singularly used to solve a business problem.

Consider the case of a shipping and logistics company planning to implement advanced analytics capabilities to optimize the scheduling, routing and utilization of its shipping vessels. In this case, the solution could potentially involve a certain level of *instrumentation* in the containers, *communication* capabilities to seamlessly transfer data collected from containers to central planning teams and *data management capabilities* to extract value from new sets of data available to achieve the business objective.

In this chapter, we will present a few composite technologies that are architected from a combination of the foundational elements discussed as part of the digital technology taxonomy. Exhibit 8.1 illustrates three key composite technologies that will be discussed discussed in this chapter. Several composite technologies are emerging through an innovative combination of digital technology elements. Especially when using cloud platforms for solving specific problems like industrial asset management or personal health solutions, a wide variety of composite technology configurations are possible. In this chapter, three composite technologies are selected for discussion based on the scope and scale of use cases and on their potential for creating business value. This chapter is intended to highlight the problem-solving and value-creation potential of composite applications of digital technology elements.

TSG Mini Case Revisited. Scenario 4: Understanding the Positioning of Composite Technologies within the Digital Taxonomy

Manu was enamoured with the taxonomy of digital technologies. He felt that the taxonomy helped in getting a solid grasp of the complex world of digital IT. Before getting into the details of the three chosen technology areas, he wanted to understand how these technology areas fitted into the taxonomy. Ishaan was struck deep in the bottom-up details; he struggled to respond convincingly. Khushi came to his rescue. Khushi had a very solid understanding of IoT due to her control systems background. She opined that the three chosen technology areas are composite in nature, constructed from several elements of the digital taxonomy. She went on to elaborate on her answer, taking the example of IoT. IoT is a composite technology that draws its constituents from all the six digital taxonomy categories, that is, it starts with instrumentation using sensors and actuators, communicates using data networks, accesses compute capability on the cloud and so on. Similarly, AI is built on data processing techniques using a variety of algorithms and depends on high-performance computing for implementing sophisticated algorithms. And so is the case with blockchain, which draws upon various elements from data storage, digital security and computational nodes. As Khushi spoke with immaculate conviction, Manu was convinced, and Aaryan was impressed.

EXHIBIT 8.1 *Composite Digital Technologies Built on the Digital Technology Elements*

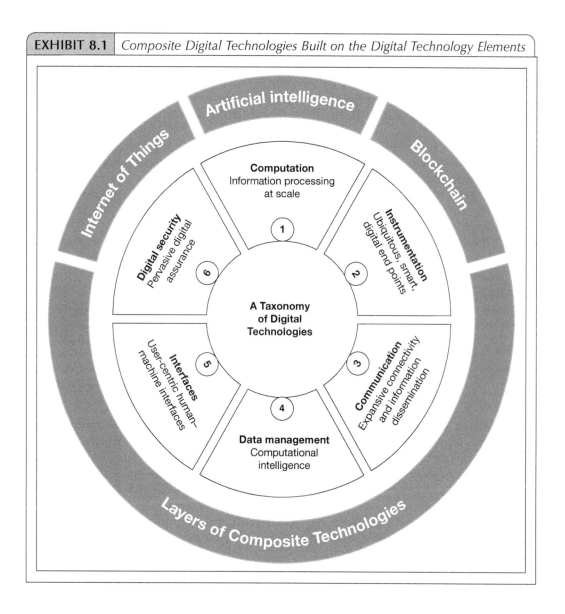

8.2. THE INTERNET OF THINGS (IOT)

IoT is one of the most pervasive and extremely diverse collections of technologies from a digital perspective, and it may be argued that IoT can be anywhere the internet is and is catalyzing the internet to reach physical spaces where it is not already present.

8.2.1. IoT Definitions

Computational devices and communication networks have predated even the internet era. Given a lot of legacy in definitions related to computational devices, it is important to define the distinct elements of IoT to discuss the capabilities enabled by IoT and the applicability of these capabilities for businesses. The ITU provides, at least, four elemental definitions related to IoT, and these definitions form the foundation of the complex and heterogeneous domain of IoT.[1] These four terms are defined as follows:

IoT thing or IoT object[2]**:** With regard to IoT, this is an object of the physical world (physical things) or the information world (virtual things), which is capable of being identified and integrated into communication networks.

IoT device[3]**:** With regard to IoT, this is a piece of equipment with the mandatory capabilities of communication and the optional capabilities of sensing, actuation, data capture, data storage and data processing.

IoT[4]**:** It is a global infrastructure for the information society, enabling advanced services by interconnecting (physical and virtual) things based on existing and evolving interoperable information and communication technologies.

Virtual thing/object in IoT[5]**:** Virtual things exist in the information world and are capable of being stored, processed and accessed. Examples of virtual things include multimedia content and application software. A physical thing may be represented in the information world via one or more virtual things (mapping), but a virtual thing can also exist without any associated physical thing.

8.2.1.1. Types of Things: Reinforcing the Idea of 'Things' in IoT

As mentioned earlier in Chapter 6, digital era instrumentation, which is miniaturized, capable and affordable, arguably creates the vast potential to connect everything to the internet. In this text, the terms IoT thing and IoT object are used interchangeably, and they are the most elementary units of IoT. When a real-world object gets connected to IoT, its digital equivalent (a virtual thing) gets created based on the attributes being measured by the object and its environment. A virtual thing may represent a real-world object, or it could be independent. 'Things' in IoT is a very key construct that is an important part of IoT. Exhibit 8.2 depicts the landscape of things in IoT to reinforce the idea of real and virtual things.

EXHIBIT 8.2 | *Landscape of 'Things' within IoT*

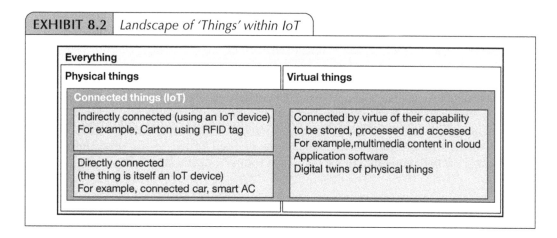

EXHIBIT 8.3 | *First-order Capabilities of an IoT Device*

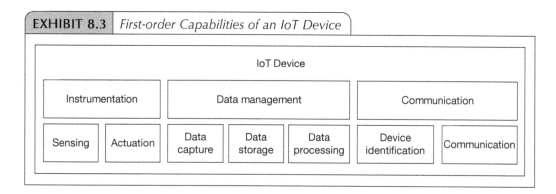

8.2.2. First-order Capabilities of an IoT Device

An IoT device is essentially an 'instrumentation' element. The capabilities of an IoT device can be understood based on the key definitions above and the first-order capabilities discussed in Chapter 6. The first-order capabilities of IoT devices are depicted in Exhibit 8.3. These capabilities enable IoT to generate data that underpin the business value potential of IoT.

There are clearly distinct digital capabilities that are typically part of IoT devices, but they are distinct from conventional computers (such as desktops, laptops and servers). The key difference is that a conventional computer is a general-purpose computing device, while an IoT device is a special purpose computing device. Computation is not the primary function of an IoT device. All things that are a part of IoT are expected to have their own specific function, which gets extended or enhanced through the addition of first-order digital capabilities.

8.2.3. Digital Building Blocks of IoT

In this section, the digital building blocks of IoT are discussed to highlight how the digital technology elements work together in this composite technology. An IoT device receives data from the environment through sensors, processes the data in the context of its specialized function and sends data after processing to actuators which in turn creates changes or executes actions in the environment. During processing, the IoT device could optionally access computational capability either in the Cloud or Edge through the Internet. The IoT system would leverage interfaces like mobile or web browsers for user interaction. Exhibit 8.4 depicts the building blocks of IoT in terms of digital technology elements.

8.2.4. IoT Architecture: A Managerial Abstraction

The power of IoT is underpinned by all the six taxonomical digital technology categories. A managerial abstraction of typical IoT architecture is depicted in Exhibit 8.5. IoT implementations are highly heterogenous from a technology perspective because their typical

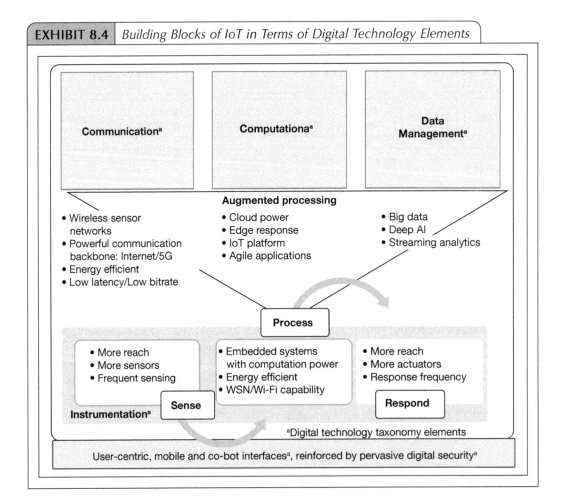

EXHIBIT 8.4 | *Building Blocks of IoT in Terms of Digital Technology Elements*

Communication[a]

Computationa[a]

Data Management[a]

Augmented processing

- Wireless sensor networks
- Powerful communication backbone: Internet/5G
- Energy efficient
- Low latency/Low bitrate

- Cloud power
- Edge response
- IoT platform
- Agile applications

- Big data
- Deep AI
- Streaming analytics

Process

- More reach
- More sensors
- Frequent sensing

- Embedded systems with computation power
- Energy efficient
- WSN/Wi-Fi capability

- More reach
- More actuators
- Response frequency

Sense

Respond

Instrumentation[a]

[a]Digital technology taxonomy elements

User-centric, mobile and co-bot interfaces[a], reinforced by pervasive digital security[a]

EXHIBIT 8.5 | *IoT Architecture: A Managerial Abstraction*

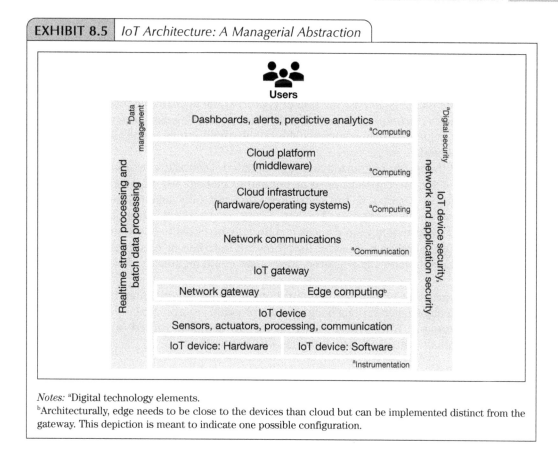

Notes: [a]Digital technology elements.
[b]Architecturally, edge needs to be close to the devices than cloud but can be implemented distinct from the gateway. This depiction is meant to indicate one possible configuration.

implementations leverage highly diverse technologies from all the six taxonomical categories for digital. This section of the text provides an overview of how various technologies are combined to create the first- and second-order capabilities enabled by IoT for business. This section elaborates on the details of various technology elements that drive business value from IoT. The technology elements and the associated capabilities they enable are examined through the lens of the six elements of the digital taxonomy.

8.2.5. Instrumentation

8.2.5.1. First-order Capabilities to Sense and Respond Using IoT

Instrumentation technologies are the last mile link between the digital and the physical world. Digitization of physical things starts with identifying them uniquely in the virtual world. Once identified, one or more virtual representations of the physical thing can be created by defining attributes that characterize the thing in the real world. For example, an air conditioner (AC) installed in a home could be identified with an IP address, connected to the home network, and its identity could be virtualized in a smart home application in the cloud. This virtual thing (a virtual manifestation of the AC) could be characterized by several of its attributes and measured through suitable instrumentation. Some examples of attributes of this connected AC include the state of operations (on/off), mode of operation for the condenser (cooling mode/fan mode, etc.), the temperature of the air, the status of the timer to sleep/start the AC, gas level detection and so on. Such attributes get measured through instrumentation and periodically communicated to the cloud to keep its virtual counterpart updated. Sensors play the role of capturing the measurable physical attributes of things and their environment and sending them for processing using the embedded computation device, which, in turn, communicates the attribute values to the cloud to keep the virtual thing updated.

The physical things are digitalized and kept updated. Digitization enables several computational logics and ML capabilities to be applied to manage IoT objects proactively. As discussed earlier in Chapter 6, the instrumentation not only enables sensing but also enables response through actuation. The act of triggering actions in the physical environment through the instrumentation devices can broadly be classified as actuation like turning on an LED or sounding a speaker. Based on the outcome of computation, necessary responses can be automatically triggered. Responses could include the following actions:

- Notify humans/users (through a smartphone app) for suitable intervention.
- Automatically trigger actions back into the physical environment
  - o For example, LED instrumented on the AC could be turned on to indicate an impending status and attract human intervention.

8.2.6. Integrating an Object in the Physical World into IoT

As discussed in Chapter 6, instrumentation refers to a category of technologies using which the necessary capabilities (identification, communication and computation) for IoT can be embedded into a real-world 'object'. An object can be made part of IoT either directly (using embedded systems) or indirectly (using data-carrying devices like radio-frequency identification [RFID] tags). In some cases, the 'thing' has built-in capabilities essential for IoT (e.g., a smartphone) and these objects function as IoT objects by virtue of themselves being IoT devices without the need for any additional embedded systems or data carrying devices like RFID tags.

8.2.6.1. Embedded Systems

Embedded systems are microcontroller-based computational devices. They are used to add computational intelligence that includes data capturing, data processing and communication capabilities to anything, thereby providing capabilities for the 'thing' to become an IoT object. This idea can be illustrated using the example of a modern-day AC. An AC fulfils its basic function of maintaining an indoor temperature that is different from the outdoor environment. While this is the primary function of an AC, its function has been enhanced by the addition of computational capability in the form of electronic control, which gets exercised using a remote control. This computational capability is made possible through embedded systems that are embedded into the AC to add the computational capability to the appliance. Such a remote-controlled AC is not yet an IoT device. The mandatory capability for an IoT device is the ability to get identified and integrated into a communication network (more specifically, the internet). Now, by adding a Wi-Fi capability to the remote-controlled AC unit, it makes it an IoT device. Using an embedded system with communication capability is a prominent method to convert any object into an IoT device.

8.2.6.2. Radio-frequency Identification (RFID)[6]

The most used instrumentation in IoT is RFID. An RFID system consists of RFID tags, RFID readers and a host computer system. The basic RFID tag is usually attached to an object which carries an identification code that provides the ability to identify the object it is attached to. An RFID reader is connected to an information or communication network, and it communicates with the tag-based at specific levels of proximity. Thus, an RFID tag, in combination with the RFID reader, helps in indirectly connecting an object to an information network. There are three types of RFID tags: active, semi-passive and passive.

A passive tag is cheaper and smaller than other types of tags since it has no battery. A passive tag uses the radio energy transmitted by a reader. Most of the radio energy from a reader is used for powering the tag, and a very small part of the energy is used for communication/signal transmission. A semi-passive tag has a small battery, and it gets activated in the presence of an RFID reader. An active RFID tag has a battery, and it periodically transmits its ID signal. Semi-passive and active RFID tags can operate with lower power radio signals from RFID readers since they use the battery power for powering the tag and for signal transmission.

8.2.6.3. Communication

IoT objects are connected to each other through device-to-device communication (within a network of IoT devices) or to other IoT devices in other connected information networks or central computational capabilities available in the cloud (or an enterprise data centre). Data captured by IoT devices need to be captured, stored, processed and acted upon to provide second-order or higher-order capabilities for business decision-making and automation. Computational and data management capabilities may be available either within the IoT device (mist computing) or in another computational device attached to the same network (edge computing) or in the cloud (cloud computing). Communication technologies provide capabilities for data flow between devices within the network and between networks. Since IoT connects billions of devices that operate in constrained computational contexts (embedded systems), these devices highly require energy-efficient communication capabilities. The IoT revolution is one of the main driving forces behind the evolution of communication technologies for the digital era discussed in the communication topic in Chapter 6. While most of the communication technologies that power IoT have been discussed in the digital taxonomy section, IoT gateways are an important additional component that requires elaboration here.

8.2.6.4. IoT Gateways[7]

IoT gateways are computational nodes that are part of a network of IoT devices. While devices may have the capability to communicate with one another directly, there are, at least, two scenarios where IoT device communication requires IoT gateways. The two scenarios are (a) when the IoT devices that need to communicate with each other use different protocols for communication or (b) when the communicating IoT devices are not part of the same network and hence require communication across networks to accomplish their communication. Hence, IoT gateways are computational and communication devices that enable two key functions: (a) 'protocol conversion' between devices when the devices use different communication protocols and (b) 'message forwarding' between networks with or without protocol conversion if the devices are not physically close enough to communicate directly.

In many cases, it is far from sufficient for gateways only to perform message forwarding and protocol translation. Gateways often need to run specific application logic to fulfil user requirements. For instance, in one case, a gateway needs to collect data from devices, analyse data and send notifications to IoT applications only if predefined conditions are met. In another case, a gateway needs to collect data from one device and trigger another device to perform some action if predefined conditions are met. These cases can be considered as examples of edge computing. IoT gateways that provide edge computing capabilities make it possible to provide real-time services by executing application logic at the network edge and reducing the stress on both the network and cloud side.

8.2.6.5. Computation

IoT is one of the biggest drivers of growth in data and the concomitant demand for computational power. The computational power can be broadly classified into hardware and software. Hardware required for processing IoT data is also called infrastructure and is available as IaaS in the cloud. Software for IoT can further be classified into platform services (PaaS) and software applications (SaaS). Capabilities provided by IaaS and SaaS categories of computation for IoT are relatively general purpose in nature and they can be understood from the capabilities and concepts discussed under the computation topic in Chapter 6. PaaS capabilities that support IoT are built to address the unique computing requirements of IoT and require elaboration here.

8.2.6.6. IoT Platforms

IoT platforms are a combination of multiple technologies that are brought together for providing a scalable foundation for bridging the diverse universe of IoT devices with that of software applications that are designed with a focus on business processes and outcomes. At a level of abstraction, IoT platforms can be considered a middleware layer that mediates across various hardware and software elements in the IoT architecture, like Instrumentation, Communication, Data Management, Computational Infrastructure, Software Applications and Digital Security. To illustrate the key attributes of an IoT platform, it will be useful to examine the high-level IoT platform offerings of leading cloud platform companies. Exhibit 8.6 depicts a simplified synthesis from the IoT platform offerings for Google Cloud Platform,[8] Amazon Web Services[9] and Azure.[10]

EXHIBIT 8.6	*Illustrative Elements of an IoT Platform and Other Mediated Cloud Services for IoT*

8.2.7. Data Management

IoT is one of the biggest sources of big data. Billions of sensors periodically scanning the environment they operate in produce a near real-time stream of data. The data, thus, collected by IoT has relevance both in real-time (for taking actions based on predefined conditions) and in the longer term where big data from sensors will feed into batch data processing applications such as data science, analytics and reporting, ML and audits. The detailed treatment of the data management topic in Chapter 7 provides the essential perspectives on how it underpins the business value of IoT.

8.2.7.1. Interfaces

Interface technologies deal with human to machine interaction or, in some special cases, physical interaction between machines (e.g., physical transfer of objects between robotic arms). Most of the ideas related to capabilities and trends in interface technologies have been described in adequate detail under the interface topic of digital technologies taxonomy in Chapter 7. As discussed earlier, in Chapter 7, the early phase of the evolution of the digital era was catalysed by touchscreen-based mobile interfaces for interaction between machines and humans. Within a few years of the proliferation of touch-based interfaces, natural language processing (NLP) capabilities matured and gave way to voice-based interfaces, like smart speakers, and voice-based digital assistants, such as Siri and Alexa. Both the touch-based inputs and voice-based interfaces were designed for engaging human beings through interfaces that facilitate modes of engagement that are more natural to human beings. Owing to the success of such natural systems of engagement, several other interface technologies are emerging further to enhance the quality of human engagement with machines. In this section, two frontier technologies, AR and VR, that are expanding the capabilities of human-to-machine interfaces have been described. This text introduces the topics of AR and VR as part of interfaces because these two technologies operate as part of the last mile, which augments user experience at the human-to-machine (smartphone, handheld device, special-purpose glasses, etc.) interface. Additionally, a brief overview of the emerging need for machine-to-machine interfaces has also been included to complete the thinking on interfaces.

AR[11]: It is a set of technologies that augments the real world around a user through juxtaposing additional information/images/animations (augmentation) to an image or a camera feed to enhance the user experience. AR is generally made available as part of an app on a mobile device that provides digital augmentation in the context of the app. One of the fun examples of AR technology is the mobile game Pokémon Go, which uses the built-in features of a mobile device such as GPS and camera to capture, train and battle virtual creatures called Pokémon. Other prominent use cases for AR can be imagined in museums. Another useful and simple use case could be imagined in tourism, to add digital explanations and information to exhibits, enhancing the visitor experience in museums or adding similar text, images and animation overlays on top of places of tourist importance. AR has unlimited potential in education, with a promise to enhance the assimilation of information and understanding of students. Given the promise AR holds, most of the leading cloud platform companies have platform services for building AR applications by providing easy access to common services that accelerate the development of AR applications through APIs for location tracking (GPS), motion tracking, light estimation and so on. AR is one of the easiest means to enhance user experience and value by adding additional experiential elements even to existing general-purpose IoT devices such as mobile phones and tablets.

VR[12]: It provides capabilities for users to experience a reality (primarily through visual and audio) that is synthesized virtually and potentially allows the users to interact with the virtual world objects through intuitive interfaces. The main difference between AR and VR is that AR augments the reality/surroundings of a user with digital content through an IoT device (usually a mobile phone or a tablet), while VR creates an entirely distinct virtual experience for the user (usually through a special purpose interface like VR headsets). The content in VR could either simulate real environments or imaginary environments. The most compelling use cases for VR are being pursued in the entertainment (video games, virtual tourism, etc.) and education sectors (medical/military training or even in immersive learning spaces for educating children). VR application in primary and secondary school education is an area of ongoing research, with concerns related to negative physiological and psychological effects being understood and addressed. VR is a very promising and continuously evolving technology area with diverse approaches to creating the user experience. Some of the interface types used in VR are as follows.

Head-mounted display (HMD)[13]**:** HMD is a display screen in front of the eyes of the user. These HMDs, also called VR headsets, are typically connected to a computational device like a personal computer, smartphone or tablet. These interfaces have high-resolution displays and are also instrumented with several sensors such as pressure, proximity sensor and temperature sensors. They also typically feature wireless connectivity to the computational devices through which they get access to high end computational and data management capabilities from a data centre or cloud-based services. HMDs are the most promising technologies that can provide a very high degree of immersive experience.

Simulators: VR simulators are equipment that includes multiple technologies, including VR glasses, 360° videos and other interfaces for interactivity with the content. Simulators experienced in amusement parks that provide multidimensional VR experience, also called 4D or X-D attractions. From an education and training perspective, simulators have been in use for aeroplane pilot training, which reduces the cost of training and improves the learning process.

Desktop-based VR: One of the simplest manifestations of VR technology is displaying a 3D visualization of the virtual world on a general-purpose computational device like a desktop or laptop. Some of the most commonly available applications can be readily experienced by users on their computer systems. The 3D imagery available on the Google Earth application is a good example of a desktop-based VR application. While this technology is available to anyone with a computer, it is not as immersive or intuitively interactive as the more advanced VR interfaces available in HMD or simulators.

Machine-to-machine interfaces: Since the industrial age, machines have been designed to interact with each other in the physical world, like in the case of a set of robotic arms performing a manufacturing operation in a coordinated fashion. These industrial settings were generally well-controlled, and the machine-to-machine interactions were not challenged to deal with a high degree of uncertainty in an uncontrolled natural world. With the growing number of mobile IoT objects, such as drones, companion robots, robots in the hospitality industry and autonomous cars, a new type of context has been created where machines will need to interact with each other in uncontrolled and natural settings. Several types of sensors and actuators are being developed, which will make machine-to-machine interfaces functional and reliable in natural settings. One instructive example of the evolving future of machine-to-machine interfaces is an IBM patent that outlines mid-air drone-to-drone cargo transfers.[14] Such an interface would have a profound impact on use cases, like drone-based cargo delivery. Drone-based delivery is limited by the range of flying a drone can cover with a single charge of the battery. With the possibility of mid-air drone-to-drone cargo transfer, the range of drone-based delivery becomes practically unlimited since drones can relay the cargo mid-air before each individual drone runs out of its battery charge.

8.2.7.2. Digital Security

Security for IoT inherits all the aspects of information security discussed under the digital security topic of the digital technology taxonomy in Chapter 7. Additionally, there are a few nuances and challenges that need to be understood with respect to security in IoT. Additional security challenges in IoT are highlighted in Exhibit 8.7.

EXHIBIT 8.7 | *Salient Security Challenges and Mitigation Approaches in IoT*

Security Aspect	Description	Mitigation Approaches
Design-level vulnerabilities	Billions of IoT devices get manufactured every year, and most of these are relatively very cheap. The quality of these devices may not be up to the mark, and they may have more security vulnerabilities and are prone to easy tampering, impacting the integrity and confidentiality of data from these devices.	Qualifying the suppliers adequately and ensuring quality at the source are one of the most effective approaches to mitigating this security issue. This could be dealt with at a policy level with adequate governance within enterprises to ensure any team that procures IoT components follows stipulated vendor selection and procurement process.
Firmware maintenance	The firmware used in the embedded systems that are a part of billions of IoT instrumentation will require to be maintained with the latest version of firmware and related patches from manufacturers. This is a humongous challenge given the volume, variety and distribuends of IoT devices.	Selecting relatively homogenous embedded system vendors and governing release management of firmware upgrades and patch management through standardized IT operations processes are key to mitigating this aspect of device security. The network architecture and the overall system design also play a crucial role in the seamless deployment and automation of firmware maintenance.
Physical security	Physically securing highly distributed implementation of IoT devices to protect from theft and physical damages.	Physical security of IoT devices is beyond the scope of this text, but it involves not only the fabrication and mounting of IoT devices but also dependent on the environment in which the devices are installed.

8.3. ARTIFICIAL INTELLIGENCE (AI)

AI is the simulation of human intelligence in machines. There are several techniques that are used for problem-solving at varying levels of complexity. The most dominant and effective techniques that have resulted in creating tremendous business value is supervised ML. Before getting into the details of this technique, this section will provide a bird's eye view of various AI definitions and capabilities.

The inspiration for AI technologies is the human brain. With a limited or incomplete scientific understanding of how the human brain works, the comparison between mainstream AI technologies and the human brain are superficial at best. However, conceptually, there are a few definitions that define AI capabilities as a continuum in terms of the degree to which AI could mimic natural human intelligence. It is important to clarify that these are mere conceptual constructs, and not all of them manifest yet in real-life, and most of them are not even deemed technically feasible. With this background, AI is generally classified into three phases of evolution and defined based on the extent to which each technology mimics human intelligence. They are as follows.

8.3.1. Conceptual Continuum of AI Capabilities

Within the context described above, AI is generally classified into three phases of evolution and defined based on the extent to which each technology mimics human intelligence. They are as follows:

Artificial narrow intelligence (ANI): ANI, also known as weak AI, is the foundation of AI. It is about performing a tightly defined set of tasks. Most use cases of AI today, including autonomous cars, swarm drones, conversational agents, such as Siri and Alexa, are examples of weak AI.

Artificial general intelligence (AGI): AGI, also known as Strong AI, is the stage where machines will possess the ability to believe and make conclusions like human beings. Currently, there are no working business/commercial examples of this possibility. A survey of experts published in 2016 has a median estimate of the period 2040–2050 for high-level machine intelligence to become a reality (Müller & Bostrom, 2016).

Artificial superintelligence (ASI): ASI is the stage of evolution where AI will completely mimic human intelligence. Currently, there are no working business/commercial examples of this possibility. A survey of experts published in 2016 predicts a lead time of fewer than 30 years after high-level machine intelligence is achieved for superintelligence to become a reality (Müller & Bostrom, 2016).

8.3.2. Machine Learning (ML)

The remaining part of this section is focused on ML, a subset of AI techniques that are creating tremendous economic value or have the potential to do so in the foreseeable future. Conventional computer programming involves providing inputs to the programme in the form of data/input variables and steps or algorithms (a function of input variables) to process the data and accomplish the desired task. For example, steps involved in a billing software could include the following three sets of inputs (1, 2 and 3) and then generate an output (4).

1. The catalogue of items with their prices
2. A function/formula for calculating the prices after applying due taxes and discounts
3. The list of items purchased by a customer
4. Generate the bill as an output using the data and the rules/formulae

This simple computational task does not involve any learning on the part of the computer programme. This can be used to automate the bill generation process for as many customers as needed if the rules/formulae do not change. Such a programmatic approach is not suitable for highly complex tasks for which it is not easy for a human expert to codify all the rules of data processing for a given task at hand. For example, when a diagnostic radiologist examines a medical image, the process is fuzzy, which could involve the following:

1. Observation of the image
2. Apply the knowledge based on their training and expertise
3. Document the factual observations
4. Arrive at a diagnostic decision on whether the medical image indicates an underlying medical abnormality
5. Present the diagnosis qualified with probabilities

If a programming goal is set to codify what the radiologist is looking for in the image (i.e., the rules of image processing), then it will be humanly impossible or extremely difficult to codify all aspects of how the image is processed by the radiologist before making their decision. For such complex tasks, ML is a modern approach to developing computer programmes that learn from data without being explicitly programmed with rules. Another way to think about ML is that it is a category AI of techniques that can be used for function approximation. A function approximation that would try to recognize patterns of relationship between independent (X) and dependent variables (Y).

8.3.3. Digital Building Blocks of ML

In this section, the digital building blocks of ML are discussed to highlight how the digital technology elements work together in this composite technology. ML receives data of independent variables (X), with or without corresponding known dependent variables (Y). With the data, ML is applied in two stages. The first stage is training: ML happens by training algorithms using the input data. The output of the first step is a trained ML model or a function that defines the relationship between X and Y. The second stage is to deploy the output from the first step (trained ML model) as part of applications to perform prediction or automation to determine Y for a given set of X's. These two stages leverage various digital technology elements, as depicted in Exhibit 8.8.

EXHIBIT 8.8 | *Digital Building Blocks of ML*

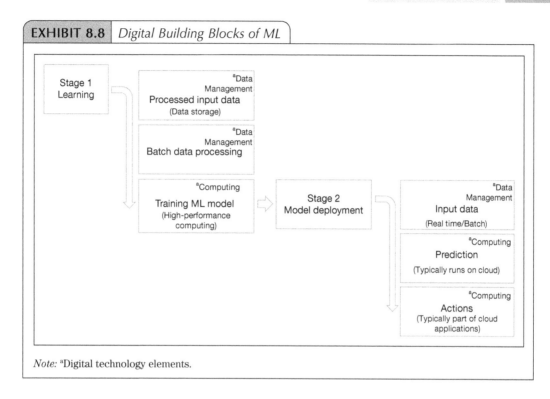

Note: ªDigital technology elements.

8.3.4. Types of ML

This task of pattern recognition can be made to occur either based on known sets of valid X and Y mapping or based only on X values without any knowledge of Y. ML can be classified into various types based on the following key characteristics of the learning process.

1. Types/combinations of inputs to an ML problem (i.e., both X and Y as inputs, only X as input)
2. Type of human feedback during the learning processes
3. Mechanics of the learning process (i.e., the process by which the computer programme discovers the rules for achieving the given computational objective)

Four types of ML approaches are at a reasonable level of maturity, and they find widespread applications in solving business problems or addressing business opportunities. They are as follows:

1. Supervised learning
2. Unsupervised learning
3. Reinforcement learning
4. NLP

8.3.4.1. Supervised Learning

Supervised learning is an ML paradigm in which the computer programme is provided with data that has the inputs along with the desired outputs. In other words, the input has data along with associated labels of 'correct' answers. When supervised learning is executed on this data along with a predefined structure (ML model) for learning the rules, the learning programme learns the parameters of the formulae in each structure. Once an adequate level of data is used to train the programme or learn the parameters, then the resulting formulae/model can be used to make predictions on input data for which the answer or classification is not known. Revisiting the example of medical imaging, the following steps provide a brief overview of the ML process.

- The input data will include a set of medical images and their corresponding classification (labelling) by a radiologist.
- An ML model should be trained adequately, say with thousands of images and their corresponding labels.
- Once the parameters of the model are learnt, then the model can be used to make the diagnosis for new sets of medical images, assisting the radiologist with a quicker and more accurate diagnosis.

There are several variations and approaches to building an ML model. Some of the most used and effective are neural networks, deep neural networks and recursive neural networks and so on. There are several nuances involved in choosing the model structure, the amount of training data, testing for errors and so on, which are beyond the scope of this text. The broad idea this text strives to emphasize is that supervised ML is a paradigm shift in computer programming. A shift that makes it possible for machines to learn the relationship between the input data and the predicted output data through supervised ML models. Most of the advancements in AI are applied in businesses, and the resulting economic value can be attributed to this one basic idea of supervised ML.

8.3.4.2. Unsupervised Learning

Unsupervised learning is an ML approach where input provided to the ML system only has data and not labels, and the output is that the programme explores the data and finds hidden patterns. Cluster analysis is one of the most used unsupervised learning approaches. Cluster analysis is also an illustrative technique that can help in understanding how unsupervised learning is different from supervised learning. In cluster analysis, an unlabelled data set is provided as an input, and the algorithm analyses the data and identifies clusters of similar data, thereby attempting to identify classes of input variables. The details of these unsupervised learning techniques are beyond the scope of this text. However, it is important to understand that unsupervised learning is used significantly in exploratory data analysis and is yet to create a large-scale impact on economic value creation in comparison to supervised learning.

8.3.4.3. Reinforcement Learning

Both supervised learning and unsupervised learning use a snapshot of data to learn or discover a classification decision automatically. The classification-based approach is tuned to discover an approximation of the relationship between X and Y variables. Reinforcement learning is a completely different paradigm whose primary purpose is to learn to make sequences of good decisions automatically. The goal for reinforcement learning is not pattern recognition, but instead, it focuses on building a type of temporal intelligence that tries to make a sequence of optimal decisions to accomplish a goal in multiple steps. One other distinct characteristic of reinforcement learning is the concept of reward. When the learning algorithm makes a decision, a human agent provides an additional input in the form of a reward or penalty based on the quality of the decision made by the algorithm. The algorithm is set up to maximize rewards, and hence, depending on the combination of an automatic decision made by the algorithm in the previous step and the reward/penalty from the human agent based on the decision, the next step tries another decision and again gets a reward or a penalty. This is the process of reinforcement learning where a reward or a penalty guides the algorithm to improve the decision it automatically makes. Reinforcement learning has potential in the application domains of robotics and gaming. AlphaGo is a computer programme built using deep learning and reinforcement learning techniques that achieved the feat of beating champion players (humans) at the game of Go. This is a landmark achievement because the attempt to beat human champions has not been very successful with other AI techniques. Reinforcement learning significantly contributed to advancing the goal of computer programmes beating human champions in this classical strategy game of Go.

8.3.4.4. Natural Language Processing (NLP)

NLP is an interdisciplinary field whose goal is to enable computers to comprehend natural language as used by humans computationally. Computational processing of natural language has attracted the attention of scientific researchers for several decades. NLP has evolved based on the computational capabilities of various technology eras. The state-of-the-art in NLP applications today heavily leverage the multiple ML approaches. NLP leverages the function approximation concepts from supervised and unsupervised learning. NLP is today effectively used in economic value, adding use cases such as speech recognition, transcription, language translation, intent parsing, sentiment analytics and language generation. Conversational agent or chatbot technologies are an effective application of NLP.

8.4. BLOCKCHAIN

Blockchain is a decentralized, encrypted ledger technology with an inbuilt security mechanism that makes the data stored in a blockchain practically tamperproof. The core aspects that underpin the properties of a blockchain are as follows:

1. Data are stored in blocks with encrypted identification.
2. All changes to the data are preserved chronologically through cross-referencing blocks.
3. Multiple copies of the chains of data blocks are stored in a peer-to-peer (P2P) network of nodes.
4. Any change to the chain requires consensus among the nodes in the P2P network.

This section is focused on describing the above attributes of blockchain technology to enable managers to appreciate the underpinnings of its capabilities.

8.4.1. Structure and Mechanism of Blockchain

Blockchain is a type of database in which data is stored in blocks and chained together as chronological blocks using a form of encryption called a hash. Each block has three pieces of information (a) data, (b) hash of the block and (c) hash of the previous block. Exhibit 8.9 provides a simplified depiction of a blockchain structure.

Hash for a block is computed by passing data from the block through an encryption function. A hash is calculated as a function of the data contained in the block, and it uniquely identifies a block and its contents. The hash of the previous block (parent hash) is the link between the blocks and thus forms a chain of blocks in a blockchain. A blockchain is valid only when the hash and parent hashes of every block in the blockchain are valid. The simple yet powerful implications of this hash and parent hash are as follows:

1. When the contents of a block get changed, its hash needs to be updated.
2. When a hash in a block is updated, then the hash reference in subsequent blocks needs to be updated to preserve the validity of the blockchain.

If the blockchain is stored and managed centrally by an organization, then it is not difficult to alter the contents of a block and update its hash and the parent hashes in the subsequent blocks in the chain. This possibility is avoided in a distributed configuration where a copy of the blockchain is stored in multiple nodes/computers owned by different owners that participate in the network. If a node wants to add a block to the blockchain or make any changes to the blockchain, it must pass the consensus mechanism. The consensus mechanism where most other nodes in the P2P network vote on/agree on the validity of the

| EXHIBIT 8.9 | *Simplified Representation of Blockchain Structure* |

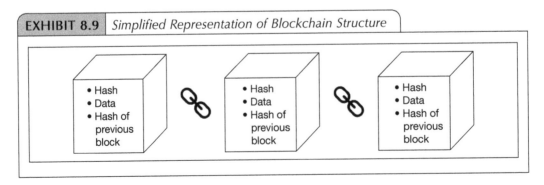

transaction. Once consensus is reached, the change/transaction is executed by the node, and distributed copies of the blockchain are updated.

8.4.2. Digital Building Blocks of Blockchain

In this section, the digital building blocks of a block are discussed to highlight how the digital technology elements work together in this composite technology. The building blocks may be understood in two stages. The first stage is the structure of a blockchain, and the second is the mechanism of a transaction in a distributed blockchain network.

In the structure of a blockchain, at least three digital elements work together, which are as follows:

1. The format and structure of data in blocks is built on data management technologies, manifesting as a new type of semi-structured data.
2. The creation of a hash to identify the block leveraged cryptography approaches from digital security.
3. When copies of the blockchain are stored in a distributed P2P network, communication technologies get leveraged.

In the mechanism of a transaction in a blockchain network, at least three digital elements work together as follows:

1. Execution of the consensus mechanism leveraged computational technologies. Nodes participating in a blockchain may be functionally equivalent to edge computing devices.
2. Validation of a new transaction using the hashes leverages digital security approaches.
3. When the valid transaction is updated across the network, communication technologies are leveraged.

The building blocks discussed above are depicted in Exhibit 8.10.

8.4.3. Types of Blockchains

Blockchain deployments require a network of nodes (owned by individuals or organizations) that participate in storing the blockchain, perform validations as part of the consensus mechanism and optionally initiate transactions to make changes/add blocks to the blockchain. Blockchain deployments are classified based on the nature of network nodes that can participate in the network. Two key deployment attributes that determine the type of blockchain network are public versus private and permissioned versus permission-less.

Public deployments are open for anyone to participate, while private deployments are controlled networks in which members of designated organizations or consortiums can participate.

Permissioned deployments require the participants to meet certain predefined criteria, while permission-less deployments do not have any predefined criteria for participation.

Types of blockchains based on the criteria discussed above are depicted in Exhibit 8.11.

EXHIBIT 8.10 *Digital Building Blocks of Blockchain*

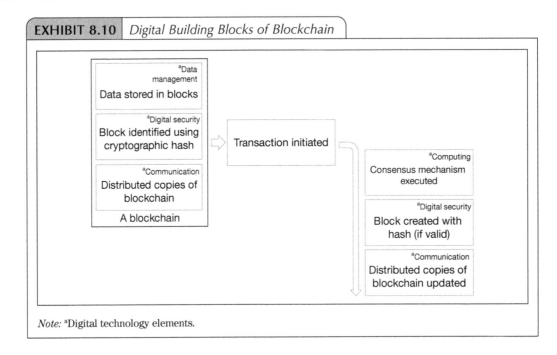

Note: [a]Digital technology elements.

EXHIBIT 8.11 *Types of Blockchain Deployments*

	Public	**Private**
Permission-less	**Who can participate?** Anyone can participate **Consensus mechanism** Proof of work **Examples** • Bitcoin (cryptocurrency) • Ethereum (cryptocurrency, smart contract)	**Who can participate?** Authorized, for example, members of a consortium **Consensus mechanism** Federated Byzantine Agreement **Examples** • Holochain • Monet
Permissioned	**Who can participate?** Based on predefined criteria **Consensus mechanism** Multiple mechanisms (called proof of stake) **Examples** • Sovrin (digital identity) • EOS (smart contract) • Ripple (settlement, currency exchange, remittance)	**Who can participate?** Anyone who is part of the private network **Consensus mechanism** Voting/Multi-party consensus **Examples** • IBM trade lens • Enterprise Ethereum Alliance

Public blockchains hold the greatest disruptive potential based on their potential to provide trust assurance in P2P transactions. Public blockchains are harder to implement as they require a substantial ecosystem to build organically without any central authority. But they have a long gestation period and sustained support from the government, corporate and consumer ecosystems to develop. In recent years, 'enterprise blockchains' have captured the imagination of innovative companies and start-ups. Enterprise blockchains are typically private and permissioned. They are comparable to private clouds, which improve the manageability and time to value by increasing the control over the resources and supporting participants within the bounds of an enterprise or a consortium of enterprises. Enterprise blockchains promise to improve the quality of products, customer service and customer experience. Given the challenges in developing thriving public blockchain ecosystems, the immediate value of blockchain is likely to be unlocked using enterprise blockchains.

8.4.4. Examples of Enterprise Blockchains

Trade lens is a supply chain platform based on blockchain. It was jointly developed by IBM and GTD Solutions. This platform promises to reduce trade friction by enabling information sharing and collaboration across the supply chain.[15]

IBM Food Trust is a supply chain solution based on blockchain for the food industry. It promises to assure brand trust and food safety through the traceability of food products along the entire supply chain. It also promises to improve supply chain efficiencies by reducing waste.[16]

Plastic Bank has built a blockchain-based backbone to create a regenerative, inclusive and circular plastic economy.[17] Working with Plastic Bank, Henkel has helped to collect over 750,000 kilograms of plastic waste through its ecosystem in Haiti.[18]

8.5. THE FRONTIER OF EMERGING DIGITAL TECHNOLOGIES

Chapters 6, 7, and 8 introduced digital technologies and how they enable new capabilities for business. Digital technologies are evolving very fast, and it would not be surprising to encounter new digital breakthroughs that enhance their transformative potential to business. There are several technologies emerging on the horizon that have exponential potential to add newer capabilities. For example, quantum computing has the potential to disrupt computing and would trivialize the high-performance computing and supercomputing of this digital era. Similarly, low earth orbit (LEO) systems will impose a paradigm shift in how communication happens at the scale of our planet. Due to the high velocity of technology evolution, practising managers would do well to keep up with the emerging trends and educate themselves proactively about emerging business potential from frontier digital technologies. Exhibit 8.12 depicts the continuous evolution of digital taxonomy and composite technologies influenced by the frontier of emerging digital technologies.

EXHIBIT 8.12	*Digital Taxonomy and Composite Technologies Juxtaposed with the Frontier of Emerging Digital Technologies*

SUMMARY

This chapter builds on the six technology elements presented in Chapters 6 and 7 and introduces the idea of composite technologies. The technology elements could be understood and used independently for addressing specific business requirements. Sometimes, these elements are combined in systematic ways to create what we call composite technologies. There are several composite technologies, and there is an ongoing innovation that is resulting in a growing number of composite technologies. The following three high impact composite technologies are discussed in detail in this chapter.

IoT: It is one of the most pervasive and extremely diverse collection of technologies from a digital perspective, and it may be argued that IoT can be anywhere the internet is and is catalyzing the internet to reach physical spaces where it is not already present. This chapter discussed in detail how the six technology elements presented as part of the digital taxonomy in Chapter 6 are systematically combined in IoT. The first- and second-order capabilities are enabled by IoT is also presented in detail.

AI: It is the simulation of human intelligence in machines. An overview of a continuum of possible levels of AI is discussed in this chapter. A specific category of AI, ANI is already a reality and is already being deployed productively in businesses.

ML is a subset of AI techniques that is creating tremendous economic value or has the potential to do so in the foreseeable future. The building blocks of ML are discussed to highlight how the digital technology elements have been systematically combined to create this composite technology.

An overview of the following categories of ML techniques has been covered in this chapter.

1. Supervised learning
2. Unsupervised learning
3. Reinforcement learning
4. NLP

Blockchain: Blockchain is a decentralized, encrypted ledger technology with an inbuilt security mechanism which makes the data stored in a blockchain practically tamper-proof. This chapter also briefly covers the digital building blocks that constitute this composite technology. Blockchain draws its power from a clever combination of technologies and the architecture used for its implementation (distributed and decentralized). These nuances are discussed briefly as part of the structure and mechanism of blockchains.

Based on types of deployment configurations, blockchain is classified into four types. These deployment configurations and their relative merits are presented in this chapter.

Finally, the chapter concludes with a brief discussion on the frontier of emerging digital technologies and what managers should anticipate and prepare for as the future unfolds at this frontier.

Discussion Questions

1. What are composite technologies? Give a few examples.
2. What are the key terms that define IoT?
3. What are the digital building blocks of IoT? How each element of the digital taxonomy powers IoT?
4. LP-WAN is one of the most disruptive technologies that enhances the potential of IoT. Would you agree? Why?

(Continued)

(Continued)

5. Theoretically, what are the various degrees of AI?
6. Define ML.
7. What are the digital building blocks of ML?
8. What are the differences between supervised ML and unsupervised ML?
9. Define the structure and mechanism of operation of blockchains.
10. What are the digital building blocks of blockchain?
11. What are the various deployment configurations of blockchain? What are their relative merits?
12. Conduct a secondary research on quantum computing (a technology emerging at the frontier of digital technologies) and discuss its potential impact on the future of computing.

GLOSSARY

5G: 5G is the fifth generation of cellular communication networks. A 5G-based communication allows high throughput/data volume to be communicated at low latency, with higher reliability and massive network capacity. This expands new frontiers of possibilities with wireless communication.[19]

Emotion AI: It is a branch of computer science that deals with detecting emotions using AI. Computers with this capability can comprehend emotions expressed in human communication.[20]

LEO systems: LEO stands for low earth orbit. LEO systems are communication systems used for data communication and use satellites that operate in low earth orbits in the range of 500 to 2,000 miles above the earth's surface.[21]

Quantum computing: It is a branch of computer science that deals with developing computers that are based on quantum theory principles. One of the main differences between quantum computing and traditional digital computing is that information is represented using two states or binary form (0 and 1) in a digital computer, while information can be expressed in more than two states in a quantum computer.[22]

NOTES

1. https://www.itu.int/rec/T-REC-Y.2060-201206-I/en
2. Ibid.
3. Ibid.
4. Ibid.
5. Ibid.
6. https://www.itu.int/en/ITU-D/Regional-Presence/ArabStates/Documents/events/2017/IoTSMW/Presentations-IoT/Session7/IoT4SSC_Session_7_Benjillali.pdf
7. https://www.itu.int/rec/T-REC-Y.4418-201806-I/en
8. https://cloud.google.com/solutions/iot
9. https://aws.amazon.com/iot/solutions/

10. https://docs.microsoft.com/en-gb/azure/?product<hig>=</hig>iot
11. https://en.wikipedia.org/wiki/Augmented_reality
12. https://en.wikipedia.org/wiki/Virtual_reality
13. https://en.wikipedia.org/wiki/Head-mounted_display
14. https://newsroom.ibm.com/2017-04-28-IBM-Inventors-Patent-Invention-for-Transferring-Packages-between-Aerial-Drones
15. https://www.tradelens.com/about
16. https://www.ibm.com/in-en/blockchain/solutions/food-trust
17. https://plasticbank.com/about/
18. https://plasticbank.com/client/henkel
19. https://www.gartner.com/en/information-technology/glossary/5g
20. https://hai.stanford.edu/news/can-artificial-intelligence-map-our-moods
21. https://www.mckinsey.com/industries/aerospace-and-defense/our-insights/large-leo-satellite-constellations-will-it-be-different-this-time
22. https://www.bcg.com/en-in/capabilities/digital-technology-data/emerging-technologies/quantum-computing

REFERENCE

Müller, V. C., & Bostrom, N. (2016). Future progress in artificial intelligence: A survey of expert opinion. In *Fundamental issues of artificial intelligence*, 555–572. Springer.

Platform Strategies

Chapters 6, 7 and 8 defined digital technologies and their role in digital transformation across business, governance and society. We also covered BMI in Chapter 4. This chapter focuses on 'platforms', which combine digital technologies to create a new business model that is ubiquitous and integral to today's businesses. By the end of the chapter, readers will be able to understand:

- History of sharing economy
- Platforms' evolution
- Classification of platforms
- Multisided platforms
- Platform native versus platform transitioned
- Leadership challenges with platforms
- Risks with platforms

Mini Case 9.1

Enel SpA (https://www.enel.com), an Italian energy company with a significant footprint in Europe and South America, was a leader in the energy industry serving millions of consumers. The company had an impressive record in leveraging renewables. In 2004, it became the first private company in the renewable power sector to be listed on the Dow Jones Sustainability Index. The company was also at the front of digitalization by introducing the world's first smart metres in 2001. Today, Enel Group is truly a global company extending to North America, Asia, Africa and Oceania. It is no longer just another power company and stands out from its peers with a ~100 Billion USD market valuation. What did the Enel Group do differently from its competitors? How did the company change its business model? What kind of a platform can an energy company build? How did its platform strategy influence the value to its customers and shareholders?

9.1. HISTORY OF SHARING ECONOMY

Sharing economy is a P2P sharing concept where individuals borrow goods from each other rather than owning them, with complementary objectives of (a) monetizing the unutilized assets and (b) avoiding owning an asset with an expected utilization of significantly less than 100%. Thus, sharing economy is also referred to as collaborative consumption.

In human history, 'sharing' dates back to the later era of the Pleistocene Epoch; always on the move, hunter-gatherers shared their food among them as the only way of living together. Sam Bowles (2003), professor at MIT, writes, 'If you didn't share, you'd be violating a basic social norm.'

As the human race progressed and moved from being hunters to farmers, private ownership of property was supposed to have existed about 11,000 years ago. However, there was a concept of 'commons' or 'common land' practised for the land, as evidenced in the world's different regions. Interestingly, in England and Wales, the land was distributed as strips to share farming tools easily. Overall, such sharing practices promoted the survival and co-existence of societies.

Things started to change drastically as society progressed further and embraced industrialization. Today, it is almost unthinkable that any part of our planet is not owned by an individual, city, state or nation. However, as society grows to be more conscious of the impact on the environment, depletion of natural resources, inequalities and the high cost of living, the concept of a sharing economy is becoming more prominent. With the advent of digital technologies in the post-internet era, collaborative consumption is taking centre stage and evolving in different shapes.

There is no single clear definition of sharing economy. However, Authors Oksana Gerwe and Rosario Silva, in their 2020 article in *Academy of Management Perspectives*, summarized some of the definitions of sharing economy from the extant literature which are given in Exhibit 9.1.

EXHIBIT 9.1 | *Definitions of Sharing Economy*

Author(s)	Definition
Botsman (2013)	An economic model based on sharing underutilized assets from spaces to skills to stuff for monetary or non-monetary benefits.
Belk (2014)	There are two commonalities in sharing and collaborative consumption practices: (a) use of temporary access non-ownership models of utilizing consumer goods and services and (b) reliance on the internet, and especially Web 2.0, differently from collaborative consumption; in sharing activities, there is no compensation involved.
Stephany (2015)	Sharing economy is the value in taking underutilized assets and making them accessible online to a community, leading to a reduced need for ownership of those assets.
Schor (2016)	Sharing economy activities fall into four broad categories: recirculation of goods, increased utilization of durable assets, exchange of services and sharing of productive assets.

(Continued)

(Continued)

Author(s)	Definition
Frenken and Schor (2017)	Consumers granting each other temporary access to underutilized physical assets (idle capacity), possibly for money.
Mair and Reischauer (2017)	We define the sharing economy as a web of markets. Individuals use various forms of compensation to transact the redistribution and access to resources, mediated by an organization's digital platform.

Source: Gerwe and Silva (2020).

The definitions, as given in Exhibit 9.1, of sharing economy in the academic literature, even though varied, have standard components which can be listed as follows.

- **P2P-based activity:** Where two parties or individuals directly collaborate for exchange, consumption or production of goods or services without intervention of third party or business entity.
- **Under-utilized assets:** Broadly refer to resources whose utilization is below their normal limits or capabilities; can be leveraged for similar or other functions/uses by others beyond the owners of the resources.
- **Monetary or non-monetary rewarding mechanisms:** Could be either monetary, tangible cash or its equivalent, or non-monetary, whose cash value may not be predetermined or may vary over time.
- **Market and non-market logics:** Markets are established (or emerging) structures in place, whereas non-market logics refer to practices such as sharing, lending and exchange of information.
- **Collaborative consumption versus pure sharing:** Collaborative consumption focuses on common access versus ownership, and normally parties involved are users themselves.
- **Temporary access or ownership:** Individuals or parties involved in the transaction provide each other with temporary ownership or access.
- **Technology enabled:** Technology infrastructure is a key enabler for awareness, community building and transactions.

9.2. PLATFORMS' EVOLUTION

Technology progress is accelerating the adoption of platforms. The presence of a platform is ubiquitous today as we experience these as individuals in our personal and professional lives. The rapid expansion of capabilities in digital technologies combined with sharing economy principles led to evolutionary progress in platform thinking.

The term platform has primarily come into management literature from the technology implementation area and is defined as: 'The extensible codebase of a software-based system that provides core functionality shared by the modules that interoperate with it and the interfaces through which they interoperate' (Tiwana et al., 2010).

However, a platform as a concept has been in existence in automotive and other manufacturing industries for a long time. In the automotive industry, car manufacturers have adapted this concept extensively. For example, they use the same chassis for multiple car models, reduce cost and complexity, and launch newer versions or models in the shortest time in the market.

Marketplaces, or two-sided markets, have also been in existence for thousands of years. We are familiar with ancient marketplaces in different civilizations and geographies where people exchanged their produce or art and craft in fairs, bazaars and so on, which typically served as two-sided markets. Today's shopping malls are a modern version of these marketplaces and perform the same purpose by functioning as a platform for multiple brick-and-mortar companies to service their *most common* consumers. Platforms of today are marketplaces, which encompass sharing economy principles and are built on the foundation of digital technologies.

We discussed digital technologies and the exponential progress made in hardware, software and network technologies in the previous chapters. Such improvement in global digital technology infrastructure has influenced platforms' popularity and growth as a business model. We will cover this in detail in the following section.

9.3. PLATFORM BUSINESS

Platform business is a type of business model, as discussed in Chapter 4 (Business Model Innovation). The platform business's primary focus is enabling the interactions between buyers or producers with sellers or consumers of goods or services (Exhibit 9.2). It is generally expected to be on a large scale. Given the adoption of technologies by both consumers and industries, these interactions are primarily digital and enabled by continuously evolving global digital infrastructure and footprint. Platform businesses, or simply referred to as platforms, are marketplaces that are enabled by digital technologies.

Platform businesses are mostly established as digital-native companies or born out of traditional brick-and-mortar industries' strategic digital initiatives. Platforms connect consumers (individuals or groups) and businesses (small or large) to exchange or share common resources. With the rapid growth of the internet and mobile connectivity, online digital platforms have become ubiquitous today. These online platforms have become intermediaries connecting people and products or services. Amazon, Google and Facebook are the most famous examples of the platforms. There are many different types and sizes of platform companies today, and they are continuously evolving.

The platform provides the infrastructure and governance for the marketplace. It helps define, set and monitor who can engage in the platform, what roles they are allowed to perform, how or with whom they can interact and so on. These standards or rules are established to facilitate interaction, collaboration and coordination among all the platform stakeholders.

Producers and consumers can exchange their roles or play both roles at the same time.

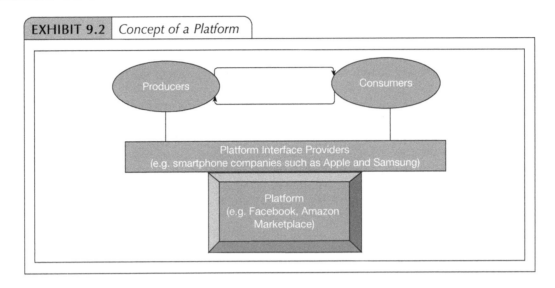

EXHIBIT 9.2 | Concept of a Platform

9.4. CLASSIFICATION OF PLATFORMS

Platforms have evolved in many different forms as digital-native companies or otherwise. There is not a single classification of platforms that can be explained appropriately. We will cover three different perspectives, encompassing academic, business and management areas.

9.4.1. Business Model-based Classification of Platforms

Karl Täuscher and Sven M. Laudien (2018) have developed a taxonomy for platform business models, identified six distinguishable types and have established a no one-size-fits-all approach to building these platforms. To create this framework, they have considered three key distinctive business model dimensions as detailed in platform specifications for business models (Exhibit 9.3).

1. Value creation (resources and activities)
2. Value delivery (value proposition, product/service, target customers)
3. Value capture (revenue and pricing model)

Karl Täuscher and Sven M. Laudien, considering the above characteristics, have evaluated 100 platform marketplaces at random using clustering to identify the six business model types as follows:

- Efficient product transactions
- Digital product community
- Product aficionados
- On-demand offline services

EXHIBIT 9.3	*Platform Specification for Business Models*

	Business model attributes	Specifications				
Value creation dimension	**Platform type**	Web-based platform			Mobile app	
	Key activity	Data services		Community building	Content creation	
	Price discovery	Fixed prices	Set by sellers	Set by buyers	Auction	Negotiation
	Review system	User reviews		Review by marketplace	None	
Value delivery dimension	**Key value proposition**	Price/Cost/ Efficiency		Emotional value	Social value	
	Transaction content	Product			Service	
	Transaction type	Digital			Offline	
	Industry scope	Vertical			Horizontal	
	Marketplace participants	C2C		B2C	B2B	
	Geographic scope	Global		Regional	Local	
Value capture dimension	**Key revenue stream**	Commissions	Subscriptions	Advertising	Service Sales	
	Pricing mechanism	Fixed pricing		Market pricing	Differentiated Pricing	
	Price discrimination	Feature based	Location based	Quantity based	None/ other	
	Revenue source	Seller	Buyer	Third party	None/ other	

Source: Taeuscher and Laudien (2018).

- Online services
- P2P offline services

The characteristics of each of these platform business model types are discussed in Exhibit 9.4.

9.4.2. Activity-based Classification of Platforms

The second type of classification (Exhibit 9.4) focuses on the nature of activities performed by platform participants and is structured as follows:

Aggregation platforms: These are platform businesses where the platform gathers a broad range of products, services or resources from various competing sources and helps

EXHIBIT 9.4 *Business Model Based Classification of Platforms*

Business Model Type	Platform Type	Platform Participants	Value Proposition	Transaction Type and Good	Revenue Model	Example
Efficient product transactions	Web-based platform	C2C, B2B	Large product variety	Physical products	Commission fee, subscription fee; mostly supply side	*Beepi* (eBay for used cars)
Digital product community	Web-based platform	C2C	Being part of a primary non-commercial community	Digital products; physical products	Commission fee; supply side, demand side	*Sellfy* (connecting 'neighbors' to share durable goods with each other)
Product aficionados	Web-based and mobile platform	B2C, C2C	Exchanging knowledge about niche products with community of like-minded people	Physical products	Commission fee; supply side	*HobbyDB* (Knowledge database and transaction platform for collectibles)
On-demand offline services	Web-based and mobile platform	B2C	Large service variety in a novel form	Offline services	Commission fee, subscription fee; mostly supply side	*StyleSeat* (connecting beauty salons and consumers)
Online services	Web-based platform	C2C, B2C	Novel online services with social networking character	Online services	Commission fee, subscription fee; mostly supply side	*iTalki* (connecting language learners with teachers for 1-on-1 online lessons)
P2P offline services	Web-based and mobile platform	C2C	Novel services with community feeling within and outside digital platform	Offline services	Commission fee (demand and supply side), subscription fee (third parties)	*Airbnb* (connecting people to list, discover, and book private accommodations)

Source: Taeuscher and Laudien (2018).

platform users to connect the most appropriate ones. These platforms tend to be transaction oriented, and the platform owner brokers transactions. There tends to be further specialization in these aggregation platforms, namely: (a) information aggregation platforms, (b) broker platforms and (c) contest platforms.

Social platforms: These are businesses where platforms focus on aggregating many people with a long-term strategic focus to monetize by getting to know them through their interactions. Instagram and Facebook are good examples of this model. These platforms differ from aggregation platforms in terms of their focus on long-term relationships, and there is no one common type of transaction that they execute on the platform. Most transactions between the platform participants may not involve the platform owner.

Mobilization platforms: These are platform businesses where common interests of platform participants are converted to actionable activities. The focus is on moving people to act in unison beyond any individual participant's ability. As the focus is on collaboration over time, these platforms tend to focus on building long-term relationships like social platforms and may leverage such platforms to gather interested participants. These platforms exist in the business context, for example, in specific industry networks where they bring in business participants to collaborate. These can exist with or without a profit motive. Open-source platforms like GitHub are a good example of a mobilization platform. Mobilization platforms could also be leveraged for social movements.

9.4.3. Internal or External Platforms

Gawer and Cusumano (2014), through their detailed analysis of a wide range of industry examples, suggested two predominant forms of platforms:

Internal (company or product) platforms: A set of assets organized in a standard structure from which a company can efficiently develop and produce a stream of derivative products.

Gawer and Cusumano note that first widespread use of the term platform seems to have been in the context of new product development and incremental innovation around reusable components or technologies. They describe that internal platforms are used to build a family of connected products by deploying reusable components. This could be by the firm themselves or in collaboration with its suppliers. As early as in 1845, the US locomotive manufacturers were standardizing locomotive parts, and these standardized components were then used across several engines.

To create a reusable infrastructure for product development, companies need a level of sophistication and planning. They have thus developed internal product platforms to meet the varying needs of customers within the overall architecture. This concept was extensively adopted in the automotive or consumer electronics industries. These thought processes extended across product development to marketing beyond manufacturing execution.

There are several potential benefits of internal platforms such as fixed cost savings, time and cost-efficiency gains in product development, expanding a product range with limited resources and so on.

However, internal platforms have limitations as they may promote only incremental innovation and constrain much broader innovation.

External or industry platforms: Products, services or technologies that are similar in some ways to the former but provide the foundation upon which outside firms (organized as a 'business ecosystem') can develop their complementary products, technologies or services.

These are similar to internal platforms as these platforms also provide a foundation of reusable components or offerings. Still, the critical difference is the founding being open to outside firms. The degree of openness varies on some dimensions such as:

- Platform governance roles
- Platform access costs
- Level of access to information and capabilities of the platform

Industry platforms, similar to internal company platforms, get developed based on a deliberate strategy and intentional managerial decisions to establish a foundational technology around which third-party firms can create or collaborate on complementary innovations. The most likely winner will not necessarily be the firm with the most dominant design but likely the owner of the 'best' platform where the majority of the industry firms are collaborating.

Some examples of industry platforms from the technology space are as follows:

- Microsoft Windows and Linux operating systems (OS)
- Intel and ARM microprocessors
- Apple's iTunes and Spotify
- App Store from Apple and Android Play Store

There are similar examples of social networking, payment technologies, IoT platforms, mobile devices and so on.

9.4.4. Transaction versus Innovation Platforms

Cusumano et al. (2020) provided their classification of platforms based on an analysis of 20 years of data from Forbes Global 2000 of public-listed platforms and compared their performance vis-à-vis a control sample of 100 non-platform companies. They observed that even though platforms have many similarities, it is possible to classify based on its principal activity's nature as Innovation and Transaction Platforms.

Innovation platforms: As the name indicates, these platforms foster innovation by facilitating new or complementary products and services built mainly by third-party organizations without formal contracts. Complementary is a keyword here that adds functionality to existing assets or value proposition of the platform by nature. This is the source of network effects, which will be covered later in this chapter. As it can be easily deciphered, more complementary products or services lead to a higher quality of platforms, making the platform more attractive to its existing and new participants.

These platforms capture value by directly selling or renting a product, or in many cases, the platform is offered free, and the company monetizes it through advertising or other services. Microsoft Windows, Microsoft Azure, Google Android, Apple iOS and Amazon Web Services have commonly used innovation platforms.

Transaction platforms: These are a digital (online) version of traditional marketplaces or intermediaries that allow participants to exchange goods and services or information. Like innovation platforms, the more participants and features and functions available on a transaction platform, the more useful it becomes to all platform constituents.

These platforms can capture value by enabling transactions that would not otherwise occur without the platform acting as an intermediary. They monetize this through either collecting transaction fees or advertising, or other related services. Google Search, eBay, Amazon Marketplace, Instagram, Twitter, Uber and Airbnb are examples of transaction platforms.

To summarize, transaction platforms are intermediaries or online marketplaces where platform participants exchange products or services. In contrast, innovation platforms enable innovation through new or complementary products or services for platform participants. However, there exist hybrid companies that contain both innovation and transaction platforms. These are far and few. Their strategies are distinct from the traditional models' cane to integrate both transaction and innovation platforms as part of their core business. A classic example would be Apple with its App Store strategy. Similar examples include Amazon Web Services, Kindle, Alexa from Amazon or Google's Android acquisition.

Start-ups or existing organizations mostly strategize to create either transaction or innovation platforms. This was true even in the offline or pre-internet era as well. However, the companies which pursue both innovation and transaction platforms, extract maximum value for themselves and their platform constituents, for example, Apple with its App Store. Such companies are adapting 'Hybrid Model' by leveraging both 'innovation' and 'transaction' platform models. It is no surprise that these hybrid companies are the most valued in the world today.

9.5. NETWORK EFFECTS

Network effects are positive feedback loops that grow exponentially as new users join the network, leading to incremental benefits for the network's existing users. The network effect can be defined as the value that an additional user of a product or service of the platform provides on that product or service value to other users or participants of the platform.

Product or service value as perceived by users or consumers has two distinct parts: (a) the value that the product or service itself provides and (b) the additional value derived from the network—leading to network effects.

These network effects can be direct or indirect. With a direct network effect, one user's purchase of a product or service has a direct impact on the other user's welfare. For example, being on the Apple iOS ecosystem allows users to communicate through iMessage directly. Every new user added will enlarge the network further. Indirect network effects are created when there is no immediate or direct impact of one user's purchase of product or service through lagging impact. Indirect network effects are more pronounced when there are two or more user groups such as buyers and sellers, producers and consumers, technology providers, users and developers. Ridesharing platforms are an excellent example of indirect network effects.

Examples of direct or same-side network effects can be observed on Facebook or Instagram, where these platforms attract users, friends of users and their acquaintances, and it goes on further. In the same context, content providers, small and big businesses, advertisers and so on are attracted to these platforms due to many users' presence, leading to indirect network effects. In some cases, indirect network effects could be even more potent than direct network effects.

However, network effects need scale, which has driven investors to become the brand that owns the network's mindshare. Platform users can move to alternate or cheaper options if it is easy to replicate or disrupt by significant parallel investments. The simplicity of platforms, which is a big attraction for users, can make it risky and hard to sustain. Thus, there is a strong need for quality to maintain scale. The value captured in the platform is transferred to each participant to make the platform successful and create a stickiness for all to continue to be a part of the platform.

9.6. MULTISIDED PLATFORMS

As it was laid out in the platforms' classification, every platform does not have to be external facing, marketplace or have a large number of participants (or users). However, two-sided or multisided platforms (MSPs) enable significant value by reducing the transaction costs for all the participants involved. Thus, MSPs are often the most valued companies in their respective industry segments and become leaders or trendsetters in their own and adjacent industries.

Over the years, multiple authors attempted to define and describe the multisided markets/platforms. For its completeness, we propose the definition by Hagiu and Wright (2015; Gerwe & Silva, 2020) which is based on two characteristics:

- Multisided businesses enable direct interactions between two or more sides
- Each side is affiliated with the platform

Direct interactions: Participating sides (two or more as the case may be) maintain the interaction's control. For example, on the Airbnb platform, there are two primary sides—rent seekers and asset owners. Owners retain control of their assets instead of one-sided intermediaries (e.g., time-share vacation companies) who control the assets.

Affiliation: Participating users pay platform-specific fees and/or make investments required to interact/trade with each other directly. For example, on the LinkedIn platform, recruiters and individual members pay premium membership fees for network expansion to meet their specific objectives. Both sides invest time and effort to develop their branding for increased visibility.

It is important to acknowledge that there is no universally accepted definition for multi-sided platforms yet. However, there is a consensus that these markets have three standard features:

- There is a multi-product firm. A platform provides distinct services to two sides (or more) of the market.
- There are cross-network effects. Users' benefits from participation depend on user participation on the other side of the market.
- Bilateral market power. Platforms are price setters on both sides of the market.

It is essential to recognize that many MSPs achieved great success as their primary target is consumers or small enterprises where they are the individual decision-makers; thus, it is easier to get them to engage in a platform. Commercial businesses, medium to large, are more cautious about contributing to a platform where they do not control or lose market power. There could be some scenarios where it may not be feasible or most appropriate to build a commercial MSP. In such cases, an industry consortium or government could build MSP as the platform's inherent benefits cannot be underscored. For example, trade platforms where one commercial vendor trying to create a platform will be competitive to incumbents and would create challenges to participation, or building a platform like the health ecosystem with providers, payers, patients and government to come together in ways that are not constrained by single interactions, which as an example would encourage prevention rather than medical intervention. There is potential for an MSP to operate that mediates the exchange of value. Still, in complex environments, this may not be a commercial business as this may create both competitive, societal and governance challenges.

9.7. PLATFORM NATIVE VERSUS PLATFORM TRANSITIONED

Among the most valuable companies today, Apple, Amazon and Facebook owe their worth to their business activity as MSPs. Many such MSPs are more valuable than companies who offer similar products or services to similar customers in the same industries. For example, Amazon is worth more than Walmart, the world's largest retail chain. However, companies like Walmart (a multibillion (https://www.lexico.com/definition/multibillion) enterprise) or an SME that were not platform native can partially turn their products/services, if not entirely, and become platform transitioned and reap the benefits of being MSPs themselves.

Hagiu and Altman (2017) developed a framework through the experience of studying and advising multiple companies in their transformation journey from product to MSPs. The framework provides four ways in which a company can transition:

1. **Open the door to third parties:** The company's product or service has a significant customer base that third-party sellers of other offerings are interested in reaching. The company could become an MSP by making it possible for those third parties to connect with its customers.
   - This scenario is where a company's product or service has a big database in which a third-party company is interested in promoting its business.

- This works when the third party's offering does not compete with its offering. The best scenario is when it complements the offering and becomes a better marketplace for the end customer by creating frequent interactions.
- It is vital to understand that customers might hold the company responsible for the third party's poor performance. The company could even lose some of its customer bases because of the third party's quality of interaction, service and pricing.
- The Forum Athletic Club is getting into an agreement with a cycling studio; the Lawson convenience store facilitates payment of utility bills, insurance and postal services for its customers. QuickBooks opened their doors to programmers who could sell software products to their customers. In India, most automobile manufacturers have tied up with insurance, financial institutes and oil suppliers to access their database.

2. **Connecting customers:** In this scenario, the company sells a product or service to two distinct customer segments that interact outside its offering. The company could become an MSP by modifying or expanding the existing offering to at least some of these interactions occur through its' product or service.
   - In this scenario, the company sells a product or service to two distinct customer segments that interact outside its offering. The company could become an MSP by modifying or expanding its offering to at least some of these interactions occur through its portfolio of product or services.
   - It works when customers interacting through the platform get better value, choice or service because there is an increase in customer traffic.
   - Customers transacting through the platform might hold the company responsible, and it is vital to have systems (payment through the company's portal, having a deposit and so on) to minimize conflicts; the value created through the transactions might be insignificant to the company though it might be significant to the participating customers.
   - QuickBooks and Garmin connected their customers to create value for their customers and themselves. Blizzard Entertainment had to withdraw its auction house in two years because it undermined the value of the game.

3. **Connecting products to connect customers:** In this scenario, the company sells its portfolio of products or services to distinct customer segments, who in turn interact outside of company's offerings. The company could become an MSP by modifying or expanding its offerings so that at least part of those interactions occurs through the company.
   - In this scenario, the company sells two products or services, each to a different customer base, two customers interact outside its offerings. The company could become an MSP by modifying or expanding its offerings so that at least part of those interactions happens through the company.
   - It works when the customers find value in transacting through the company; the value might be a better choice, ease of transaction and safety.
   - The value created might be very little compared to the platform's investments; optimizing the customer products' interactions might limit the growth potential.
   - Brick-and-mortar credit bureaus could become or clone themselves as MSPs, where consumers could obtain their credit scores and banks or insurance

companies can offer their products. Traditional credit bureaus in this avatar could expand their offerings to enable consumers to maintain their digital data along with their credit scores to apply to these products offered by these institutions.

4. **Supplying to an MSP:** In this scenario, the company can become an MSP by creating an offering for its customers, enhancing the value of the product or service they buy from its customers.

- Although this strategy is logically possible, there are not many examples of successful execution. It is important to note that this is not similar to the 'Intel Inside' nature of branding but directly to customers' products/services. As it is evident, it is likely to negatively affect the company's customers unless there are some potential network effects for them through this approach.

- Shopify is a leading provider of e-commerce tools today and is the fast-growing online store builder. It powers over 1,000,000 businesses worldwide, and if it were to convince its customer's customers to agree on a single sign-on, then it would lead to Shopify becoming an MSP, also known as another Amazon. Shopify's valuation in November 2020 was at ~$120 billion (stock price increased from ~300 to ~900 in the last 12 months) vis-à-vis Amazon valuation is upwards of $1.5 trillion. Of course, whether such a move by Shopify being successful would largely depend on how its customers' and customers' customers—merchants and the online stores—anticipate the network effects.

9.8. LEADERSHIP CHALLENGES WITH PLATFORMS

Platform business models are relatively new, and business leaders need to equip themselves with toolkits to understand, establish and lead them. In the earlier section, we covered a framework to analyse the business and identify opportunities for transitioning to platform businesses. The platform strategy of a firm includes deciding how to build and manage a platform, strategize the transactions with adjacent platforms and anticipate potential competitive platforms. Some of the unique challenges for the leaders are as follows:

Closed versus open architectures: Platform businesses mandate open architectures supporting a large user base. It requires the leaders to govern this with the right policies to attract and retain by incentivizing the users appropriately. This requires leaders to think about collaboration and competition differently from what they are traditionally taught or practised.

Broader optimization responsibility: As leaders in the conventional industries, leaders are well equipped to optimize and focus on increasing internal operations' efficiency such as manufacturing, distribution and product mix. Platform business model would need to think beyond the firm's boundaries for maximizing value creation by looking beyond the firm's immediate influence areas. This is likely to acquire different expertise and change in mindset.

Exponential growth: Digital technologies that enable the platforms are changing every day, and their capabilities are increasing exponentially, creating opportunities to rework or create new business models. As we discussed earlier in the chapter, there is always a significant risk to replicating existing platforms with similar or better value propositions as the long-term loyalties are challenging to attain in this business model. There is still a danger of overestimating the value of the current strengths and underestimating future technologies' potential.

Metrics: Leaders' familiarity with current metrics may lead to wrongly adapting similar but modified metrics for the platform business. They require to develop new metrics and new ways of measuring their business and people's growth and performance.

9.9. RISKS WITH PLATFORMS

Platform-based businesses are experiencing regulatory challenges globally as regulators take an in-depth look at socio-economic costs, particularly in economies where these platforms are expanded at a large scale.

Network effects are at the core of the issue. The platform requires a minimum scale to realise the network effects, and in the process, there has been a massive explosion of investments to buy out the competitors to get that scale. This leads to a monopolistic environment, and governments slowly realise the platforms' negative impact. They are imposing fines for anti-competitive behaviour, with regulatory scrutiny is continuously increasing. Geo-political conflicts and the spread of nationalistic agenda are compounding the intensity of review on platform businesses.

Platform companies like Amazon started to build their product range and offering it through their marketplace, which is again being seen as a conflict of interest as Amazon's choice products are likely to show up in the first few products for the consumer, leading to seemingly unfair advantage. This is likely to impact small businesses in the short term and affect medium to large companies as well in a long time.

Data privacy legislation such as GDPR in Europe and other similar legislation in most countries focuses on how the platforms collect, process, and use data to combat some of the platforms' challenges. In some countries, there are calls for some platforms to be broken up to clip some of the powers that these platforms start to yield in the market. However, excessive regulations can stifle innovation, and that closer collaboration among the industry, platforms, and government can help set the course for continued innovation in the platform business.

MINI CASE 9.1. DISCUSSION

In 2016, Enel Group's revenues decreased by about 6 per cent from the previous year. Since the high of ~85 billion euros in 2012, the company experienced a drop in revenues for the next four years. This was more of a reflection of the volatile external environment than its strategy or execution, as evidenced by improvement in operating income during this period (Exhibits 9.5a and 9.5b).

During this period, the company's most crucial information was not reflected in the numbers but in terms of their strategy. Enel had continued its focus on sustainable energy and global expansion. The fundamental strategy was about how the company started to unlock the actual value of its overall assets, not just its physical or financial assets.

EXHIBIT 9.5A | *Enel's Revenue*

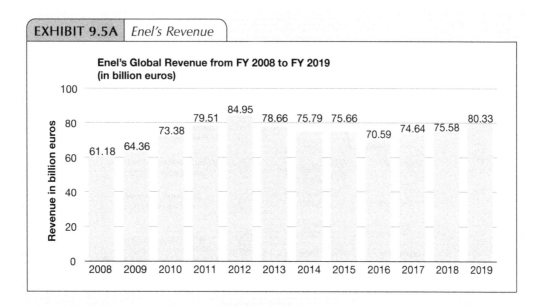

Enel's Global Revenue from FY 2008 to FY 2019 (in billion euros)

EXHIBIT 9.5B | *Enel's Operating Income in 2016*

	Millions of Euro			
	2016	**2015 Restated**	**Change**	
Italy	4,387	4,588	(201)	–4.4%
Iberia	1,766	1,473	293	19.9%
Latin America	2,163	2,320	(157)	–6.8%
Europe and North Africa	286	(569)	855	–
North and Central America	565	338	227	67.2%
Sub-Saharan Africa and Asia	(5)	4	(9)	–
Other	(241)	(469)	228	48.6%
Total	**8,921**	**7,685**	**1,236**	**16.1%**

Source: Enel Annual Report 2016, https://www.enel.com/content/dam/enel-com/documenti/investitori/informazioni-finanziarie/2016/annuali/en/annual-report_2016.pdf

In early 2017, the Enel Group introduced a new global business line, 'Enel X', by adopting a new organization structure with 'platform' at its core of the strategy. Even though the company only mentioned digitization and customer focus as its focus areas, it built the foundation for the platform through those initiatives.

Enel Group focused on decoupling its assets—customers, physical assets, people from business needs, products and geographical regions through digitization. This enabled the group to accelerate innovation and extract additional value from existing assets by selling third-party services. This helped the group create new shared value for all the stakeholders of the platform ecosystem (Exhibit 9.6).

EXHIBIT 9.6 | *Enel's Digital Platforms*

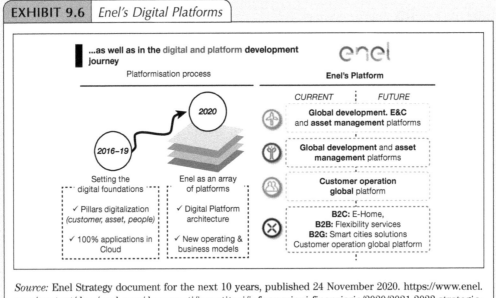

Source: Enel Strategy document for the next 10 years, published 24 November 2020. https://www.enel.com/content/dam/enel-com/documenti/investitori/informazioni-finanziarie/2020/2021-2023-strategic-plan.pdf

SUMMARY

Platforms are ubiquitous in today's world—prominent already for businesses and consumers for B2B and business-to-consumer (B2C) transactions, expanding to non-traditional areas such as G2C and C2C interactions. Core principles of the sharing economy have been in existence in some form or the other for many generations and have moved to a different era of adoption through digital technologies in the internet era. The growth of platforms has been unprecedented in the last decade. It can be observed from the data of the most-valued companies building or transitioning to platform-based business models. Whether a company is facing competition from a platform in their industry or not, most companies in any sector must evaluate how they can build or transition their business to a platform approach to extract value through network effects. Most industries today are being disrupted by platform companies. Only those who understand and internalize the concept of shared economy and network effects are likely to survive in the future.

Discussion Questions

1. Define a sharing economy. Explain the relevance of platforms in sharing economy.
2. Describe the different types of platforms with examples.
3. What are network effects? How are these different in one-sided versus multi-sided markets?

4. How can an existing company develop a platform business? Explain through a case example.
5. Identify similarities and differences between innovation and transaction platforms.

GLOSSARY

B2B: Business to business, where transactions are between companies or organizations.

B2C: Business to consumer where businesses sell goods or services directly to consumers.

Brick and mortar: Denotes a business that operates traditionally rather than over the internet.

C2C: Consumer to consumer; citizen to citizen.

Ecosystem: A network of an interconnected system.

G2C: Government to citizen; services or interactions between any level of government and the citizens.

GDPR: General Data Protection Regulation, data privacy law of the European Union; https://gdpr.eu

IoT: Internet of Things; a network of physical things which are connected on digital networks through sensors and other software, hardware and network technologies.

Peer to peer: Individuals interact with each other without any intermediary.

Platform native: A business that started as a platform, also known as native app.

Platform transitioned: A business that transitioned to being a platform.

SME: Small and medium enterprise; businesses that are below a threshold level of turnover, capital or employees and these limits vary across countries

REFERENCES

Bowles, S., & Choi, J. K. (2003, January). *The first property rights revolution*. Workshop on the Co-evolution of Behaviors and Institutions, Santa Fe Institute, Santa Fe.

Cusumano, M. A., Yoffie, D. B., & Gawer, A. (2020). The future of platforms. *MIT Sloan Management Review, 61*(3), 46–54.

Gawer, A., & Cusumano, M. A. (2014). Industry platforms and ecosystem innovation. *Journal of Product Innovation Management, 31*(3), 417–433.

Gerwe, O., & Silva, R. (2020). Clarifying the sharing economy: Conceptualization, typology, antecedents, and effects. *Academy of Management Perspectives, 34*(1), 65–96.

Hagiu, A., & Altman, E. J. (2017). Finding the platform in your product. *Harvard Business Review, 95*(4), 94–100.

Hagiu, A., & Wright, J. (2015). Multi-sided platforms. *International Journal of Industrial Organization, 43*, 162–174.

Täuscher, K., & Laudien, S. M. (2018). Understanding platform business models: A mixed-methods study of marketplaces. *European Management Journal, 36*(3), 319–329.

Tiwana, A., Konsynski, B., & Bush, A. A. (2010). Research commentary—platform evolution: Coevolution of platform architecture, governance, and environmental dynamics. *Information Systems Research, 21*(4), 675–687.

CHAPTER

10

Digital Use Cases

Learning Objectives

Chapters 6, 7 and 8 covered digital technologies (individually and as composite technologies) and their uses. At an industry level, multiple composite technologies are deployed to create industry and process-specific solutions. This chapter focuses on four use cases where digital technologies are being extensively deployed—financial services, healthcare, retail and smart cities. In Chapter 11, we deal with another specific use case—manufacturing. In Chapter 12, we focus on digital marketing, where once again, various digital technologies have been integrated to develop new methods of marketing products and services. By the end of this chapter, readers will be able to:

- Understand how digital technologies can be combined to develop use cases
- Understand how such technologies have become an integral part of various industries
- Learn specific examples of global companies that have leveraged digital technologies

---

10.1. FINANCIAL SERVICES

Financial services is a vast industry that includes banks, card issuers, insurance, stock brokerages, investment funds, mortgage and consumer finance companies. According to a report by Gartner, one-third of CIOs listed digital as their top business priority. This shift to digital has meant that incumbent companies have had to take a relook at their strategy, business models and processes. In the last five years, a new genre of financial services companies known as financial technology (fintech) companies, which combine technology with financial services, have emerged as disruptors to traditional institutions.

Mini Case 10.1

The Royal Bank of Canada (RBC), founded in 1864, is a Canadian financial services company and the largest bank in Canada by market capitalization. The bank serves over 16 million clients and has 86,000+ employees worldwide. In its 150 years of history, RBC demonstrated that it could stay in tune with the times by investing early in emerging technologies. In 2016, RBC embarked on an ambitious plan to deliver personalized customer engagement through its digital channels. Beginning with developing a mobile platform, the bank launched a series of initiatives that provided its customers with personalized customer experiences. Internally, RBC focused on changing its culture, resulting in increased customer-focused outcomes.

10.1.1. Digital Transformation across the Value Chain

As discussed above, the financial services industry is diverse, and processes are distinct across each subcategory of the industry. However, at a very broad level, financial services companies have a few common functions that have been the focus of digital transformation.

Customer related: At the forefront of the transformation of most financial services companies are customer acquisition- and customer service-related processes. Some of the processes that have already been digitalized are the use of digital marketing to acquire customers, online and mobile account opening, mobile apps to onboard customers and digital know your customer (KYC). Customer service through mobile apps and the use of technologies ranging from interactive voice response (IVR) to customer bots have replaced traditional call centres and branch banking. Many banks are also using video for customer meetings to replace physical meetings. Digital interactions also help generate data that can be analysed and provide better and more customized products.

Back-office processes: Financial services companies have had back offices to process the large volume of transactions generated by their customers. Until a decade ago, these transactions were mostly paper based. Over the last decade, most of these paper-based processes have been automated by scanning equipment and workflow software. The digital transformation of customer-facing processes is forcing financial institutions to accelerate back-office automation. RPA enables increased efficiencies and further lowers operating costs. Most legacy financial institutions have disconnected information silos, manual processes and (expensive) legacy IT systems. This transformation of the front-end has also led to connected systems, all the way from data capturing to intelligent information management, analysis, and customer service. The newer systems are also lighter, more agile, and flexible in dealing with customer-facing processes.

    Digital technologies are also being implemented extensively across back offices. For example, blockchain distributed ledgers are being used in trade finance, supply chain validation processes and other areas. Vast volumes of structured and unstructured data contain insights that are being analysed using advanced data analytics tools. AI tools like NLP help parse and review contracts. Deep learning and cognitive analytics are being used to proactively guide customer service representatives in their conversations with clients.

Regulation and compliance: Regulation and compliance play a critical role ranging from front-office KYC protocols to capital management. Every process in the financial services industry is strictly monitored and regulated to ensure security and stability. Firms are using technologies like AI for regulatory mapping to monitor the financial universe for all the regulatory changes that are impacting their global operations.

Along with AI, data mining algorithms based on ML and visualization tools are used to organize, analyse and report large sets of data. These tools help present data in an organized manner to decision-makers, thereby enabling efficient decision-making and problem-solving. An entire industry, often called regulatory technology (regtech), has emerged that is helping financial services companies streamline their regulatory and compliance processes.

Administrative processes: In addition to core financial services processes, institutions are also implementing digital in their administrative processes. These include accounting, payroll, internal helpdesks and office maintenance.

Employee processes: The financial services industry has relied primarily on leveraging digital capabilities to enhance the customer experience. They have not made investments to the same extent in employee experience. However, this is changing. From employee self-service to collaboration tools for knowledge sharing, institutions are implementing technologies that enable digital employees. Companies are also investing in digitalizing the entire employee life cycle process from hiring to retention. As millennials form a larger proportion of both customers and employees, institutions are realizing a need to build a digital culture across their organizations.

10.1.2. Financial Technology (Fintech)

A new breed of technology-intensive companies is disrupting the financial services industry (Das, 2010). These digital-native companies are often referred to as fintech companies. Fintech companies either provide standalone financial services that compete with traditional institutions or develop technologies leveraged by these institutions. As a corollary, larger financial services institutions view fintechs as both collaborators and competitors. Fintechs are changing the way capital is raised, transferred and allocated. Kickstarter is a crowdsourcing fintech that helps in raising capital. Payment technologies and companies are good examples of fintechs involved in capital transfer, and robo-advising is an example of capital allocation.

10.1.2.1. Growth of Fintech

There are several reasons for the growth of fintechs:

Availability of digital technologies: Fintechs solutions are based on newer technologies such as blockchain, AI, IoT, location-based services and mobile apps, which are backed by analytics.

Penetration of digital devices: Widespread availability of the internet, devices, like mobile phones, and apps allowed fintechs to provide customer-oriented solutions like payments.

Innovation: Financial services companies were not investing in innovation and transformation before the financial crisis of 2008. The crisis led to disenchantment among customers of these companies' inability to keep pace with their needs. The gap between customer requirements and offerings from legacy financial institutions led to the evolution of fintechs.

Lower transaction cost: One of the primary reasons for customer dissatisfaction with legacy financial institutions was the high transaction costs being passed on to them. Using technology and innovative business models, fintechs were able to reduce these costs.

Disintermediation: The availability of newer technologies helped fintech disintermediate traditional channels, increase transactions speed and reduce costs.

Democratization: Fintechs focused on underserved markets such as emerging markets, SMEs and low-value payments largely ignored by traditional institutions.

10.1.2.2. Challenges with Fintechs

While the fintech industry has been growing rapidly, it also faces several challenges.

Regulatory: The biggest challenge faced by the industry is the lack of proper regulations. Most countries do not have a suitable regulatory framework within which fintechs can operate. The most common example of this is blockchain-based currencies like bitcoin. While these currencies provide many benefits, their usage has not been approved in many countries as they bypass traditional networks and regulatory frameworks.

Data security: Many fintech solutions are cloud based, and there are concerns about the threat of hacking as well as protecting sensitive consumer and corporate financial data.

Competition: As the number of fintech companies in every area grows, there is a severe competition among fintechs and between fintechs and financial services companies. For example, in India, there are over 300 payment start-ups.

Lack of standardization: In addition to the number of start-ups in each area of fintech, there is also a lack of standardization of technologies and processes.

Financial viability: Fintechs have high start-up costs and low transaction costs. As many companies have a platform business model, they depend on network effects to scale up. Many fintechs are aggressively adding customers by providing very incentives that impact their profitability. As a result, most fintechs are not profitable, and their business viability is questionable.

10.1.2.3. Technologies in Fintech

The following technologies form the core of fintech companies:

AI: AI in fintech works best with the combination of big data solutions. AI helps in analysing the performances and creating insights of a financial institution and its customers. AI also helps automate essential organizational processes (administration, documentation and client communication).

Blockchain: Blockchain has been at the core of the fintech revolution. It provides several benefits. Each transaction is encrypted, and every network stakeholder must approve a transaction, thus reducing the possibility of fraud and hacking. It also allows for detailed audit trails of transactions. Tokenization helps international businesses to use universal currencies instead of country-specific money.

Cloud: Cloud platforms enable fintech companies to build data lakes, data aggregation and create data compliance frameworks.

Mobile: Mobile devices are the backbone of most fintech applications and provide convenience, access to the internet and other tools such as Bluetooth, near-field communication (NFC) and GPS that enable fintech solutions.

MINI CASE 10.1. DISCUSSION

RBC was proactive with its digital transformation strategy. Instead of aiming to offer all things to all people, it chose to focus on the best use of technology in areas where there was a real friction point and a problem to be solved. After its transformation, more than four out of five of its active customers engaged with the bank digitally, even though RBC still had about 1,300 branches. Further, RBC witnessed 17–20 per cent year-over-year growth in mobile banking utilization from 2015 to 2020.[1]

According to Rami Thabet, VP of mobile at RBC,

> The mindset here at RBC is that we want to have a digitally-enabled relationship with our customers. We want this relationship to be meaningful and offer a blend of channels that makes for a much better user experience than when customers use single channels. But instead of looking at cutting-edge technology that is at the early stage we look to innovate in areas where we can tackle everyday issues that our customers have. In this way we offer something that actually adds value to our customers.

RBC launched a large-scale implementation of an AI-based digital service, NOMI. This service offered its customers insights into their personal financial habits and the ability to automate their savings. The service also included P2P capabilities and loyalty programmes for its customers.

To help Canadian businesses transform themselves digitally, the bank, in partnership with Microsoft, launched RBC's Go Digital programme.[2] The programme is designed to remove key barriers which businesses have cited as preventing or delaying their digital transformation. RBC was the first bank in Canada to offer immersive, remote video chat to its small business customers across North America at no extra cost to their clients.

With these initiatives, RBC transformed itself from a traditional bank to being at the forefront of digital transformation.

Note: The case is created from publicly available sources, press releases and articles.

10.2. RETAIL

The retail industry has been at the forefront of digital transformation. The COVID-19 pandemic accelerated this transformation.

10.2.1. Evolution of the Industry

The retail industry was traditionally brick and mortar with shoppers visiting standalone stores or mall-based outlets to purchase products. In developed markets, like the USA, small retailers have been replaced by large chains and franchises. In emerging markets also, like India, large retailers are making their presence. However, the lack of infrastructure to set up large malls, limited roads and highways and public transport has resulted in smaller retail outlets and malls in emerging markets. The local small retailers, especially for groceries, continue to be the preferred format in these markets.

The availability of the internet and mobile devices led to the development of e-commerce in the retail industry. Customers now have the option of either going to a store or buying online via computers or mobile phones. This option is referred to as multichannel retail.

The next phase of retail is omnichannel retail. The term 'omnichannel' was first used in IDC Global Retail Insights reports in 2010 to describe an evolution from multichannel where customers use multiple channels in parallel to omnichannel that involves more channels and allows the customer to switch from one channel to another during their buying process. As an illustration, a customer may initiate a product search on a retailer's web portal, find the nearest store and purchase the product through a mobile app and pick up the purchase, all seamlessly.

10.2.2. Digital Technologies in Retail

Several digital technologies are enabling retailers to evolve from brick and mortar to move towards multi and omnichannel. As each of these retail formats coexists, digital technologies are being used across both online and offline stores, making the experience seamless. Some of the technologies and their uses are highlighted in this section. These technologies have been classified based on where they are being deployed.

In-store: These are digital technologies that are being deployed in-store. In addition to the essential point-of-sale systems and self-checkouts, retailers are implementing several unique solutions to make the customer experience easier.

QR codes: Customers can scan QR codes on products to get more information on the products, including date of manufacture, expiry, calories and so on.

Smart shopping carts: These carts follow customers around the store instead of having to be pushed.

Beacon technologies: Some of the largest retailers, such as Walmart and Target, are using beacon technology to send personalized messages to enhance the brick-and-mortar experience of a customer while in-store.

Mobile apps: Many large retailers use mobile apps and augmented reality to help find the proper aisle and shelf for the exact items required by the customer.

The Amazon Go stores in the USA use a combination of computer vision, deep-learning and sensor-fusion technology to automate the payment and checkout process. This means that customers can enter the store, pick up items and leave without queuing or checking out, while the payment is automatically made through the Amazon Go app.

Online: These are technologies that are enabling online and mobile shopping. The online experience of shoppers is being augmented with digital tools, like VR, where customers can see and 'test' a product. Online shopping is also being integrated with voice-activated devices, such as Google Home, Alexa and Siri. The mobile shopping experience is being enhanced by providing customers with location-based shopping ideas and deals. Online shopping is also being highly personalized using analytics and AI-driven recommendations.

Supply chain: These are processes that allow for efficient ordering and dispatch of goods from suppliers to customers. Given the criticality of the supply chain to retail, the industry is moving to digital supply networks (DSN). These are dynamic and 'always-on' leveraging IoT sensors, applications and AI to make real-time decisions. DSNs are interconnected with end-to-end visibility, centrally linking information and decisions from other nodes and flows in the network as well as suppliers, partners and customers. Blockchain technologies are also playing a role in building DSNs. DSNs allow for end-to-end analytics, network inventory visibility, integrated demand forecast and supplier and carrier connectivity. This topic is covered extensively in Chapter 11.

Analytics: Analytics forms the backbone of the retail industry. It is used to analyse customer behaviour, track in-store experience, allow for targeted promotions, track the customer journey and optimize the supply chain process. With predictive analytics and targeted promotions, retailers determine what offers and products are most popular. Retailers also continue to test and analyse new ways to capture customer interest, both in-store and through e-commerce. In-store, analytics using sensors, beacons and mobile applications are used to track customer movements throughout the store and provide a better shopping experience.

Payments: Cash and card-based payments dominated retail payments a decade ago. Today, digital payments have become the preferred payment method for retailers and customers. Technologies such as contactless payments leveraging NFC and mobile wallets provide the consumer with the convenience of easy payments. At the same time, they provide retailers with greater access to data. Mobile apps and wallets also have multiple security layers that reduce payment fraud that was rampant with card-based payments. Loyalty programmes and discount coupons have also been integrated into these newer payment options.

Digital marketing: Digital marketing is used extensively by online and offline retailers to reach customers through activities such as display advertising, SEO and marketing. Retailers also use social media platforms such as Facebook and Instagram to build their brands, generate leads and sell products. Digital channels allow for two-way interaction between retailers and their customers. Chapter 12 covers this topic in detail.

MINI CASE 10.2. DISCUSSION

Since 2011, Target has made significant investments in its digital transformation. This included strengthening its e-commerce platform and bringing e-commerce logistics in-house.

The company relaunched Target.com online through a mobile app that provided a much better experience for its customers. In addition to its flagship mobile app, the company developed the Cartwheel app. This app allowed users to build shopping lists that helped them find everything within Target's brick-and-mortar locations. The app also had features relating to coupons and discounts.

In 2017, the company CEO Brian Cornell stated at a conference, 'The future of retail is digital.' At this point of time, more than 5 per cent of its $75 billion in revenue was from digital channels. Cornell stated that his vision for Target in the omnichannel world was as a 'hyperlocal, shoppable distribution centre'. With a store within 4 miles of 50 per cent of the US population, the company was transforming its stores to be convenient pick-up centres for items ordered online. This was reflected in the design of Target's future stores that had separate entrances for the two activities.[3]

By 2020, Target's digital performance revenues had exceeded $5 billion in annual sales, and a majority of the company's overall sales growth was from digital sales (Q3 2020 report).

10.3. HEALTHCARE

Digital is transforming healthcare across the globe. Processes, as varied as drug discovery, hospital management, patient care and surgery, have all incorporated digital technologies.

Mini Case 10.3

PK Hospitals is one of the largest hospitals in the city of Udaipur in India. Udaipur is a small city located in the state of Rajasthan. PK Hospitals was founded by Dr Parikh about four decades ago and is now run by his son and daughter-in-law, who are both doctors. PK Hospitals is the largest multi-speciality hospital in the region, and for patients within a 300 km radius of the city, this is the only hospital with any sophisticated facilities. By 2020, the hospital had reached its full capacity of 300 beds, and unless they opened a new facility, it would not be able to handle any further patients. Dr Parikh and his family had a lot to think about. Should they just add a new building in Udaipur? What can they do to provide better healthcare in the towns and villages surrounding the city? How can they reduce the need for patients to travel great distances to reach their facilities? Once the patients were at their facility, how could they make their experience better?

10.3.1. Industry Overview

The healthcare industry is one of the largest and fastest growing sectors in the world. It consists of several sub-sectors, including pharmaceuticals, medical equipment, drug distribution including pharmacies, healthcare providers including hospitals and clinics and healthcare payers like insurance companies.

10.3.2. Challenges in the Industry

The healthcare industry has been facing many challenges over the last few decades, which are as follows:

High costs: The industry has high costs across the value chain. The drug discovery and approval processes are very complex. According to a recent study done by the Tufts Center for the Study of Drug Development published in the *Journal of Health Economics*, it is estimated that successful drug costs around $2.5 billion to develop. Increasing and ageing populations are adding to the stress on healthcare systems and costs.

Inefficiencies: The number of sub-sectors involved in the industry leads to improper data flows and duplication of efforts. Even within a sector, the mix of manual processes, digital processes and system multiplicity aggravate these inefficiencies. For example, a hospital may have a hospital management system, financial system and electronic health record system that are not interoperable.

Government policies: Most governments find it challenging to balance the different stakeholders' priorities in delivering healthcare. As a result, there is a constant modification and churn in healthcare policies that result in the players' inability to make long-term investments. The US healthcare system is an example of such policy shifts.

Access: In emerging economies, access to healthcare is limited to large urban centres. This causes challenges for a large proportion of the population who are located in semi-urban or rural areas.

Trained resources: In most countries, there is a shortage of trained resources, especially those relating to patient care. These include doctors, nurses and other support staff.

Lack of patient focus: Many of the issues discussed above also result in the absence of a patient-focused healthcare system. There is also less focus on preventive healthcare that reduces the strain on the system.

10.3.3. Digital Transformation of Healthcare

The healthcare industry has invested in various technologies over the last two decades. They have helped reduce some of the challenges discussed above, but there is still a considerable gap between patient requirements and what the industry can deliver. The digital transformation of the industry is helping to further reduce these gaps. This section outlines some of the steps taken by the various players in the industry.[4]

Pharmaceutical and biotech industry: AI and data analytics play a significant role in reducing the cost and time taken to market the drug discovery process. With real-time information from both clinical trials and patients, drug companies are gaining a better understanding of the impact of a drug on patients, and how they can optimize their effects and minimize side effects. AI and big data are also helping organize and analyse vast data sets available from previous research and trials and then applying the learning to future research. Pharma companies are also making their production processes more efficient using IoT and advanced control systems. On the drug distribution side, these companies have been implementing digital in their supply chain processes to allow for more efficient drug distribution. Pharma companies also have large salesforces. The entire marketing and salesforce management processes have been moved to digital platforms.

These companies are also gradually moving to become platform companies where their role will evolve from owning all parts of their ecosystem to becoming orchestrators of the ecosystem. The efficiencies gained from all these processes will help companies reduce their costs and deliver drugs at the right place at the right time.

Bio-medical equipment: This sector deals with equipment ranging from artificial limbs and customer sensors to diagnostic and testing equipment. The industry has significantly evolved with the advent of digital technologies. Some examples include the following:

Robotics: With tremendous growth expected in the industry, the global medical robotics market is expected to reach $20 billion by 2023. This includes rehabilitation with prosthetics and micro-bots that can target therapy to a specific part of the body, like radiation to a tumour.

Computer and machine vision: Machine vision is being used for viewing scans and medical images, like CT scans. The applications help leverage past data and reduce human error.

Wearable technology: Wearable fitness devices promote exercise and fitness. The devices measure steps taken, calories burnt and other personal data. Other forms of wearable devices include electrocardiogram monitors that detect atrial fibrillation, blood pressure monitors and self-adhesive biosensor patches that track temperature and heart rate. Wearable tech helps consumers proactively get health support by detecting anomalies and promoting preventive healthcare by encouraging exercise and diet.

3D printing: 3D printing enables surgeons to replicate patient-specific organs. Also, many medical devices, prosthetics and dental implants are 3D printed.

Extended reality: In addition to being used for training and surgery simulation, these technologies help patients with visual impairment and autism.

Providers: Providers, including hospitals, are using many of the technologies discussed in the previous section for patient care. Telepresence has helped doctors examine and treat patients in remote areas. The roll-out of 5G will enhance these capabilities as doctors will be able to transmit and receive large files and use AI, IoT and mixed reality for remote and reliable monitoring of patients. AI and data analytics are also helping to integrate patient information lying across multiple systems.

Cloud-based patient management systems have resulted in lighter and more agile hospital and patient management systems. Mobile apps are being used to increase patient convenience. This includes doctor search, appointment scheduling and management, prescription management, integration with pharmacies and post-visit reminders.

Pharmacies: Pharmacies play an important role in delivering prescriptions to patients. Pharmacies are trying innovative approaches such as integrating prescriptions with hospitals, online order placement, home delivery with tracking and 'prescriptions as a service' models. The entry of e-commerce giant Amazon is expected to disrupt this part of the healthcare industry further.

Payers: Payers or insurance companies are integrating digital strategies into their customer-facing and back-office activities. AI-based customer tools are used to handle queries relating to policies, educate customers on policies and benefits and provide 24×7 customer service. AI is also being used to analyse the vast amount of data that payers have access to, for predictive and preventive healthcare. Payers are incorporating mobile solutions with apps to track the status of payments and claims. Payers are also increasingly using robotics process automation in their back offices to enhance claims processing with speed and accuracy.

MINI CASE 10.3. DISCUSSION

Dr Parikh and his family had a discussion on the future of PK Hospitals. They realized that instead of setting up another hospital in Udaipur, their patients would be better serviced by providing primary healthcare in their villages. They then hired a digital consultant with knowledge of the Indian healthcare provider industry to help them build and implement a digital strategy. Based on the advice received from the consultant, they decided to roll out their digital plan in phases.

Phase 1 was focused on making the experience of walk-in patients better. PK Hospitals transitioned from its legacy software to an integrated cloud-based hospital and patient management system. This system was also integrated into its billing and accounting platforms. With this implementation, the hospital managed to get a single view of a patient across all their interactions with the hospital. The system features were also mobile-enabled and had both a mobile app and an SMS-based push notification for patients who did not have smartphones or were in remote areas with limited data coverage. Through these features, patients can schedule and manage appointments as well as receive basic reports and prescriptions. As the local pharmacies were not digitally transformed, the app was not integrated with pharmacies. Instead, patients could show their prescriptions on their phone and purchase medication. Pre-scheduling appointments led to a dramatic decrease in wait times and increased utilization of available doctor time. This, in turn, increased the capacity of the hospital.

In Phase 2, PK extended its services to non-Udaipur locations. This was done through a combination of voice and video conferencing. The service included triage between doctors at the hospital, local healthcare workers and primary healthcare centres. This service reduced the need for patients to travel to Udaipur for ailments that did not require them to do so.

In the next phase, PK decided to implement AI technologies to analyse the vast patient data they had and develop customized preventive healthcare strategies. The hospital also wanted to explore robotics for surgery and prosthetics. As the 5G roll-out was still some time away, PK decided not to venture into remote surgery and radiology at this stage.

10.4. SMART CITIES

Mini Case 10.4

Austin is the capital of Texas, one of the largest states in the USA. It is also among the fastest-growing cities, attracting large investments from major corporations, especially in the technology sector. The population has doubled in the last 30 years, and Austin was among the few major cities that grew even during the financial crisis of 2008. However, the exceptional growth also brought with it some challenges. The economic growth the city witnessed was not uniform across its geographic spread, society and ethnicities. The influx of an affluent workforce drove real-estate prices up and made housing unaffordable for many sections of society. Many people had to move away from the city to distant neighbourhoods and commute long distances to work. This, in turn, resulted in mobility challenges with a lack of public transport and a high volume of traffic. To address these challenges and build a city for the future, city officials decided to launch a 3Es plan: equity, economic opportunity and environmental stewardship. To implement this plan, the city decided to leverage technology and data analytics.

10.4.1. Introduction

'Smart cities' are urban areas that use digital technologies to improve their residents' quality of life. There are hundreds of smart cities being developed worldwide, and eventually, most urban areas will be 'smart'. There is no single roadmap for converting a city into a smart city. Every country and city has prioritized different elements of a smart city based on their pressing needs.

Studies have identified three key elements (3Is) of a smart city: instrumented, interconnected and intelligent (Harrison et al., 2010).

Instrumented refers to the devices that gather data across a city, including cameras, IoT devices as well as smartphones, wearables and social media as a network of human sensors.

Interconnected refers to the integration of this data into a central computing platform that manages various city services. Public Wi-Fi and 5G provide the backbone for interconnectivity.

Intelligent refers to the analysis and visualization of this data to help make decisions that are efficient for the citizens and the city at an overall level. To allow for continuous innovation, most smart city networks have been created as open platforms that allow for data flow from multiple sources.

Many large technology companies have launched comprehensive smart city solutions. These include Sidewalk Labs by Google, CityNext by Microsoft and City Brain by Alibaba.

10.4.2. Smart City Solutions

The 3Is of smart cities are used to transform many aspects of urban living digitally. According to a study by the World Economic Forum,[5] some of the more common solutions include the following:

Governance and planning: Cities provide a range of services to their citizens. Providing these services efficiently and inclusively is among the key priorities for local governments. These services could range from urban planning to citizen engagement. As an illustration, urban planners can analyse the data from various sources to develop plans that balance physical, social and economic requirements. There are several examples of this, including the Dubai government's initiative to launch a Smart Dubai Happiness Meter based on feedback from its residents on the quality of services they receive from various government bodies across thousands of touchpoints.

Society: The next set of solutions revolves around enhancing societal needs. These include education, healthcare, public safety and social inclusion. Smart technologies help cities deliver services to their citizens and create a comfortable, healthy and safe environment. For example, in Singapore, a growing number of older people live alone and need support. The government wanted to provide wellness and health monitoring services to improve the quality of care delivered to them. Home monitoring solutions were implemented through a private partnership that combined smart technologies (IoT, motion and sound sensors, data analytics and AI) and 24×7 personal assistance. The data generated from these systems helped the government, healthcare providers and insurance companies provide better services to the elderly.

Monitoring citizens' safety using devices such as cameras and drones combined with digital technologies such as AI and facial recognition is one of the most widely deployed smart-city solutions.

Improving the quality of education is another key agenda of smart cities. For example, in India, IBM is launching a 'Smarter Education' programme, and Microsoft is introducing its CityNext initiative, which promotes an 'Educated Cities' programme. Many cities have already implemented advanced infrastructure for educational institutions. These initiatives help in digitalizing the classroom, providing access to global resources to students, and assisting in evaluating and monitoring educational objectives.

Infrastructure and services: All large cities face several infrastructural challenges. Through smart initiatives, cities tackle issues relating to water, waste management, mobility and transport, real estate and energy, among others. Using digital technologies such as IoT and AI combined with analytics, cities and local governments are managing utilities and optimizing traffic and public transport schedules.

In Singapore, solar panels are being embedded into building facades in addition to rooftops to generate solar power in a country that has no natural resources. In the UK, IoT-enabled sensors collect real-time data on water distribution and leakages. This enables optimizing water facilities by detecting leaks or monitoring how water is being distributed across the network.

Waste management is a massive challenge from both a logistics and cost perspective for most municipalities. IoT-powered smart waste management solutions are addressing these challenges. An everyday use case is route optimization of waste disposal trucks to increase efficiencies and reduce fuel consumption. Sensors are also being embedded into dumpsters to detect the level of waste generated and schedule pick-ups.

In the Nordics, significant efforts have been made to integrate public transport schedules into other services, such as traffic lights, traffic monitoring and parking. For example, in Stockholm, if a bus is running late, traffic lights along the route are adjusted to allow for the bus to speed up. Also, passengers waiting for the bus can track its location and arrival time. Smart traffic management solutions are being implemented worldwide to smoothen the flow of traffic and reduce the wait time at signals. The data from these systems are also being used to develop new roads and introduce additional public transport.

In Dubai (UAE), several blockchain-based initiatives have been launched through multi-stakeholder engagement and participation. Initiatives such as digital payments reconciliation and land title management were made significantly more efficient using 'blockchain as a service'.

Environment: Environmental sustainability is one of the critical goals of smart cities. Many of the initiatives discussed earlier, including traffic management, waste management, power and water management, contribute to sustainability. Other solutions include monitoring air and water pollution and creating green spaces through better urban planning. Satellite surveys and drones help urban planners develop a picture of the green space in their cities and identify areas for additional green spaces. IoT-backed irrigation and monitoring of green spaces for encroachment and destruction are being used to create greener smart cities.

Economy: Smart-city technologies can have a dramatic impact on the local economy. Better infrastructure, road connectivity and telecom connectivity all attract new investors and businesses. Smart-city investments have been found to trigger economic growth by attracting businesses, residents and talent. They have become the new centres for innovation and research. According to a report by ABI Research,[6] smart cities can see an incremental growth of almost 3 per cent, resulting in more than $20 trillion in additional economic benefits over the next decade.

MINI CASE 10.4. DISCUSSION

As part of this smart-city vision, several pilot initiatives were launched in Austin, which are as follows:

- Smart stations bring together a variety of mobility services and a platform for other services useful to commuters.
- Connected corridors link these smart stations with new transit services. The corridors also have a sensor-rich environment that allows for rapid deployment of connected-vehicle technology.
- A mobility marketplace connected commuters to their best-packaged mobility options and provided an ecosystem for the development of newer mobility services. The marketplace also included payment options and a travel information service, all backed by an analytics platform.
- All three of the above pilots are integrated into a set of ladders of opportunity initiatives that use smart stations, connected corridors and the mobility marketplace to improve access to jobs, education, healthcare, healthy food and other areas.

The initiatives were backed by the 'one-system' regional operations and management concept, leading to the integration and enhancement of travel management operations around the city. An extensive network of intelligent sensors was set up to provide data to the central systems, a two-way open data portal, known as the Data Rodeo, that integrated data from multiple public, private and non-profit sources. The data was made available to enable research and education as well as support application and tool developers. The urban analytics and policy research platform plays an integrated role in the performance management metrics and evaluation for the entire smart city effort.

Some of the other smart city initiatives in the city include updating its electric grid to a more efficient digital meter system. The updated electric grid makes it easier to incorporate renewable energy sources and a growing electric car network. The city also launched trials of free Wi-Fi in public parks and 5G throughout the city.

Source: ausstintexas.gov (2016).

SUMMARY

Digital strategies and technologies have been implemented across industries. Cloud, IoT, mobile and platforms are the most deployed technologies followed by AI and blockchain. Technologies such as extended reality, 3D printing, 5G and edge computing are in the early stages of implementation and are currently being used for high-value processes. In almost all use cases, a combination of these digital technologies is enabling companies' digital strategies. Digital is also transforming all aspects of a company, customer-facing processes, including acquisition and customer service, back-office processes, such as human resources and accounting, and core operations, including manufacturing and supply chain. Digital strategies allow industries and companies to launch new business models (e.g., omnichannel in retail), extend services to newer segments (e.g., mobile banking to the unbanked), reduce costs (e.g., through crowdsourced innovation) and increase efficiencies (e.g., robotics automation in banking back office). While this chapter focused on four large sectors, most other industries are undergoing similar transformations.

Discussion Questions

1. What is the difference between traditional financial services companies and fintech companies? Are they competitors or collaborators? Please provide examples.
2. This chapter describes the evolution of Target from a brick-and-mortar retailer to multichannel and omnichannel. Please describe an example of another retailer who has gone through a similar transition. What was similar and different about their respective evolutions?
3. What are some of the challenges in the healthcare industry? How have digital strategies helped address these challenges?
4. What are some key solutions that form an integral part of smart cities?
5. Describe the role of digital transformation in college education. What are some of the challenges, and how has digital transformation helped address these challenges?

GLOSSARY

Financial services industry: This is a vast industry that covers banks, credit cards, insurance, mortgage, consumer finance companies, stock brokerages and investment funds.

Fintech: Fintech is a technology and innovation that aims to compete with traditional financial methods in delivering financial services.

Omnichannel: This form of retail is an evolution from multichannel (where customers use multiple channels in parallel) to a model that involves more channels and allows for a customer to switch from one channel to another during the buying process seamlessly.

Smart city: A city that optimizes its functioning and promotes economic growth while also improving the quality of life for citizens by using smart technologies and data analysis.

NOTES

1. https://www.fintechfutures.com/2018/06/mobile-banking-case-study-rbc-farewell-friction/
2. https://www.bloomberg.com/press-releases/20110-06-18/rbc-and-microsoft-launch-new-program-to-accelerate-the-digital-transformation-of-canadian-businesses
3. https://www.cio.com/article/3183486/targets-reimagined-store-aims-to-win-in-the-digital-world.html

4. https://www.forbes.com/sites/bernardmarr/20110/11/01/the-10-biggest-technology-trends-that-will-transform-medicine-and-healthcare-in-2020/?sh<hig>=</hig>43cbdcf372cd
5. http://www3.weforum.org/docs/WEF_Smart_at_Scale_Cities_to_Watch_25_Case_Studies_2020.pdf
6. https://www.chordant.io/white_papers/abi-research-role-of-smart-cities-for-economic-development

REFERENCES

austintexas.gov. (2016). Live from Austin, Texas: The smart city challenge. https://austintexas.gov/sites/default/files/files/Transportation/Austin_SCCFinal_Volume1_5.25.pdf

Das, S. R. (2010). The future of fintech. *Financial Management, 48*(4), 1081–1007.

Digital Initiative. (2018). Target transforms for the digital age. https://digital.hbs.edu/platform-digit/submission/target-transforms-for-the-digital-age/

Harrison, C., Eckman, B., Hamilton, R., Hartswick, P., Kalagnanam, J., Paraszczak, J., & Williams, P. (2010). Foundations for smarter cities. *IBM Journal of Research and Development, 54*(4), 1–16.

11

Digital Supply Chains

Learning Objectives

Supply chains are being disrupted globally across industries due to the increasing application of digital technologies. This chapter provides perspectives on value creation opportunities by the strategic application of digital technologies and supply chains. At the end of the chapter, students will gain an understanding of the following:

- A review of supply chain fundamentals to examine the impact of digital technologies
- Capabilities enabled by digital technologies for supply chain management
- Digital transformation potential of supply chains
  - o Salience of critical digital technologies for managing supply chains
  - o Understand the impact potential of IoT, blockchain, analytics and AI
- How digital technologies have been used to create business value across the following use-case categories:
  - o Procurement
  - o Track and trace
  - o Industrial asset management
  - o Facilities management
  - o Service management
- Anticipating, preparing for and defining the future of digital supply chains
- Balancing efficiency versus resilience in the post-pandemic world

Mini Case 11.1

The SKF Group is a market leader in the bearings and rotating equipment market. The company's portfolio of offerings includes technical support, maintenance, engineering consulting and training services. The company is present in more than 130 countries and has about 17,000 distribution locations around the world. With an employee base of over 45,000, the company generated revenue of approximately $8.7 billion in 2017. In 2015, the company assessed its growth potential and needed to transform itself to perform to its potential in a growing market; the global bearings market is expected to grow at a 7.2 per cent compounded annual growth rate (CAGR) from 2017 to2023. Despite its strong competitive position and vibrant market, the company identified the need to transform its supply chain to support its future growth. The threat of potential digital disruptors such as Airbnb in the hospitality industry and Uber in public transportation served as the inspiration to transform even when there was no real crisis for SKF.

The opportunity to transform the supply chain arose from the fact that SKF has grown both organically and through acquisitions, leading to several complexities due to the assimilation of several manufacturing locations, distribution centres and warehouses. There were diverse deployments of enterprise planning systems across different regions. Any transformation to such a complex network would entail new demands on the workforce both in terms of change management and reskilling. A team of specialists and consultants was involved in setting the vision for the transformation. Directionally, the highest priority was to implement a global planning structure that will maximize efficiencies across the supply chain, a shift from local planning and reduce friction between internal organizations.

Source: How SKF Uses a Supply Chain Twin to Enable Integrated Planning, 14 December 2018. *CSCMP's Supply Chain Quarterly.* https://www.supplychainquarterly.com/articles/1806-how-skf-uses-a-supply-chain-twin-to-enable-integrated-planning

11.1. SUPPLY CHAIN MANAGEMENT: A CONCEPTUAL FOUNDATION

11.1.1. Overview

This chapter focuses on the applications of digital technologies in a broad category of business processes that fall under supply chain management (SCM). SCM is the coordination of activities within and between vertically linked firms for the purpose of serving end customers at a profit (Larson & Rogers, 1998). This definition implies two things: (a) SCM would broadly include processes that deal with activities that businesses undertake to produce and supply their offerings (goods, services or a combination of goods and services) to fulfil customer needs at the most optimal cost and (b) while the fulfilment of the customer needs creates customer value, for the business to be sustainable, the part of the value extracted as the price of the offering needs to exceed the supply chain costs, thus the general purpose of serving end customers at a profit. A prerequisite for profit is that the value generated for the customer, a part of which would be extracted as the price of the offering, should exceed the supply chain costs. For the purposes of this chapter, we define the value generated by a supply chain as the value generated for the end customer, net of all the costs in the supply chain, a metric called supply chain surplus:

Supply chain surplus (Chopra et al., 2013) = Value generated for end customer
– Supply chain cost

It is important to note that this section is not intended to provide a comprehensive treatment of the theory and the practices of the vast area of SCM. Instead, it intentionally focuses only on illustrative essentials to examine the impact and potential of digital technologies in this domain.

11.1.2. Anatomy of Supply Chains

At a macro level, processes that come under the scope of SCM can be conceived as a network of activities that include, but not limited to:

- Receiving or anticipating demand for offerings
- Acquisition of inputs (raw materials, information, etc.)
- Processing of inputs to incrementally transform them into finished offerings.
- The flow of inputs, semi-finished offerings and finished offerings between various stages in the network (suppliers, factories, service providers, warehouses, retail outlets, customers, etc.)
- Life cycle support for the offerings (technical assistance, maintenance, recycling physical products, etc.)

These processes and associated activities are performed using various assets, physical and intellectual resources, such as skilled personnel, machinery and equipment, information systems, know-how and patents. The endeavour to produce and supply to customers typically leverage assets and capabilities both within and outside the boundaries of a business entity (firm).

In a typical supply chain, there are five types of entities that participate. They are supplier, producer, distributor, retailer and consumer. These entities are present in a typical good supply chain where products are produced using raw materials as input. Then, finished goods are moved downstream to the end user (consumer) through intermediaries such as distributors and retailers. Exhibit 11.1 depicts a typical supply chain's anatomy, including the key stages, elements and flows involved in fulfilling customer needs. Depending on the nature of offerings, the configuration of entities in a supply chain would differ. For example, the supply chains of a car manufacturer, a health care provider like a hospital, and a telecom service provider are distinct from one another. In this text, the objective of a generalized representation of a supply chain is to examine and understand the potential impact of digital technologies on its performance. This chapter leverages the capability view of digital technologies (Exhibit 11.3, adapted from Chapter 6, Exhibit 6.2) to appreciate the transferability of the potential impact of digital technologies in one context (say a product/goods supply chain) to other diverse and complex supply chain contexts.

11.1.3. Supply Chain Performance Frontier

Supply chain performance can be viewed along two broad dimensions: The first is responsiveness to market demand and the second is costs incurred in serving the demand. Costs are incurred in the supply chain to produce and supply various offerings to the market. Supply chain responsiveness (Chopra et al., 2013) may be defined across multiple dimensions such as the volume of demand, variety of demand and lead time to supply. The following are some examples of how responsiveness manifests in a supply chain.

EXHIBIT 11.1 *Supply Chain Anatomy: Key Stages, Elements and Flows*

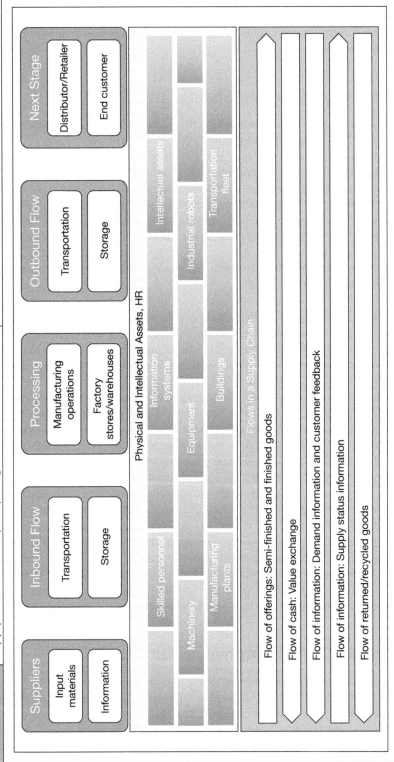

Note: Illustrative depiction of key stages, elements and flows in goods supply chain.

- In the supply chain of a car manufacturer, once the demand for a particular car model has been forecast or known from customer orders, responsiveness means how quickly operational processes in the factory can respond to set up and produce the required model in required quantities.
- In the context of a call centre, operations responsiveness would mean how quickly a customer who is calling gets responded to (response time) and how quickly the customer's request is fulfilled (resolution time).
- In the context of a mobile app, development responsiveness would mean how quickly a feature demanded by the users gets developed, tested and deployed for the users to download.

Costs involved in a supply chain could include capital expenditure for setting up production, transportation and storage capacities and operational expenditure, such as labour costs, fuel costs and rent for real estate. A higher level of responsiveness requires a higher level of capacity and capability, which drives up the supply chain costs. Costs are inversely proportional to the productivity of various factors of production involved in a supply chain such as plant and machinery, skilled workers and intellectual assets. For example, excess production capacity would make the supply chain more responsive to spikes in demand but will reduce the productivity of the capacity when the demand spike recedes. There are also opportunity costs of not fulfilling a part of the demand due to supply chain constraints.

Thus, supply chain performance is characterized by its responsiveness to meet market demand and the costs incurred in fulfilling the demand. The inverse relationship (trade-off) between the desirable levels of Responsiveness and Costs is depicted in Exhibit 11.2. Supply chain strategy, planning and operational decisions need to optimize the trade-offs between performance and costs of various factors in a supply chain, in the context of the demand environment.

EXHIBIT 11.2 | *Performance Frontier: Illustrative Relationship between Responsiveness and Costs in a Supply Chain*

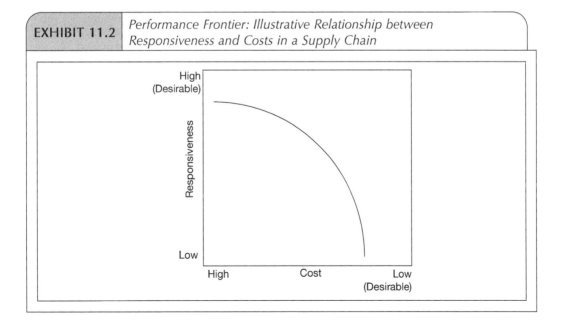

11.1.4. Supply Chain Dynamics and Uncertainties

11.1.4.1. Dynamics of Demand

Demand for a particular offering is either known in advance (when the product or services is made to order) or anticipated by the businesses. In either case, several variables characterize demand, including, but not limited to, quantity, physical location (where the customer's need requires fulfilment) and time (the time by which the demand needs to be fulfilled). For example, a customer on an e-grocery platform may require two units of a detergent liquid delivered at their home address, by 8 AM the following day. Thus, the three variables that characterize this demand for the detergent liquid are the quantity (2 units), physical location (home address) and time (8 AM the following day). Demand for an offering is inherently uncertain, and this uncertainty is due to uncertainty in quantity, location and time.

11.1.4.2. Dynamics of Supply

Supply for a particular offering is generally constrained by a capacity to produce in time or available inventory of goods. Several variables characterize supply, including, but not limited to, available capacity to produce, inventory of goods, location of production capacity, availability and capacity for moving goods from the point of production to the place of demand on time and so on. For example, to fulfil the demand of a customer on an e-grocery platform for two units of a liquid detergent, it must be available in the inventory that is at reasonable proximity to the delivery address of the customer and the door delivery capacity (i.e., delivery agent, delivery truck, etc.) must be available to be able to deliver the product on time. The supply capacity for an offering is relatively inelastic, that is, it is typically fixed for a duration of time irrespective of the demand. For example, in the context of the e-grocery business, the production capacity of a factory that produces the liquid detergent is fixed, the storage capacity of a warehouse is fixed, locations at which distribution warehouses are present are relatively fixed, several delivery vehicles and delivery personnel available are relatively inelastic in short to medium term and so on. Thus, the most important implication of all these dynamics of supply is that the supply capacity is relatively fixed or inelastic in the short to medium term.

The second important aspect of supply dynamics is performance uncertainty driven by issues in the supply capacity. For example, a machine used for manufacturing may malfunction, resulting in either an availability problem or a quality problem, that is, the supply capacity exhibits availability or performance uncertainty, which adds an element of uncertainty on the supply side.

11.1.4.3. Uncertainties in Supply Chains

In the preceding sections, various aspects of uncertainty were introduced. This section brings forth the uncertainties in supply chains as the central problem in SCM. Supply chain literature calls out four types of uncertainties. They are as follows:

1. Uncertainty in demand
2. Uncertainty in supplier performance
3. Uncertainty in manufacturing/service operations
4. Uncertainty in customer deliveries

Demand uncertainty could be influenced by cyclicality in demand, random variation in customer purchasing behaviour, competitive actions, weather changes, variations in the regulatory environment (taxation rules, free trade agreements, etc.), long-term and short-term impacts of macro-economic events, such as demographic changes, wars and pandemics, and many more. Uncertainty in demand exists not only at an aggregate level for an offering but also at a more granular level involving location and time attributes of demand as discussed under the heading 'Dynamics of Demand' in this chapter. Uncertainty in supplier performance could involve various aspects such as quantity, quality and timeliness. Uncertainty in production affects process quality, employee availability and productivity, equipment availability and so on that eventually impact the quantity, quality and timeliness of output.

When the uncertainties in demand and supply are juxtaposed, it becomes evident that matching supply with demand is a challenging and ongoing exercise that requires a significant amount of resources in the form of cost, expertise and practice.

11.1.5. Levers to Manage Supply Chain Performance

There are several levers which help in matching supply with demand, which include, but not limited to, production capacity, inventory and supply speed. These levers act as buffers in the supply chain to optimally overcome the mismatch between demand and supply at any point in time. In addition to these levers, economic theory postulates price as a critical lever to match supply with demand (Davis, 1993). However, price as a lever is dominantly considered as a part of the marketing processes and is not discussed in this chapter. The following subsections introduce the levers to manage supply chain performance which will be examined for the impact potential of digital technologies in the subsequent sections in this chapter.

11.1.5.1. Capacity

The capacity to produce a portfolio of offerings is an essential lever for managing supply chain performance. Building up capacity to produce generally takes time. Hence, the capacity of a supply chain is relatively rigid, and this rigidity is a constraint for maximizing responsiveness and minimizing costs in supply chains. If there is a spike in demand, existing capacity may not cater to the spike, reducing responsiveness. Alternatively, if there is adequate capacity to cater to spikes in demand, such capacity will be idle or less productive in the absence of peak demand, resulting in increased costs. An example of design capacity to handle demand spikes is a peak load powerplant. Seasonal peaks in electricity demand are catered to using peak load power plants. Peak load power plants run only when demand for electricity peaks, either due to weather cycles or heightened industrial activity.

While these peak load power plants cater to demand spikes, they also simultaneously reduce the productivity of installed capacity. Capacity related decisions are critical in SCM to manage the uncertainties in both the demand and supply side.

The ability of decision-makers to make a capacity decision is predominantly a function of insights about future demand. Hypothetically, suppose there is absolute information about future demand in terms of volume and product mix, location and time. In that case, managers will make operationally optimal choices on how much capacity to mobilize and where to make it available. However, information about future demand is rarely known with certainty, inducing a certain degree of subjectivity on capacity decisions. Reducing the subjectivity in critical supply decisions enhances value by optimizing capacity decisions, considering both the costs of excess capacity and the opportunity cost of unfulfilled demand. The second-order capabilities enabled by digital technologies (Exhibit 11.3) play a significant role in reducing subjectivity and optimizing capacity-related decisions in a supply chain.

11.1.5.2. Inventory

Inventory occurs in the form of raw materials, works in progress and finished goods. Inventory is the lever which bridges the gap between production and consumption in terms of both rate and volume. Typically, demand fluctuates and goes through peaks, troughs and other random variations. When planning for inventory, managers need to forecast demand and forecast production and supply capacity. Such forecasts are made either based on known market or historical data or predicted data based on market information. Goods produced in anticipation of demand manifest in a supply chain are known as finished goods inventory. There are several nuances involved in inventory types and inventory decisions. For this text, inventory is broadly treated as a mechanism in the supply chain to bridge the mismatch between demand and supply. Inventory is less rigid than capacity, and hence inventory decisions are made both for the short term and long term.

The ability of decision-makers to make optimal inventory decisions is predominantly a function of (a) visibility about the current state of capacity, inventory and demand and (b) insights about anticipated variations in both demand and supply. Hypothetically, suppose there is granular, real-time information about the status of capacity, inventory and demand and perfect information about future variations in demand and supply capacity. In that case, inventory management decisions will be most objective and optimal. However, none of this information is known with certainty, inducing a certain degree of subjectivity in inventory decisions. Reducing inventory decisions' subjectivity enhances value by optimizing inventory, considering both the excess inventory costs and the opportunity cost of unfulfilled demand. The second-order capabilities enabled by digital technologies (Exhibit 11.3) play a significant role in reducing subjectivity and optimizing inventory management decisions in a supply chain.

In addition to improving decision-making, digital technologies offer the possibility to automate inventory management actions. For example, when inventory in a particular warehouse or store for a specific product falls below the required level and when certain other conditions are met, then robotic process automation can be applied to initiate the actions to replenish inventory. Such automation reduces human errors and avoidable delays in initiating inventory replenishment.

11.1.5.3. Time

Time lever in SCM relates to the time taken for demand fulfilment. It is a lever to deal with uncertainties in a supply chain from two perspectives. First, the ability to produce and supply with speed directly influences the supply chain's responsiveness, and hence, higher speed means greater ability to deal with uncertain variations in demand. Alternatively, if customers are willing to wait for fulfilment after they placed their order, it again improves the ability to manage the residual uncertainty on the supply side. This time could range from several years for complex products, like an aircraft, or several weeks or days for a high-volume automobile manufacturer. Time to fulfil is also influenced by the speed at which produce can be transported and supplied to the customer after it is produced. Time to fulfil is relatively lower for locally produced goods and could run into several months for products sourced through a global supply chain spanning several countries.

Supply chain decisions relating to the time dimension are typically a trade-off between the cost of faster supply and the cost of making a customer wait for fulfilment. Processes optimized primarily for fulfilment typically entail higher supply costs, which could manifest in unscheduled transportation trips, using more expensive air freight for faster transportation and so on. On the other hand, processes optimized for cost could lead to poor customer experience, or even lost demand due to a longer time to fulfil demand.

The second-order capabilities enabled by digital technologies (Exhibit 11.3) play a significant role in providing near real-time and granular information to supply chain managers, allowing them to make balanced trade-offs between cost and speed of demand fulfilment.

11.2. CAPABILITIES ENABLED BY DIGITAL TECHNOLOGIES

There are two broad categories of capabilities that are enhanced by digital technologies in the supply chain. The first category of capabilities manifests in the form of appropriate information at the appropriate time (enhanced visibility), enabling better supply chain decisions to optimize the trade-off between timely fulfilment of demand and optimization of factors in the supply chain. The second category of capability manifests in the execution of actions in the form of partial or complete automation. With better information regarding emerging demand and the status of the supply chain, decisions can be more targeted. This information reduces the extent of buffers and supply chain costs while increasing the supply chain surplus. The various capabilities enabled by digital technologies are depicted in Exhibits 6.2 and 6.3 in Chapter 6. They are further contextualized for Digital Supply Chains in Exhibit 11.3, and the scope and impact of digital technologies on supply chains are depicted in Exhibit 11.4.

These capabilities provided by digital technologies can enable businesses to operate at the frontier of supply chain performance and promise to create new possibilities and eliminate inefficiencies, thereby expanding the frontier. Later sections in this chapter explore some examples of digital technology applications that demonstrate their potential to expand performance frontiers. These two types of potential improvements are depicted in Exhibit 11.5.

EXHIBIT 11.3 *Digital Technologies: Mechanism of Impact in Digital Supply Chains*

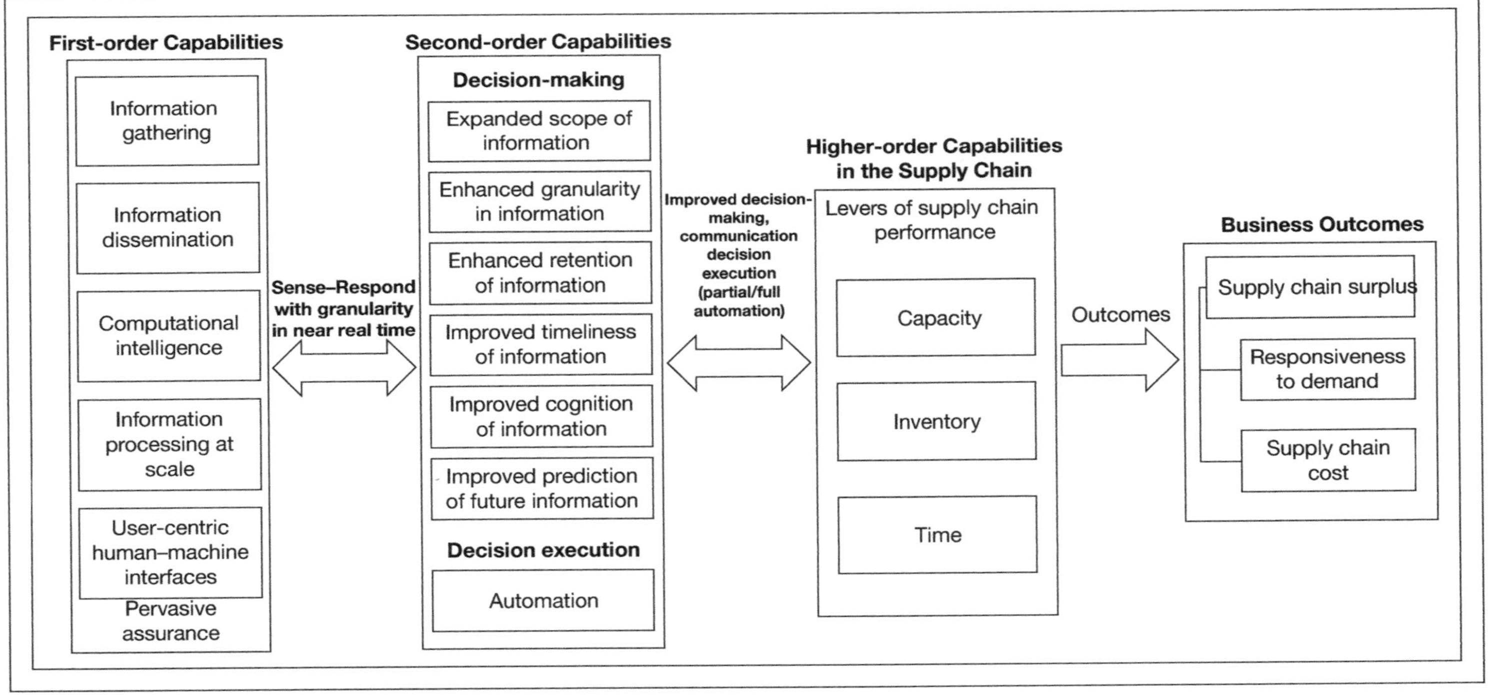

EXHIBIT 11.4 Scope of the Impact of Digital Technologies across Supply Chains

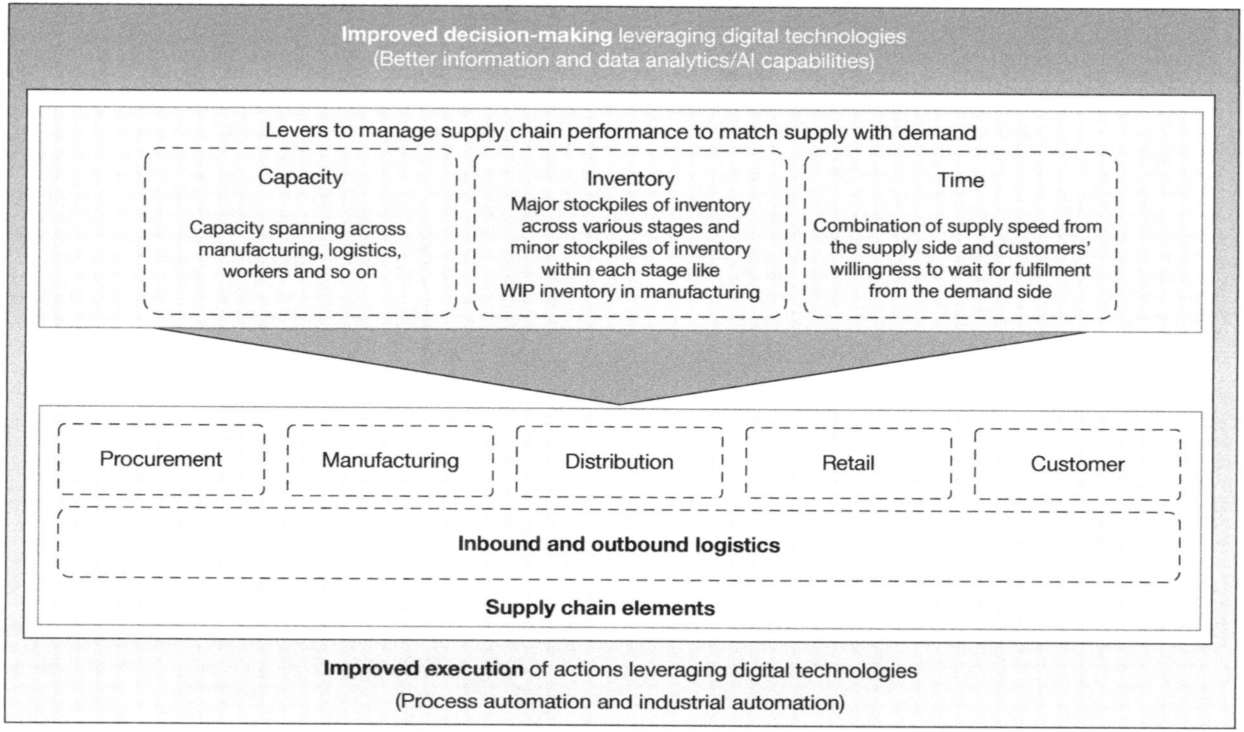

Improved decision-making leveraging digital technologies
(Better information and data analytics/AI capabilities)

Levers to manage supply chain performance to match supply with demand

Capacity

Capacity spanning across manufacturing, logistics, workers and so on

Inventory

Major stockpiles of inventory across various stages and minor stockpiles of inventory within each stage like WIP inventory in manufacturing

Time

Combination of supply speed from the supply side and customers' willingness to wait for fulfilment from the demand side

Procurement — Manufacturing — Distribution — Retail — Customer

Inbound and outbound logistics

Supply chain elements

Improved execution of actions leveraging digital technologies
(Process automation and industrial automation)

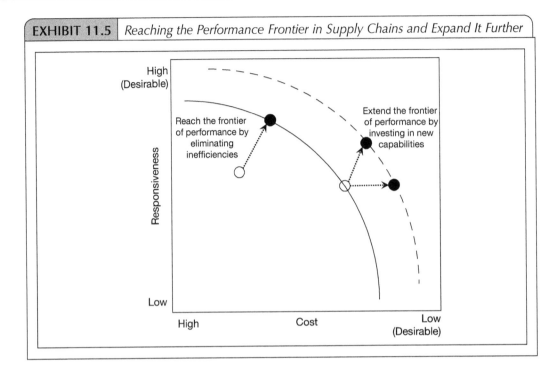

EXHIBIT 11.5 | *Reaching the Performance Frontier in Supply Chains and Expand It Further*

At this point in the chapter, it is important to review the fundamentals of digital technologies presented in Chapters 6, 7 and 8. These digital technology fundamentals are very relevant to examine the impact of digital technologies on SCM.

11.3. DIGITAL SUPPLY CHAINS: TRANSFORMATION POTENTIAL

Digital technologies are applied to solve problems and address opportunities across the various stages in the supply chain. The transformation potential emerges from the strategic use of digital technologies. This transformation potential is underpinned by the capabilities enabled by a combination of several technologies, including, but not limited to, cloud computing, IoT, analytics, AI and blockchain. This section examines the potential to apply these capabilities in high-impact use-case categories at various stages in a supply chain.

11.3.1. Procurement

Digital technologies create the potential for transforming the procurement function through insights from across the supply chain on past trends, current state and predictive insights, enabling timely and optimal procurement decisions and automation of contracting and ordering processes.

Procurement is the process of purchasing necessary inputs for the business to produce and supply its goods and services to the market. This includes the procurement of direct materials and services that are part of the business' offerings (like raw materials in manufacturing) and indirect materials that support the business, for example, computer systems, ACs, power equipment like generators. In large global enterprises, the procurement function spans multiple company locations, countries and suppliers. For example, IBM operates in 170 countries and has over 13,000 suppliers, making the procurement function very complex and critical to its business. This is a critical function because effective procurement controls the costs (both direct and indirect costs) incurred by a business and influences responsiveness in its supply chain, thereby influencing the supply chain surplus. In complex procurement operations, where typically large volumes of data are involved in several decision-making stages, there is a significant potential for gainfully applying digital technologies. Digital procurement can lead to sizable business value, delivering cost savings of 5–10 per cent and efficiency improvements of 30–50 per cent.[1] Some of the illustrative examples of digital procurement are presented in examples as follows:

Examples

IBM reported transformation of its procurement function leveraging analytics and AI solutions are realized $67 million in savings, reducing procurement costs by 13 per cent and, at the same time, improving net promoter score by four points.[2]

A global consumer goods company transformed its procurement function into a data-driven procurement and realized $1 billion in savings over a period of three years. Performance improvement manifested in reduced contract cycle time from 15 days to 2 days, with 99 per cent of contracts being drafted right the first time and 60 per cent of suppliers signing contracts digitally. This also resulted in consistent buyer satisfaction scores.[3]

Intel was awarded the Supply Chain Innovation Award 2020 for their innovation in contract auditing using digitization and advanced analytics. The initiative improved speed by 99 per cent and saved the company $19 million.[4]

In early 2020, Walmart Canada worked with Toronto-based DLT Labs on 'the world's biggest blockchain solution' for transportation payments, the two companies said. DLT Labs claims its blockchain-based supply chain system has produced 'dramatic savings' for Walmart Canada's annual shipments by reducing invoicing disputes between trucking companies and Walmart from 70 per cent down to less than 2 per cent.[5]

A global beauty care company increased its efficiency in indirect procurement with 90 per cent of all indirect procurement transactions visible to managers enabled by analytics and reporting and realized savings of $50M in the sourcing. This was made possible by leveraging digital technologies to standardize processes, automate buying and other self-service capabilities.[6]

11.3.2. Track and Trace

Digital technologies enable capabilities to track and trace critical aspects of objects in a supply chain (raw materials, works in progress, finished goods, goods purchased by customers, etc.) throughout their life cycle by leveraging exponential growth in the instrumentation of objects (IoT) coupled with immutable provenance of digital assets enabled by blockchain.

Track and trace is a dominant use-case category in the supply chain application of digital technologies, especially IoT and blockchain. This category of use cases concern the process of identifying, tracking and tracing the present and past locations (and other associated parameters) of unique items/objects in a supply chain. This could include tracking and reporting the location and other attributes of interest (temperature, humidity, etc.) of transportation vehicles, containers, individual cartons or any other items being transported. Conventionally, barcodes were used to identify objects being tracked, which provided limited track and trace capabilities. With the advent of digital technologies, RFID tags are increasingly used to identify objects and integrate them into a communication network through the RFID readers, thereby enhancing the scope, granularity and timeliness of information about the location and status of the objects of interest. Sometimes the track and trace capabilities manifest as value-added services to end customers, like in the case of courier services where a customer can gain visibility into the location or status of the parcel being couriered. More than technical possibilities, it is customer expectations that are the driving requirements like real-time tracking in logistics. In shipping services real-time tracking of shipment, status was rated as the third most important metric in shipping services: While 44 per cent rated ability to track real-time status among the top three priorities, 17 per cent of shippers identified real-time tracking as the most important metric.[7] Some of the illustrative examples of track and trace using digital technologies are presented in examples as follows.

Examples

Walmart Canada is applying IoT-based sensing and AI-based sense-making tech to ramp up capacity across its distribution centres. The new $3.5 billion investment covers asset tracking sensors in 2,200 truck trailers to give real-time data around the quality and freshness of deliveries, plus a new analytics partnership with Texas-based o9 to predict and plan retail volumes.[8]

DHL and Accenture developed a proof of concept for blockchain in the healthcare industry to address counterfeit medications. Interpol estimates that about one million lives are lost due to counterfeit medicines, and up to 30 per cent of pharma products sold in emerging markets are fake.[9]

iPoint Systems uses blockchain to trace minerals sourced from conflict-affected areas such as Congo and Rwanda. iPoint uses a digital twin approach coupled with an immutable record of minerals and their source information, thereby providing the capability for its clients to keep conflicted minerals out of their raw material supply chain. This use case caters to responsible sourcing as a corporate policy and helps companies comply with regulations like the US Dodd-Frank Wall Street Reform and Consumer Protection Act.[10]

Walmart worked with IBM to implement Hyperledger Fabric, a modular blockchain framework to trace the origin of 25 products from five different suppliers. The business challenge was when a foodborne disease erupted, the business needs to quickly identify the origin of its products to take due safety measures. One of the products chosen by Walmart during an initial pilot was mangoes sourced from the USA. Using the new solution, the trace time needed for the provenance of mangoes went from 7 days to 2.2 seconds.[11]

11.3.3. Industrial Asset Management

Digital technologies create the potential for a new frontier of asset performance enabled by a wide variety of data from industrial assets, collected at a granular level using IoT instrumentation and insights through the application of advanced analytics and AI techniques.

Managing industrial equipment is a very critical activity that ensures optimal utilization and performance of the equipment. There are innumerable varieties of industrial equipment, including, but not limited to, computer numeric control (CNC) machines, material handling equipment, like cranes, earth-moving equipment and a whole range of transportation vehicles, such as forklifts and trucks. Industrial equipment is critical to producing and supplying goods as part of supply chains; they are expensive, have a long lifespan and are subject to wear and tear. Industrial asset management includes several activities over the equipment life cycle, such as commissioning, operation, maintenance, upgradation and disposal. These tangible industrial assets represent the capacity to perform work within supply chains, and their availability and performance significantly impact the capacity level of supply chains to produce and supply.

The application of digital technologies in industrial asset management has demonstrated great potential in improving availability, reliability and extending the life of industrial assets, resulting in both cost reduction and improved responsiveness in supply chains. Maintenance of an industrial asset is one of the most significant and critical endeavours in industrial asset management. Across industries, maintenance costs as a share of operating expenses are as high as 20 per cent, which translates to about 4–7 per cent of gross revenues.[12] Applying digital capabilities to transform maintenance and reliability of industrial assets has the potential for businesses to increase asset availability by 5–15 per cent and reduce maintenance costs by 18–25 per cent.[13] Data-driven proactive maintenance not only improves availability and maintenance costs but also results in up to 30 per cent energy savings.[14] Predictive maintenance also has a significant impact on industrial safety; for example, in the coal mining industry in China, 3,000 people die every year due to workplace incidents, and 80 per cent of these deaths are attributed to equipment failure.[15] One of the most critical factors contributing to such potential is reduced uncertainty resulting from improved information regarding asset performance and the need for maintenance. Digital technologies provide capabilities to gain predictive insights about asset performance trends, enabling optimal decisions regarding timely and efficient maintenance of these assets, thereby increasing their availability, reliability and lifespan.

Exhibit 11.6 depicts the continuum of capabilities that enhance the performance of the asset maintenance process, resulting in benefits across both the dimensions of responsiveness and cost. Advancements in proactive asset maintenance capabilities are underpinned by digital technologies such as IoT, analytics and AI.

EXHIBIT 11.6	Continuum of Capabilities for Industrial Asset Maintenance

Reactive	Proactive	Optimized Proactive	Smart Proactive
Breakdown Maintenance	Preventive Maintenance	Basic Predictive Maintenance	Advanced Predictive Maintenance
• Unplanned downtime • Reactive: Takes higher time and cost to fix • More expensive trade-offs with other competing priorities	• Planned downtime based on a time-based schedule • Based on pre-defined specifica-tions from product design or experience • Reduces unplanned downtime • Does not take into account the current state of the system and its likelihood to fail	• Planned downtime based on data from equipment • Data in the form of leading indicators of failure (such as vibration and heat) • Significant margin of safety in proactive response to limited ability to monitor (of parameters, warning lead time) • Limited automation	• Higher level of ability to monitor (more sensors) • More reach into remote locations due to the evolution of instrumen-tation capabilities and lower cost • Near real-time sensing due to wireless sensor networks • Near real-time response due to AI/analytics • Greater processing power of embedded systems • Greater analytics power in the cloud

Some of the illustrative examples of industrial asset management using digital technologies are presented in examples as follows:

Examples

A global healthcare technology company leveraged digital supply chain solutions to improve back-office productivity by 12 per cent working with Accenture. The initiative delivered a business impact of over $130 million, including $45 million savings in corrective maintenance, $17 million of inventory reduction by reducing supplier lead times, $5 million through reverse supply chain inventory reduction and more.[16]

Michelin uses IoT instrumentation in trucks, including tires instrumented with sensors, analytics and high-order human expertise to provide recommendations to truck fleet managers and coaching to drivers of truck fleets. This service, when implemented, can provide savings of about 2 litres of diesel for every 100 kilometres per truck.[17]

Cheniere Energy uses IoT for managing enterprise assets in LNG operations, resulting in a high level of operational control in planning and scheduling. The maintenance team is able to work with improved efficiency, analyse resource availability and align the right expertise to address issues, leading to improved response times and reduced rework. Once Cheniere collects enough data over a couple of years, they expect to acquire capability maturity to perform preventive maintenance, optimize maintenance activities, improve asset life, reduce unplanned downtime and overall costs.[18]

Shell Nigeria uses an IoT solution to provide digital capabilities to manage its oil fields. The solution offers remote monitoring capabilities to perform surveillance on Shell's oil pipeline and monitor the wellhead in the delta of the Niger River. The solution is underpinned by instrumentation and automation technologies to perform efficient data management and faster analysis for insights. The key benefits included efficient and safe oil field operations. Additionally, the connectivity technology that leveraged a low-power wide-area network saved about $1 million in infrastructure investments for Shell.[19]

11.3.4. Facilities Management

Digital technologies have made the processes of managing buildings and industrial plants more proactive. They have elevated the process objectives from providing safe and hospitable enclosures to providing enhanced occupant experience and improving employee productivity and satisfaction.

Facilities management includes provisioning and maintaining real-estate property, buildings, furniture, power, heating, ventilation and air conditioning (HVAC), lighting, telecommunication, tenant-specific appliances and so on. Real-estate costs are often one of the highest costs for any organization. Space utilization is a very important metric that needs to be managed effectively to reduce supply chain costs. Office spaces have a significant impact on the productivity of employees, and hence need to be managed for workplace ergonomics and experience. Digital technologies enable integrated management of various systems within facilities, extending the frontier of performance both from a cost and efficiency perspective and from an occupant experience perspective. Digital technologies expand the frontier of facilities management by providing integrated, real-time, granular visibility into the performance parameters and utilization of globally distributed facilities. Globally distributed organizations leverage such unprecedented visibility to make, implement, monitor and govern facility management decisions. The COVID-19 pandemic drastically altered the performance expectations of facilities in terms of social distancing, surveillance, workplace safety and hygiene. Some of the organizations that are pioneers in using digital technologies for facilities management have demonstrated the agility and resilience needed to adapt to the new normal in the post-pandemic world. Enhanced level of efficiency, safety and occupant experience have been enabled by unhindered visibility into enterprise-wide data from real-time monitoring of facility environment, equipment and occupancy parameters through appropriate instrumentation (IoT) and application of advanced analytics and AI for dynamic space planning and implementation. Some of the illustrative examples of facilities management using digital technologies are presented in examples as follows.

Examples
When the COVID-19 pandemic hit in March 2020, the IBM Global Real Estate (GRE), which manages 78 million square feet of space across 1,300 locations spread over 100 countries,

had to facilitate 95 per cent of its 430,000-employee base to work from home. For the remaining 5 per cent essential staff, GRE had to provide a safe workplace in line with emerging government guidelines, including providing personal protective equipment (PPE) kits and much more. GRE was able to respond effectively based on granular data from its integrated workplace management system with time-to-insights on global occupancy within minutes (which could have taken several days in the absence of the digital workplace management system).[20]

Elbphilharmonie, a building that includes three concert halls, one hotel, luxury apartments and a public square in Hamburg, Germany, leveraged digital energy and built solutions to provide premium visitor comfort as a top priority and energy efficiency. One of this building's salient features is that it offers air conditioning suitable for people and musical instruments in the concert halls. The digital technologies implemented in this building included 5,210 sensors and actuators, 89,000 communication points, and more than 648,000 meters of cables. The building was called out as one of the 'best reference projects' by the jury of the 'Architects Darling Award' in 2018.[21]

UST Global, an IT services company, decided to upgrade its smart building in Trivandrum, India, into a green building by integrating digital technology and sustainability goals. The company implemented a digitized building, resulting in multifold benefits. An already Leadership in Energy and Environmental Design (LEED) and Indian Green Building Council (IGBC) gold-rated building improved its efficiency further with an additional cost savings of 15 per cent, within two years.[22]

11.3.5. Service Management

Service management is being disrupted by digital technologies, especially automation powered by AI. Intelligent automation in services creates value both by automating tasks and augmenting human workers. Autonomous customer engagement created by conversational agents powered by AI expand the frontier of customer experience.

Services include most activities spanning a broad continuum of low wage services from domestic help to high-value services, such as consulting and audit, and constitute a large proportion of economic activities in both developed and emerging economies. Services are delivered to customers both as stand-alone offerings, such as beauty care and financial audit services, and as part of product-service packages that include annual maintenance services for home appliances. Distinguishing characteristics of services include intangibility and simultaneous consumption (Bordoloi et al., 2019). In most cases, real-time information is critical to service operations. Digital technologies enhance service performance through three key mechanisms.

- First, through enriched information presented to service workers (like a unified information portal for service personnel) and through intuitive and ubiquitous interface technologies such as mobile and other handheld devices (augmenting human capability to perform work)

- Second, through the application of analytics and AI to synthesize relevant insights to augment the knowledge and information available to the worker, like in the case of insights on investment products to a financial advisor, providing investment advice to clients
- Third, through partial or complete automation of service performance, as in the case of conversational agents like chatbots

The above mechanisms enhance service delivery efficiency, service quality and service experience of customers. McKinsey Global Institute estimated about 34 per cent of time spent on all US occupations is spent on activities related to data collection and data processing, the equivalent of about \$2 trillion in wages in 2014—these activity categories have high automation potential from a technical feasibility perspective.[23] Digital technologies that deal with data management, AI and analytics can impact these work activities, either through automation or work or augmentation of work performed by human workers. Some of the illustrative examples of service management using digital technologies are presented in examples as follows.

Examples

AMEX Global Business Travel modernized its IT systems to enable simplified information access to employees through a unified information portal. This system supports local expertise in 140 countries powered by a global knowledge base that holds a range of information from general travel information like flights or information like meeting rooms, which are a part of localized knowledge. This system also automates some part of the customer support using AI-based conversational agents, that is, chatbots that handle about 500 interactions every day. The system has resulted in 18,000 hours of productivity gains and about \$500,000 in cost savings.[24]

Dell Technologies implemented RPA to automate high volume, repetitive transactional HR processes that not only to helped improve efficiency and cost-effectiveness but also resulted in freeing up HR employees for higher-value activities. The automated processes include offer status management, onboarding process reminders, expense error reports, talent acquisition, employee travel invitation letters and many more. As a result of these efforts, Dell realized up to 85 per cent productivity gains in HR productivity.[25]

Automation Anywhere implemented RPA in contract operations that included contract signing and approval, order status updating in customer relationship management software and order status notification. This helped the contract operations team to effectively deal with a spike in workload, resulting in 10 times improvement in contract processing time.[26]

DBS Bank deployed its virtual banking assistant KAI to handle customer queries. In the first six months, the bot was only able to handle conventional queries but was able to learn over a period to address more complex questions. The virtual assistant has been able to take 80 per cent of the queries received by the bank with 80 per cent accuracy, resulting in reduced human worker requirements in the bank's call centre operations. KAI uses conversational AI technology and can respond to customer queries in less than 0.5 seconds. This AI-based conversational agent also enhanced customer experience. It saves the customer from the pain of navigating through the bank's IVR or waiting for a call centre agent to speak with.[27]

MINI CASE 11.1. DISCUSSION: THE DIGITAL TWIN

To execute successful centralized planning, it is essential to gain reliable and timely visibility into inventory levels, production outputs, staff capacity and transportation options. Within SKF's supply chain, with its scale and complexity, it was challenging to make an optimal trade-off between supply chain levers consistently. Timely and reliable information is a prerequisite to gain the right level of visibility to enable the supply chain managers to make optimal decisions. SKF's realized the need to have a digital copy of the supply chain that describes the key elements and attributes in its supply chain with timely information of the status of various operational parameters in the supply chain. The team defined this need or the solution to gain visibility as 'the digital twin of the supply chain'. Such a digital twin would provide the necessary visibility to perform advanced analysis and make data-driven decisions.

Implementation

The idea of digital twins was implemented in three broad steps. First, it was to create a digital structural representation of the end-to-end supply chain, including how the offerings are produced, stored, transported and sold globally. This involved normalizing and consolidating data on approximately 500,000 stocks, keeping units from 40 ERP system instances. One item could potentially be produced in one facility, stored in 20 different warehouses and sold through 40 sales operations. The first step in implementation ensured that data about all relevant aspects of the supply chain, including each stock keeping unit (SKU), are defined and interpreted consistently across the entire network. With this, the supply chain team of SKF has readily available information about their supply chain at a very granular level.

The second step was to augment the digital supply chain representation with operational data which brings the digital twin to life. Operational data includes inventory data, data about in-transit goods, customer orders and so on. Once the second step is implemented, then it will be possible to get answerers to visibility-related questions in near real time. For example, how many specific SKUs are currently being transported in all of SKF's transportation lanes?

The third step was to feed all relevant information from the digital twin's data repository to the supply chain planning software (ToolGroup's SO99+). As part of the third step, SO99+ became a part of daily operational planning. Once the third step was implemented, SO99+ enabled the supply chain team to optimize supply chain performance for all SKUs across all the locations in SKF's supply chain.

A Phased Approach to Transformation

The ambitious transformation was going to be implemented in one production line at a time, including the transformation of adjacent departments such as customer service, manufacturing and human resources. In 2018, there were two factories (one in Austria and the other in France) at which the new system was operational. At these two factories, global planners were using the SO99+ system to balance global supply with demand for their products. From a central location, these planners are responsible for their respective SKF products which are stocked globally in more than 20 warehouses. The warehouse locations stretched across the USA, Europe, the UAE, Russia, China, Singapore and a few smaller warehouses in New Zealand and Thailand.

The Impact

The factories which started leveraging the enhanced data and new capabilities from the digital twin can automate several information processing tasks such as forecasting external demand, factoring in the supply chain lead times, forecasting for net inventory for each warehouse based on actual stock levels and estimated safety-stock levels and creating of replenishment plans to satisfy future customer demand. The system also augmented the capabilities of supply chain planners by proactively alerting them of potential problems such as disruptions in warehouses and unusual demand patterns. This helps them to make better decisions and proactively solve problems before they become a real crisis. With this kind of visibility and decision capabilities, SKF was soon expected to achieve a high level of supply chain capability maturity with one global forecast, globally consistent planning method and a true end-to-end single point global accountability for every product.

Source: How SKF Uses a Supply Chain Twin to Enable Integrated Planning,14 December 2018. *CSCMP's Supply Chain Quarterly.* https://www.supplychainquarterly.com/articles/1806-how-skf-uses-a-supply-chain-twin-to-enable-integrated-planning

To achieve the objective of centralizing the planning, the most important input is adequate and timely information. This information was made available in the following two steps during implementation.

In the first step, the digital twin was modelled in the form of structural digital representation. One way to visualize this step is to view the structural digital representation as a combination of entities, attributes that define the entity's status and relationships between entities. Exhibit 11.7 presents a perspective on how capabilities enabled by digital technologies could potentially be applied in Step 1.

In the second step, operational data is fed into the digital representation. Once the operational data is captured, it represents the status of various entities over time, in terms of various attributes that define the entities. Exhibit 11.7 presents a perspective on how capabilities enabled by digital technologies could potentially be applied in Step 2.

Once the first and second steps are accomplished, then they manifest the second-order capabilities of digital technologies discussed earlier in the chapter (Exhibit 11.3). These second-order capabilities manifest in the form of centralized-near-real-time visibility.

With the visibility generated from the first two steps, coupled with advanced analytics and AI, process level decision-making is enabled, which in this case is centralized global planning using one global forecast, globally consistent planning method and a true end-to-end single point global accountability for every product.

11.4. ANTICIPATING, PREPARING FOR AND DEFINING THE FUTURE OF DIGITAL SUPPLY CHAINS

With the advent of digital technologies, granularity and real-time and predictive insights have become the two key dimensions of organizational capability. SCM leveraging digital is capable of granular and predictive insights in real-time, expanding the frontier of

Second-order Capabilities

Step 1: Structural digital supply chain representation — at the global level

Step 2: Structural representation overlayed with operationaldata, coupled with analytics and AI

Automation of information processing tasks such as forecasting external demand, forecasting inventory and levels

Decision-making

Expanded scope of information

Enhanced granularity in information

Enhanced retention of information

Improved timeliness of information

Improved cognition of information

Improved prediction of future information

Decision execution

Automation

Sense–Respond with granularity in near real-time

First-order Capabilities

Information gathering

Information dissemination

Computational intelligence

Information processing at scale

User-centric human–machine interfaces

Pervasive assurance

SO99+ supply chain software and all associated data bases, hardware, user interfaces (mobile, web) and so on performance in terms of both responsiveness and cost. In 2020, the COVID-19 pandemic comprehensively disrupted global supply chains, making them dysfunctional for prolonged periods of time due to lockdowns and other protocols to manage the pandemic. The global supply chains which were typically tuned for minimal cost with optimal responsiveness were tested for resilience during shock induced by the pandemic. This adverse event has raised several questions regarding the performance priorities and trade-offs in supply chains. While on the supply side, the pandemic tested the resilience of global supply networks, on the demand side, customers are impacted by an uncertain and shifting job environment, making the market more competitive. Measures to improve resilience in the supply chain such as increased local or near-shore sourcing and increased buffers/inventory levels increase costs in the supply chain. Due to these competing drivers of resilience and cost, supply chains are likely to be reconfigured to arrive at an optimal balance between affordability and resilience. Digital technologies will play a crucial role in expanding the frontier of performance of global supply chains to meet the new normal in the post-pandemic world.

SUMMARY

SCM is a very fertile domain for applying digital technologies. The transformation potential of applying digital in supply chains has been demonstrated in several examples. Observing and studying these examples is a quick way to understand the potential of digital supply chains.

The following five aspects of the supply chains are presented in this chapter as the theoretical context to examine the potential impact of digital technologies:

1. Goal of a supply chain is to maximize supply chain surplus
2. Anatomy of supply chains which captures the key sages, elements and flows involved in a typical supply chain
3. The relationship between responsiveness and cost in supply chains
4. Uncertainties in a supply chain
5. Levers to manage supply chain performance

The capabilities enabled by digital technologies are contextualized for supply chains, and this chapter discusses how the first-order, second-order and higher-order capabilities enabled by digital technologies are linked to the business outcomes in supply chains.

Examples of application of these capabilities in high impact domains/use-case categories within supply chains are discussed to highlight the manifestation of digital impact. The following domains are discussed with examples: procurement, track and trace, industrial asset management, facility management and service management.

The chapter discusses the case of a global supply chain transformation using digital technologies and finally concludes with a peek into the future with the performance expectations that shift as the world recovers from the COVID-19 pandemic. A few ideas have been presented as motivations to promote managerial thinking on the future of global supply chains enabled by digital technologies.

Discussion Questions

1. Describe the anatomy of supply chains. What are the key stages, elements and flows involved in a typical goods/manufacturing supply chain?
2. What are the two dimensions that define the supply chain performance frontier? How are they related to each other?
3. What are the sources of uncertainties in supply chains?
4. What are the levers of SCM? How do they help manage the uncertainty of demand and supply?
5. How do the first and second order capabilities enabled by digital technologies get applied in SCM? Describe their scope and impact.
6. What are the top three highlights of the digital transformation potential of the following domains?
   a. Procurement
   b. Track and trace
   c. Industrial asset management
   d. Facility management
   e. Service management
7. Based on your understanding of the supply chain performance frontier and the potential of digital technologies, what is your anticipation of the future of global supply chains?

GLOSSARY

AI: AI has several connotations, ranging from narrow intelligence manifested in ML applications to ASI that imagines a state where machine intelligence far exceeds human intelligence. For the purposes of this text, we may define AI as a high-level machine intelligence as one that can carry out most human professions at least as well as a typical human.[28]

Analytics: Analytics refers to software tools and techniques to analyse data and generate insights from data. They are broadly classified into descriptive analytics, diagnostics analytics, predictive analytics and prescriptive analytics. Techniques to perform predictive and prescriptive analytics typically involve the application of AI.

Blockchain: Blockchain is a system of recording information (called blocks) and recording the changes to information by chaining (cross referencing) of blocks. A blockchain system stores specific chained blocks of information that are duplicated across a distributed computer network. Changes to the transactions and modifications to the blocks are governed by algorithms that make it nearly impossible to fraudulently change the status of these chained blocks of information. More details on Blockchain are presented in Chapter 8 (Composite Technologies).

Cloud computing: Cloud computing is a type of computing technology that enables on-demand availability of computing resources over the internet or other long-distance networks. The computing resource could include computer hardware or storage hardware or various types of software such as operating systems, database and user applications (office productivity applications, enterprise applications, etc.).

CNC machine: CNC stands for computer numeric control. It is used for automatic control of machine tools by using computational intelligence that is embedded as part of the machine. CNC machines process a piece of material based on codified programming instruction, without being controlled by a manual operator directly.

HVAC: HVAC stands for heating, ventilation and air conditioning. HVAC systems are used for controlling the environmental temperature and other attributes like humidity within the building and vehicular environments like containers. The goal of HVAC systems is to provide comfort for occupants and to provide acceptable levels of air quality.

IGBC: IGBC stands for Indian Green Building Council. IGBC is a part of the Confederation of Indian Industries. The council offers a wide set of services with the goal of enabling a sustainable built environment for all. IGBC's offerings include developing new green building rating programmes, and related certification and training services.

IoT: It is a global infrastructure for the information society, enabling advanced services by interconnecting (physical and virtual) things based on existing and evolving interoperable information and communication technologies.[29] More details on IoT are presented in Chapter 8 (Composite Technologies).

LEED: LEED stands for Leadership in Energy and Environmental Design. It is the building rating system in the world. LEED provides a framework for healthy, highly efficient, and cost-saving green buildings.[30]

ML: It is the field of study in computer science that gives computers the ability to learn without being explicitly programmed (Park et al., 2018).

PPE kits: PPE stands for personal protective equipment. It is a kind of protective clothing that includes goggles, helmets and other garments designed to protect the wearer from infections or injuries.

RFID: RFID stands for radio frequency identification. It typically consists of adhesive tags that use electromagnetic fields to identify and track objects to which these tags are attached to.

RPA: RPA is a category of software applications that execute repetitive tasks based on triggers or inputs from real-time data processing applications or AI applications or any other business or IT applications. Sometimes, RPA is paired with AI to embed a certain degree of learning into the RPA use cases. A brief contextual overview of RPA is presented in Chapter 7 (Digital Technologies: Data Management Section).

NOTES

1. https://www.bcg.com/en-in/capabilities/procurement/digital
2. https://www.ibm.com/services/client-stories/procurement-transformation
3. https://www.accenture.com/in-en/case-studies/operations/reinventing-procurement-function
4. https://www.supplychainquarterly.com/articles/3944-intel-takes-home-cscmp-innovation-award

5. https://enterpriseiotinsights.com/20200722/channels/news/walmart-canada-invests-in-iot-ai-blockchain-smart-logistics
6. https://www.accenture.com/in-en/case-studies/operations/transforming-source-to-pay
7. https://www.ups.com/us/en/services/knowledge-center/article.page?kid<hig>=</hig>art170d3b3c382
8. https://enterpriseiotinsights.com/20200722/channels/news/walmart-canada-invests-in-iot-ai-blockchain-smart-logistics
9. https://www.dhl.com/global-en/home/press/press-archive/2018/dhl-and-accenture-unlock-the-power-of-blockchain-in-logistics.html
10. https://www.ibm.com/blockchain/use-cases/success-stories/#section-10
11. https://www.hyperledger.org/learn/publications/walmart-case-study
12. https://www.accenture.com/_acnmedia/pdf-21/accenture-intel-connected-asset-mgmt-intel-solution-brief.pdf
13. https://www.mckinsey.com/business-functions/operations/our-insights/digitally-enabled-reliability-beyond-predictive-maintenance
14. https://new.siemens.com/global/en/products/buildings/services/asset-performance-services.html
15. https://www.shell.com/business-customers/lubricants-for-business/industry-insights/the-benefits-of-predictive-maintenance.html
16. https://www.accenture.com/in-en/case-studies/operations/intelligent-supply-chain-boosts-productivity
17. https://www.accenture.com/_acnmedia/pdf-1/accenture-driving-unconventional-growth-through-iiot.pdf
18. https://www.ibm.com/case-studies/cheniere-energy-inc
19. https://www.businesswire.com/news/home/20160330005357/en/Ingenu-and-KON%C4%8CAR-Partner-with-Shell-to-Deliver-Digital-Oilfield-Connectivity-to-Nigeria-Pipeline-Facility
20. https://www.ibm.com/case-studies/ibm-global-real-estate-tririga-watson
21. https://www.boschbuildingsolutions.com/xc/en/news-and-stories/elbphilharmonie/
22. https://www.se.com/in/en/work/campaign/life-is-on/case-study/ust-global.jsp
23. https://www.mckinsey.com/~/media/mckinsey/featured%20insights/Digital%20Disruption/Harnessing%20automation%20for%20a%20future%20that%20works/MGI-A-future-that-works-Executive-summary.ashx
24. https://www.servicenow.com/customers/amex-gbt-portal.html
25. https://www.automationanywhere.com/solutions/bpo/dell-uses-rpa-for-hr-processes
26. https://www.automationanywhere.com/resources/customer-stories/automation-anywhere-aworks
27. https://www.dbs.com/lm/how-dbs-banks-kat-banking-chatbot-is-setting-a-new-benchmark-in-customer-service.html
28. https://www.researchgate.net/publication/280838978_Future_Progress_in_Artificial_Intelligence_A_Survey_of_Expert_Opinion
29. https://www.itu.int/rec/T-REC-Y.2060-201206-I/en
30. https://www.usgbc.org/help/what-leed

REFERENCES

Bordoloi, S., Fitzsimmons, J., & Fitzsimmons, M. (2019). *Service management: Operations, strategy, information technology* (9th edition). McGraw Hill.

Chopra, S., Meindl, P., & Kalra, D. V. (2013). *Supply chain management: Strategy, planning, and operation* (vol. 232). Pearson.

Davis, T. (1993). Effective supply chain management. *Sloan Management Review, 34*, 35–35.

Larson, P. D., & Rogers, D. S. (1998). Supply chain management: definition, growth and approaches. *Journal of Marketing Theory and Practice, 6*(4), 1–5.

Park, C., Took, C. C., & Seong, J. K. (2018). Machine learning in biomedical engineering. *Biomedical Engineering Letters, 8.* https://doi.org/10.1007/s13534-018-0058-3

Digital Marketing

Learning Objectives

Digital marketing is gaining a more significant share of marketing budgets compared to traditional marketing across all types of industries and companies. These include large corporations to small enterprises, products and services companies and companies focusing on business and consumer markets. Digital marketing offers many benefits, including the ability to attract larger and targeted audiences at lower costs and generate data for analytics. This chapter will help the reader understand:

- What digital marketing is and how it is different from traditional marketing
- The importance of a digital marketing strategy
- How to build a digital marketing campaign
- The use of digital and social media in brand building, customer acquisition, customer service and retention

---

Mini Case 12.1

Nancy Sharp was the Director of Sharp Hardware Supplies (SHS), a company located in Marietta, Georgia, that sold hardware supplies and equipment to home consumers, tradespersons such as electricians, carpenters and plumbers and small construction companies across the greater Atlanta area.

Started by Nancy's father, SHS, the 30-year-old business has expanded to four stores across the Atlanta Metropolitan Area. The company sold a wide range of products, including hand tools, power tools, hardware, electrical supplies, lawn maintenance and plumbing equipment. SHS sold some of its own branded products and also stocked most national brands.

The hardware equipment supplies business in Atlanta was on a general decline due to the presence of national chains which had set up large retail outlets across the city and were able to sell products that were priced lower than those sold by SHS. The company was also witnessing competition from online hardware stores and multi-product e-commerce platforms like Amazon that also stocked hardware products. The highly profitable consumer business of SHS has been declining over the last decade, losing out to e-commerce and the national chains. With a new generation of tradespeople replacing its long-time customers, the company had started to lose this part of the business to the e-commerce platforms.

Nancy realized that to survive, SHS would need to rebuild its brand among the new generation of customers. The company needed to launch a digital marketing campaign, in addition to its traditional marketing methods. Nancy had to put together a marketing strategy for SHS.

12.1. CREATING A MARKETING STRATEGY

Peter Drucker (1971), the doyen of modern business thinking, wrote that a company's only reason for existence is its customers, and therefore marketing and innovation are the only two functions that matter. According to him, the rest is detail. While, 50 years later, this statement can be debated, marketing remains one of the most critical functions in any company.

The process of developing a marketing strategy has not changed over the last many decades. Exhibit 12.1 provides a widely used framework for marketing strategy development.

EXHIBIT 12.1 *Marketing Strategy Framework (Dolan)*

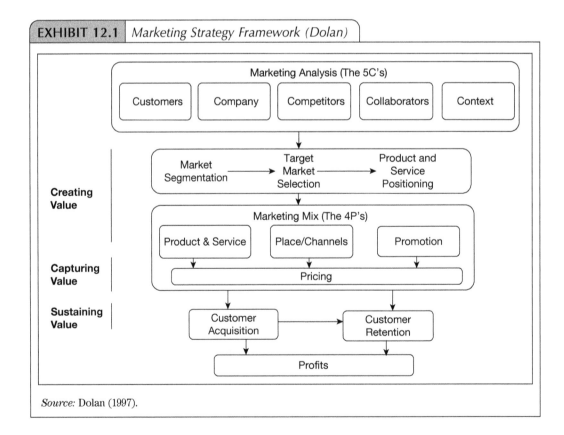

Source: Dolan (1997).

As per the framework, marketing strategy begins with an analysis of the market ecosystem in which a firm operates (5Cs). The next step is to develop strategies that create value for customers through segmentation, product selection and positioning. The operational elements of a market strategy consisting of the 4Ps help in capturing value. Finally, the value is sustained through customer service and retention.

12.2. GOING DIGITAL

As discussed briefly in Chapter 2 (Exhibit 2.5), digital technologies have had a significant impact on the 4Ps of marketing (Kotler, 2003).

Product: In its traditional definition, a product means a well-defined object or service targeted at a specific set of industries or clients. Digital is changing the boundaries of this definition to include products as part of platforms. Let us take an example of a simple electric switch. In the traditional model, a company made electric switches, and these were marketed to consumers or businesses (builders). In the digital world, this is changing. Switches come inbuilt with IoT devices and are an integral part of 'hubs' that manage other appliances such as thermostats and refrigerators through a single device like a mobile phone. This shift has significant implications for designing all the 'Ps'. Some questions organizations need to ask themselves are:

- What are the redrawn industry boundaries? (Is a mobile phone now a competitor for an electric switch?)
- What are the disruptions that are happening in the company's industry or adjoining industries?
- How does the company digitally evolve its products to be a part of these platforms as platforms change the fundamental way business is done, away from linear models to networks?
- Should a manufacturer focus only on the company's original products or focus on a set of related products that fit into a platform offering?
- How does a company focus on building a network of partners for the other products, assuming they do not have the competency to build all of them independently as some of these partners may be competitors in the old world?

Place: The place is the location where a product is marketed and sold. In the example of electric switches, there was an element of push (advertising for brand building) and then the pull (via distributors and electric retailers) in the traditional model. In the digital model, a platform owner becomes an important distribution partner. For example, a Google Nest or an Amazon Alexa become important channel partners/influencers. Even if not part of a hub, switches will now have to be sold through e-commerce platforms such as Amazon and Alibaba.

Platforms have also made globalization relatively easier. Companies need not launch exclusive operations in international markets and can instead leverage global platforms. Some key questions that companies need to ask themselves are:

- What are the platforms that are relevant to the products/services?
- How do companies participate in these platforms?
- How can companies leverage these platforms to expand to new markets and customer segments?

Price: As discussed in Chapter 4 (Business Model Innovation), digital has transformed the way products/services are priced. Subscription-based or annuity models are becoming more and more prevalent than one-time pricing. For example, traditional products ranging from razor blades to personal automobiles are now available on subscription models. The power of pricing has shifted to the platforms that dictate pricing and revenue shares. Pricing conflicts across channels have taken new dimensions with the aggressive discounting strategy of e-commerce platforms. Key questions include:

- How to price product/services in models that increase customer stickiness?
- How can a company modify its pricing model to make its products/services suitable for newer segments?

Payment methods have also changed due to digital and companies need to accommodate receiving payments from multiple payment platforms.

Promotion: The most visible change digital has brought about is how products are promoted, both in B2C and B2B contexts. Companies need to have a comprehensive digital marketing presence to reach their customer base. This includes:

- Online presence (website)
- Online marketing on e-commerce platforms
- Mobile applications
- Search marketing including SEO and SEM
- Social media marketing through social media such as LinkedIn, Facebook and Instagram
- Online reputation management
- Whitepapers/news articles/blogs

12.2.1. Data Is the New Oil

One of the most significant impacts of digital marketing is the availability of rich customer behaviour data. Historically, acquiring customer data was expensive as companies needed to collect data from formal surveys and market research. Digital ensures that data is generated everywhere and continuously. Experiments on a customer's reactions to modifications of any of the 4Ps are relatively easier to conduct. However, the ease of data generation has created a new problem, converting it into actionable information. The other challenge of digital media is ownership of data and who it belongs to—the customer, the platform or the product company. Finally, a large proportion of data generated through digital marketing is in unstructured formats (e.g., data on review platforms) and needs new tools and technologies like AI to harness.

In summary, the overall process of creating a marketing strategy has remained constant. However, digital has revolutionized the way value is captured and sustained.

The remaining chapter focuses on the use of digital media in brand building and lead generation.

12.3. DEFINING DIGITAL MARKETING

Digital marketing refers to promotions delivered through digital channels such as search engines, websites, social media, email and mobile apps. It is different from traditional channels such as television or print media in multiple ways (Exhibit 12.2).

Digital marketing leverages digital medium and provides marketers with many benefits such as targeted communications, instant interaction and an ability to measure effectiveness. In developed markets, like the USA, digital media accounts for close to two-thirds of media spending. Even in emerging markets, like India, where the overall penetration of digital marketing is lower, it is growing three times faster than traditional media.[1]

12.4. THE DIGITAL MARKETING PROCESS

Digital marketing begins with defining the client's objectives and target segments (Exhibit 12.3). Once the market is determined, the next step is to identify the suitable digital channels to be used to reach the target segment and develop content for each of these channels. As will be discussed later in this chapter, the content varies based on its purpose and channel used.

The next phase of a digital campaign is to develop a budget and timelines for each of the activities. The final stage in the process is to monitor the campaign's effectiveness using tools, like Google Analytics. The process is iterative, which means that the content, campaigns and channels are modified based on results achieved.

As a customer goes through the buying process, each of the components of digital and traditional media plays an important role (Exhibit 12.4).

EXHIBIT 12.2 | *Digital versus Traditional Marketing*

Attribute	Traditional	Digital
Medium of communication	Print, outdoor, paper based	Electronic/Digital
Direction of communication	Unidirectional	Multi-directional
Communication style	Formal, legal	Formal and casual
Availability	During specific hours or times slots	24 × 7 customer dependent
Customer response	Long	Instant or short
Measurability	Proxy measures	Structured

EXHIBIT 12.3 | *Digital Marketing Process*

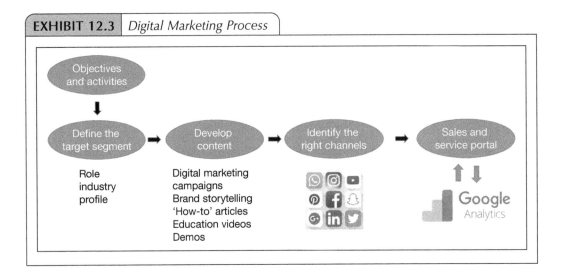

EXHIBIT 12.4 | *Media across a Customer Journey (Illustrative)*

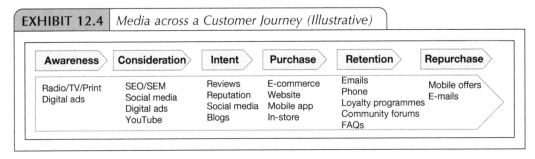

Activities such as online advertising and search marketing are essential during the awareness and consideration phases. Websites, portals and e-commerce sites are important in the purchase phase, and social media and blogs form an important part of post-sale customer feedback.

12.5. TYPES OF DIGITAL MARKETING

The types of digital campaign are vast and often confusing (Exhibit 12.5).
Some of the typical components of a digital campaign include:

Search marketing: Leveraging search engines, such as Google and Bing, to market products through a variety of techniques
Social media marketing: Use of social media, such as Facebook and LinkedIn, for brand building and lead generation
Mobile marketing: Use of mobile technologies to market products. The mechanisms could be on the device (e.g., pushing an advertisement onto a phone) or off-device (e.g., scanning a QR code for receiving promotional material)

EXHIBIT 12.5 | *Types of Digital Campaigns*

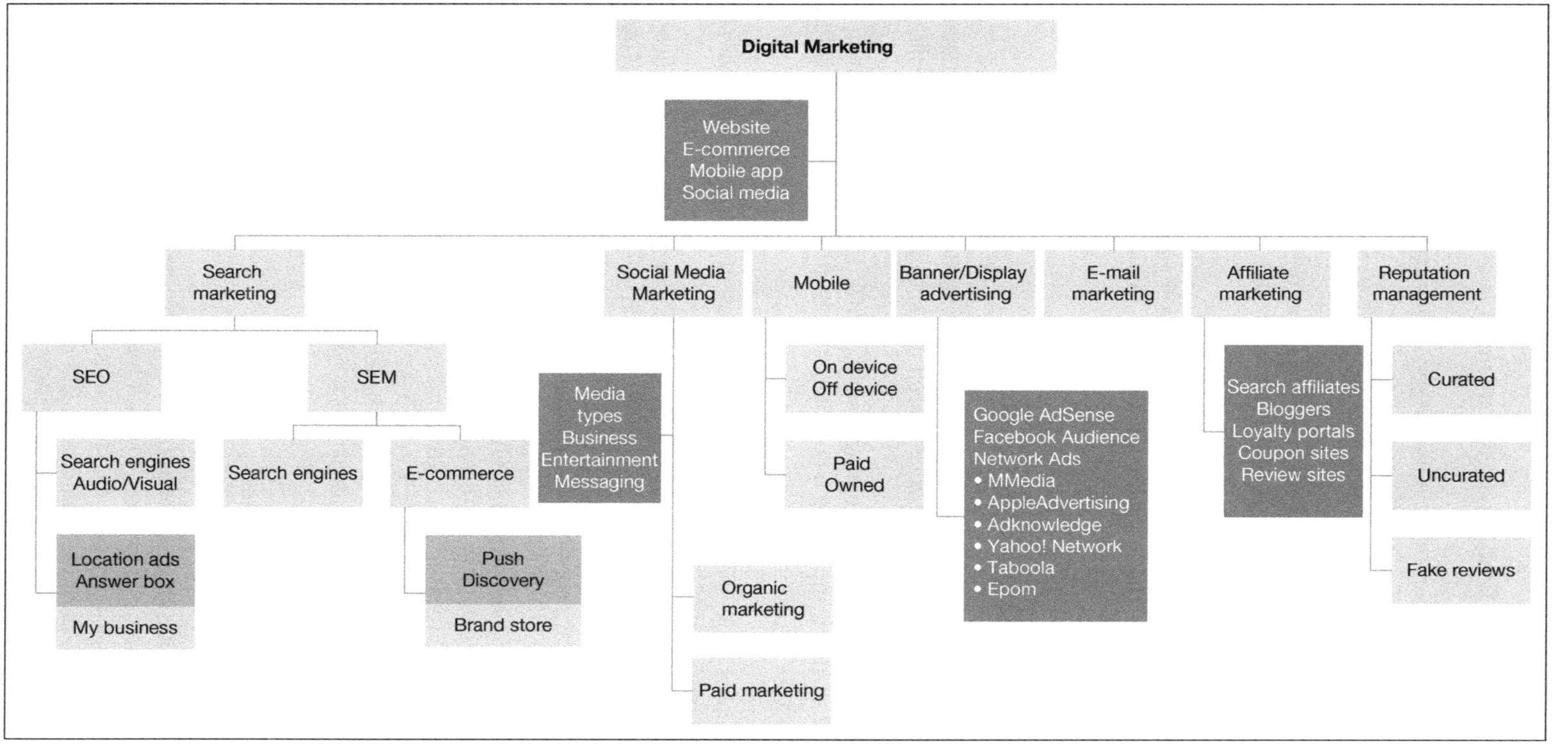

Digital Marketing

Website
E-commerce
Mobile app
Social media

Search marketing

SEO

Search engines
Audio/Visual

Location ads
Answer box
My business

SEM

Search engines

E-commerce

Push
Discovery
Brand store

Social Media Marketing

Media types
Business
Entertainment
Messaging

Organic marketing

Paid marketing

Mobile

On device
Off device

Paid
Owned

Banner/Display advertising

Google AdSense
Facebook Audience
Network Ads
● MMedia
● AppleAdvertising
● Adknowledge
● Yahool Network
● Taboola
● Epom

E-mail marketing

Affiliate marketing

Search affiliates
Bloggers
Loyalty portals
Coupon sites
Review sites

Reputation management

Curated

Uncurated

Fake reviews

Display marketing: Posting advertisements in target online publications (e.g., CNET or CNN)

Email marketing: Deploying email-based campaigns for lead generation and information sharing

Affiliate marketing: Incentivising other sources, including websites and portals, to divert traffic and leads

Reputation management: While online reputation management is not strictly a tool for creating awareness or generating leads, a lack of proper reputation management processes can impact a company's sales

The above list is not exhaustive but covers a significant proportion of a digital marketing strategy. The rest of the chapter provides a high-level overview of each of these components.

12.5.1. Search Marketing

Search marketing is digital marketing based on terms used in search engines like Google or Bing. There are two primary forms of search marketing, which are as follows:

- **SEM:** It is the process of gaining website traffic by purchasing ads on search engines.
- **SEO:** It involves improving a company's website to increase its visibility for relevant searches.

Google dominates SEM, with over 90 per cent share of search in most countries worldwide other than China, where Baidu is the leader.

While Google has dominated the search market for close to two decades, it is now facing a threat from competitors such as Facebook and e-commerce giant Amazon. More and more customers are moving specific types of searches directly to these platforms. For example, a significant proportion of product searches have moved to e-commerce search engines like Amazon.

SEO and SEM have different benefits, and a company needs to have a strategy for both. Exhibit 12.6 provides the key differences between the two forms of search marketing.

SEO is an organic form of marketing and takes a longer time to have an impact but also has an impact that lasts longer. It is relatively inexpensive and perceived to be more trustworthy by customers. SEM, on the other hand, is instant as it is a form of paid advertising. Its impact is immediate, and an advertiser pays for an ad only when the audience clicks on the advertisement.

12.5.1.1. Search Engine Marketing (SEM)

SEM is used to provide short-term or immediate results. It attracts users who have an intent to purchase a product or services. From a buyer's perspective, it is easy to transact with just a click. Advertisers pay only for the customers who click on their link, and it is easy to control costs by pre-defining a budget. SEM also provides useful analytics such as click-through rates (CTR) and cost per click (CPC).

EXHIBIT 12.6	*SEO versus SEM*

Parameter	SEO	SEM
Results	Takes time as it is organic	Immediate as it is paid advertising
Cost	No direct cost; only cost of creating content/websites and so on	Pay per click; can get expensive
Visibility	Shown to anyone searching keywords	Shown to select/targeted audience
Search results	Shown as organic search; more trust and permanence	Shown as ad; limited to time of campaign
When to use	Long-term impact Brand building	When quicker results are required Lead generation

One of the most critical parameters in SEM is ad rank. Ad rank is defined as the position of an ad in a search engine result. A company needs to achieve a high ad rank as studies have shown that 60–70 per cent of clicks are for the top three links. Google defines the ad rank as the CPC bid × quality score.

Quality Score

- Quality score is an estimate of the quality of ads, keywords and landing pages. Higher quality ads can lead to lower prices and better ad positions.
- The quality score is reported on a 1–10 scale and includes expected CTR, ad relevance and landing page experience.
- The more relevant ads and landing pages are to the user, the more likely it is that you will see higher quality scores.

Source: Google.com

CPC bid: This is the cost-per-click bid by the advertiser for specific keywords.

A website, to receive a high ad rank, needs both a high CPC bid and a high-quality score. At the same time, websites with a high-quality score can afford to bid a lower CPC and yet achieve a good ad rank. This makes it essential for companies to have an effective SEM strategy focusing on improving their quality score.

To achieve a higher quality score, a website needs to have the following, as a minimum.

- Good landing page
    - o Original content on the home page
    - o Inclusion of keywords in headline and content
- Higher CTR
    - o High-historical CTR results in better quality scores
    - o As a corollary, new advertisers may have to pay higher

- Relevance
  o High linkage of search terms with keywords on the landing page
  o Content that is relevant to the most frequent search terms

Some of the key characteristics of a good ad are as follows:

- Three clear components: headline, URL and description
- Different landing pages for each product category
- Rich content includes advanced features such as video, audio and other elements that encourage viewers to interact and engage with the content
- A clear call to action
- All keywords are clearly included

Keywords

Keywords are words and phrases that help define what the content on a website is about. In terms of SEO, they are the words and phrases that searchers enter into search engines. Keywords are the matching links between searches and results. The ad rank for a page on a search engine result page and keywords determine what kind of traffic a website gets. Therefore, identifying the right keywords and bidding the optimum price for them is critical for SEO and SEM success.

Keywords are typically classified into short tail and long tail. Short-tail keywords are shorter terms that generate higher volume but are not specific to a product. Long-tail keywords are longer phrases and more specific. As expected, these keywords drive a lower volume of high-quality traffic. For example, 'SUVs' is a short tail keyword that will drive high but non-specific traffic. On the other hand, the 'SUV Land Rover Defender' will drive lower traffic but only from people looking specifically to buy this or other premium SUVs, thus resulting in a greater probability of sales conversion (see Exhibit 12.7).

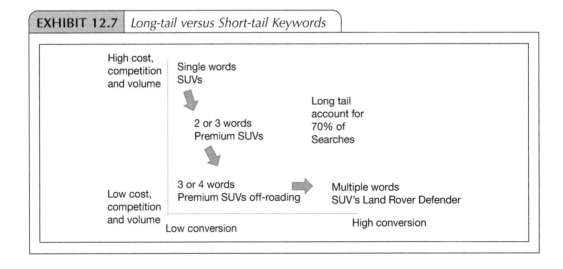

EXHIBIT 12.7 | *Long-tail versus Short-tail Keywords*

Keyword matches can be set up to be an exact match or broad matches depending on the advertiser's requirements.

Advertisers can evaluate and adjust the performance of their campaigns using the flexible reporting provided by Google Analytics.

12.5.1.2. SEM on E-commerce Sites

As discussed earlier in the chapter, e-commerce platforms are gaining share from traditional search engines.

The advertisements on e-commerce platforms can be of three types. Push ads are ads pushed out to customers based on keywords. Discoverable ads are ad suggestions for other products that a customer might be interested in purchasing. For example, a consumer searching for toothpaste on an e-commerce website might be shown ads for soaps. E-commerce platforms also allow brands to create exclusive brand stores.

12.5.1.3. Search Engine Optimization (SEO)

SEO is the process of increasing the visibility of a website or a web page in a search engine's unpaid results. As discussed earlier, it is unpaid and organic, and therefore, searchers find SEO more credible. However, SEO takes a long time to implement and grows organically.

Achieving a high search engine ranking (SER) is not an exact science. However, some obvious factors impact ranking across each search engine. At a broad level, SER is dependent on authority and relevance. Authority refers to how authoritative a domain or page is and is determined by the quality and quantity of external links that refer to that domain on specific topics. For example, if a technical support site is referred to by microsoft.com or similar sites, its authority will be enhanced. Relevance refers to the significance of the domain or page to the keywords being searched. This has been discussed in the SEM section above.

Implementing an SEO Strategy. As outlined in Exhibit 12.8, SEO implementation can be categorized into six steps (Gupta, 2020), which are as follows.

Audit: The first step is to audit the current website/URL for its effectiveness. Several free tools are available to conduct this audit. The key elements of an SEO audit include the following:

- **Keyword position:** Position and frequency of keywords in the title and content of the website
- **Keyword cloud:** Visual representation of keywords used on the website
- **Sitemap:** Availability of a clear structure of the website in the form of a sitemap
- **Brower/operating system/device compatibility:** Compatibility with multiple browsers and devices such as mobile, tablets and computers
- **Backlinks:** Ensuring that all backlinks are functioning and real
- **Domain authority:** Authority and relevance of the site in its specific area of interest

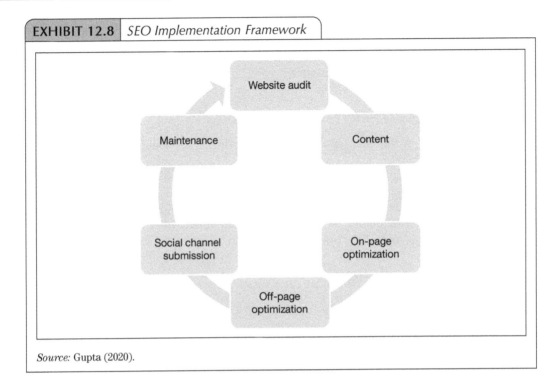

Source: Gupta (2020).

- **Speed audit:** Speed of loading and refreshing
    Content: Content refers to all the information available on a website. To achieve a higher SEO, the content needs to be unique, original and refreshed frequently. The greater the variety of content, the better, and this could include text, hyperlinks, images, videos and audio files. While text allows for faster load times, images, videos and audio attract a greater number of users. Another feature of good content is the robots.txt file. The robots.txt file, also known as the robot exclusion protocol, is a text file that tells web robots which pages to crawl and not crawl. This helps search engines crawl the right pages that have the keywords that have been searched for.
    On-page optimization: An effective SEO strategy requires optimization on the website. Some of the factors that help in this process include the following:
- **Site performance:** The site should load in less than two seconds
- **Domain name:** Domain names and URLs should be easy and intuitive to find and remember
- **The 404/500 errors:** Errors on navigation should have 'easy to find' links leading back to the home page
- **HTML tags:** HTML tags on the webpage provide a structure. Generally, there are three types of tags, which are as follows:
- Meta tags provide information about the webpage
- Heading tags are titles or subtitles that are displayed on a webpage. It is recommended that up to six such layers are clearly identified (h1–h6)

- Anchor tags are used to link a webpage to other webpages
- **Image/video optimization:** If the site has images and videos, these need to be optimized for faster loading and for access across operating systems and devices
- **Schema.org standards:** Schema.org is a collaborative community activity that helps create, maintain and promote schemas for structured data on the internet.
- **RSS feeds:** RSS feed items will not enable much better ranking as their content is syndicated and therefore not unique. However, the increase in traffic generated as a result of the site being the place to go for information will help SEO.
- **Microsites:** Creation of microsites for specific products or services that a company wants to promote that have its own unique set of keywords

  Off-page SEO: This refers to all the activities done away from the website to raise the ranking of a page with search engines, like, for instance, the creation of backlinks as these provide source diversity and source independence. Some techniques to increase the number of backlinks are inclusion in directories and social media profiles. Creating forums, newsletters and outreach through social media and influencers also helps increase the number of backlinks. An easy way to develop a backlink strategy is to study competitor links.

  Social media reach: This is becoming increasingly important for SEO. Therefore, it is essential to create a social media presence on multiple platforms and create links to the website through cross-posting. The use of social media is discussed in a separate section later in this chapter.

  Maintenance: SEO is not a one-time activity, and its impact decays within a short period, primarily driven by competition activity. While it is important to understand what techniques positively impact SEO, it is equally important to understand that techniques referred to as 'Black-Hat' techniques can harm a website's SEO. Therefore, SEO managers need to understand what some of these Black Hat techniques are and avoid using them. Duplicating content and overloading the website with keywords (keyword stuffing) are some examples of such techniques.

12.5.1.4. Other SEOs

Some other forms of SEOs include local search SEO, answer box SEO and Google 'My Business'.

Local search: 'Near me' is a very common part of search terms. Google allows for map-based marketing, where the nearest businesses relevant to the search terms are highlighted. These businesses can be ranked based on proximity, ranking or rating in google reviews.

Answer box SEO: These appear above organic search results and are referred to as position zero. Some tips to appear in answer boxes are as follows:
- Target relevant keywords. 'Long-tail keywords' trigger most answer boxes.
- Create content using a question-and-answer format.
- Include lists, graphs and tables.
- Maintain SEO best practices.

Google 'My Business': This is a platform used extensively by small businesses to highlight their business. Companies can register themselves on this platform and provide information on the company's name, type of business, brief description and links to contacts and a URL. This information is shared across all Google platforms.

12.5.1.5. Voice and Visual Search

Voice and visual search are becoming increasingly relevant in SEO. Visual search is the leading trend as 90 per cent of the information transmitted to the human brain is visual. Google, Pinterest, eBay and Amazon are all investing heavily in visual search. Some tips to achieve better SEO in visual search are the inclusion of clear images with title and name tags. Voice search is also growing, with 55 per cent of teenagers primarily using this mode. Voice searches are heavy on long-tail keywords and are conversational. SEO techniques must be adjusted to accommodate these differences.

12.5.1.6. Google versus Bing

Google and Bing form two large search engines. The way SEO works across these two platforms differs (Exhibit 12.9).

While Google search is more contextual, Bing focuses on a match of keywords. Another key difference is that Google prefers fast-loading text pages, while Bing prefers multimedia content.

12.5.2. Social Media Marketing

Social media is any digital tool that allows users to create and share content with others quickly. The usage of social media is increasing and, therefore, an ideal platform for marketing. In 2018, there were around 2 billion unique social media users around the globe.

Some of the unique characteristics of social media are as follows:

- It is digital based and growing rapidly.
- Unlike traditional media, it is location independent.

EXHIBIT 12.9 | *Google versus Bing Search*

	Google	Bing
Keywords	Based on searcher's intent Contextual cues Semantic search	Match of keywords
Meta keywords or meta tags	Less relevant	Very important
Backlinks	Page rank of the linked site	Focus on domain age and some specific extensions
Multimedia	Fast loading pages	Preference for heavy multimedia

- It is collaborative with significant interaction between users.
- It is instant and allows for feedback on products and services.
- There is a large volume of user-created content.

Social media marketing leverages these strengths of social media to provide a cost-effective medium for both brand building and lead generation. It is less intrusive and more effective than traditional channels like email or telephone campaigns. Social media marketing also contributes to better SEO, and there are several options available for advertisers depending on their end goals for campaigns.

Exhibit 12.10 summarizes some of the popular social media platforms and the benefits they offer.

All B2B companies must have a LinkedIn strategy and B2C companies a Facebook strategy at the minimum. Both these platforms are explored in greater detail in this section.

EXHIBIT 12.10 | *Marketing on Social Media Platforms*

Medium	Features	Benefits
LinkedIn	Real people Lead generation tools	Best suited for B2B marketing Brand building and lead generation Thought leadership through groups and posts
YouTube	The second biggest search engine Largest for 'how to' (70%) Educational videos, brand telling videos, entertainment videos	Suitable for brand building 'How-to' videos, product demos and videos
Facebook	2.5 billion active users Broad-based user profile Average FB users have 200 friends (viral) Mostly real profiles (businesses can see who their viewers are and good for analytics) FB ads integrated with WhatsApp and Instagram Powerful ad platform	Suitable for brand building across all types of companies Lead generation for SMEs through FB marketplace and pages
Twitter	Interacting versus broadcasting Sharing information/driving engagement/building brand Search for clients directly Social listening	Good for brand building Useful to showcase a company and its leadership
Instagram	Visual content Suitable for brand building—humanizing a brand Growth tools for businesses Influencer marketing	Brand building Most used platform for influencer marketing

12.5.2.1. Facebook Marketing

Facebook allows for two types of marketing.

'Organic marketing' is where a company sets up its Facebook page and posts company, product and brand information at regular intervals. Some of the tactics to increase organic (unpaid) reach include the following:

- **Finding the right content mix in advance:** The content could be from:
  o Own website or blog content
  o Other people's content (including influencers)
  o Brand images
  o Funny pictures
  o Facebook live video
- **Posting times to suit the end customers:** For example, a brand focusing on baby products could find that the ideal time to post is late evening as that is when new mothers have time to check their accounts.
- **Becoming the 'Go To' page for users:** The page becomes the authoritative destination for certain types of information.

Facebook also has a highly structured and easy to set-up 'paid marketing' process through its ad manager. The Facebook ad manager has three steps, which are as follows:

- Ad campaign—defining ad goals
- Ad set—defining targeting and bidding
- Ad launch

Campaigns can be set with three objectives: Awareness is for introducing a company and its brands and products; consideration is for getting customers to think more about the product/service, and conversion is about getting them to buy or use the product or service.

Facebook provides several ad types, including single ads, multiple or carousel ads, videos and slideshows. Companies can either participate in auctions that will determine their ad placement or buy a fixed number of advertisements for a pre-determined budget. Facebook also has a powerful insight tool to help advertisers analyse their ads' reach and effectiveness and make necessary changes.

Facebook allows the integration of specific features across all its platforms, such as Instagram and WhatsApp.

WhatsApp is primarily a chat platform, but it has large numbers of business users across the world. To leverage this opportunity, WhatsApp has launched 'WhatsApp for Business' focused on small businesses. Small and mid-sized businesses can now create a catalogue to showcase products and services. It also provides tools to automate, sort and quickly respond to messages and integrate with websites and portals for communication.

12.5.2.2. LinkedIn

LinkedIn hosts over 700 million+ users across 200 countries. The profiles on this platform are mostly real, and the platforms are best suited for B2B and P2P relationship building.

LinkedIn profile pages and groups are some of the basic features of this platform. The platform offers LinkedIn's Sales Navigator tool that has 22 different filter categories for sales and lead generation. These categories include geography, keywords, relationship, industry, job and function, job title, seniority, years in the position, years at the company, years of experience, company and company headcount. Sellers can shortlist profiles based on these categories and generate a lead list. LinkedIn also offers InMail to reach these profiles and provides backward integration into popular CRMs.

There are several newer social media platforms, like TikTok, that are also gaining popularity. Social media marketing is expected to continue to grow and become a large part of companies' digital marketing strategies.

12.5.3. Display Advertising

This is the most common type of digital advertising where digital advertisements (as against physical advertisements) are displayed on various websites, portals and social media platforms. The advertisements can be in the form of banners, images and videos. The media can be static, animated (e.g., GIFs), interactive (clickable) or videos. Some of the large display advertising networks are Google Display Network and Facebook Audience Network.

Google Display Network allows advertisers to place their ads on over two million websites. This network is different from the Google Search Network that was discussed in the previous search marketing section. Display networks focus on audience networks and profiles and not on keywords. Using this network, advertisers can target audiences both on Google sites as well as partner networks such as news channels and other websites. There are several methods to target audiences. Some of the most common ones are as follows:

Affinity audience: This is targeting people based on their lifestyles, tastes and passions. Google qualifies and categorizes audiences based on data obtained from various sources. For example, the ad for a new car may be displayed to an audience with a demonstrated affinity for automobiles.

In-market audience: These are audiences who are in the market to buy a product. The audience may be researching products or have demonstrated that they are actively considering purchasing a service or product. These audiences are targeted by advertisers focused on getting conversions.

Remarketing: A remarketing list is a collection of website visitors or app users who have previously interacted with a company's website or mobile app. Remarketing is created by adding codes to websites that allow tracking such audiences. The code also stores information on what the audience has interacted with (e.g., a specific product on the website), the time spent on the website or even abandoned carts.

Demographic audience: As the name suggests, Google Ads allows an advertiser to reach a specific set of potential customers who are likely to be within a particular age range, gender, parental status or household income. For instance, an advertiser for women's cosmetics can reach an audience of women of a particular age group and geographic location.

Custom audience: Advertisers can also create custom segments to target. This can be based on keywords, apps or URLs.

12.5.4. Mobile Marketing

Mobile devices are becoming the primary tools for accessing the internet. In 2020, there were 5.2 billion unique mobile phone users worldwide, with India and China leading the growth. Android is the primary platform in most countries. Spends on mobile devices are projected to reach a share of 64 per cent of digital ad spends by 2022. As a result, companies must have a mobile marketing strategy.

Mobile marketing offers many benefits. It is low cost and targeted. The messaging is real-time and two-way. Mobile offers multiple messaging formats allowing for various types of marketing configurations. Since everyone carries their mobile phone, marketing on this platform is instant, two-way and has mindshare. Using GPS and other location-based tools, mobile marketing is also contextual. For example, a person may receive a restaurant promotion when they are in geographic proximity of that restaurant. Mobile phones have also integrated payments as app-based payments, which are gaining popularity across the globe.

Mobile marketing is broadly classified into two groups, which are as follows:

- On-device advertising
    o Network-based (via SMS and Wireless Application Protocol [WAP])
    o Off network—unrelated to a network provider, for example, social media, apps and so on
- Off-device advertising (typically call to action)
    o Barcodes/QR code
    o Missed calls to a number

It can also be 'paid advertising' or 'owned advertising'. Exhibit 12.11 provides examples of paid mobile advertising.

On the other hand, 'owned advertising' is advertising on a company's own website or mobile app.

Good mobile apps are clutter-free. Good mobile apps include features such as location-based sensors, proximity-based marketing features and QR code integration to payment apps. Some steps a company can take to increase the visibility of its mobile apps are as follows:

- Build an app landing page
- Encourage app reviews and ratings
- Freemium
- Optimize for all app stores (Android, iOS)
- Enhance visual appeal with image and video content
- Run app store ads
- Press releases to talk about the app
- Social media presence/blogs and so on to promote apps

12.6. DIGITAL MARKETING ANALYTICS

As discussed earlier in the chapter, one of the critical benefits of digital marketing is the generation of data that can be analysed. All digital platforms provide comprehensive analytical tools to analyse the effectiveness of marketing activities.

EXHIBIT 12.11 | *Paid Advertising on Mobile Platforms*

	Type	Illustration
SMS	SMS Push	160-character text message
	SMS footers	20–60-character text below a non-advertising message
	USSD	Message with links
	Short codes	Voting, activating channels on OTT platforms
	Enquiry services	Rail, weather, astrology and so on
Voice	Outbound dialer calls	Pre-recorded messages (e.g., COVID-related messages)
	Mobile radio	Used in rural areas
	CRBT/AdRBT	Caller ring back tones
	Enquiry services	Rail, airline, weather and so on
WAP	Mobile sites	WAP banner adds
In-app	Mobile apps	Adds/Ads inside an app
Videos	Pre-app	Video ads that play before an app opens
	Live advertisements	Adds/Ads inside apps (e.g., inside media apps)

Source: Adapted from Gupta (2020).

The metrics used to track digital marketing can be broadly classified into three categories: behaviour, experience and outcome.

12.6.1. Behaviour Analysis

This was traditionally called clickstream data analysis and measures visitors' intents on pages they visit, what they click and in what order. Some of the key metrics are as follows:

(Confusing definitions highlighted below.)

- A visit is a single browsing session. If a visitor views another page on the site within 30 minutes of the last page view, it is counted as the same visit.
- 'A page view' is defined as an instance of a page being loaded (or reloaded) in a browser. Repeated views of the same page are counted as separate page views.
- 'Time on site' reflects the level of engagement of a visitor. The more time spent on a site, the greater the engagement.
- 'Bounce rates' represents the percentage of visitors who enter the site and then leave (bounce) rather than continuing to view other pages on the same site.
- 'Heat map analysis' shows the percentage of people who interacted with different parts of a web page. The most-used parts of the page are often displayed in dark red and with less viewed parts displayed as lighter red, orange, yellow and so on.

- 'Exit pages' is a metric for determining which page users are exiting the page. Businesses need to understand why users exit and how they can be retained.
- 'Traffic sources' to a website reflect whether the stream of traffic is from direct visitors, search visitors or referral visitors.
- 'Search type' indicates the type of search, including voice, text or image.

12.6.2. Outcome Analysis

- 'Conversion rate' is the percentage of users who perform the required action like a sale.
- 'Average order value' is the total revenue generated divided by the number of orders.
- 'Multichannel funnel' reports answer these on how marketing channels (i.e., sources of traffic to the website) work together to create sales and conversions.
- 'Micro conversion' are transactions that lead to a sale eventually. For example, a visitor who provides her information and downloads a demo or white paper.
- 'Macro conversion' is the final sale or conversion.

12.6.3. Experience Analysis

Customer experience analysis is a method for measuring whether the website, app, product or service meets or exceeds consumer expectations.

'Site surveys' help in understanding the value of a web page. The surveys can appear in different forms, from pop-ups to full-page overlays. These surveys can also appear on places on a site, depending on the pages that need to be improved.

'Usability surveys' help determine the ease of navigating the site and finding the right products or services.

'Website experimentation and testing exercises' conduct various tests, including A/B testing or split testing where two versions of an ad are tested among similar profiles of the customers to determine which of them is more effective.

Google Analytics and Facebook Insights provide formats for standard and customizable reports to track the metrics discussed in this section.

MINI CASE 12.1. DISCUSSION

SHS catered to three different segments of customers. There were end customers who bought spares and other equipment for 'do-it-yourself' repairs. The second were tradesmen who were individual contractors, and the third were small construction companies. The marketing plan that Nancy had to put together needed to address all these segments.

End customers, currently, are people who live within 10 miles of any of the SHS stores. To retain and expand this profitable segment, Nancy felt that SHS should continue attracting customers who walked into their stores and target customers who were buying supplies online from the greater Atlanta region. As a first step, Nancy worked with a local digital marketing agency and created an SHS website and portal. The agency helped in managing and improving the SEO of the website by focusing on search terms, such as 'local hardware store', 'hardware store near me' and 'hardware suppliers'. The geographic limit for SEO was set within the greater Atlanta region. SHS also tied up with a local logistics company to deliver supplies to their customers' homes. To being with, Nancy felt that SEM was an expensive option for SHS. Instead, she chose to list SHS through Google Local Search and Google My Business. The company also created several 'how-to' videos that were hosted on the SHS website as well as on YouTube. Finally, Nancy decided to advertise through a combination of spots on local radio and display advertising among targeted audiences in Atlanta. The display ads were a mix of brand-related ads and also of discounts on purchasing products online through the SHS website.

Nancy felt that she needed a different strategy to attract tradespeople. This segment was very mobile and spent a lot of time coordinating and scheduling customer appointments. Nancy realized that if SHS could develop a mobile app for tradespeople, it would make their lives easier. Within a short period of six months, SHS launched a mobile app that was available free for tradespeople. The app had several features, including appointment scheduling, a basic CRM, GPS tracking and spares ordering. Every tradesperson had the option of creating a co-branded customer interface with their company name and the SHS brand visible to users. Tradespeople were encouraged to get their regular customers to download the app to schedule any repairs and monitor the progress. The app was integrated into various payment options. The app also provided access to the SHS mobile store. As a tradesman received or confirmed an appointment, they had the option of ordering the required hardware and chose if these items should be delivered on-site or if they would collect them from the nearest SHS store. The app became very popular among tradespeople and their clients as it made coordination much easier. For SHS, it provided brand visibility, loyalty from tradespeople as well as increased sales volumes. SHS used a combination of radio spots and banner advertising in online trade journals to popularize this app.

For small construction companies, SHS chose to use a combination of radio spots, banner advertising and email campaigns to increase brand awareness. SHS also ran a series of webinars explicitly focused on using various types of hardware and invited speakers from its customer base as panellists.

Within a year of launching a highly targeted digital, mobile and radio campaign, Nancy had driven SHS to become the growth leader in the hardware business in the Atlanta Metropolitan Area.

SUMMARY

Digital has had a significant impact on the marketing of products and services. While the process of developing a marketing strategy has not changed, the implementation of the 4Ps has changed significantly due to the availability of digital technologies. Products and services that were distinct have now been combined. Promotions that were largely print and paper-based are now done online through digital platforms. Digital marketing has several advantages over traditional marketing. It allows for instant and targeted communication with tools for interaction with potential customers. A digital strategy consists of many components. Display advertising is about moving ads away from traditional media to digital media. Given the large number of websites and webpages, companies such as Google and Facebook provide platforms for distributing display ads across their own and partner platforms.

Search marketing is one of the strategies and has two sub-components: SEO and SEM. SEO is organic and takes time to build but has greater credibility. SEM, on the other hand, is faster to roll-out and is based on payment for keywords. Google has dominated the search engine for close to two decades and has a significantly larger market share than the next largest search engines, such as Bing and Yahoo. In recent times, however, it has begun to lose share to e-commerce search engines such as Amazon and app-based searches.

Keywords form an integral part of the search and can include short words or terms referred to as short-tail or longer phrases called long-tail terms. Long-tail keywords are less expensive, leading to more conversion but drawing a lower volume of traffic.

Social media marketing is another form of digital marketing. Several platforms are available for marketing, each tailored to a specific type of messaging and customer segment.

Mobile marketing is another form of digital marketing that is growing rapidly due to the proliferation of mobile devices and extensive access to the internet through mobile phones, especially in emerging economies. Companies need to consider integrating the various forms of mobile-based marketing into their digital marketing strategies.

One of the critical differentiators of digital marketing is the availability of data and the potential of analytics. There are three types of analytics in digital marketing. These are behaviour-, experience- and outcome-related analytics. Digital marketing is no longer an option, and all companies, both large and small, need to have a digital marketing strategy.

Discussion Questions

1. What is digital marketing? What are some key activities in a digital marketing strategy?
2. Outline all the ways where SEO and SEM are different. Why should a company pursue both strategies?
3. What are the types of keywords in search marketing? In what scenarios should companies use the various types of keywords?
4. Why is mobile marketing necessary for a company? Describe the various types of mobile marketing.
5. What is social media marketing? What are some of the key platforms available for B2B and B2C marketing?
6. Describe the three types of digital marketing analysis/analyses and provide examples of each

GLOSSARY

Ad rank: It is defined as the position of an ad in a search engine results. Google defines the ad rank as the CPC bid × quality score.

Affinity marketing: It refers to marketing through companies that have a similar customer profile or products.

CPC bid: It is the cost per click bid by the advertiser for specific keywords.

Digital marketing: It refers to promotions delivered through digital channels such as search engines, websites, social media, email and mobile apps.

Display marketing: It is the posting of advertisements in target online publications (e.g., CNET or CNN).

Keywords: These are words and phrases that define the content of a website.

Mobile marketing: It is the use of mobile technologies to market products. The mechanisms could be on the device (e.g., pushing an advertisement onto a phone) or off-device (e.g., scanning a QR code).

Off-page SEO: It refers to all the activities done away from the website to raise the ranking of a page with search engines. Backlinks are an example of this type of SEO technique.

On-page optimization: Techniques used directly on a website for SEO including good headlines and content, tagging and so on.

Quality score: It is an estimate of the quality of ads, keywords and landing pages. Higher quality ads can lead to lower prices and better positions.

Search marketing: It is the leveraging of search engines such as Google and Bing to market products through various techniques.

SEM: It is the process of gaining website traffic by purchasing ads on search engines.

SEO: It is the process of improving a company's website to increase its visibility for relevant searches.

Social media marketing: It is the use of social media such as Facebook and LinkedIn for brand building and lead generation.

NOTE

1. https://www.financialexpress.com/industry/technology/digital-surpasses-print-to-become-2nd-largest-advertising-medium-after-tv/1857934/

REFERENCES

Dolan, R. J. (1997). Note on marketing strategy. Harvard Business School Background Note 598-061.

Drucker, P. F. (1971). *Drucker on management.* Harper & Row.

Gupta, S. (2020). *Digital marketing.* McGraw-Hill Education.

Kotler, P. (2003). *A framework for marketing management.* Pearson Education India.

13

Implementing Digital Technologies

Learning Objectives

This chapter focuses on the implementation of digital technologies. It covers topics such as conducting a digital audit and determining the degree of digital maturity of a company, identifying process and technology gaps and finally prioritizing implementation. This chapter will help readers understand:

- Assessing the digital maturity of organizations
- Mapping the customer journey
- Developing an implementation road map
- Prioritizing digital implementation
- Risks in digital implementation
- Concepts of change management
- Ethics in the digital world

Mini Case 13.1

Asian Paints is the leader in the Indian paint industry with a revenue of over $2 billion. The company is the third-largest paint company in Asia and among the top five players in decorative paints worldwide. The company's operations span 16 countries (mainly emerging markets), with 25 paint manufacturing plants worldwide and servicing customers in over 60 countries. In India, Asian Paints distributes its products through 45,000 dealers spread across the country. A decade ago, the company began transforming from a brick-and-mortar product manufacturer into an agile and adaptive enterprise that provided value-added services to help its customers make their homes beautiful.

How did the company make this transformation? How could/did the company map its customer journey? What technologies would/did it need to incorporate to support new business models?[1]

13.1. INTRODUCTION

As discussed in the previous chapters, developing a digital strategy requires a combination of BMI, people innovation product and process innovation, all enabled by digital technologies. Digital technologies are, therefore, deeply interlinked with the other elements of digital transformation/strategy. This chapter focuses on how a company can digitally transform based on customer and business needs. It delves into how these needs can be translated to process and product innovations, and the digital technologies that enable these innovations.

Implementing digital technologies can be broadly divided into the following three phases:

1. **Digital maturity assessment:** This refers to understanding where a company is on its digital journey.
2. **Customer mapping and road map development:** The next step is to map/identify the underlying business processes that will drive a digital strategy and the technologies that will enable these processes. In most traditional companies, several digital interventions are required to bridge the identified gaps. Companies need to prioritize these implementations based on the company's maturity, its competitors, pain areas, costs, time, the complexity of execution and risk management.
3. **Implementation and scaling:** Once the processes and technologies are identified, the next phase comprises developing and implementing a digital road map. Implementation also involves testing the solutions in a pilot environment before scaling the road map.

As discussed in the earlier chapters, the digital landscape is evolving rapidly. Therefore, for a company to be competitive, the steps described above must be iterative and ongoing.

13.2. DIGITAL MATURITY ASSESSMENT

A digital maturity model is a framework used to assess how digitally mature an organization is currently and what is required to build a road map for the future. Several frameworks have been developed by consulting and technology companies. Some frameworks focus on specific functions like marketing, while others are holistic and can be used across an organization. Some of the proprietary frameworks are discussed in this section.

The **Deloitte-TM Forum model**[2] is an organization-wide framework and provides benchmarks against peers and competition. The model measures digital maturity across 5 core dimensions and 28 sub-dimensions. These sub-dimensions are further broken down to 179 individual criteria (Exhibit 13.1).

The **Forrester digital maturity model**[3] assesses a company along the following four dimensions.

1. **Culture:** A company's approach to digitally driven innovation and how it empowers employees with digital technology
2. **Technology:** A company's use and adoption of emerging technology

---

EXHIBIT 13.1 | *Deloitte: TM Forum DMM Model*

Customer	Strategy	Technology	Operations	Organization and Culture
Engagements	Brand management	Applications	Agile change management	Culture
Experience	Ecosystem	Connected things	Automated resource management	Leadership and governance
Insights and behaviour	Finance and investment	Data and analytics	Integrated service management	Organization design and talent management
Trust and perception	Market and customer	Delivery governance	Real-time analytics and insights	Workforce enablement
	Portfolio ideation and innovation	Network	Smart and adaptive process management	
	Stakeholder management	Security	Standards and governance	
	Strategic management	Tech architecture		

*Source:*Adapted from tmforum.org.

---

3. **Organization:** How aligned a company is to support digital strategy, governance and execution
4. **Insights:** How well a company uses customer and business data to measure success and inform strategy

The model requires companies to score their status on a set of questions on each of the four dimensions. The final score determines the digital maturity of the company.

McKinsey Digital 20/20's[4] survey-based diagnostics leverages expert-developed questions to assess an organization's current capabilities, benchmark answers against peer results and best practices. The tool assesses companies across seven dimensions: strategy, analytics, technology, marketing, people and operations.

BCG's Digital Acceleration Index (DAI)[5] is a diagnostic tool that lets companies conduct a digital capability assessment and compare their digital performance with peers, the industry average, best-in-class digital leaders and everyone in between. It also assesses their readiness to become a bionic company, that is, to blend new technologies with human capabilities to power growth, innovation, efficiency and resilience. DAI assesses digital maturity across 36 categories such as customer journeys, digital supply chain and marketing personalization.

EXHIBIT 13.2 | *Digital Adoption Stages*

Stage	Definition
Digital unaware	Unaware of digital transformation or digitalization. Basic awareness of digitization and automation.
Digital aware	Aware of digitalization. However, the company does not have a digital strategy or has implemented digital technologies.
Digital starter	Has a basic digital strategy. Has begun implementing some digital technologies.
Digital proficient	Has a clear digital road map. In the process of implementing multiple digital technologies. Focusing on BMIs.
Digital expert	Fully digital (these are typically only born-digital or digital-native companies).

While these tools have nuances, they all focus on key elements covered as part of the digital model discussed in Chapter 1. These are customers, product/services, processes, people including culture, organizational design, technologies and strategies. The tools provide companies benchmarks of their digital journeys in comparison to their peers.

Based on its digital maturity, a company can be classified into one of the following categories (Exhibit 13.2).

Other than some SMEs, there are very few companies in the unaware phase that have never explored digital strategy or technologies. Most traditional companies are in the starter and proficient phase with a few companies in the expert phase. Most newer companies that are born digital or are digital native are in the expert phase.

Digital maturity also varies by industry. Industries such as financial services, retail, travel and hospitality are ahead in their transformation, while process manufacturing, agriculture and utilities are relatively behind.

13.3. CUSTOMER MAPPING

A customer journey is a way a customer interacts with a company. For a B2C company, this could be how a customer decides on a product and then purchases it from one of many channels. For B2B companies, this could be how a customer makes a buying decision, orders a product, tracks the order's status or interacts with the vendor. It is essential to map the entire customer journey to determine what is working well, what pain points need to be improved and what is working but is not required. Mapping a customer journey allows a company to determine the priorities for its digital transformation.

Exhibit 13.3 is an illustrative customer journey mapping that led to the concept of ridesharing.

The journey can be mapped by talking to several customers individually or in group discussions.

EXHIBIT 13.3 *Customer Journey Mapping*

Activity	Current Process	Pain Point	Customer Need
Search for a taxi service	Yellow pages/directory Get a number from a reference Use a previously used taxi service	May not be able to find the yellow pages/direct number	A universal way to contact a taxi service irrespective of one's location
Contact the service	Call the service and speak to the dispatch representative	Not easy to get through Service may not be available 24 × 7	24x7 contact Not dependent on human contact
Order the taxi	Provide the current location and destination details	Long process Potential to get the address wrong	An automated way to send location and destination
Schedule the services	Provide time for the cab	A taxi may not be available If not available, the customer must repeat the entire process with another service	Increase the availability of service Eliminate the need to contact multiple services
Wait for taxi	Wait at the scheduled location	If there is any change in location, it is not easy to make the change	Ability to change the location at the last minute
Taxi status	Call the taxi service to follow up	Need for constant follow-up	Ability to track the status of the booking
Interact with the taxi driver	Inform the taxi driver of the destination	Duplicated effort	Eliminate the need to repeat details of the destination
Drive to location	Provide directions to the driver	Need for the customer to be constantly alert and interact with the driver	GPS-based system that automatically guides the driver to the destination
Determine the cost of a trip	Driver or dispatch clerk pre-informs the customer or fare is based on a metre	Lack of transparency on the method used to calculate the fare and distance	An automated and transparent system of fare calculation Pre-inform customer of the charges
Payment	Cash or credit card (only if a driver has the provision)	Time-consuming The driver may not have exact change	Automated payments
Customer feedback	No current process A customer has to call back the taxi service	Lack of an easy process to provide feedback	Automated and instant method for feedback
Customer loyalty	No process	No process for taxi service to maintain a relationship with its customers No incentive for a customer to use the same service	Loyalty programmes Method for constant interaction between the service provider and customer

13.3.1. Design Thinking

There are several frameworks for customer journey mapping but one of the most frequently used methodologies is design thinking. The concepts of design thinking have been used in qualitative market research and product design for decades. Its current form is associated with David Kelly, a Stanford professor and founder of leading design firm IDEO. Since the early 1990s, many companies across multiple industries have successfully applied design principles to strategy and innovation.

Design thinking moves companies away from a linear approach where solutions are decided upfront based on a superficial understanding of customer needs and the focus is on implementation. It helps companies explore alternative solutions by asking four questions: Where are they today? Where all can they be? How can they get there? What is the best way?

Design thinking is human centric, with customers and stakeholders co-creating the solutions. It allows for multiple possibilities to emerge out the discussions with customers. It is also iterative and leverages concepts like rapid prototyping (Exhibit 13.4).

The design thinking processes require companies to observe what their customers do rather than what they say they do. This helps uncover real issues they never knew existed and leads to innovative digital and non-digital solutions.

Key elements of the design thinking methodology include early and frequent interaction with customers, agile process design, rapid iterations involving building prototypes early in the process and testing with customers. Design thinking teams need to have a balance of creative, intuitive, process-driven and analytical individuals. This allows for creative conflict and multiple perspectives to problems and solutions. The concepts of design thinking can be used at a functional or organizational level. Innovation, product development, sales and marketing, and customer services are functions that are common users of the methodology. However, design thinking is as relevant for production, supply chain, HR and finance functions. As an example, design thinking can be used by the HR function to improve the recruitment process or by the finance function to improve the supplier payments process.

EXHIBIT 13.4 | *Design Thinking Process*

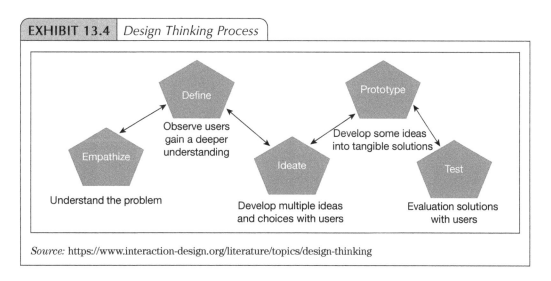

Source: https://www.interaction-design.org/literature/topics/design-thinking

13.4. ROAD MAP DEVELOPMENT

Once the customer's pain points are determined, the next step is to find solutions to alleviate these pain points. Exhibit 13.5 illustrates the steps to be taken once the needs of a customer are defined in the ridesharing illustration.

As can be seen from Exhibit 13.5, the customer requirement is a service, in this case a mobile phone-based app, with features such as GPS and payments. The app needed to consolidate individual drivers and cab services to increase the availability of rides and eliminate the need to contact multiple providers. The customer journey mapping also showed that three versions of the app are required: cab services company, drivers and customers. Data should be seamlessly shared across the three versions of the app. The entire service has to be backed by analytics. This is what we know today as ridesharing services.

The next step for a company is to create a road map for implementing the solutions highlighted in Exhibit 13.5. In the case of the ridesharing illustration, MVP may involve

EXHIBIT 13.5 | *Developing a Solution Road Map*

Customer Needs	Solutions
A universal way to contact a taxi service irrespective of one's location	One universal solution that works across any location
	Mobile phone based
24 × 7 contact	Mobile app with all features
Not dependent on human contact	
An automated way to send location and destination	GPS-based solution
Increase the availability of service	Consolidate all service providers under one app
Eliminate the need to contact multiple services	
Ability to change the location at the last minute	GPS and App
Ability to track the status of the booking	GPS-based tracking
Eliminate the need to repeat details of the destination	A driver is provided with an app as well and data automatically updated in driver's app
System that automatically guides the driver to the destination	GPS-based system
An automated and transparent system of fare calculation	App to provide a cost estimate based on previous trips on the same route
Pre-inform customer of the charges	
Automated payments	App-based payments linked to card or other payment methods
Automated and instant method for feedback	App-based feedback
Loyalty programmes	Analytics
Method for constant interaction between the service provider and customer	Loyalty programmes
	Chat feature

rolling out all the features outlined in Exhibit 13.5. In more complex scenarios, companies may prioritize the roll-out. For example, in the ridesharing illustration, customer and driver-facing mobile apps receive priority over loyalty programmes or internal processes like payroll or accounting.

13.5. IMPLEMENTING DIGITAL TECHNOLOGIES

Implementing a digital strategy involves making changes to a company's organizational structure, developing new products or services, adapting processes and deploying digital technologies. In this section, some of the methods used to build and deploy digital technologies are highlighted.

13.5.1. Agile Methodologies

Agile methodologies go hand in hand with design thinking in implementing digital technologies. Agile methodology is a people-focused and a result-focused approach to software development that respects our rapidly changing world. It is centred around adaptive planning, self-organization and short delivery times.

In traditional software development frameworks such as the waterfall model, requirements for a project must be agreed upfront. The entire scope of the project is planned, and timelines agreed between the stakeholders. These methodologies provide a structure to the development and save the customer's time. However, such methods are rigid and do not have the flexibility to adapt to customer and market changes that may happen along the development process. The methodologies require a relatively longer time to take a solution to market and have no mechanism for interim feedback. The methods also disconnect the customer from the development process. Agile development overcomes many of the weaknesses of these traditional methodologies.

Agile has existed since the late 1950s but became mainstream only in the 2000s. Reducing product life cycles and a customer's need to connect with the development processes has increased agile development usage. Agile methods make the following trade-offs:

- Individuals and interactions over processes and tools
- Working software over comprehensive documentation
- Customer collaboration over contract negotiation
- Responding to change over following a plan

Some of the popular methods used in agile include Scrum, Extreme Programming (XP) and rapid application development (RAD).

13.5.1.1. Scrum

According to Scrum.org,[6] Scrum is a framework within which people can address complex adaptive problems, while at the same time productively and creatively delivering products of the highest possible value. It was co-created by Ken Schwaber and Jeff Sutherland.

EXHIBIT 13.6 | *Scrum Framework*

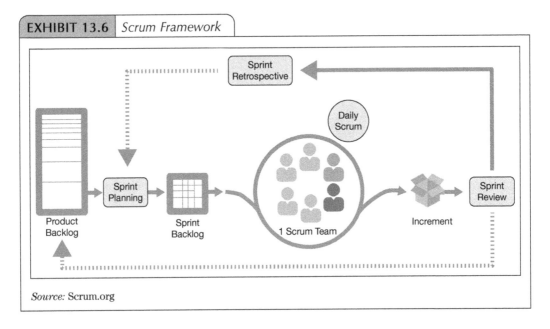

Source: Scrum.org

The Scrum framework (Exhibit 13.6) replaces a programmed algorithmic approach with a heuristic one to deal with unpredictability and focuses towards solving complex problems. Scrum defines three roles, the product owner, Scrum master and development team member. The framework follows a set of prescribed events to create a schedule and reduce additional meetings. All meetings are timeboxed. The Scrum events include:

- **Sprint:** A sprint is a timebox of one month or less during which a 'done', useable and potentially releasable product increment is created. Sprints have consistent durations throughout a development effort.
- **Sprint planning:** Sprint planning is timeboxed to a maximum of eight hours for a one-month sprint. For shorter sprints, the event is usually shorter.
- **Daily Scrum:** The daily Scrum is a 15-minute timeboxed event for the development team to synchronize activities and create a plan for the next 24 hours.
- **Sprint review:** A Sprint review is held at the end of the sprint to inspect the increment and adapt the product, if needed.
- **Sprint retrospective:** This provides an opportunity for the Scrum team to inspect itself and create a plan for improvements to be enacted during the next Sprint.

13.5.1.2. Extreme Programming

XP[7] is an agile software development framework that aims to produce higher quality software as well as a higher quality of life for the development team. Often used with Scrum, XP is an example of how agile can heighten customer satisfaction. Rather than deliver everything the customer could ever want far in the future, it gives them what they need now, fast.

XP is different from Scrum in some ways. Scrum teams typically work in sprints that are from two weeks to one month long. XP teams usually work in iterations that are one- or two-week long. Scrum teams do not allow changes in their sprints. XP teams are much more amenable to change within their iterations. XP teams work in strict priority order. Features to be developed are prioritized by the customer (Scrum's product owner), and the team is required to work on them in that order. By contrast, the Scrum product owner prioritizes the product backlog, but the team determines the sequence in which they will develop the backlog items. Scrum does not prescribe any engineering practices, while XP does. For example, XP focuses on automated testing and test-driven development. In Scrum, the Scrum master is responsible for communication with the customer; in XP, the customer is always available and directly communicates with the team.

Most agile development teams use a combination of agile and XP techniques.

13.5.1.3. Rapid Application Development

RAD is another agile project management strategy. RAD's pace is made possible by minimizing the planning stage and maximizing prototype development. By reducing planning time and emphasizing prototype iterations, RAD allows project managers and stakeholders to accurately measure progress and communicate in real time on evolving issues or changes. The four stages of RAD include the following:

- **Define requirements:** Rather than developing specifications with users, RAD begins by defining a loose set of requirements. The client provides their vision for the product and agrees with developers on the requirements that satisfy that vision.
- **Prototype:** In this phase, the goal is to build something that can be demonstrated to the client. This can be a prototype that satisfies all or only a portion of requirements (as in early stage prototyping).
- **Receive feedback:** RAD developers present their work to the client or end users and collect feedback on everything from interface to functionality.
- **Finalize product:** During this stage, developers implement the feedback and make the product scalable.

13.5.2. Low and Zero Code

Gartner defines a low-code application platform (LCAP) as one that provides RAD and deployment using low-code and no-code techniques like model-driven application design and development.[8]

Low and zero code platforms democratize the roll-out of technology applications and allow business users to build and roll out apps as MVPs based on customer's needs. These tools eliminate the need for complex and expensive software coding.

LCAPs use a visual design format rather than coding. This allows business users to evolve processes without having to know code or going back to the technology teams every time a change is required. A user-friendly interface also lets designers get changes completed faster and more efficiently, saving time and money on labour resources. Low code allows for flexibility to meet the customer's needs of fast and personalized experiences.

Beyond customer experience, LCAPs help automate even the most complex processes with drag-and-drop process modelling. Users can leverage the built-in features like instantaneous launch on a portal or mobile app. Most low-code software has in-built security features that allow for their deployment in industries such as financial services and healthcare.

13.5.3. Choice of Digital Technologies

As companies develop their digital road maps, they have two choices on how these road maps can be developed (Caetano & Amaral, 2011).

1. **Market pull:** In a market pull strategy, companies base their technology plan on external factors such as industry and markets and are looking for brand new opportunities to target. Therefore, the road map starts at the market layer, working through the product layer, towards the technology layer. For example, a market pull strategy could emerge from a customer journey mapping exercise. This is a less risky approach and is less innovative. Most competitors would follow a similar process.
2. **Technology push:** The technology push approach, unlike the market pull approach, looks to identify opportunities for a specific technology. Most of the current work around blockchain is technology push as companies are still looking for use cases for this upcoming technology. This approach is riskier as there is no obvious market need. However, companies like Apple have made this approach their hallmark.

Most companies adopt a mix of the two strategies with 70–80 per cent based on market pull and the balance from technology push.

13.6. BALANCING LEGACY WITH DIGITAL

Unlike born-digital companies, traditional organizations already have large investments in legacy technologies and infrastructure. These technologies have helped service internal and external users for decades and have undergone regular upgrades. The technologies that have thus been established have proven to be reliable and scalable. Migrating from these technologies to less conventional digital technologies pose considerable challenges. Markets and companies are being disrupted by born-digitals and need to transform. However, there is no established path nor is there certainty as to which technologies will eventually be the industry standards. Legacy companies also need to simultaneously manage their legacy business models with digital models. To successfully manage this dichotomy, legacy companies need to focus on the following four areas (Bossert et al., 2014):

1. **Two-speed architecture:** A two-speed architecture has a digital front end that is customer centric backed by a slower-speed legacy back end. Such architecture was very common in the early days of digital. The customer-facing front end or system of engagement was designed with flexibility and agility in mind, while the legacy back end or system of record was designed for stability. Such architectures allowed for legacy companies to launch their digital journeys quickly. However, this mode had

many challenges.[9] Companies had to maintain two teams. One was the 'fancier' digital team and the other was the less glamorous back end. This led to issues relating to employee morale and retention. Second, as the front end rapidly evolved, the back end eventually could not keep pace leading to disconnects between the two systems.

2. **Develop the low-speed architecture:** Companies are investing in developing their back-end architecture to cope with the changes in the front end. However, the speed and process are still different from the front end as the systems of record require rigorous development and testing methodologies and must be managed for resilience and scalability.

3. **Develop common principles:** While the front-end and back-end technologies are changing, companies need to develop some common philosophies around areas such as information security, privacy and testing to integrate the entire architecture.

4. **Use of blended methodologies:** Legacy systems have been built using the waterfall model, while the newer digital technologies are being developed using agile methodologies. Companies are blending the benefits of agile (iterative development, continuous delivery) into the waterfall model.

13.7. RISK MANAGEMENT

Implementing digital strategies is high risk. Therefore, it is critical to understand these risks and develop mitigation strategies for each of the identified risks. While some of the risks are common to any strategic or technological changes, others are unique to digital transformation.

- **Strategic risks:** Digital strategies are, in most cases, venturing into the unknown. They are transformational in nature and require changing almost all aspects of a business. In a fast-changing business world, a company may invest large sums of money and time on a strategy that is disrupted by newer competitors and technologies even before the implementation is complete.

- **Technology obsolescence risks:** As discussed previously, digital technologies form the backbone of digital strategies. As digital technologies are still evolving, companies need to be careful about the technologies they adopt. If the technology becomes obsolete or the industry standards change, the entire transformation is put at risk. Microsoft's failed attempt to build its phone on a Windows CE platform is an example of a company betting on the wrong platform.

- **Security risks:** Digital technologies, by design, are connected. This raises the challenges relating to security. Data breaches and cyberattacks are common in digital companies and they not only cause service outages but also impact the reputation of the company.

- **Third-party risks:** Many digital companies operate with tight integration with vendors and suppliers. Failure to provide service by any member of the ecosystem impacts the entire ecosystem. For example, any issues with a third-party logistics partner can impact the sales of an e-commerce company. Managing third-party risks becomes more critical for companies that have moved away from being fully integrated into ecosystems and platforms.

- **HR risk:** This refers to a company's inability to source and retain manpower with the required digital skills. This can lead to delays in digital implementations.
- **Regulatory and legal risks:** As discussed in Chapter 9, many countries have not yet set up the regulatory frameworks for digital companies to operate in. These frameworks range from licences and permissions to operate to data protection and privacy laws. Any changes or introduction of new policies can severely impact the working of a digital company. For example, in a country like India, changing regulatory frameworks and policies for digital payment companies (like the introduction of mandatory KYC) caused severe turbulence.
- **Financial risks:** As discussed in earlier chapters, digital companies, especially platform companies, focus on winning against the competition based on network effects. There is a greater focus on user growth than profitability and cash flow. The high 'burn rate' of digital companies, especially start-ups, is a considerable risk for both the company and its ecosystem partners and customers.
- **Operational risks:** Digital companies are scale oriented and promise customers instant and real-time access to products and services. Any downtime in a digital company can lead to customer dissatisfaction and customer attrition, in addition to immediate revenue loss. For example, the downtime on a mobile app will have a greater impact than the downtime in a bank's branch operation.

While implementing digital strategy, a company needs to build specific risk mitigation plans for each of the above risks.

13.8. MANAGING CHANGE

Change management is the structured approach to proactively manage the impact of transformation on a corporation.

As can be seen in Exhibit 13.7, digital transformation causes change across an organization.

The changes include process and product changes, inter-organizational changes that involve other stakeholders within the organization and inter-organizational changes that require new ways of interacting with external stakeholders. Digital transformation also requires changes at every level of the technology stack including hosting and infrastructure, security, privacy and even the skills required to manage technology. To succeed in their digital transformation, companies, therefore, need robust change management processes.

Several change management frameworks have been developed by academics and professionals. One of the seminal works on change management was done by John Kotter of Harvard in his book *Accelerate* (2012). According to Kotter, there are eight critical steps that a company needs to take to transform and sustain this change successfully.

1. **Establishing a sense of urgency:** The first step to successful change management is to create a vision for change and emphasize the need to implement the change

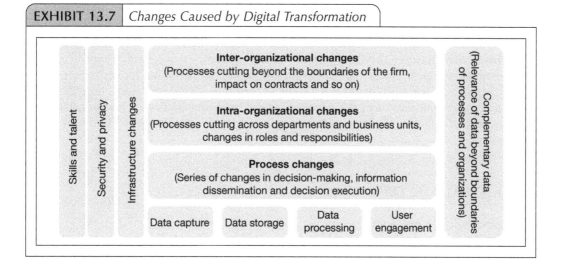

EXHIBIT 13.7 | *Changes Caused by Digital Transformation*

Skills and talent

Security and privacy

Infrastructure changes

Inter-organizational changes
(Processes cutting beyond the boundaries of the firm, impact on contracts and so on)

Intra-organizational changes
(Processes cutting across departments and business units, changes in roles and responsibilities)

Process changes
(Series of changes in decision-making, information dissemination and decision execution)

Data capture | Data storage | Data processing | User engagement

Complementary data (Relevance of data beyond boundaries of processes and organizations)

rapidly to avoid being disrupted. This step also involves communicating the need to change and the potential downsides of not changing from the status quo. People need to be moved off their comfort zones and their mindsets moved away from the fear of failure and downside risks to the upsides of the transformation.

2. **Creating the guiding coalition:** As discussed in Chapter 5, transformation starts with the CEO. However, to implement the change, the CEO needs to enlist a team of leaders who span the organization. This could include CXOs and divisional heads. Through workshops and brainstorming sessions, the extended team's views need to be incorporated into the transformation plan. The team needs to develop ownership for the success of the plan.

3. **Developing a vision and strategy:** In Chapter 2, the need for a digital vision was discussed. The vision needs to be clear and concise and interpreted uniformly across the leadership team and the organization. Studies on failed transformations have shown that the digital plan was a series of programmes and projects with no overall vision tying them together. This led to disparate implementations of the programmes and the eventual failure of the transformation programme.

4. **Communicating the change vision:** While it is essential to have a vision for the transformation, it is equally important that this vision is visible and communicated through the organization. Communication must be continuous and include important updates on the overall progress of the transformation progress.

5. **Empowering employees:** All change will encounter obstacles. These obstacles could be in the form of resistance from employees, lack of processes and policies or even lack of knowledge of overcoming some challenges. Employees need to be empowered to overcome these challenges using innovative methods. A highly centralized decision-making structure will result in delays and eventual disenchantment among the teams.

6. **Generating short-term wins:** Transformation is a long process and causes employee fatigue and morale issues. It is, therefore, important to generate short-term wins. These wins need to be communicated and celebrated.

7. **Sustain acceleration:** All transformation projects take time. While it is important to generate short-term wins, it is equally important to sustain the momentum till the completion of the programme.

8. **Institute change:** The final step of managing change is to ensure that the change is sustainable. It is easy for the company to slip back to the 'legacy' way of handling processes. Employees need to be shown that digital processes help the company grow, become more profitable and lead to more satisfied customers. The new organization also needs to reflect leadership and employees who embrace this change.

13.9. ETHICS IN DIGITAL

Digital technologies are shaping the way humans and corporations function. While digital strategies bring many benefits, that have been discussed in earlier chapters, to both companies and their customers, they have also led to several ethical issues. Some of these challenges are discussed in this section.[10]

- **Data privacy and misuse:** Data and analytics form a critical role in the success of digital strategies. While these provide great opportunities to innovate, they also expose customers and corporations to data misuse. The way data is collected, managed and used raises several legal and ethical issues. The sharing can be intentional or unintentional. The sharing of data by Facebook to Cambridge Analytica is a well-documented illustration of this issue where customer data was used for political advertising. Organizations need to assure their customer that the data they collect is subject to robust governance and audit procedures.

- **Biases:** These are typically imbibed subconsciously and can influence human behaviour. Confirmation bias is probably the most well-known example where individuals seek or interpret information in a way that confirms their beliefs and hypotheses. This becomes critical in analytics-based decision-making that drives digital companies.

- **Inference models and algorithms:** Technologies such as AI and ML are influenced by data used to train and build models. Any bias in the training data may lead to perpetuating the bias.

- **Unintentional use of technologies:** Technologies like 3D printing allow for rapid manufacturing. While these technologies can be used to develop customized artificial limbs, they can also make illegal weapons. Similarly, bitcoin, using blockchain technologies, has unintentionally become the prevalent currency for illegal activities.

- **Substituting human intuition:** As machines and robots take over complex decision-making processes, it takes away the ability for human intuiting to intervene. An example is the decision a self-driving car must make when it has a choice to save the passengers in the car or the pedestrian who has come in the car's path.

MINI CASE 13.1. DISCUSSION

Asian Paints' services transformation began with their 'painting-as-a-service' offering. This change emerged from the company's understanding of the painting-as-a-service ecosystem and the number of customer touchpoints involved. It emerged out of design-thinking workshops that the company conducted.

To provide a consistent customer experience across multiple touchpoints and offer optimal product and service delivery, the company needed to ensure strong digital enablement across the value chain. To achieve this goal, Asian Paints digitalized its functions end to end, from customer engagement systems to all front-end CRM and dealer management systems as well as all supply chain and manufacturing operations. Data analytics was another foundational element across the value chain.

The company had been using JDA Software's advanced supply chain planning solutions for over two decades. However, to cope with the rapid changes in the front end, the company developed an advanced Supply Chain Management application using IBM Watson, which allowed for effective decision-making amid continuing uncertainty. The SAP HANA platform-based solution reinvented the company's order servicing by empowering the sales team with timely information about the current stock and the distribution team about inventory levels and possible product shortages. The company mapped the customer journey across channels and built a data architecture and an IT platform powered by SAP Enterprise Application Software. This was combined with Adobe's Experience Manager platform to provide a robust IT architecture covering both the softer aspects of customer experience and transactional and process requirements.

Given their propensity for continual reinvention, the company understood that early and pioneering adoption of IT is critical to success. Early adoption of an API-driven architecture worked very well for the company. While the front end kept changing rapidly, the back end system remained supportive. Asian Paints also evaluated emerging technologies annually and plotted them across the business areas to determine possible opportunities and selectively execute them.

Today Asian Paints is recognized globally for its digital transformation.[11]

SUMMARY

This chapter focuses on the implementation of digital technologies. The process begins with assessing an organization for its digital maturity and determining its position within its industry and competitors. Several models to evaluate digital maturity exist in the industry, and most of them are proprietary to consulting and IT companies. However, the elements covered in these models are similar. The assessment determines the gaps in digital maturity of an organization. One of the most critical elements of digital maturity is customer experience. Techniques such as design thinking help organizations map their customer/customers' journey and determine their digital strategies and prioritize aspects of implementation. Agile development methodologies go hand in hand with design thinking. Agile methods are customer centric and in contrast to traditional waterfall development methodologies are more flexible and help develop prototypes faster. Scrum, RAD and XP are examples of agile methodologies. The chapter also discusses technology implementations and market pull and push. Implementing digital technologies brings about several risks, change management challenges and ethical issues. Companies need to consider these before embarking on implementation and ensure that mitigation strategies are in place.

Discussion Questions

1. Describe some of the key elements of a digital maturity model.
2. With an illustration, explain how design thinking helps in developing a new product/service and a business model.
3. How is agile development different from the traditional waterfall method?
4. Provide scenarios where a waterfall method may still be the preferred method for software development.
5. What is two-speed IT? Discuss its benefits and disadvantages.
6. Describe three key risks in digital implementation and potential mitigation strategies.
7. What is change management? Why is it critical in digital implementation?
8. How can companies deal with the ethical issues that arise out of digital implementation?

GLOSSARY

Agile methodology: It is a people-focused, results-focused approach to software development that respects our rapidly changing world. It is centred around adaptive planning, self-organization and short delivery times.

Design thinking: It is one of the most popular frameworks for customer journey mapping. Its current form is associated with David Kelly, a Stanford professor and founder of leading design firm IDEO.

Digital maturity model: It is a framework used to understand how digitally mature an organization is currently as well as what is required to build a road map for the future.

Low code: LCAP is a technology that provides RAD and deployment using low-code and no-code techniques such as declarative, model-driven application design and development together with the simplified one-button deployment of applications.

Market pull: In a market pull strategy, companies base their technology plan on external factors such as industry and markets.

Scrum: According to Scrum.org, it is a framework within which people can address complex adaptive problems, while productively and creatively delivering products of the highest possible value.

Technology push: The technology push approach, unlike the market pull strategy, looks to identify opportunities for a specific technology.

Two-speed architecture: A two-speed architecture has a digital front end that is customer centric backed by a slower-speed legacy back end.

NOTES

1. https://www.cognizant.com/perspectives/asian-paints-the-digital-odyssey-of-a-serial-reinventor
2. https://www2.deloitte.com/content/dam/Deloitte/global/Documents/Technology-Media-Telecommunications/deloitte-digital-maturity-model.pdf
3. https://go.forrester.com/blogs/assessing-your-digital-maturity-what-does-excellence-look-like/
4. https://www.mckinsey.com/business-functions/mckinsey-digital/how-we-help-clients/digital-2020/overview
5. https://www.bcg.com/capabilities/digital-technology-data/digital-maturity
6. https://www.scrum.org/
7. http://www.extremeprogramming.org/
8. https://www.gartner.com/reviews/market/enterprise-low-code-application-platform
9. https://www.mckinsey.com/business-functions/mckinsey-digital/our-insights/a-two-speed-it-architecture-for-the-digital-enterprise
10. https://www.consultancy.uk/news/16602/the-top-five-ethical-moral-principles-for-digital-transformation
11. https://www.cognizant.com/perspectives/asian-paints-the-digital-odyssey-of-a-serial-reinventor

REFERENCES

Bossert, O., Laartz, J., & Ramsøy, T. J. (2014). Running your company at two speeds. *McKinsey Quarterly*.

Caetano, M., & Amaral, D. C. (2011). Roadmapping for technology push and partnership: A contribution for open innovation environments. *Technovation, 31*(7), 320–335.

Kotter, J. P. (2012). Accelerate!. *Harvard business review, 90*(11), 44–52.

Dhanashree Agro: Transforming a 'Farmer-first' Model*

INTRODUCTION

Mahesh Damodare, the director of Dhanashree Agro Industries (DAI), left his home in Pune, in western India, early morning of late May 2020. He had three-hour drive ahead of him as he headed to his warehouse in Nashik where he was meeting his head of sales, Ravi Kelkar. The journey took him past some of India's most extensive vineyards, many of whom were his customers. The roads were quiet, and Damodare had time to contemplate about his business. DAI was a company that focused on speciality crop nutrients and protection. The Damodare family had been in trading agri-inputs for over 60 years. Over two generations, the company had built trust among farmers in the western region of Maharashtra, one of the most agriculturally advanced states in India. The business had grown by CAGR of 85 per cent in the last five years (Exhibit C.1) and was very profitable.

However, the recent COVID-19-induced lockdown had shaken up the business. The products distributed by DAI were stuck in the high seas or at ports. For the products available at their warehouses, they did not have the necessary packaging or logistics. For 60 days, DAI had come to a complete halt. While he and Kelkar had taken some innovative measures to keep in touch with their customers, Damodare realized that this was a wake-up call for him and the company.

At an operational level, the company needed to quickly move away from manual processes and implement supply chain and other technologies. At a more strategic level, Damodare required to take a relook at how he could scale and de-risk the business. DAI had built its reputation on trust and one-on-one relationships with its customers (farmers). Over the years, the company had worked with these farmers on customized productivity plans through a curated portfolio of plant nutrients. Damodare was keen to transform the company. He had tried to introduce technology in the past, but Kelkar had resisted any change, especially on the sales side of the business.

---

* This case has been published with the permission of Emerald Emerging Markets Case Studies.

For the case and teaching note please refer to: Pingali, S. R., & Korem, J. R. (2021). Dhanashree Agro: transforming a "Farmer First" model. Emerald Emerging Markets Case Studies.

EXHIBIT C.1	Dhanashree Agro Industries Revenue Growth

Year	Net Sales (₹)	No. of Dealers
2007–2008	2,000,465.00	74
2008–2009	2,922,000.00	50
2009–2010	6,484,794.00	82
2012–2013	18,653,130.59	66
2013–2014	34,842,150.80	64
2014–2015	51,596,559.77	71
2016–2017	197,006,057.71	96
2017–2018	243,368,266.67	150
2018–2019	331,752,093.00	161
2019–2020	476,651,886.19	185

Source: Company presentation (2020).

Note: July 2020, ~₹75 = 1 USD.

As Damodare reached his warehouse in Nashik, he was greeted by Kelkar, whom he had not met for over two months since the lockdown.

'Good morning, Ravi. Glad to see you after a while. I know we have a lot of things to catch up but the one thing I do want to discuss with you is how we can implement changes in the supply chain and sales processes. We cannot let incidents like this shut us down completely.'

Later in the evening, Damodare and Kelkar met in his office to discuss the options available for DAI.

AGRICULTURE IN INDIA (2018)

Agriculture was still a significant part of the Indian economy. Although declining, more than 58 per cent of the country's population still cited agriculture as their primary source of income. Agriculture accounted for close to 20 per cent of the Indian GDP and 10 per cent of all exports from India in 2020. While India was self-sufficient in food, agricultural exports had failed to take off due to the inability of farmers to diversify beyond commodities like rice to high-value produce such as fruits and processed foods.[1] To enhance this, a comprehensive overhaul of the agricultural value chain from farming methods and marketing would be required.

Agriculture was widely distributed across the country with each region specializing in certain types of crops depending on factors such as soil conditions, weather, availability of water and local government incentives. States such as Uttar Pradesh, Punjab and Madhya

Pradesh ranked high in terms of production. However, when it came to high-value or cash crops, each state had its strengths. States such as Maharashtra and Rajasthan contributed significantly to oilseed production; Maharashtra, Gujrat and Telangana to cotton; and Maharashtra and Karnataka to sugarcane. In fruit production, Maharashtra (grapes), Andhra (mangoes), Uttar Pradesh (mangoes) and Tamil Nadu (bananas) were some leading states.

Agri-inputs were critical for the growth of agriculture and had two major components: crop nutrients or fertilizers and crop protection.

Crop Nutrients (Fertilizers)

Crop nutrition is essential for optimum growth and production of crops. There are 16 elements necessary for crop production (Exhibit C.2). Although macro and micronutrients are required in smaller quantities, they are equally important for crops to ensure balanced fertilization.

A fertilizer is any material of natural or synthetic origin that provides soil with any of these 16 elements. Fertilizers can be single nutrients (N, P or K) or multi-nutrient.

The most common forms of fertilizers used in India are **urea** (accounts for 82% of total nitrogen consumption) and **diammonium phosphate** (DAP, accounts for 63% of phosphate consumption).

Speciality nutrients are a subgroup of crop nutrients and are different from the mass nutrients such as urea and DAP. These are high-value products and have designer properties tailored to specific needs. For example, when applied, urea and DAP are lost to soil and atmosphere through chemical reactions, and their effectiveness cannot be controlled. Through improved formulations, production and application, speciality nutrients overcome

---

EXHIBIT C.2 *Essential Nutrients*

Supplied from Air and Water	Supplied from Soil and Fertilizers	
	Macronutrients	Micronutrients
Carbon	Nitrogen	Zinc
Hydrogen	Potassium	Copper
Oxygen	Phosphorus	Iron
	Sulphur	Manganese
	Calcium	Boron
	Magnesium	Chlorine
		Molybdenum
		Cobalt

Source: Company presentation (2020).

many of these issues. Speciality nutrients can be classified broadly into four buckets, though this is not exhaustive:

- Compounded fertilizers containing multiple nutrients to provide specific actions
- Water-soluble fertilizers that can be applied through fertigation and foliar sprays
- Fertilizers using efficiency promoters like slow release or control release using coatings
- Most macro and micronutrients

Speciality nutrients were still in the early stages of development and use in India. They were far more expensive than standard nutrients, and most farmers were not convinced about the value they offered. They are mainly used in fertigation (mixed with water and administered through drip irrigation) and foliar application (directly applied to leaves), both of which also had low penetration in the country.

Crop Protection

Crop protection went together with crop nutrients. Crop protection is a collection of tools, products and practices farmers use to defend their crops against weeds, disease and harmful insects and fungi (https://www.bayer.com/en/). There are broadly three types of protection required:

1. **Pest and insect management:** Insects and pests that eat up the crop
2. **Weed management:** Undesirable plants that steal the nutrients, sunlight, water and other resources from the crops and affect their growth
3. **Plant disease management:** Fungal and bacterial diseases that could damage crops

In India, injudicious use of chemical pesticides in agriculture had resulted in several associated adverse effects such as environmental pollution, ecological imbalances, pesticides residues in food, destruction of plant beneficial biocontrol agents and development of resistance in pests.

There was a drive from the Indian government to create awareness of these hazards, control the use of harmful chemicals and enhance the use of biopesticides and biocontrol agents in plant pest management.

FARMERS IN INDIA

Even in 2018, India contained a mix of basic primitive subsistence farming (where farmers grew crops to meet the needs of their families and neighbourhoods) and intensive subsistence farming (where more extensive areas of land are cultivated using fertilizers and crop protection). Both these forms of agriculture were still mostly manual and focused on commodity grains. Commercial farming, using the latest techniques and automation, was at a nascent stage in the country.

The average size of landholdings was very small (less than three acres) and adoption of modern agricultural practices was inadequate and hampered by lack of awareness of such practices and their impracticality for small landholdings. Illiteracy and general socio-economic backwardness were very prevalent among a large section of farmers. However, there were a small proportion of farmers who took it upon themselves to overcome these issues and be at the leading edge of farming. These were mostly commercial farmers and are spread across the states of Maharashtra, Andhra and Telangana, Gujarat, Punjab, Haryana and Tamil Nadu. Cotton, sugarcane, corn, vegetables, flowers and fruits such as grapes and bananas, and tea and coffee were all examples of crops grown commercially in India. These commercial farmers were educated, more aware of the latest developments in agricultural techniques and were technology savvy. They used modern techniques such as fertigation and foliar application. They also leveraged the recent availability of cellular networks and data services in remote locations to be connected to the global agricultural ecosystem. In addition to productivity and quality, these farmers were also investing in areas such as sustainability and organic farming.

DHANASHREE AGRO AND ITS CUSTOMERS

1960–2006

Damodare's grandfather started the family business of agri-inputs trading in the 1960s. His father, Nana Damodare, further expanded the business, Damodare Agro Marketing, across several districts in Maharashtra. Nana Damodare rose to become a leading figure in the agri-inputs industry and was instrumental in propagating latest seed, plant protection and fertilizer technologies to the agriculturally significant districts of western Maharashtra. Nana Damodare was very popular among the farmers as he was always available for help on all matters, agricultural or otherwise. He was a strong proponent of innovation in crop patterns, cultivation practices and inputs. He strived for getting maximum economic benefits for the growers. The Damodare business was built on trust and personal connection.

2007–2014: 'Crossing the Chasm'

After receiving his mechanical engineering degree from Pune University, Mahesh Damodare went on to complete first master's degree from the prestigious National Institute of Industrial Engineering in Mumbai. He then went to Stanford University and got a second master's degree in manufacturing engineering. Post his graduation from Stanford in 1997, Damodare worked for a few years at Oracle Corporation before starting his own software company focusing on supply chain management. In 2004, Damodare returned to India and formally joined the family business. At that point of time, the family business, Damodare Agro Marketing, was trading in bulk nutrients and crop-protection chemicals, as a distributor for a large German agriproducts company. The products were sold through a network of dealers in multiple districts in western Maharashtra. Damodare realized that this was a low-margin and commodity business. The company was operating in a highly competitive market where large players were dumping products to gain market share. To sustain in the industry, he needed to move the family business to the higher end of the value chain.

It was a coincidence that in 2007, the German agriproducts company divested its speciality nutrients company. The now separate entity was seeking a distributor in India and Damodare jumped at the opportunity to sign up as its non-exclusive distributor. Then, speciality nutrients was a tiny part of the family portfolio of agriproducts. Still, Damodare saw an opportunity to build what he felt would be a growth business with high margins. He quickly separated the family business into two entities. Damodare Agro Marketing continued to focus on the traditional bulk products business. In contrast, the newly formed DAI focused on speciality nutrients (Exhibit C.3).

Damodare focused his time on DAI as he felt it would require time to establish itself. The initial days for DAI were a struggle. Speciality nutrients were, at the minimum, 30 per cent more expensive than bulk products and in many cases, 30–50 times more expensive. The market was tiny, and farmers were not very aware of its potential. Damodare realized that unless farmers were educated about the benefits of speciality nutrients, they would not buy the products.

In 2007, two kinds of sales models existed in the agri-inputs market. Nutrients were sold in bulk by large global and Indian manufacturers. These manufacturers created brand awareness among farmers through advertising and by incentivizing local agri-inputs dealers. The manufactures did not have any direct connection with the farmers. As the products were standard, this approach was cost-effective. Crop protection, on the other hand, was very personalized to the specific issues faced by a farmer. Crop-protection companies had field sales executives who interacted with farmers and educated them on the right products to use.

To expand the market for speciality nutrients, Damodare decided to adopt the highly personalized approach being used to sell crop protection. Another decision he took was not

EXHIBIT C.3 *Product Mix*

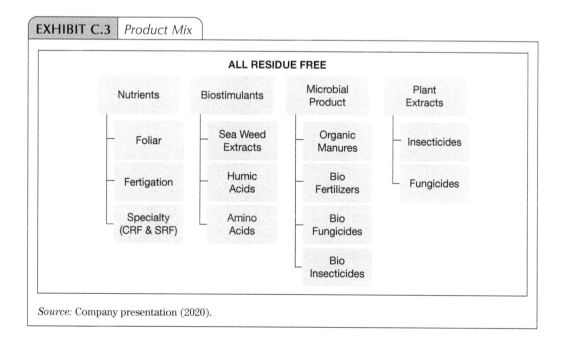

Source: Company presentation (2020).

to rebrand the products he was importing to a DAI brand. While he did realize that building his own brand may be beneficial in the long run, he decided against this for two reasons. First, he felt that given the nascent stage of the market, he would have more credibility if he represented global brands. Second, by not rebranding to a DAI brand, he could represent multiple global brands.

His first hire in DAI was Kelkar. Kelkar was a recent graduate with a bachelor of science degree in agriculture from a local college in Nashik. His father had been a long-term employee in Damodare Agri-Products and was very keen that Kelkar also joined the company. He was very familiar with the local markets as he had travelled extensively, with his father, across the state. Damodare knew that while Kelkar may not be able to contribute to the strategy of DAI, he would be a good operations leader and be able to build relationships with local farmers effortlessly.

In the initial days of DAI, Damodare and Kelkar personally approached some farmers who had been long-standing customers of the family business and offered speciality nutrients to them. While some farmers bought the products due to the relationship, Damodare realized that they were sceptical about the cost–value equation, and this was not a sustainable approach.

At Stanford, Damodare had been significantly influenced by *Crossing the Chasm* by Geoffrey Moore. The book was about selling high-tech products to mainstream customers and classified customers into five buckets (Exhibit C.4). While agri-inputs were not high-tech, Damodare felt the concepts outlined in the book applied to his industry as well. He knew that through existing relationships, he could attract the 'innovators' and maybe even the 'early adapters' to speciality nutrients. However, to build the business, he would need to cross the chasm and get to the 'majority'. Speciality nutrients would always be a niche

---

EXHIBIT C.4 | *Crossing the Chasm*

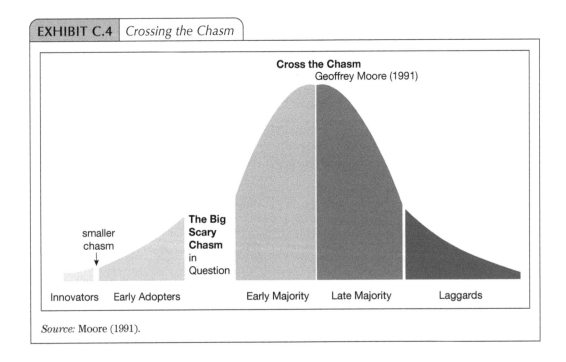

Source: Moore (1991).

market. However, if he could attract the 'majority' of the target segment, he could become a dominant player in a niche market.

As an industrial engineer, Damodare had also been exposed to concepts of design thinking. He had used these principles while working at Oracle and at his supply chain start-up. Damodare decided to apply these principles to this new market and include farmers as co-creators to his strategy and product portfolio building. This decision laid the path to the growth and differentiation of DAI over the next decade.

We will not have a product management team. The farmer is our product management team.

Another key decision Damodare took was to focus only on the region of western Maharashtra where his family already had a good reputation. He also decided to focus on commercial farmers who were growing grapes and pomegranates, the two large cash crops grown in that region (Exhibit C.5).

To implement his strategy, Damodare and Kelkar hired a team of 10 agricultural graduates as 'development associates'. These associates were familiar with the area and spoke the local language of Marathi. Each of the 10 associates was assigned a set of farmers and was expected to know the specific crops being grown, and the challenges being faced by their farmer customers, intimately. By organizing workshops and training programmes for farmers, the team built strong relationships with their respective customers.

As Damodare said,

'I don't want to tell the farmers what to buy. I want them to approach their development associate for whatever issues they have and then co-create a solution.'

Once he received an idea from a development associate team, Damodare tied up with global suppliers of speciality agri-inputs to source the right product. A typical farmer would initially buy one product and test it out. Once successful, the farmer bought four to five products in the next season. It was only in the third season that a farmer bought a full bouquet of products from DAI. As a result, the typical sales cycle with an individual farmer was more than two years.

This 'farmer-first' approach was tremendously successful, and soon DAI tied up with six global suppliers and serviced over 12,000 farmers. The German supplier had tried four

---

EXHIBIT C.5 | *DAI Crop Mix*

	(% of DOI Revenue)		
Crop	**2009**	**2019**	**Average Sale Acre/Year (₹)**
Grapes	95	50	12,000
Vegetables		25	300
Pomegranates	05	07	1,500
Citrus		04	1,500
Bananas		02	300
Others		11	500

Source: Company presentation (2020).

other distributors in the state of Maharashtra. All of them had used the traditional agri-nutrients sales approach and failed.

By 2015, eight years after he had applied his industrial engineering knowledge to agriproducts, Damodare felt that DAI had 'crossed the chasm'.

2015–2019: The Consolidation Years

As the company grew, Damodare focused on managing the relationships with the suppliers, and he left Kelkar to manage the farmer relationships. By 2015, the number of development associates grew to 50. While the team was organized by region and sub-region, Damodare insisted on having a uniform job title for all his field employees. He felt that everyone in DAI should be equally empowered and developed a flat organization structure with all development associates directly reporting to Kelkar.

During this period, DAI consolidated its presence by strengthening its relationship with the farmers. The farmer workshops had been formalized into a Plant Nutrition Learning School. It now included global experts from various countries ranging from Germany to Chile and Spain. The company also started to organize field trips for farmers to visit their counterparts in other countries. For example, grape farmers were taken to Chile and Peru, global leaders in grape exports. The Indian farmers met their counterparts in these countries to discuss common issues and learn from them. The 'farmer as a co-creator' concept remained deeply rooted in the business model and any ideas that emerged from these workshops were quickly implemented.

Damodare felt that he needed to give back to the community where he operated. He created the Shri Nana and Sou. Sharada Damodare Charitable Trust, named after his parents. The trust focused on four activities: (a) education and sports, (b) financial support for the underprivileged, (c) agricultural support for marginal farmers and (d) animal shelters for the preservation of Indian cattle breeds. Damodare started to spend a significant amount of his time on the activities of the trust.

The business was steadily growing. The Plant Nutrition Learning School had covered over 25,000 farmers. Damodare had achieved the goal he had set for himself in 2007—become the largest player in the speciality agriproducts business in western Maharashtra. While most of the business was focused on speciality nutrients, the speciality crop-protection business also began to grow.

Several global and Indian speciality agri-inputs companies started manufacturing operations in India or were importing products (Exhibit C.6). However, given the relatively nascent stage of the industry and the lack of product knowledge among farmers, these companies were struggling to distribute their products. Many of the international companies approached DAI to become their distribution partner. Damodare did not want to spread his resources across multiple companies and, at any point, did not expand beyond five to six brands to represent. The choice of brands and products was made in conjunction with DAI's customers. The Indian companies, on the other hand, primarily developed in-house distribution capabilities, though a few tied up with DAI.

There were several independent agri-inputs distributors in Maharashtra and the rest of the country, and the distributor market was highly fragmented. However, these distributors

EXHIBIT C.6	*Speciality Agri-nutrient Manufacturers in India*

Global		
Manufacturer	**Country of Origin**	**Represented by DAI**
Compo Expert	Germany	Yes
Tradecorp	Spain	Yes
Idai Nature	Spain	Yes
Arysta	Japan	Yes
Mosaic	USA	No
Nutrien	Canada	No
ICL	UK	No
Domestic		
Manufacturer	**Country of Origin**	**Represented by DAI**
SEA6	India	Yes
Fishfa	India	Yes
MAPCO	India	No
Tata Chemicals	India	No
Indogulf	India	No
Nagarjuna	India	No

Source: Company presentation (2020).

neither understood speciality agri-inputs nor did they have the depth of farmer relationships that DAI had developed.

2019–Present: The Crisis

In the last couple of years, Damodare had spent time thinking about how to take the business to its next phase. While the development associate model was highly successful, he was unable to scale the team. Newer industries such as IT and high-tech manufacturing had made it very difficult for DAI to recruit bright graduates. These graduates felt agriproducts was an old-world business, and they did not want to time travel through rural India. Damodare had briefly explored using digital technologies to increase farmer connect. However, Kelkar was not convinced that farmers would trust digital communication.

DAI had also not invested in robust supply chain processes. He was sourcing material in bulk from six global locations (Germany, Chile, South Africa, Poland, Spain and Japan) to its two warehouses in Maharashtra. The bulk material was then repacked into customer-size packing and sold through dealers. The entire process was left mainly manual. Damodare was personally supervising the work, and error rates were low.

Retailers offered credit to farmers who purchased multiple products from them, and Damodare did not want to disturb this relationship. DAI's direct connection with the farmer created a pull for DAI's products, who then physically purchased them from the dealers. Given the high profit margins of speciality nutrients, the business was able to absorb the additional layer between DAI and its customers.

Finally, DAI had seen so much growth among the fruit farmers of western Maharashtra that Damodare had not diversified beyond this market. He also felt that he could not scale his 'farmer-first' model outside this region as it was highly relationship dependent. At the same time, he knew that the market for speciality nutrients was enormous and largely untapped. Very few suppliers had managed to 'cross the chasm', and most farmers across the country were unaware or had not used speciality nutrients. With the right resources, he could easily grow his business tenfold.

Damodare had been reading about platforms and how they are disrupting distribution across industries. He had wondered if DAI could aggregate its customers onto a technology platform where it could provide other value-added services like information on weather and potential pest attacks. Also, he could use the platform for farmers to actively collaborate with each other and interact with DAI. He had spoken to a technology start-up which was willing to provide him with a white-labelled platform. However, Damodare was not sure if his customers were ready to adopt the technology.

On multiple occasions, Damodare had mulled over these plans, but he got very quickly drawn back into day-to-day issues and his work at the Damodare Trust. Lack of support from Kelkar on any of the new ideas was also a hindrance. However, given the tremendous job Kelkar was doing in western Maharashtra, Damodare never considered any drastic actions.

Early 2020

Early 2020 saw the world being hit by the COVID-19 pandemic. By the middle of March, India was locked down. After about six weeks of complete shutdown, the government allowed farmers to get back to their farms as it was the beginning of the most critical crop season for the country. Most of DAI's customers were back at their farms. However, the company was not operational. Shipments of crop nutrients were stuck on the high seas or at the ports. For the material at the warehouses, there was not enough packaging material, nor were they geared for logistics. The dealers themselves were shut, and DAI's products could not reach the farmers. Kelkar and his team were also locked down at their homes.

For the first time in many years, Damodare felt unprepared. Farmers were heading into the critical sowing season and DAI needed to re-establish its connection with the farmers. As they had no other option, they organized a video conference with all DAI's customers to understand their situation and see how best DAI could support them during the crisis. To their surprise, almost 200 farmers joined the first conference that was conducted jointly with the local farmer association. Having seen the success of this conference, DAI organized an education workshop for farmers. This time, almost 2,000 farmers attended the virtual workshop, and more than 8,000 unique visitors watched the recording within a few weeks of the programme.

It struck to Kelkar and Damodare that it usually took a development associate a month to meet 200 farmers. Had they underestimated the power of digital communication among rural customers?

Back to Present Day

Damodare and Kelkar met in the evening to discuss the options that DAI had. Kelkar, who had recently witnessed the power of digital, was more open to looking at the possibilities. Damodare started the meeting.

'We have many options and each has its own opportunities and risks. Doing nothing is no longer an option. We do not know how long this crisis will last and if there will be others like this. We were caught unprepared this time and cannot afford to lose the trust of our farmers. We also need to re-evaluate the roles you and I play in the organization. I think DAI is too depended on us personally. We need to build robust processes and make the company less person dependent. We have discussed many options in the past but right now I have more questions than answers. Let us go through them one by one.'

Damodare outlined the options that were available for the company.

The first option was to fix operational issues using digitization and automation and grow within the existing market. This would ensure that the supply chain process became efficient and scalable. It would be able to handle future business shocks within the existing markets.

The second option was to go beyond digitization to launch the platform Damodare had explored previously. The COVID experience had demonstrated that farmers were open to using digital platforms, especially high-end farmers. DAI could transform itself from a traditional distributor to a platform company that provided a range of value-added services to the farmers.

The third option for DAI was to go beyond western Maharashtra. How could DAI expand its business beyond the current market? Would it need to first build a development associate team like the one in Maharashtra? What role would Kelkar play in the new markets, if at all? Could DAI afford to wait for 5–10 years to build relationships? How could the digital platform be leveraged to speed up DAI's entry to these new markets?

Damodare and Kelkar had much to think about. Which of these options or a combination of options would be optimal for DAI? Dhanashree was a family-owned and operated business. Damodare was keen to de-risk and grow the company, but he was unwilling to cause any damage to the trust built over six decades. He had achieved what he had set out a decade ago to do. He and Kelkar had built DAI into an undisputed market leader in western Maharashtra, and both the company and they individually were financially secure. Damodare was spending more time with his family and the Trust. Was there really a need to start all over again?

Discussion Questions

1. Analyse the market for speciality agri-inputs in India in 2018 using Porter's five forces framework. What are some of the challenges and opportunities?
2. How does Damodare lead DAI 'across the chasm'? What innovative methods did he use? What alternate paths could Damodare have chosen?
3. In 2020, Damodare had three options: (a) digitalize and strengthen his current operations within the existing business model, (b) expand within the existing market using digital technologies and (c) expand to newer markets using a combination of digital and physical presence. Discuss the advantages and risks of each of these models and recommend the alternate or combination of alternates he should take.
4. Assume you are a vendor pitching to Damodare to help build his platform. What kind of a platform would you recommend (one-sided versus two-sided)? What are the key features you will include in the platform? How would you overcome the key concern that Damodare had about the platform not being able to replicate the one-to-one relationship his team currently had with their customers? How would the 'farmer-first' philosophy be built into the platform?

NOTE

1. http://www.marketexpress.in/2020/04/can-agriculture-exports-lead-to-farm-income-growth. html#:~:text=Linking%20agricultural%20production%20to%20export, market%20and%20enhance%20 income%20opportunities.&text=In%202018%2C%20India's%20exports%20in, USD%2027.3%20 Billion%5B2%5D

REFERENCE

Moore, G. (1991). *Crossing the chasm*. HarperCollins.
Pingali, S. R., & Korem, J. R. (2021). Dhanashree Agro: transforming a "Farmer First" model. Emerald Emerging Markets Case Studies.

Index